Shojo Beat

Story & Art by
Aya Nakahara

2

love★com

contents 2

The Story So Far...

First-year high school student Risa Koizumi is 5'7". She and Atsushi Ôtani (5'1") are considered their class's lopsided comedy duo, but actually all they do is quarrel. However, when Risa falls for Suzuki, a guy in a different class, and Ôtani falls for Risa's friend Chiharu, the two of them team up to get the love they want. Unfortunately, Suzuki and Chiharu are attracted to each other, and Risa and Ôtani end up kissing their hopes goodbye when the other two start going out—with Risa and Ôtani's help. So the mismatched duo make a bet over who can get together with someone first! But one day after school, the "love fortune" machine they play just for laughs tells them they're 100% compatible! It's true they have a lot in common...except it turns out that Ôtani's pretty popular, and Risa isn't. Starting to panic, she goes to a party to meet people—only to run into Ôtani! Although Risa does her best to find herself a boyfriend at the party, all that happens is she discovers she gets along with Ôtani much better than she ever expected...

♥ To really get all the details, check out Love★Com Vol. 1, available at bookstores everywhere!!

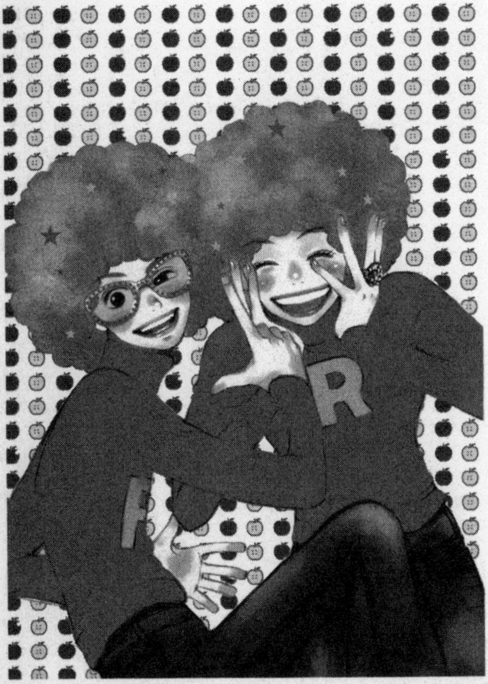
R
R

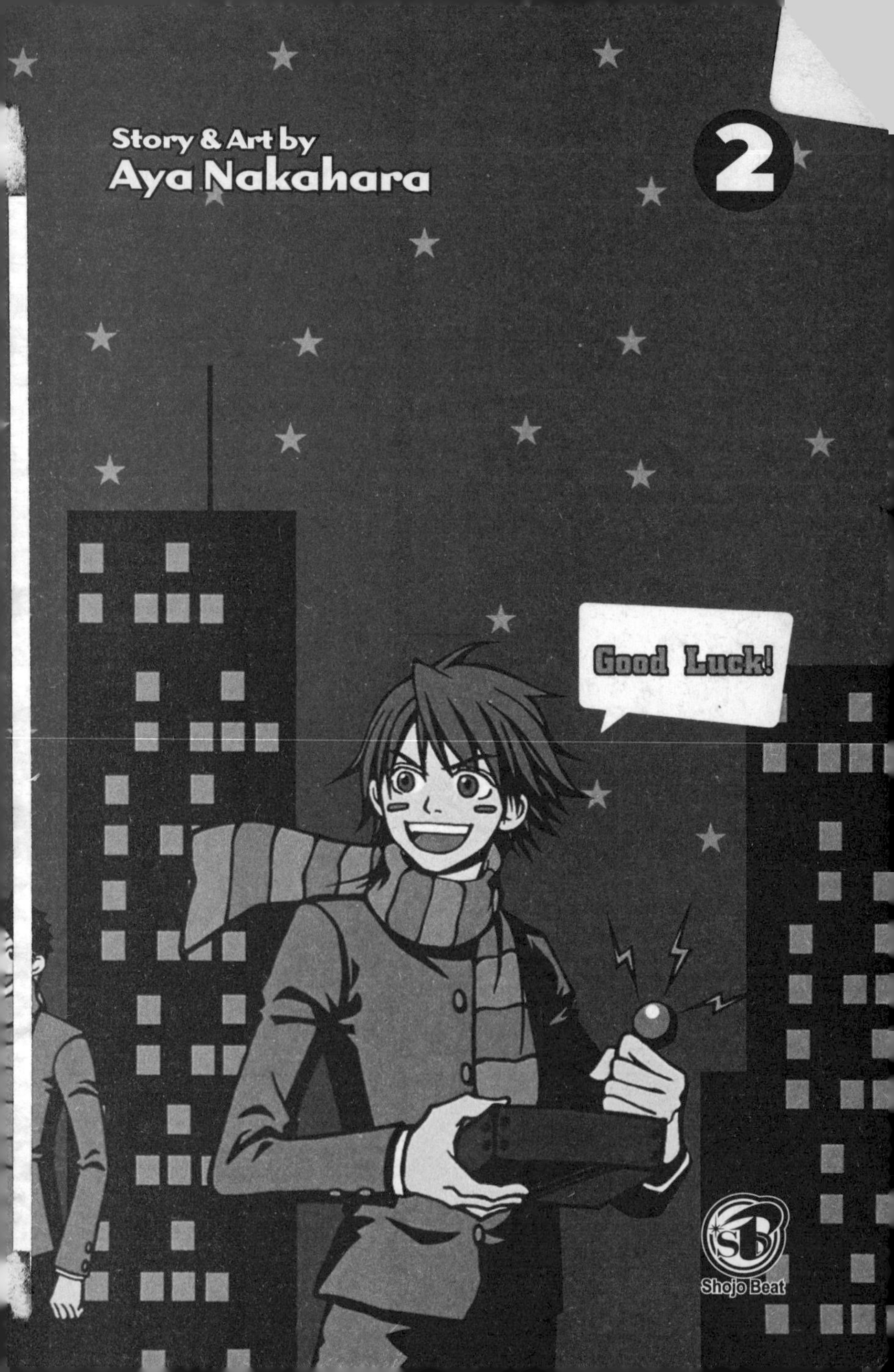
Story & Art by
Aya Nakahara
2
Good Luck!
Shojo Beat

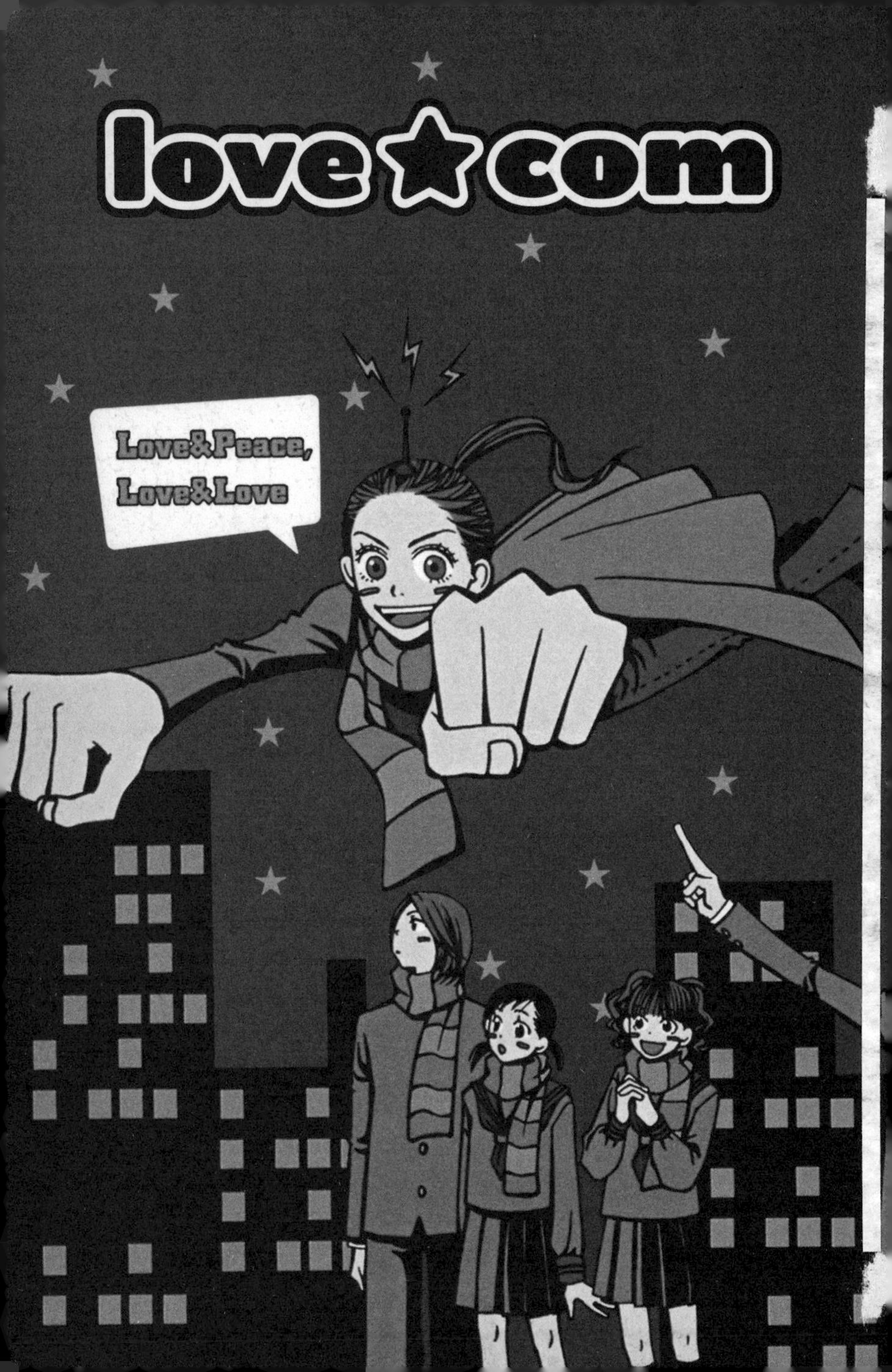
love★com
Love&Peace,
Love&Love

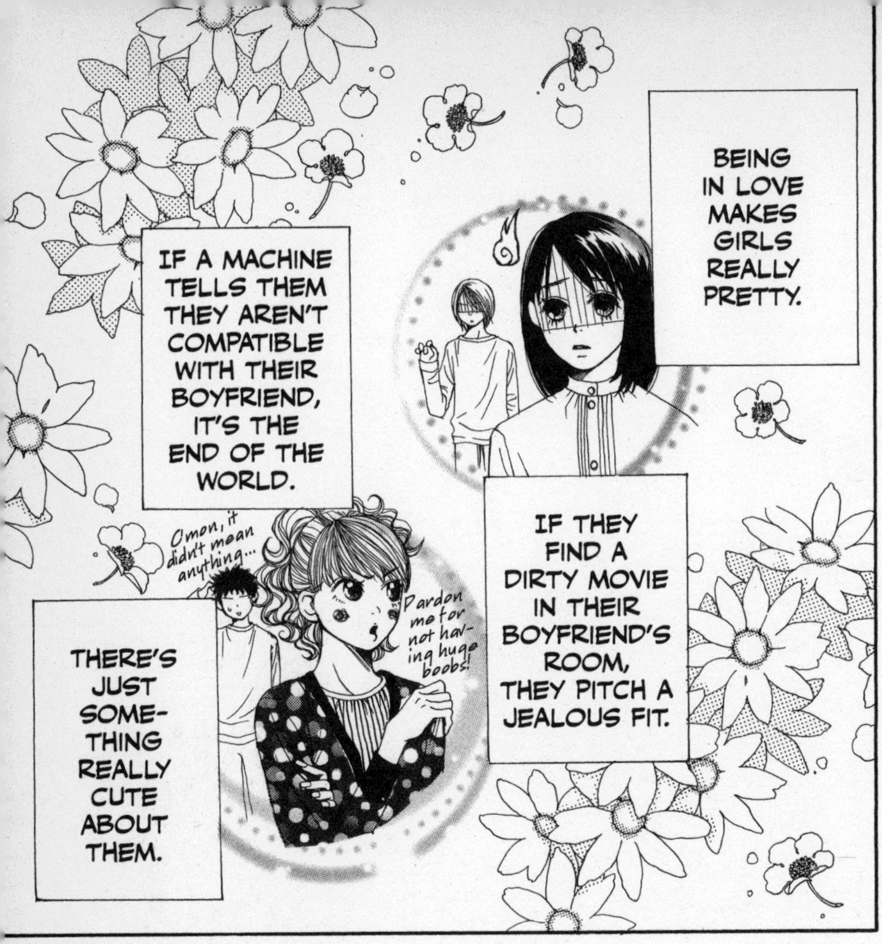
BEING IN LOVE MAKES GIRLS REALLY PRETTY.
IF A MACHINE TELLS THEM THEY AREN'T COMPATIBLE WITH THEIR BOYFRIEND, IT'S THE END OF THE WORLD.
IF THEY FIND A DIRTY MOVIE IN THEIR BOYFRIEND'S ROOM, THEY PITCH A JEALOUS FIT.
Pardon me for not having huge boobs!
C'mon, it didn't mean anything...
THERE'S JUST SOMETHING REALLY CUTE ABOUT THEM.

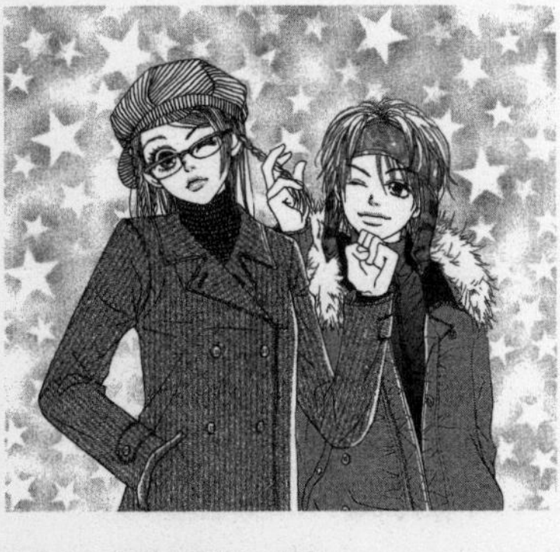

CHAPTER 5

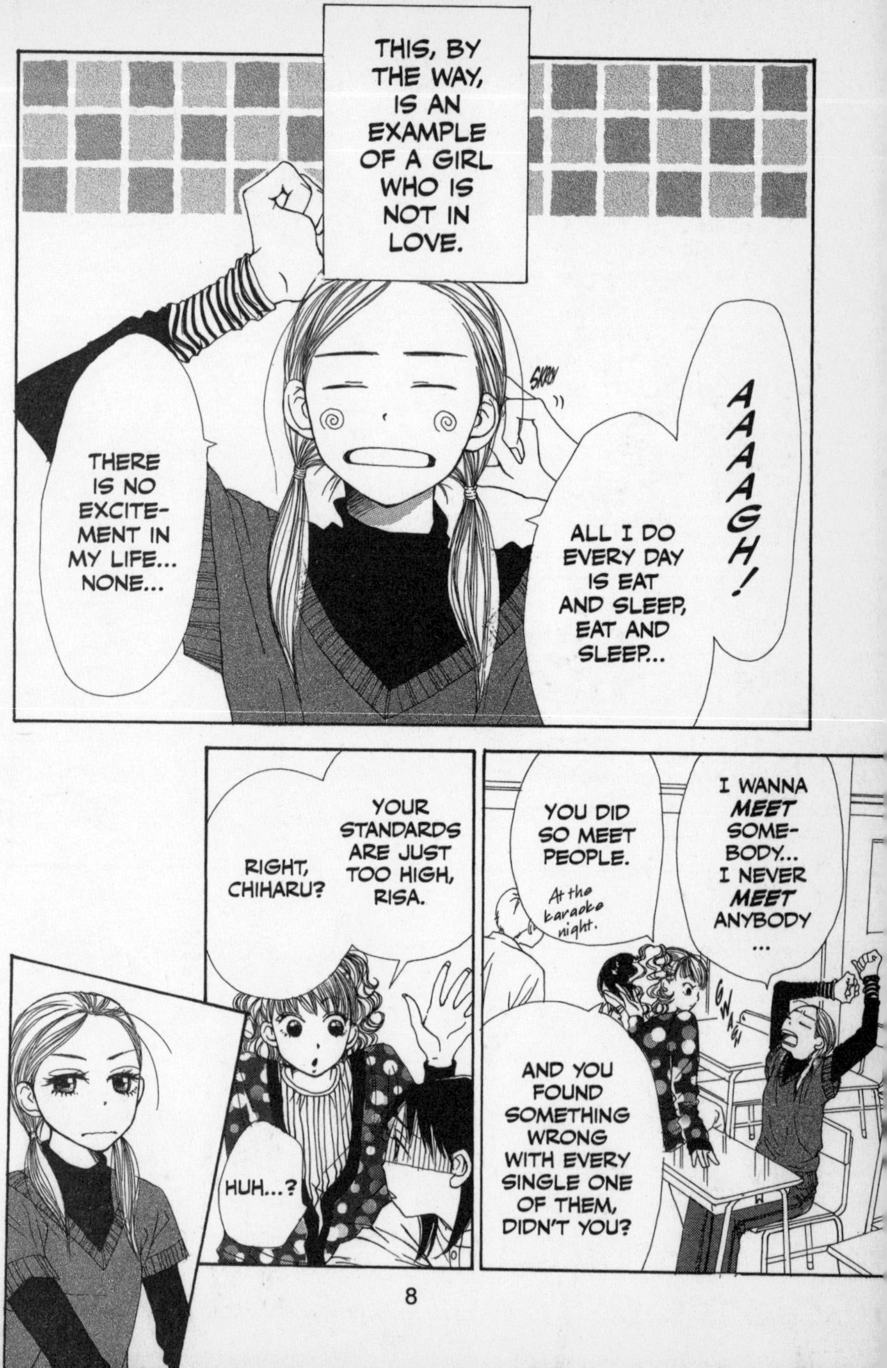
THIS, BY THE WAY, IS AN EXAMPLE OF A GIRL WHO IS NOT IN LOVE.
AAAAGH!
ALL I DO EVERY DAY IS EAT AND SLEEP, EAT AND SLEEP...
THERE IS NO EXCITEMENT IN MY LIFE... NONE...
I WANNA MEET SOMEBODY... I NEVER MEET ANYBODY ...
YOU DID SO MEET PEOPLE.
At the karaoke night.
AND YOU FOUND SOMETHING WRONG WITH EVERY SINGLE ONE OF THEM, DIDN'T YOU?
YOUR STANDARDS ARE JUST TOO HIGH, RISA.
RIGHT, CHIHARU?
HUH...?

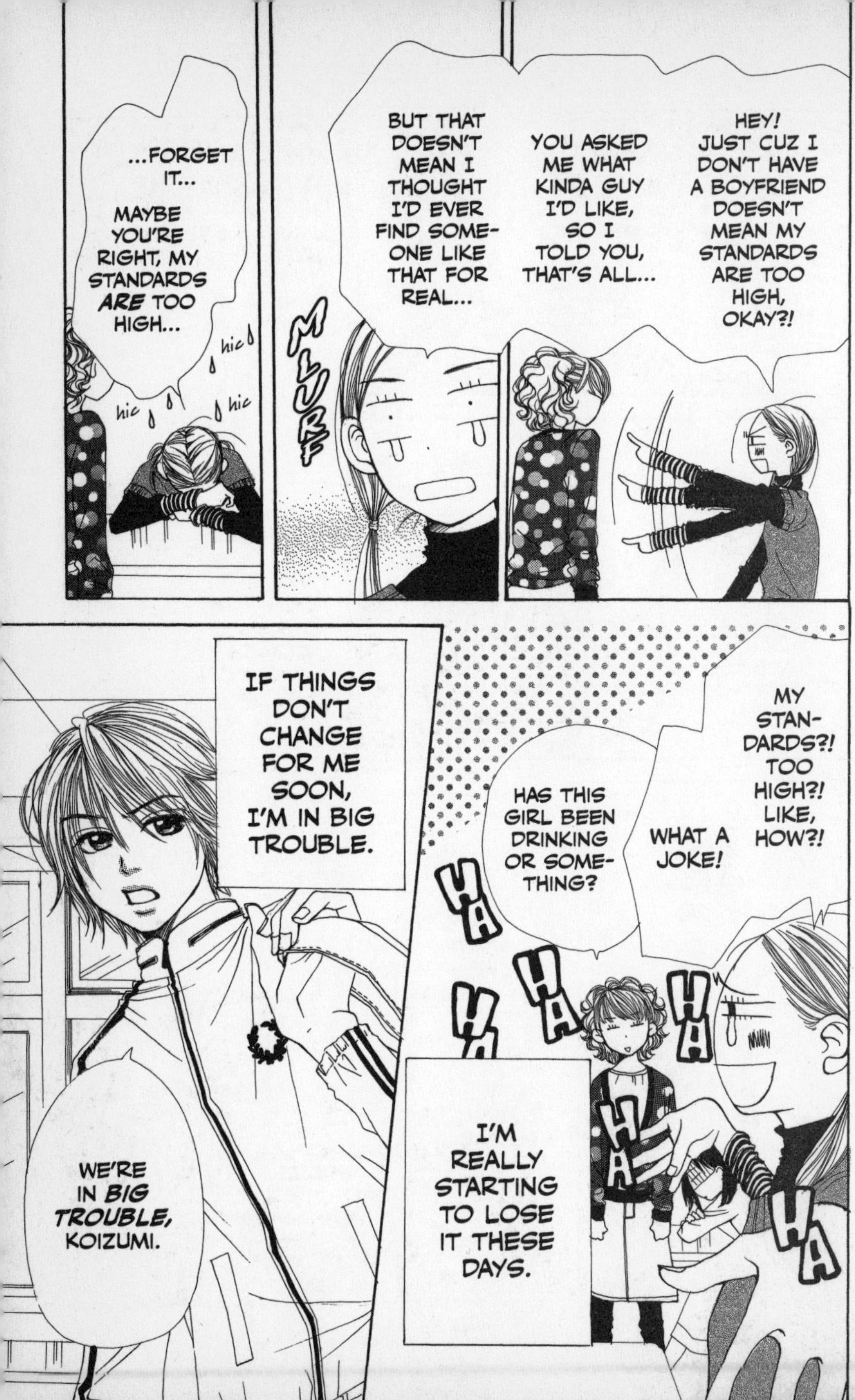
HEY! JUST CUZ I DON'T HAVE A BOYFRIEND DOESN'T MEAN MY STANDARDS ARE TOO HIGH, OKAY?!
YOU ASKED ME WHAT KINDA GUY I'D LIKE, SO I TOLD YOU, THAT'S ALL...
BUT THAT DOESN'T MEAN I THOUGHT I'D EVER FIND SOME-ONE LIKE THAT FOR REAL...
MYURF
...FORGET IT...
MAYBE YOU'RE RIGHT, MY STANDARDS *ARE* TOO HIGH...
hic
hic
hic
MY STAN-DARDS?! TOO HIGH?! LIKE, HOW?!
WHAT A JOKE!
HAS THIS GIRL BEEN DRINKING OR SOME-THING?
HA
HA
HA
HA
HA
HA
I'M REALLY STARTING TO LOSE IT THESE DAYS.
IF THINGS DON'T CHANGE FOR ME SOON, I'M IN BIG TROUBLE.
WE'RE IN *BIG TROUBLE,* KOIZUMI.

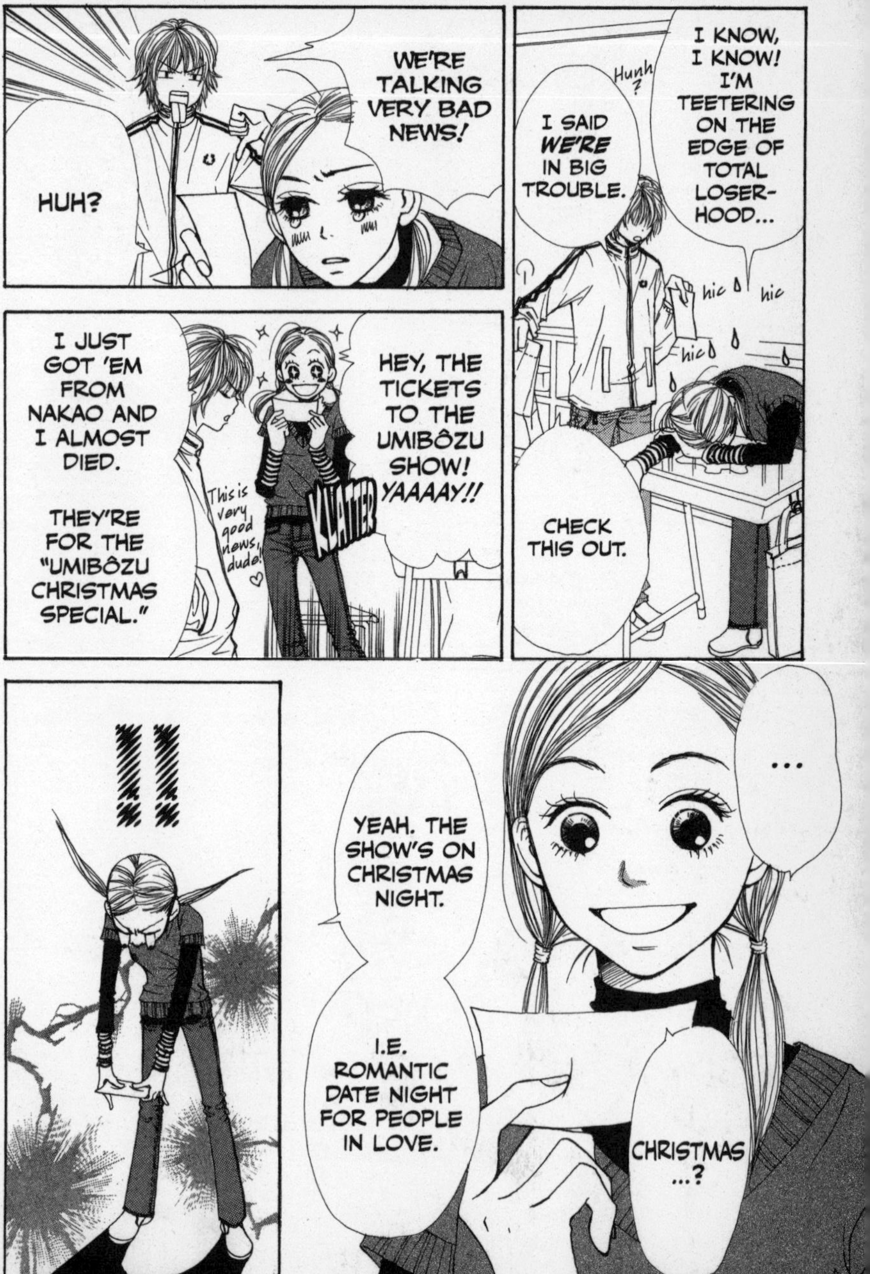
I KNOW, I KNOW! I'M TEETERING ON THE EDGE OF TOTAL LOSER-HOOD...
Hunh?
I SAID *WE'RE* IN BIG TROUBLE.
hic hic
hic
CHECK THIS OUT.
WE'RE TALKING VERY BAD NEWS!
HUH?
HEY, THE TICKETS TO THE UMIBÔZU SHOW! YAAAAY!!
KLATTER
This is very good news, dude!
I JUST GOT 'EM FROM NAKAO AND I ALMOST DIED.
THEY'RE FOR THE "UMIBÔZU CHRISTMAS SPECIAL."
...
CHRISTMAS ...?
YEAH. THE SHOW'S ON CHRISTMAS NIGHT.
I.E. ROMANTIC DATE NIGHT FOR PEOPLE IN LOVE.
!!

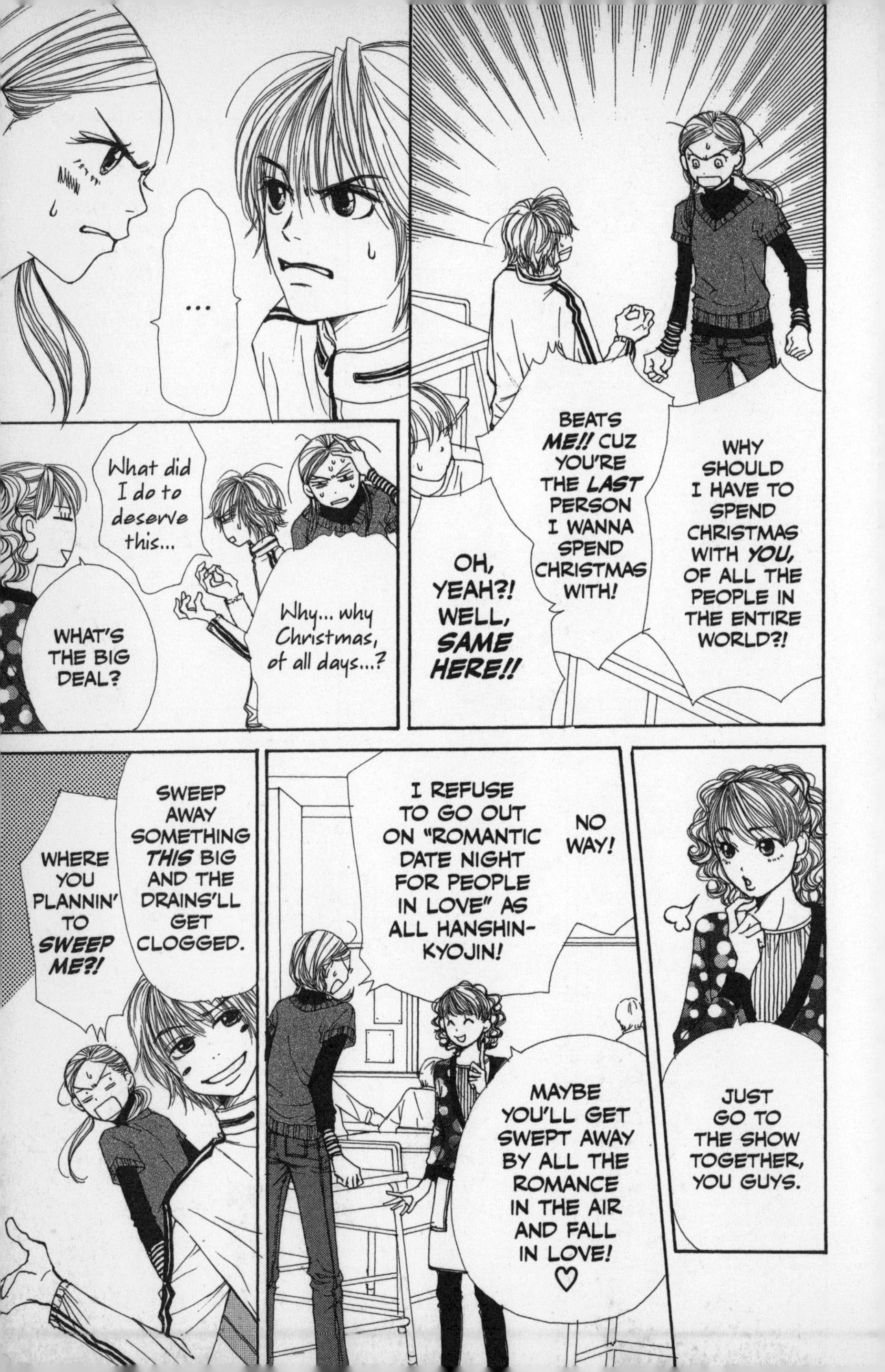
WHY SHOULD I HAVE TO SPEND CHRISTMAS WITH *YOU*, OF ALL THE PEOPLE IN THE ENTIRE WORLD?!
BEATS *ME!!* CUZ YOU'RE THE *LAST* PERSON I WANNA SPEND CHRISTMAS WITH!
OH, YEAH?! WELL, *SAME HERE!!*
...
What did I do to deserve this...
Why... why Christmas, of all days...?
WHAT'S THE BIG DEAL?
JUST GO TO THE SHOW TOGETHER, YOU GUYS.
NO WAY!
I REFUSE TO GO OUT ON "ROMANTIC DATE NIGHT FOR PEOPLE IN LOVE" AS ALL HANSHIN-KYOJIN!
MAYBE YOU'LL GET SWEPT AWAY BY ALL THE ROMANCE IN THE AIR AND FALL IN LOVE! ♡
SWEEP AWAY SOMETHING *THIS* BIG AND THE DRAINS'LL GET CLOGGED.
WHERE YOU PLANNIN' TO *SWEEP ME?!*

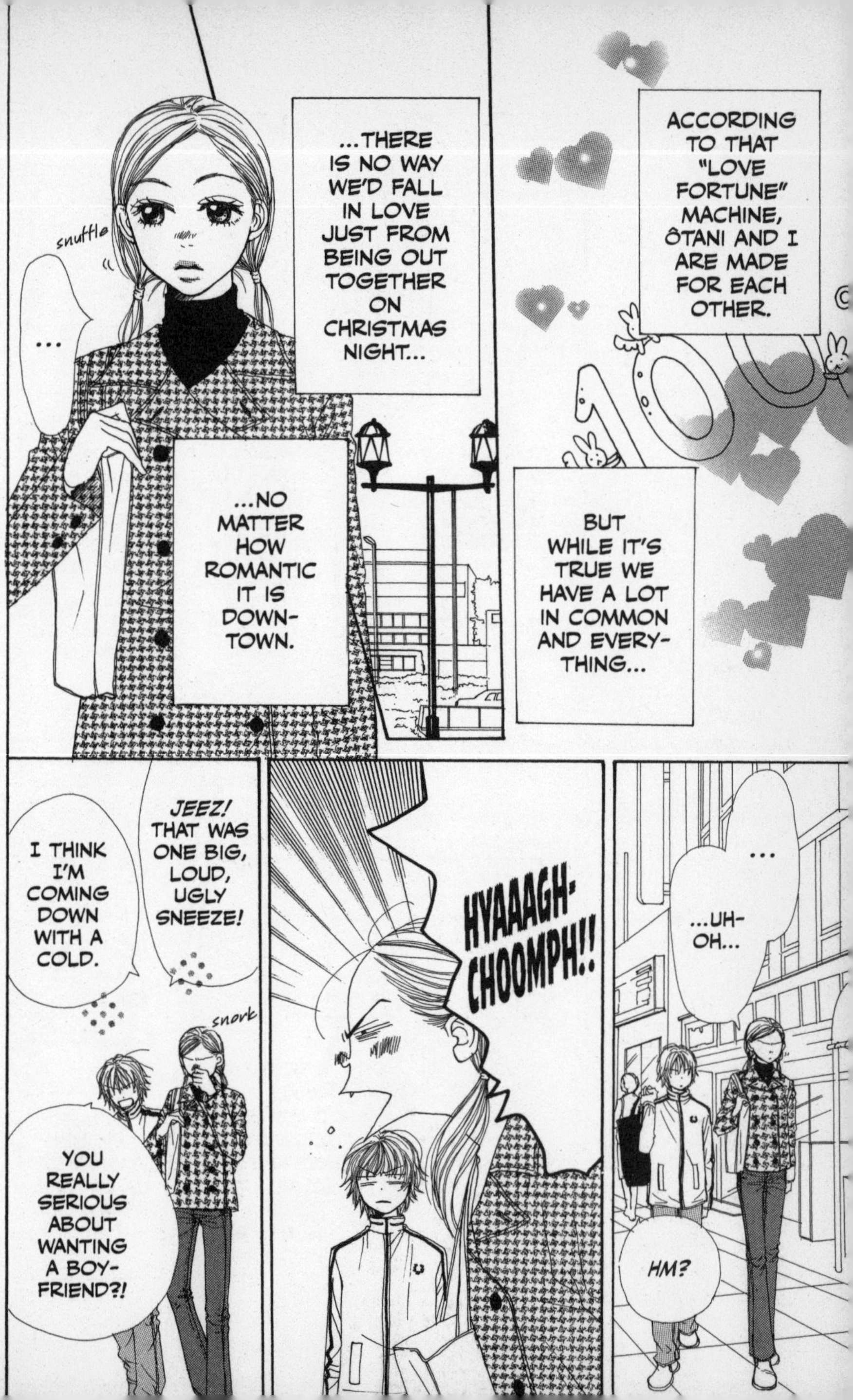
ACCORDING TO THAT "LOVE FORTUNE" MACHINE, ÔTANI AND I ARE MADE FOR EACH OTHER.
BUT WHILE IT'S TRUE WE HAVE A LOT IN COMMON AND EVERY-THING...
...THERE IS NO WAY WE'D FALL IN LOVE JUST FROM BEING OUT TOGETHER ON CHRISTMAS NIGHT...
snuffle
...
...NO MATTER HOW ROMANTIC IT IS DOWN-TOWN.
...
...UH-OH...
HM?
HYAAAGH-CHOOMPH!!
JEEZ! THAT WAS ONE BIG, LOUD, UGLY SNEEZE!
I THINK I'M COMING DOWN WITH A COLD.
snork
YOU REALLY SERIOUS ABOUT WANTING A BOY-FRIEND?!

1.

Hello, Nakahara here with Volume 2...ta-da!

Lately, every time I see somebody I haven't met in a while, they say "Gosh, you've lost weight..." and give me this pitying look.

I think it's because I've been staying up all night and generally leading an unhealthy life. So, I joined a sports club to try and get some exercise. I started taking Tai Chi classes, which is something I've always wanted to do.

But breathing is kind of complicated in Tai Chi, and I get all mixed up. The teacher will say, "Breathe in while you do this and that..." and I keep breathing in until I just about keel over.

Maybe I'm just not cut out for this sorta thing... I was hopeless at aerobics too...

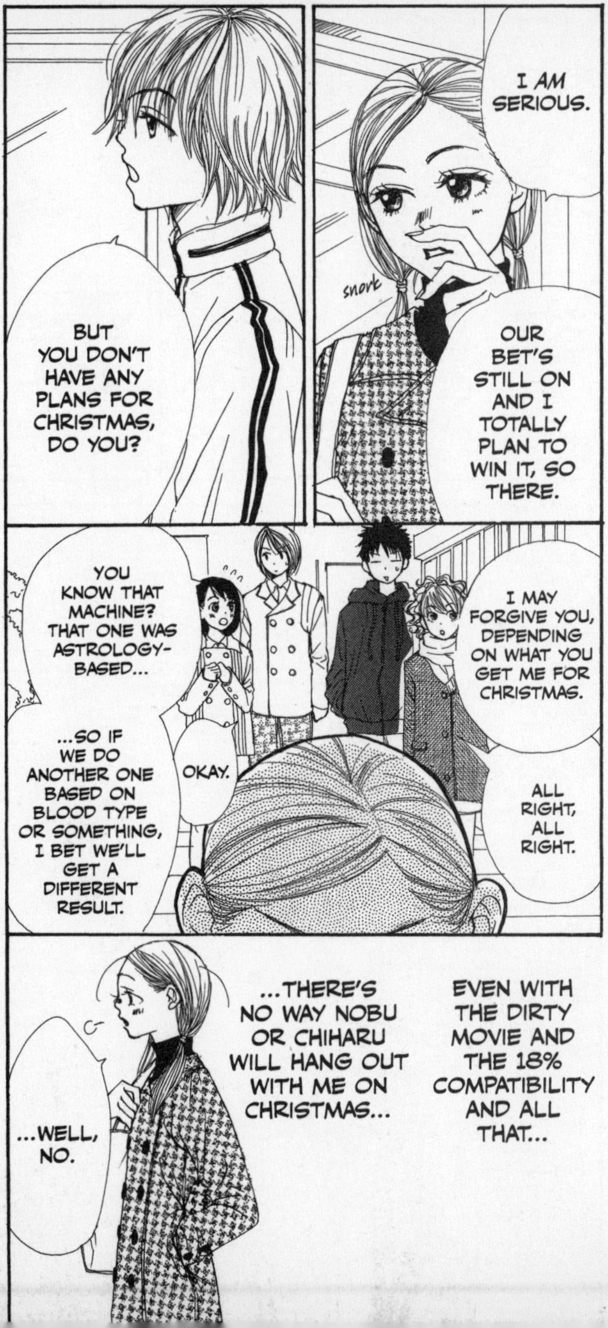
I AM SERIOUS.
snork
OUR BET'S STILL ON AND I TOTALLY PLAN TO WIN IT, SO THERE.
BUT YOU DON'T HAVE ANY PLANS FOR CHRISTMAS, DO YOU?
I MAY FORGIVE YOU, DEPENDING ON WHAT YOU GET ME FOR CHRISTMAS.
YOU KNOW THAT MACHINE? THAT ONE WAS ASTROLOGY-BASED...
ALL RIGHT, ALL RIGHT.
OKAY.
...SO IF WE DO ANOTHER ONE BASED ON BLOOD TYPE OR SOMETHING, I BET WE'LL GET A DIFFERENT RESULT.
EVEN WITH THE DIRTY MOVIE AND THE 18% COMPATIBILITY AND ALL THAT...
...THERE'S NO WAY NOBU OR CHIHARU WILL HANG OUT WITH ME ON CHRISTMAS...
...WELL, NO.

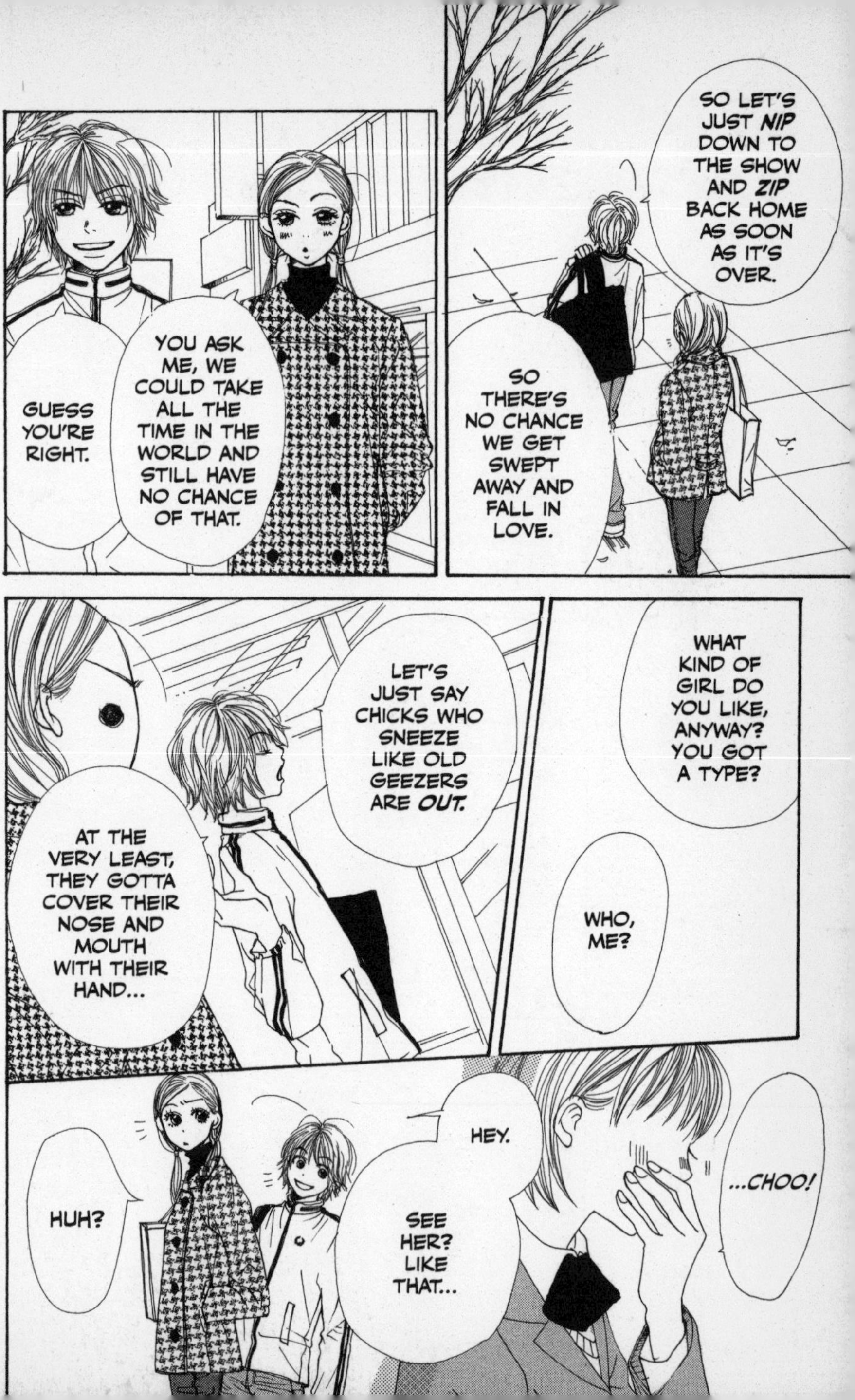
SO LET'S JUST *NIP* DOWN TO THE SHOW AND *ZIP* BACK HOME AS SOON AS IT'S OVER.
SO THERE'S NO CHANCE WE GET SWEPT AWAY AND FALL IN LOVE.
YOU ASK ME, WE COULD TAKE ALL THE TIME IN THE WORLD AND STILL HAVE NO CHANCE OF THAT.
GUESS YOU'RE RIGHT.
WHAT KIND OF GIRL DO YOU LIKE, ANYWAY? YOU GOT A TYPE?
WHO, ME?
LET'S JUST SAY CHICKS WHO SNEEZE LIKE OLD GEEZERS ARE *OUT.*
AT THE VERY LEAST, THEY GOTTA COVER THEIR NOSE AND MOUTH WITH THEIR HAND...
...CHOO!
HEY.
SEE HER? LIKE THAT...
HUH?

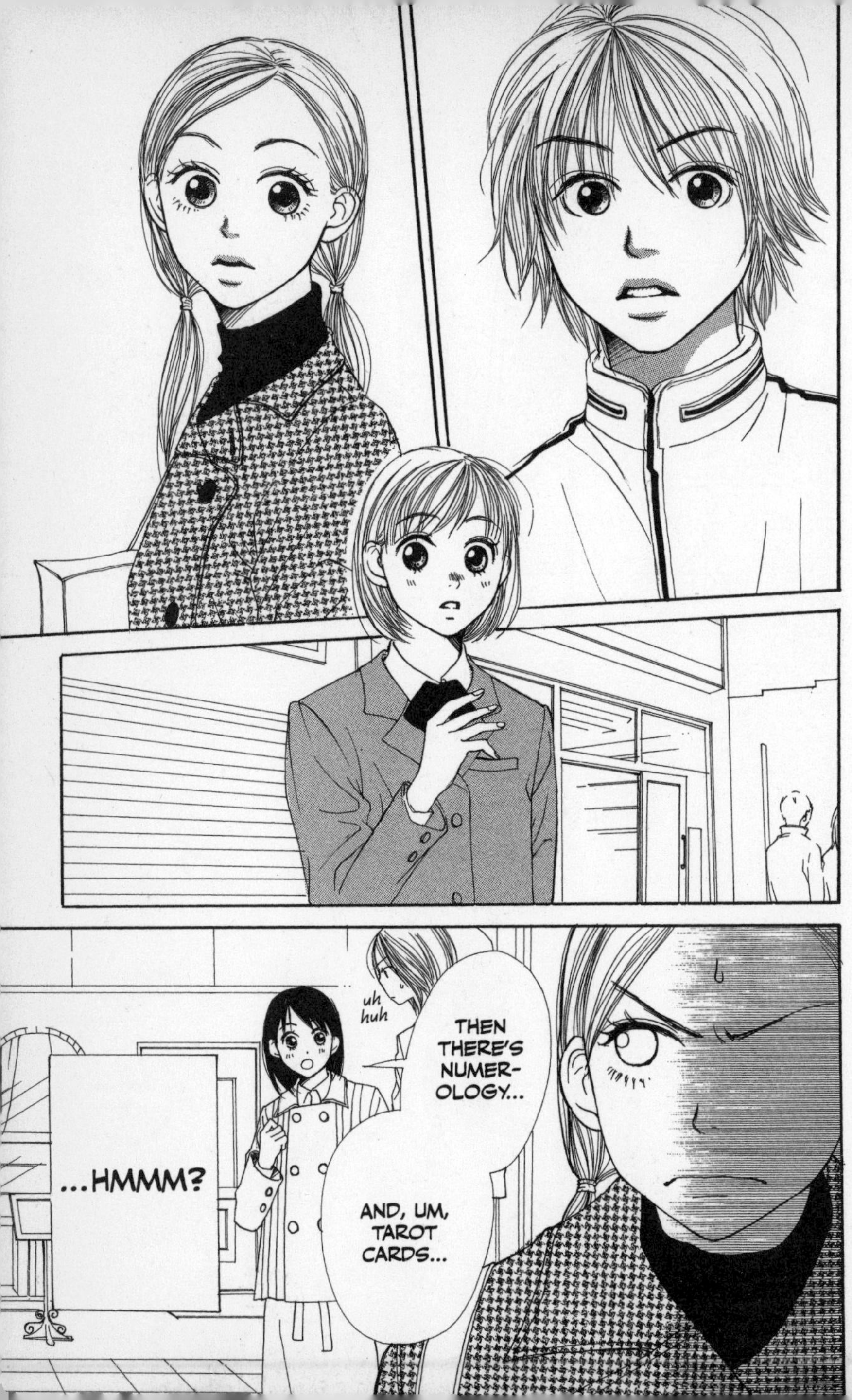
THEN THERE'S NUMER-OLOGY...
AND, UM, TAROT CARDS...
uh huh
...HMMM?

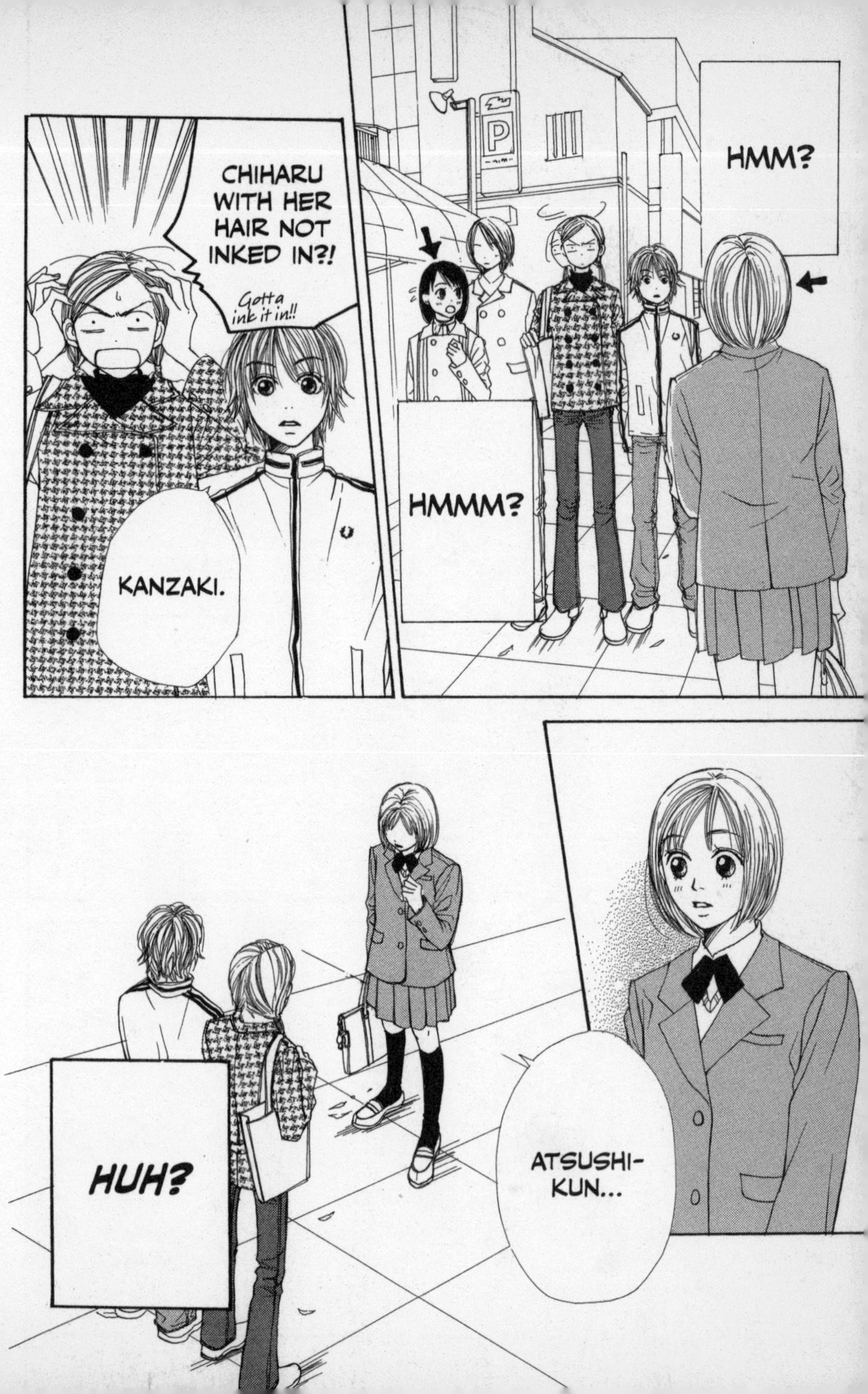
HMM?
HMMM?
CHIHARU WITH HER HAIR NOT INKED IN?!
Gotta ink it in!!
KANZAKI.
ATSUSHI-KUN...
HUH?

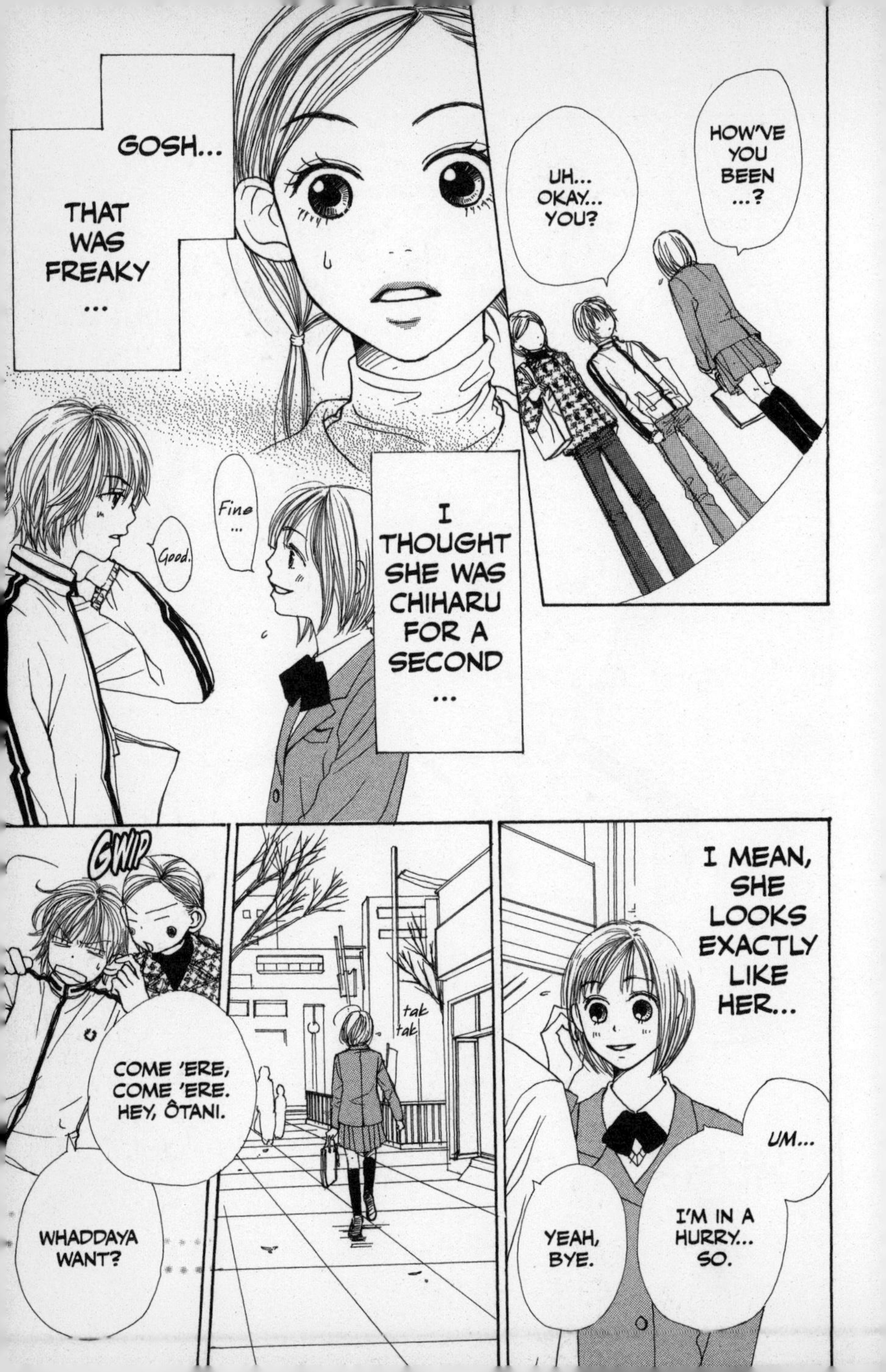
HOW'VE YOU BEEN ...?
UH... OKAY... YOU?
GOSH...
THAT WAS FREAKY ...
I THOUGHT SHE WAS CHIHARU FOR A SECOND ...
Fine ...
Good.
I MEAN, SHE LOOKS EXACTLY LIKE HER...
UM...
I'M IN A HURRY... SO.
YEAH, BYE.
tak tak
GWIP
COME 'ERE, COME 'ERE. HEY, ÔTANI.
WHADDAYA WANT?

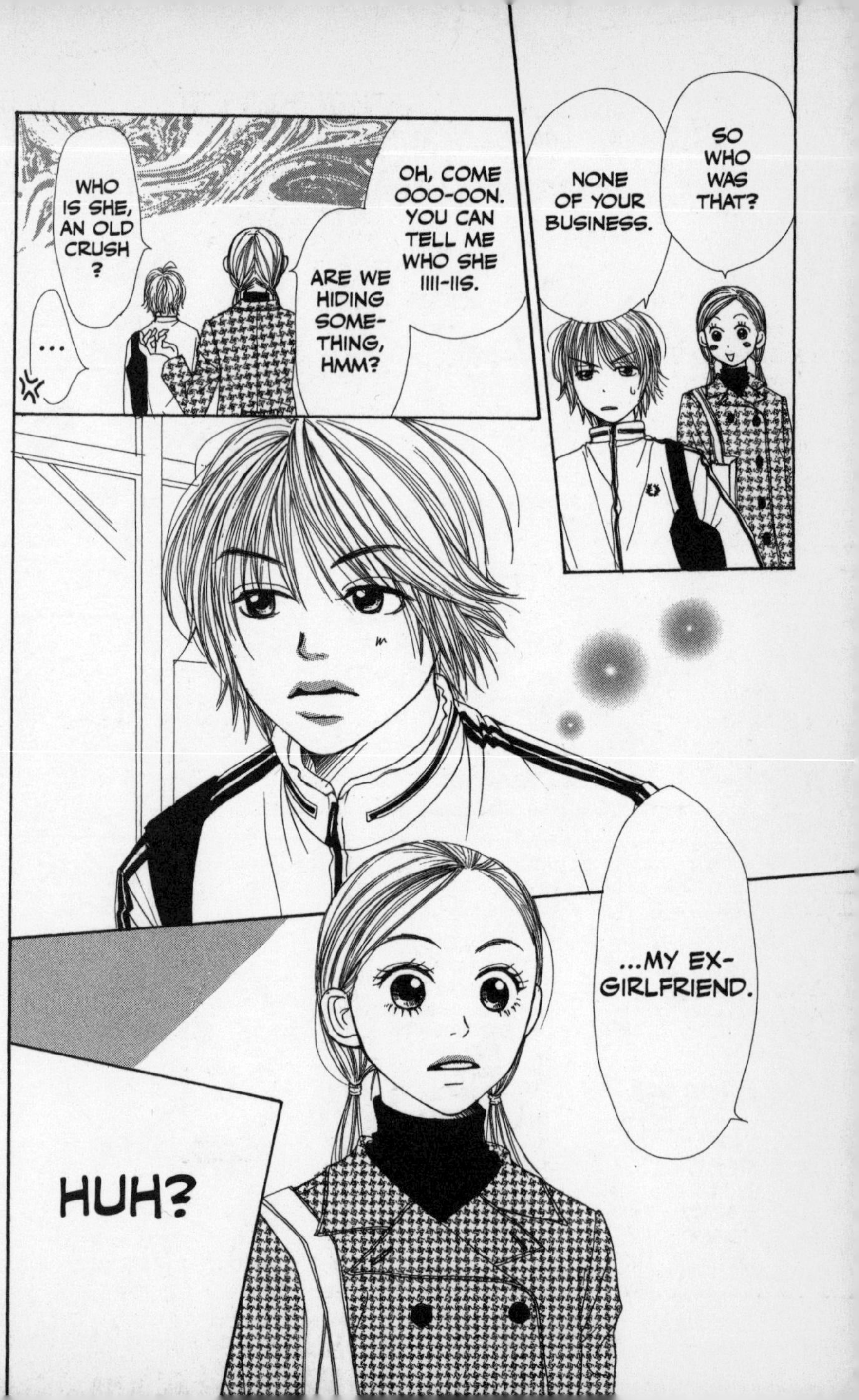
SO WHO WAS THAT?
NONE OF YOUR BUSINESS.
OH, COME OOO-OON. YOU CAN TELL ME WHO SHE IIII-IIS.
ARE WE HIDING SOME-THING, HMM?
WHO IS SHE, AN OLD CRUSH?
...
...MY EX-GIRLFRIEND.
HUH?

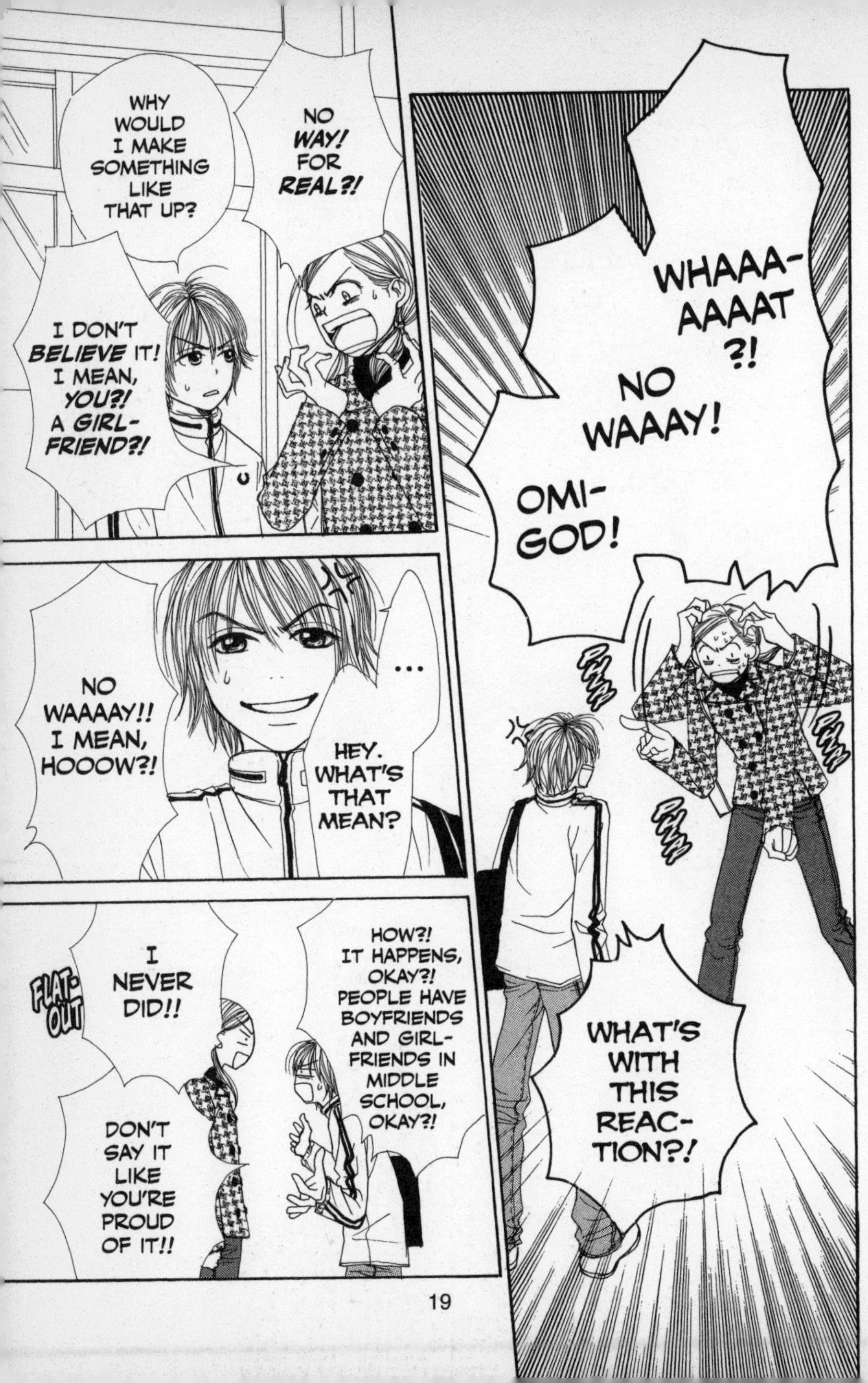
WHAAAA-AAAAT?!
NO WAAAY!
OMI-GOD!
WHAT'S WITH THIS REACTION?!
NO WAY! FOR REAL?!
WHY WOULD I MAKE SOMETHING LIKE THAT UP?
I DON'T BELIEVE IT! I MEAN, YOU?! A GIRL-FRIEND?!
...
NO WAAAAY!! I MEAN, HOOOW?!
HEY. WHAT'S THAT MEAN?
HOW?! IT HAPPENS, OKAY?! PEOPLE HAVE BOYFRIENDS AND GIRL-FRIENDS IN MIDDLE SCHOOL, OKAY?!
I NEVER DID!!
FLAT-OUT
DON'T SAY IT LIKE YOU'RE PROUD OF IT!!

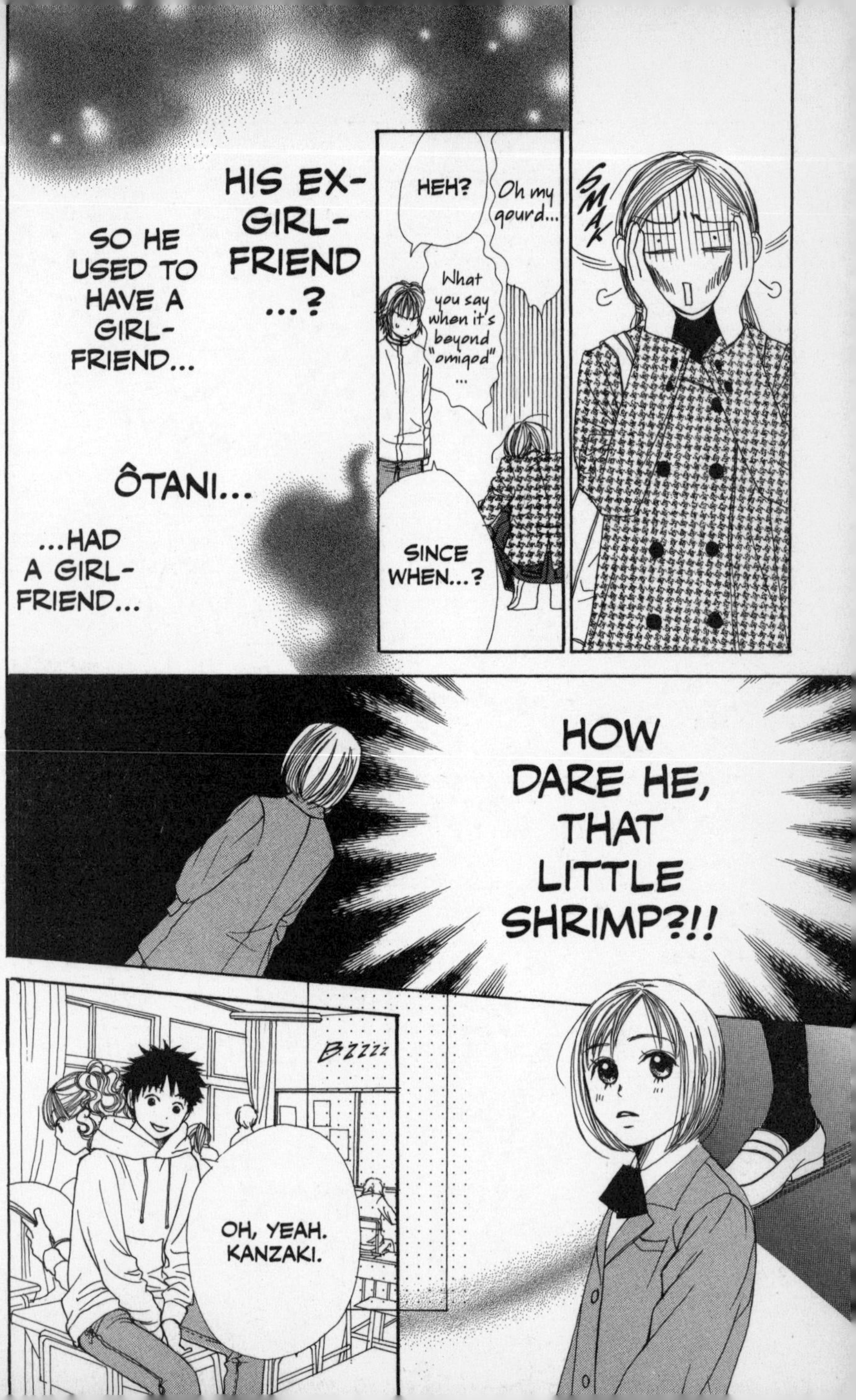
SMAK
Oh my gourd...
What you say when it's beyond "omigod"...
HEH?
SINCE WHEN...?
HIS EX-GIRLFRIEND...?
SO HE USED TO HAVE A GIRLFRIEND...
ÔTANI...
...HAD A GIRLFRIEND...
HOW DARE HE, THAT LITTLE SHRIMP?!!
B-zzzz
OH, YEAH. KANZAKI.

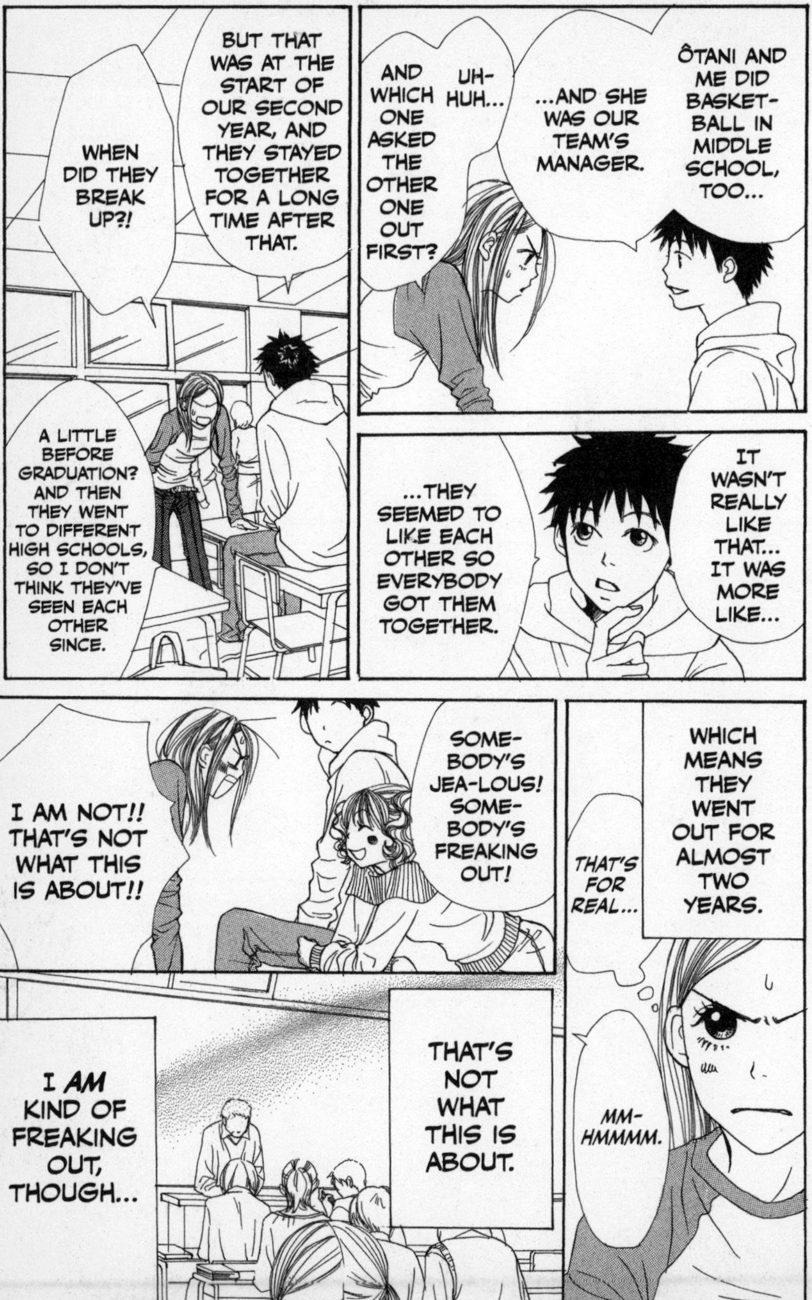
ÔTANI AND ME DID BASKET-BALL IN MIDDLE SCHOOL, TOO...
...AND SHE WAS OUR TEAM'S MANAGER.
UH-HUH...
AND WHICH ONE ASKED THE OTHER ONE OUT FIRST?
IT WASN'T REALLY LIKE THAT... IT WAS MORE LIKE...
...THEY SEEMED TO LIKE EACH OTHER SO EVERYBODY GOT THEM TOGETHER.
BUT THAT WAS AT THE START OF OUR SECOND YEAR, AND THEY STAYED TOGETHER FOR A LONG TIME AFTER THAT.
WHEN DID THEY BREAK UP?!
A LITTLE BEFORE GRADUATION? AND THEN THEY WENT TO DIFFERENT HIGH SCHOOLS, SO I DON'T THINK THEY'VE SEEN EACH OTHER SINCE.
WHICH MEANS THEY WENT OUT FOR ALMOST TWO YEARS.
THAT'S FOR REAL...
MM-HMMMM.
SOME-BODY'S JEA-LOUS! SOME-BODY'S FREAKING OUT!
I AM NOT!! THAT'S NOT WHAT THIS IS ABOUT!!
THAT'S NOT WHAT THIS IS ABOUT.
I AM KIND OF FREAKING OUT, THOUGH...

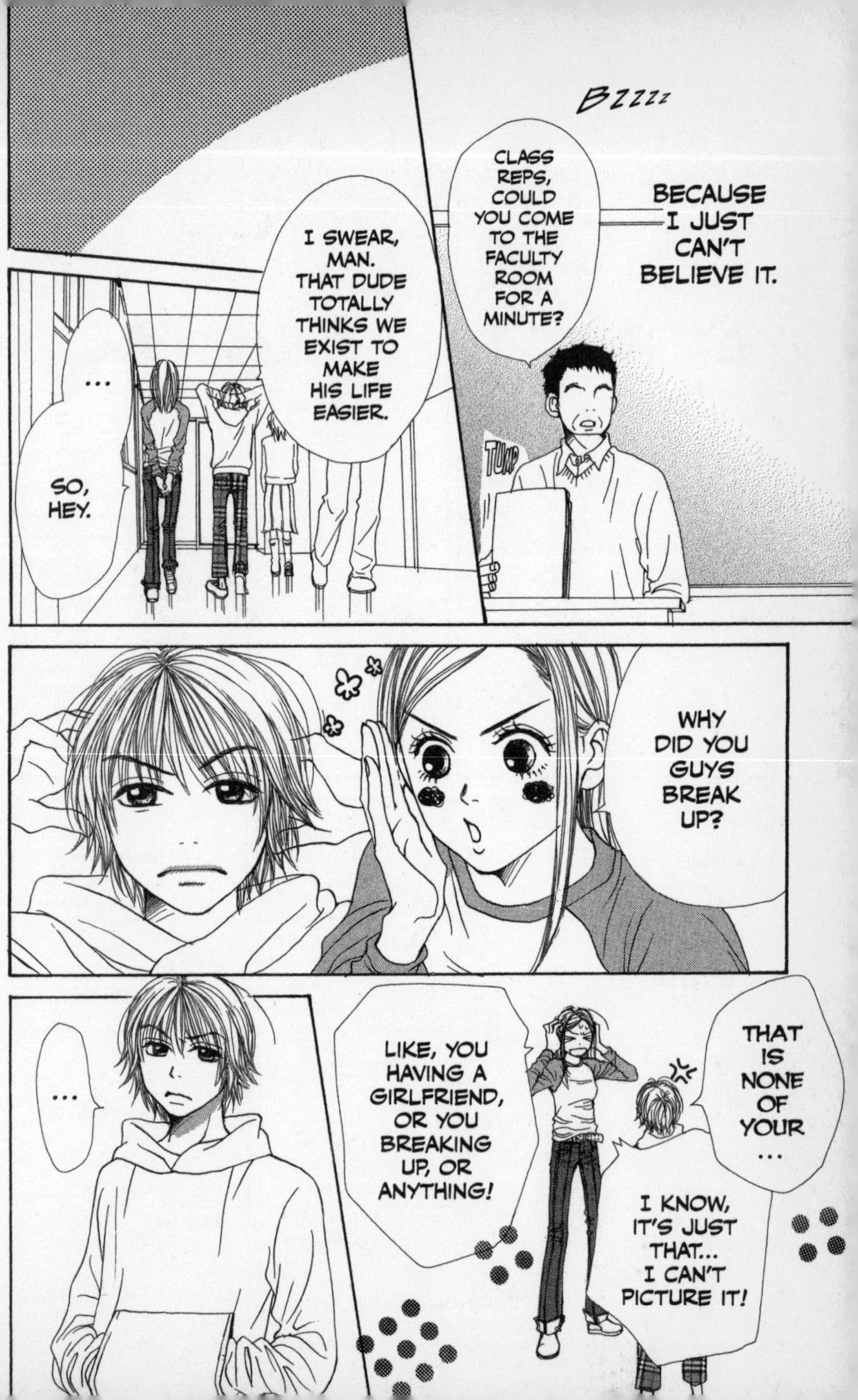
Bzzzz
BECAUSE I JUST CAN'T BELIEVE IT.
CLASS REPS, COULD YOU COME TO THE FACULTY ROOM FOR A MINUTE?
TUMP
I SWEAR, MAN. THAT DUDE TOTALLY THINKS WE EXIST TO MAKE HIS LIFE EASIER.
...
SO, HEY.
WHY DID YOU GUYS BREAK UP?
THAT IS NONE OF YOUR ...
I KNOW, IT'S JUST THAT... I CAN'T PICTURE IT!
LIKE, YOU HAVING A GIRLFRIEND, OR YOU BREAKING UP, OR ANYTHING!
...

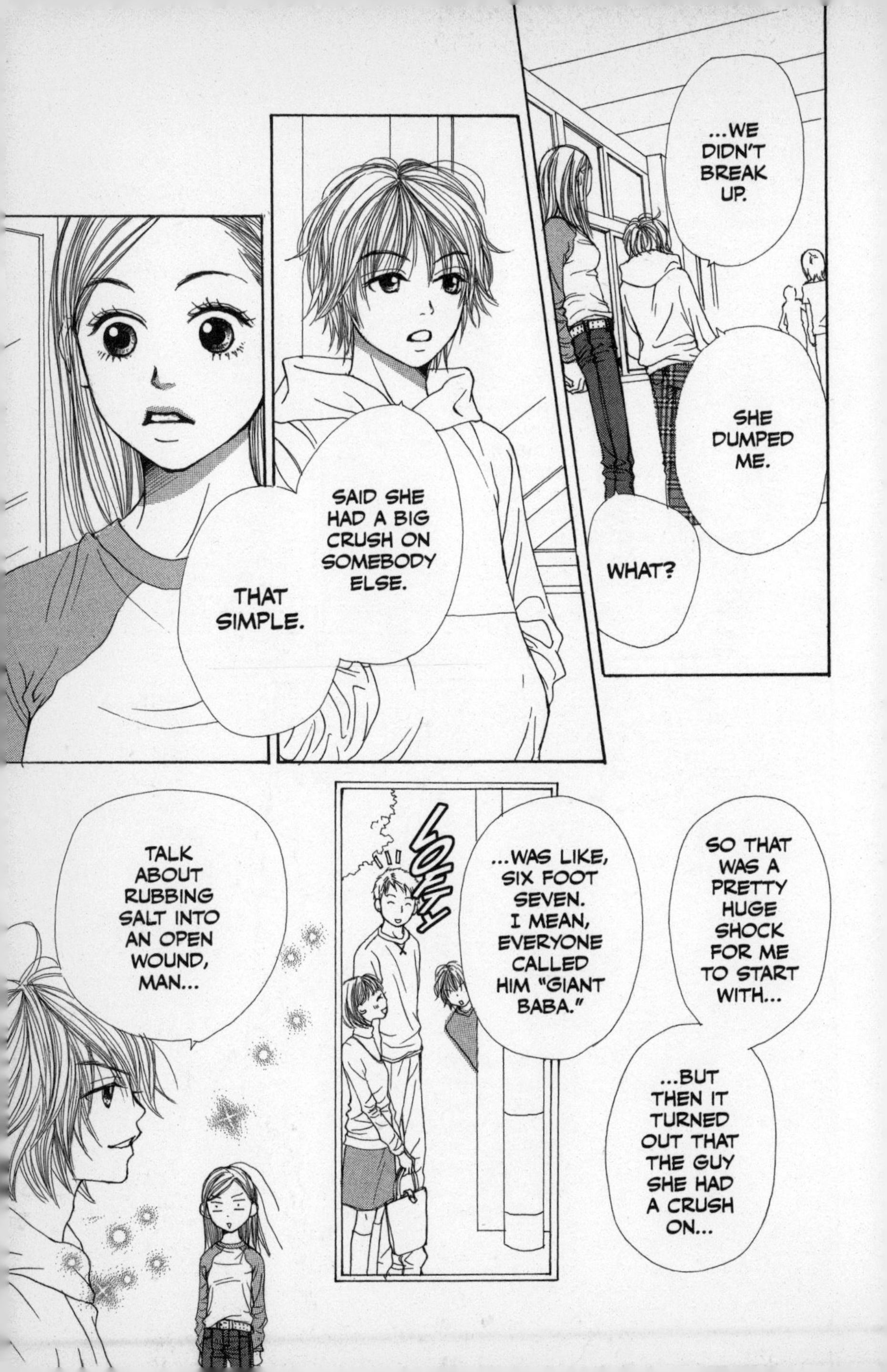
...WE DIDN'T BREAK UP.
SHE DUMPED ME.
WHAT?
SAID SHE HAD A BIG CRUSH ON SOMEBODY ELSE.
THAT SIMPLE.
SO THAT WAS A PRETTY HUGE SHOCK FOR ME TO START WITH...
...BUT THEN IT TURNED OUT THAT THE GUY SHE HAD A CRUSH ON...
...WAS LIKE, SIX FOOT SEVEN. I MEAN, EVERYONE CALLED HIM "GIANT BABA."
TALK ABOUT RUBBING SALT INTO AN OPEN WOUND, MAN...

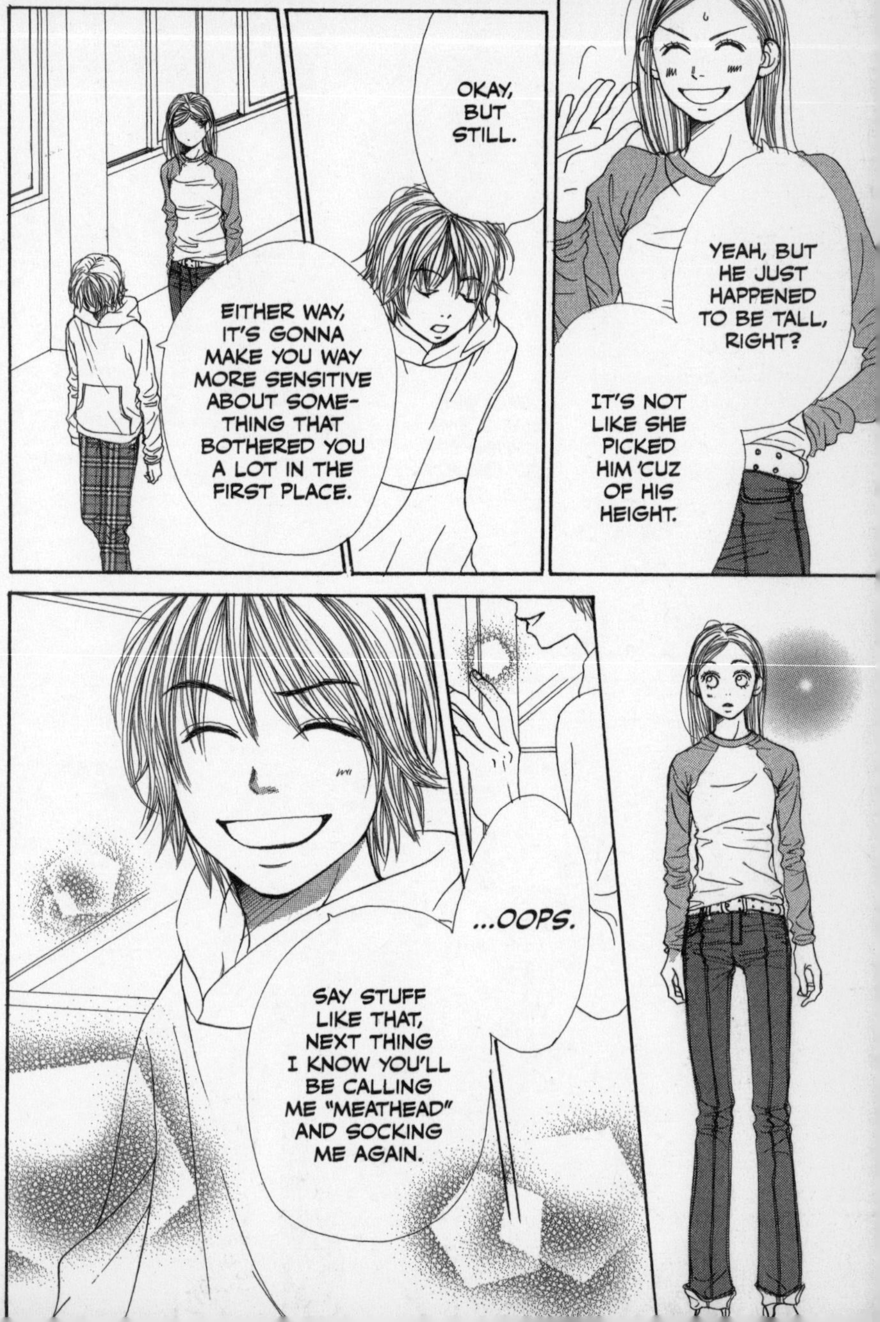
YEAH, BUT HE JUST HAPPENED TO BE TALL, RIGHT?
IT'S NOT LIKE SHE PICKED HIM 'CUZ OF HIS HEIGHT.
OKAY, BUT STILL.
EITHER WAY, IT'S GONNA MAKE YOU WAY MORE SENSITIVE ABOUT SOME-THING THAT BOTHERED YOU A LOT IN THE FIRST PLACE.
SAY STUFF LIKE THAT, NEXT THING I KNOW YOU'LL BE CALLING ME "MEATHEAD" AND SOCKING ME AGAIN.
...OOPS.

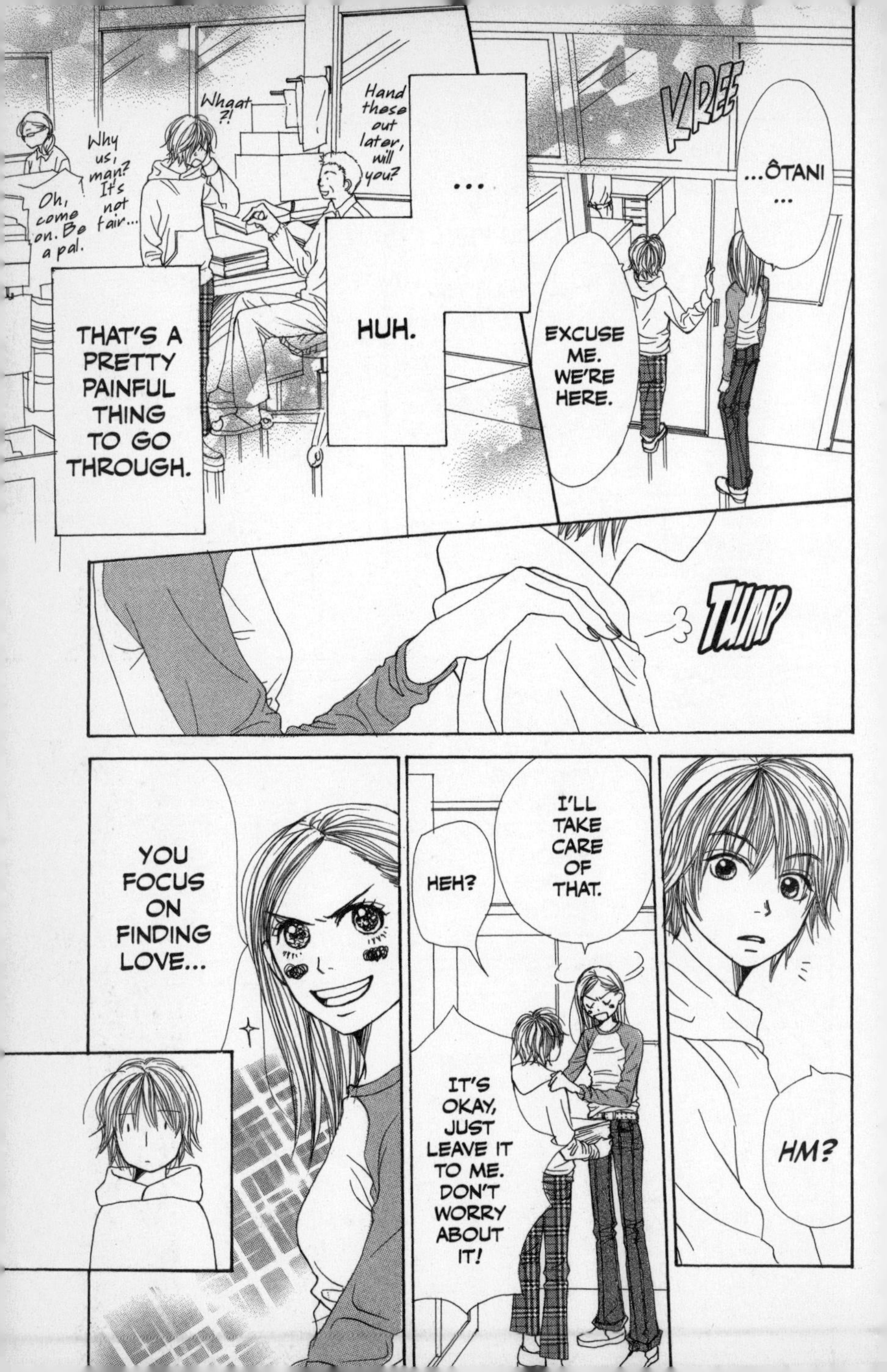
KREE
...ÔTANI ...
EXCUSE ME. WE'RE HERE.
...
HUH.
Hand these out later, will you?
Whaat?!
Why us, man? It's not fair...
Oh, come on. Be a pal.
THAT'S A PRETTY PAINFUL THING TO GO THROUGH.
THUMP
HM?
I'LL TAKE CARE OF THAT.
HEH?
IT'S OKAY, JUST LEAVE IT TO ME. DON'T WORRY ABOUT IT!
YOU FOCUS ON FINDING LOVE...

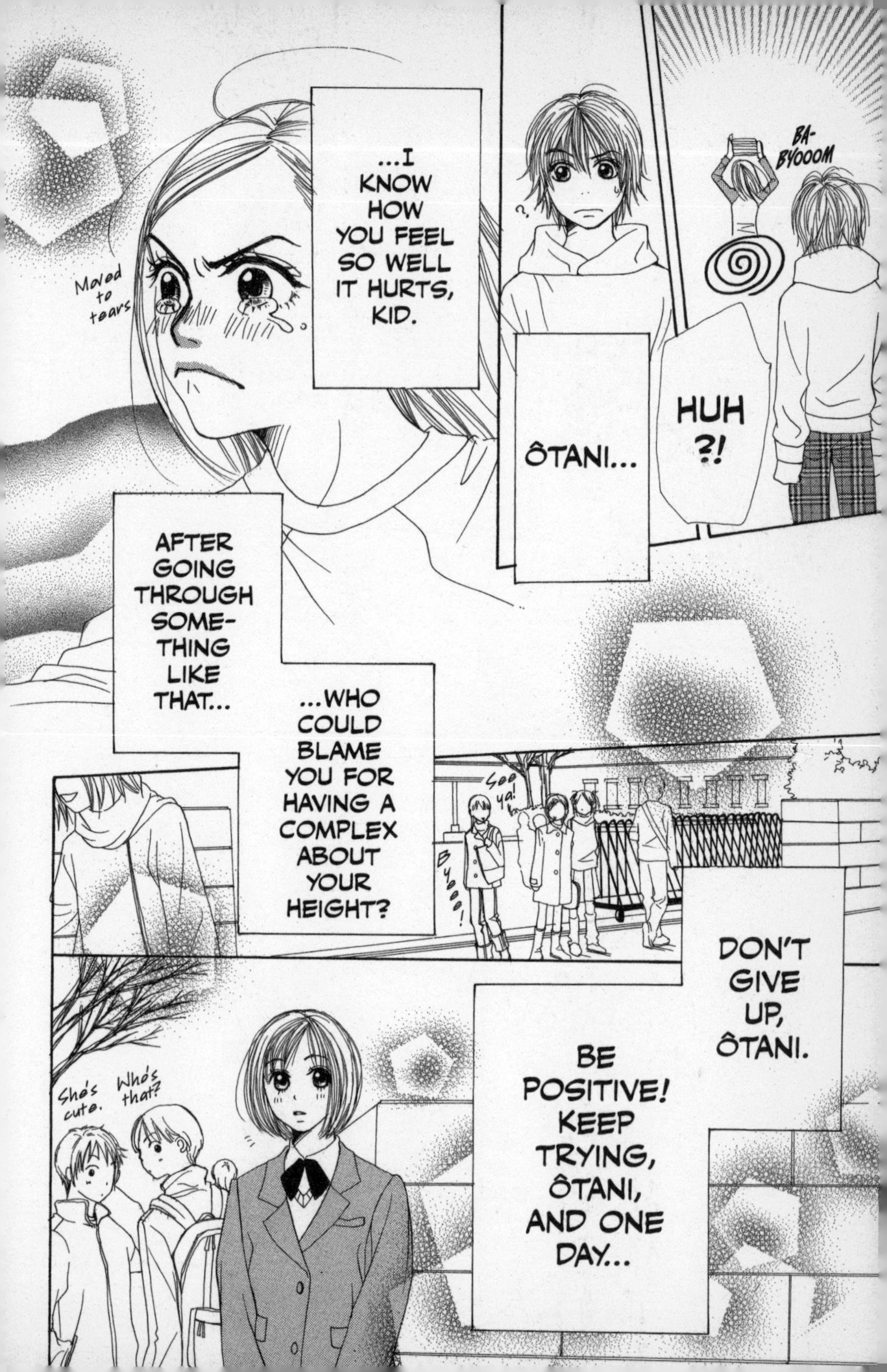
BA-BYOOOM
HUH ?!
ÔTANI...
...I KNOW HOW YOU FEEL SO WELL IT HURTS, KID.
Moved to tears
AFTER GOING THROUGH SOME-THING LIKE THAT...
...WHO COULD BLAME YOU FOR HAVING A COMPLEX ABOUT YOUR HEIGHT?
See ya!
Byeee!
DON'T GIVE UP, ÔTANI.
BE POSITIVE! KEEP TRYING, ÔTANI, AND ONE DAY...
Who's that?
She's cute.

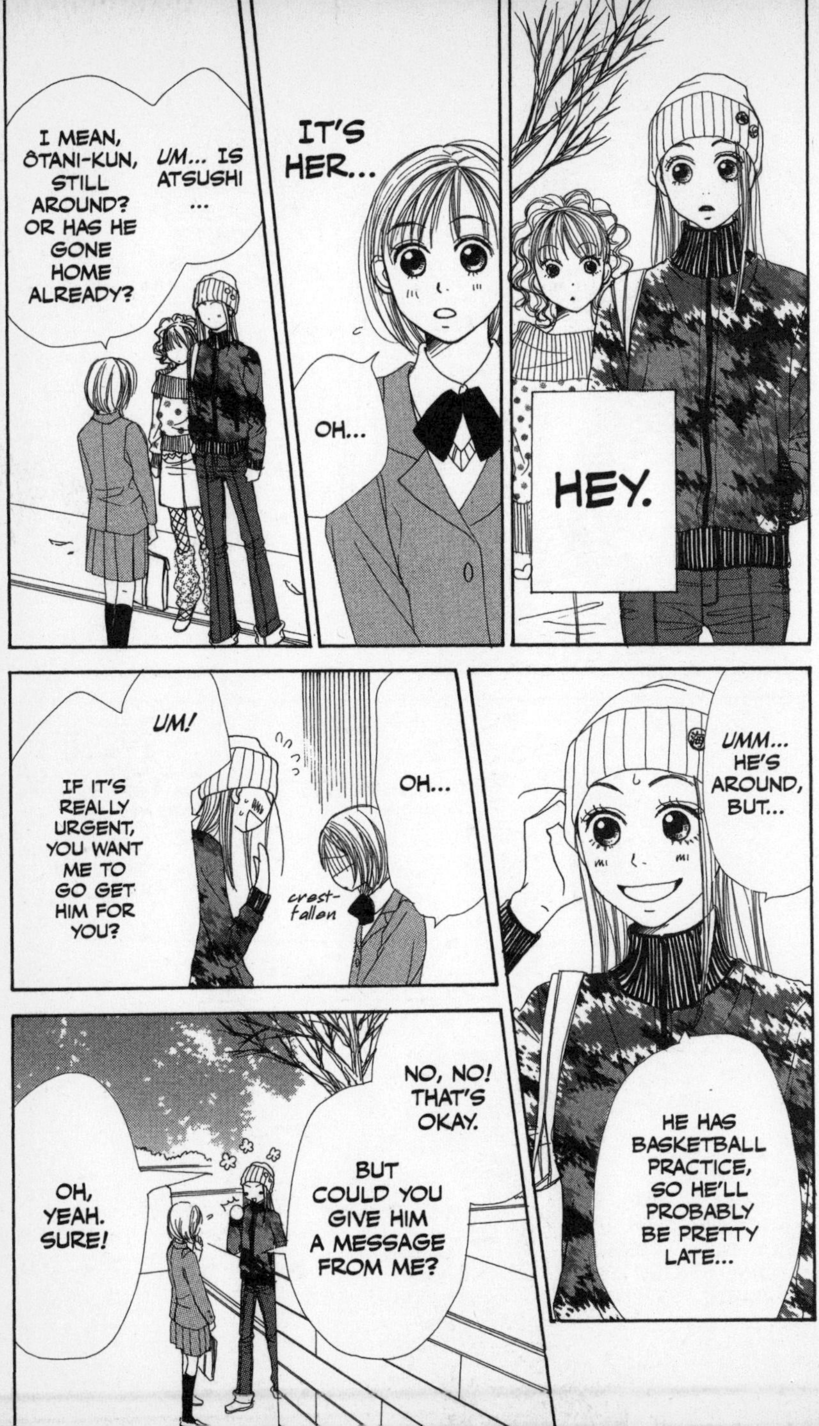
HEY.
IT'S HER...
OH...
UM... IS ATSUSHI ...
I MEAN, ŌTANI-KUN, STILL AROUND? OR HAS HE GONE HOME ALREADY?
UMM... HE'S AROUND, BUT...
HE HAS BASKETBALL PRACTICE, SO HE'LL PROBABLY BE PRETTY LATE...
OH...
crest-fallen
UM!
IF IT'S REALLY URGENT, YOU WANT ME TO GO GET HIM FOR YOU?
NO, NO! THAT'S OKAY.
BUT COULD YOU GIVE HIM A MESSAGE FROM ME?
OH, YEAH. SURE!

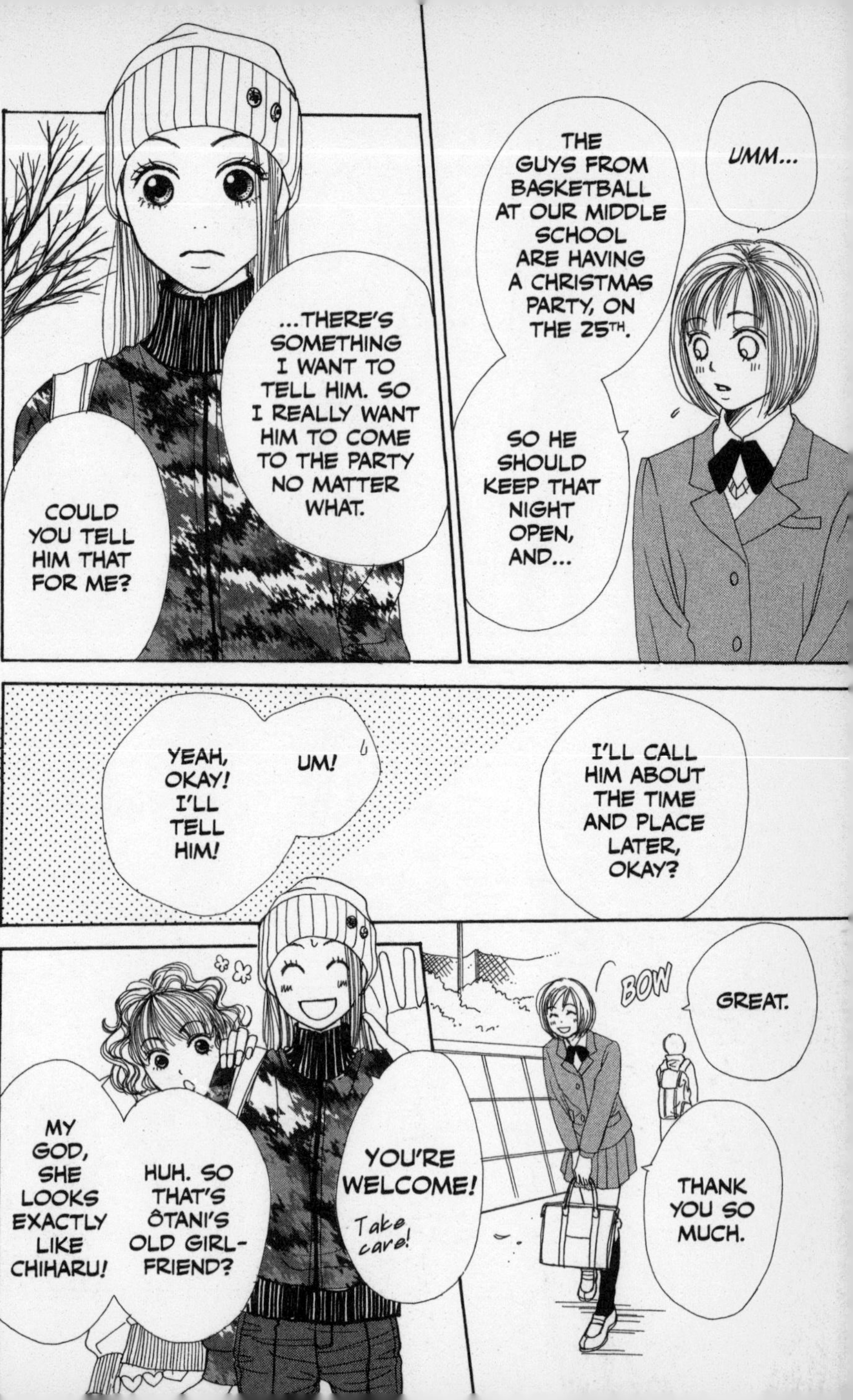
UMM...
THE GUYS FROM BASKETBALL AT OUR MIDDLE SCHOOL ARE HAVING A CHRISTMAS PARTY, ON THE 25TH.
SO HE SHOULD KEEP THAT NIGHT OPEN, AND...
...THERE'S SOMETHING I WANT TO TELL HIM. SO I REALLY WANT HIM TO COME TO THE PARTY NO MATTER WHAT.
COULD YOU TELL HIM THAT FOR ME?
I'LL CALL HIM ABOUT THE TIME AND PLACE LATER, OKAY?
UM!
YEAH, OKAY! I'LL TELL HIM!
GREAT.
BOW
THANK YOU SO MUCH.
YOU'RE WELCOME!
Take care!
HUH. SO THAT'S ÔTANI'S OLD GIRLFRIEND?
MY GOD, SHE LOOKS EXACTLY LIKE CHIHARU!

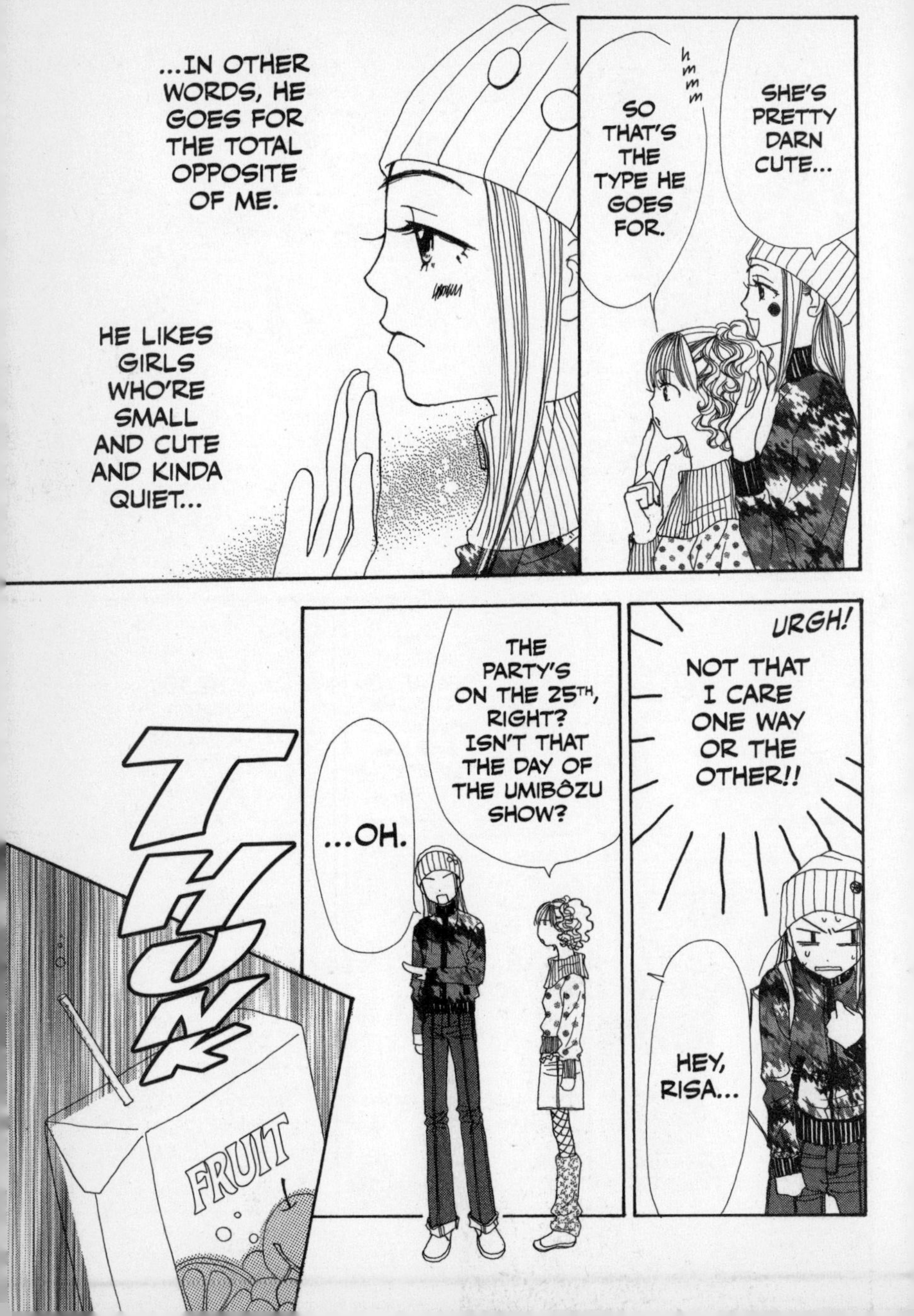
SHE'S PRETTY DARN CUTE...
hmmm
SO THAT'S THE TYPE HE GOES FOR.
...IN OTHER WORDS, HE GOES FOR THE TOTAL OPPOSITE OF ME.
HE LIKES GIRLS WHO'RE SMALL AND CUTE AND KINDA QUIET...
URGH!
NOT THAT I CARE ONE WAY OR THE OTHER!!
HEY, RISA...
THE PARTY'S ON THE 25TH, RIGHT? ISN'T THAT THE DAY OF THE UMIBÔZU SHOW?
...OH.
THUNK
FRUIT

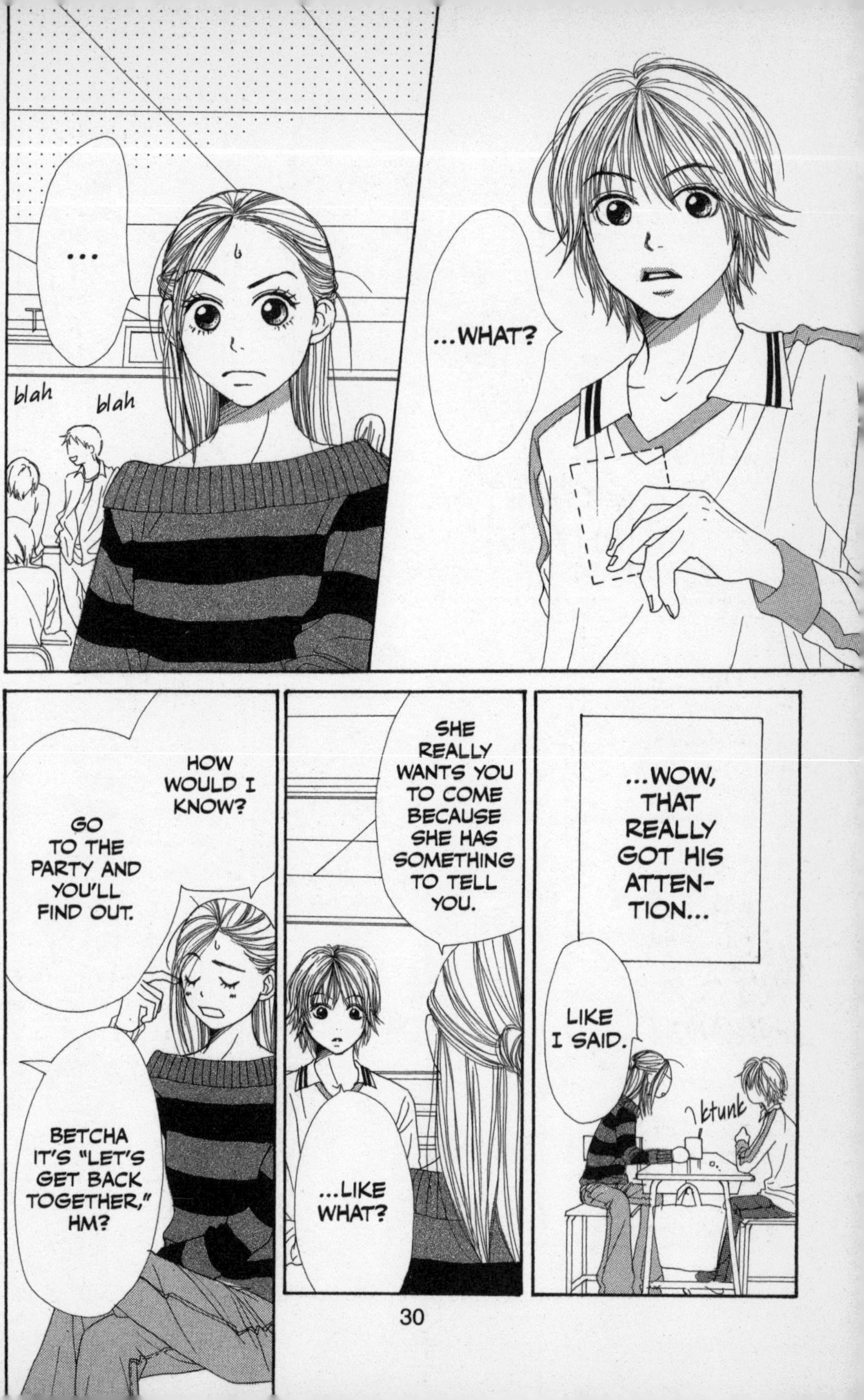
...WHAT?
...
blah
blah
...WOW, THAT REALLY GOT HIS ATTEN-TION...
LIKE I SAID.
ktunk
SHE REALLY WANTS YOU TO COME BECAUSE SHE HAS SOMETHING TO TELL YOU.
...LIKE WHAT?
HOW WOULD I KNOW?
GO TO THE PARTY AND YOU'LL FIND OUT.
BETCHA IT'S "LET'S GET BACK TOGETHER," HM?

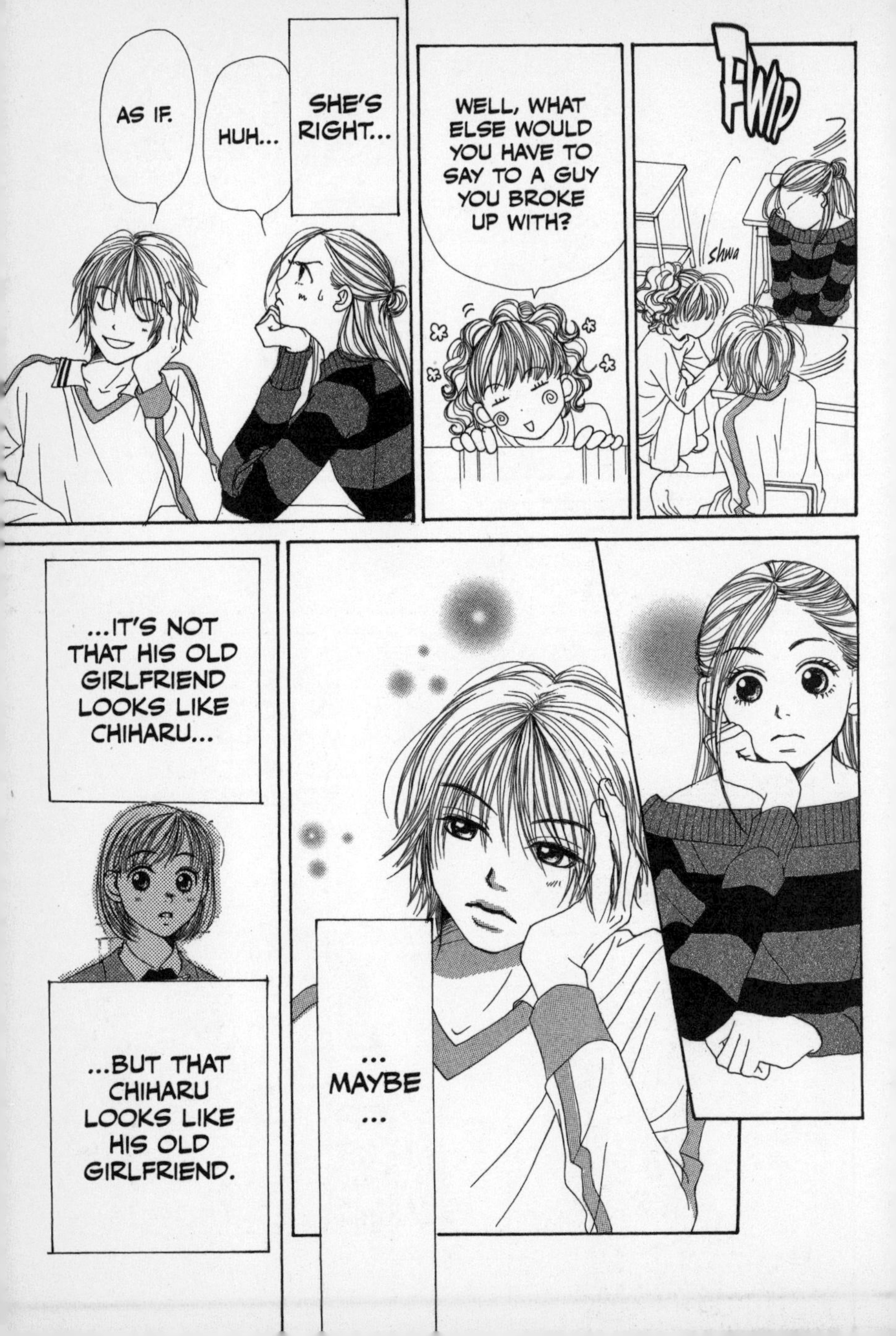
F-WIP
shwa
WELL, WHAT ELSE WOULD YOU HAVE TO SAY TO A GUY YOU BROKE UP WITH?
SHE'S RIGHT...
HUH...
AS IF.
... MAYBE ...
...IT'S NOT THAT HIS OLD GIRLFRIEND LOOKS LIKE CHIHARU...
...BUT THAT CHIHARU LOOKS LIKE HIS OLD GIRLFRIEND.

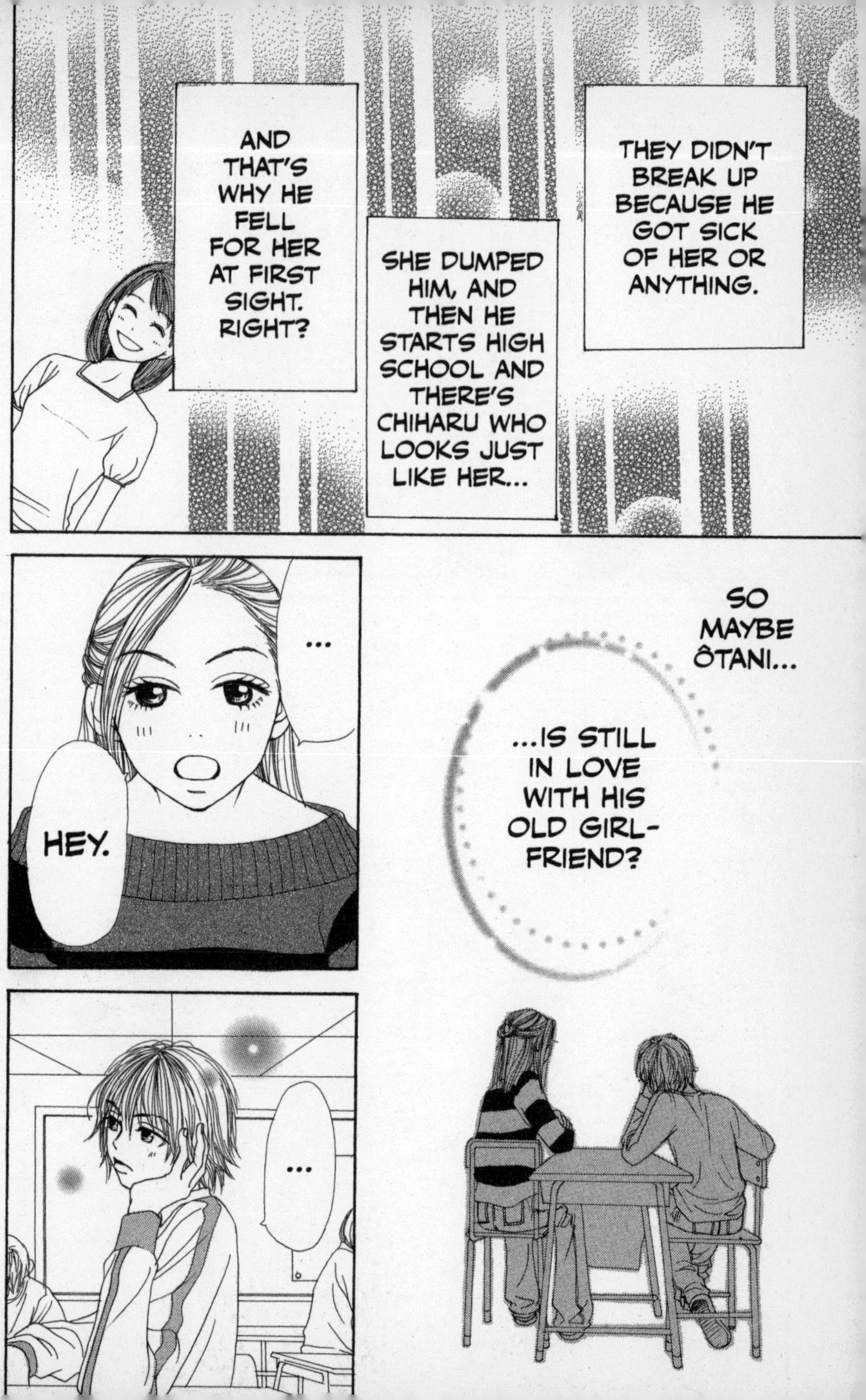
THEY DIDN'T BREAK UP BECAUSE HE GOT SICK OF HER OR ANYTHING.
SHE DUMPED HIM, AND THEN HE STARTS HIGH SCHOOL AND THERE'S CHIHARU WHO LOOKS JUST LIKE HER...
AND THAT'S WHY HE FELL FOR HER AT FIRST SIGHT. RIGHT?
SO MAYBE ÔTANI...
...IS STILL IN LOVE WITH HIS OLD GIRL-FRIEND?
...
HEY.
...

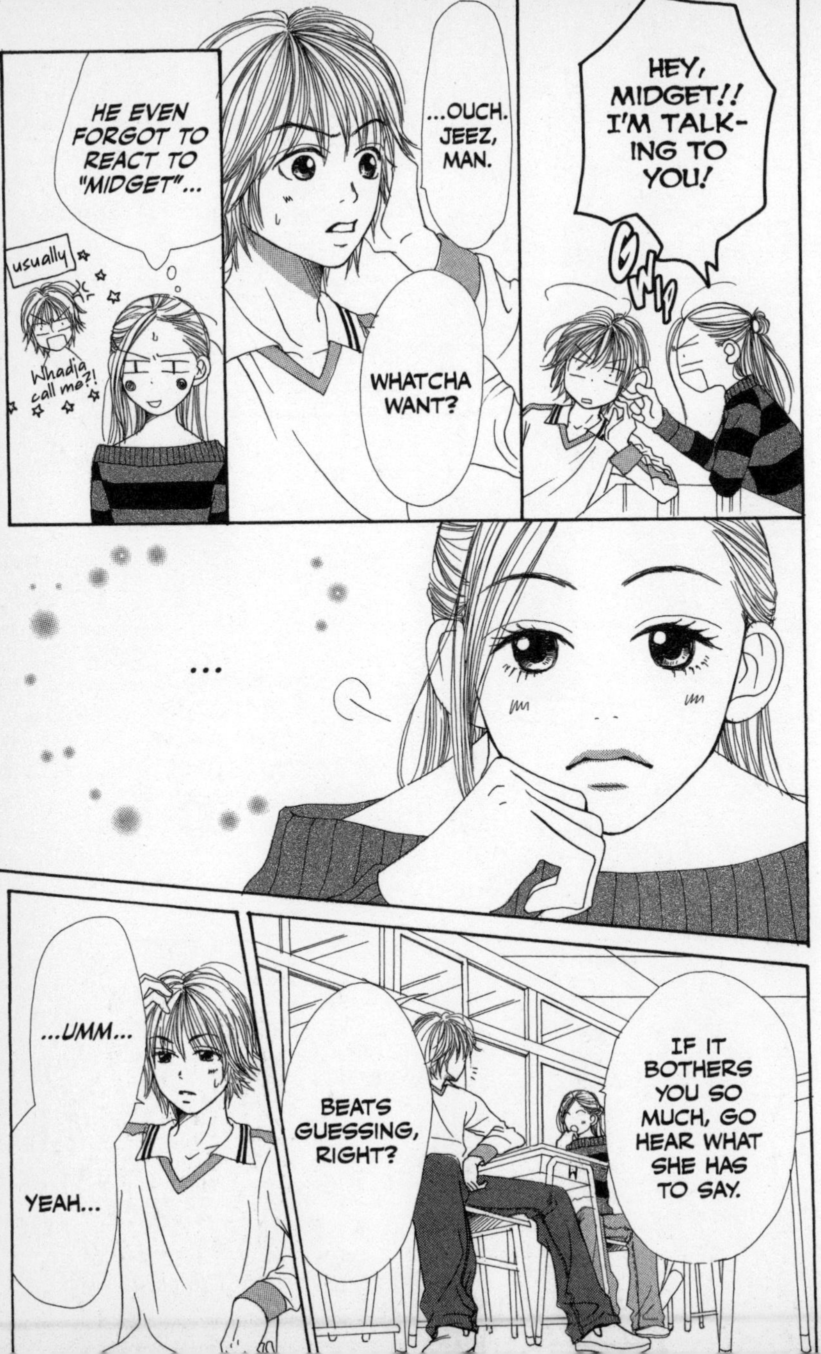

HEY, MIDGET!! I'M TALKING TO YOU!
...OUCH. JEEZ, MAN.
WHATCHA WANT?
HE EVEN FORGOT TO REACT TO "MIDGET"...
usually
Whadja call me?!
...
IF IT BOTHERS YOU SO MUCH, GO HEAR WHAT SHE HAS TO SAY.
BEATS GUESSING, RIGHT?
...UMM...
YEAH...

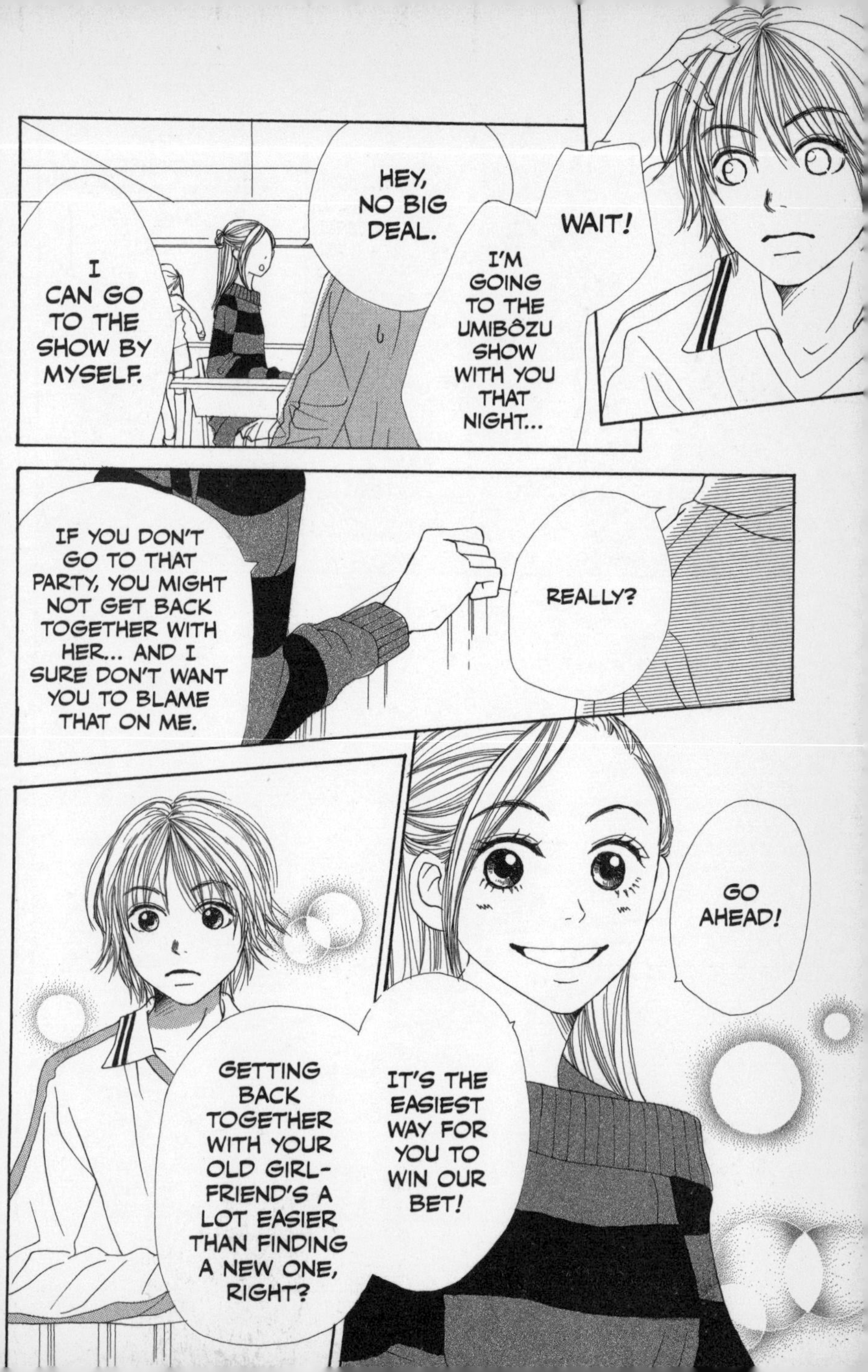
WAIT!
I'M GOING TO THE UMIBÔZU SHOW WITH YOU THAT NIGHT...
HEY, NO BIG DEAL.
I CAN GO TO THE SHOW BY MYSELF.
REALLY?
IF YOU DON'T GO TO THAT PARTY, YOU MIGHT NOT GET BACK TOGETHER WITH HER... AND I SURE DON'T WANT YOU TO BLAME THAT ON ME.
GO AHEAD!
IT'S THE EASIEST WAY FOR YOU TO WIN OUR BET!
GETTING BACK TOGETHER WITH YOUR OLD GIRL-FRIEND'S A LOT EASIER THAN FINDING A NEW ONE, RIGHT?

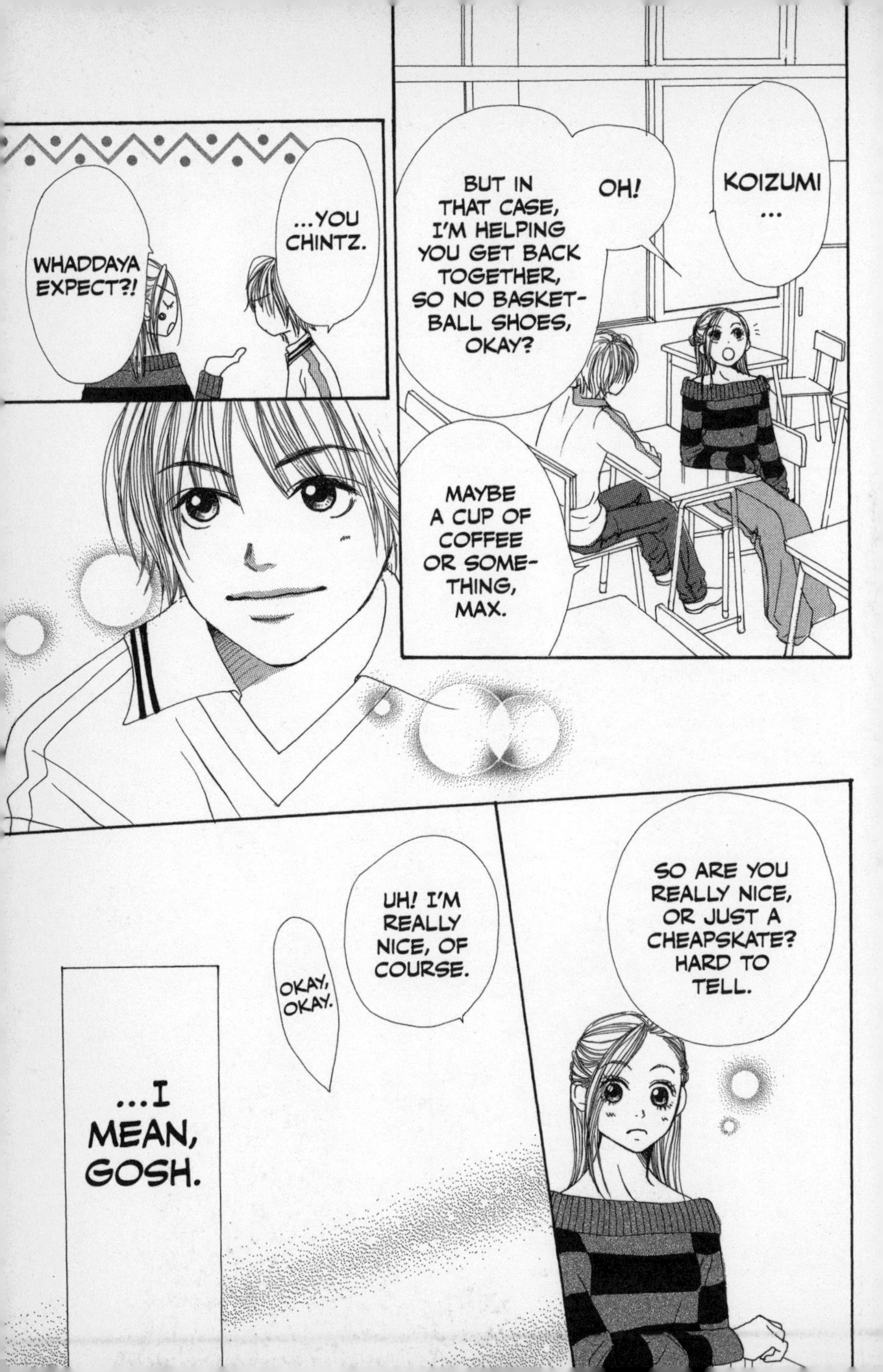
KOIZUMI ...
OH!
BUT IN THAT CASE, I'M HELPING YOU GET BACK TOGETHER, SO NO BASKETBALL SHOES, OKAY?
MAYBE A CUP OF COFFEE OR SOMETHING, MAX.
...YOU CHINTZ.
WHADDAYA EXPECT?!
SO ARE YOU REALLY NICE, OR JUST A CHEAPSKATE? HARD TO TELL.
UH! I'M REALLY NICE, OF COURSE.
OKAY, OKAY.
...I MEAN, GOSH.

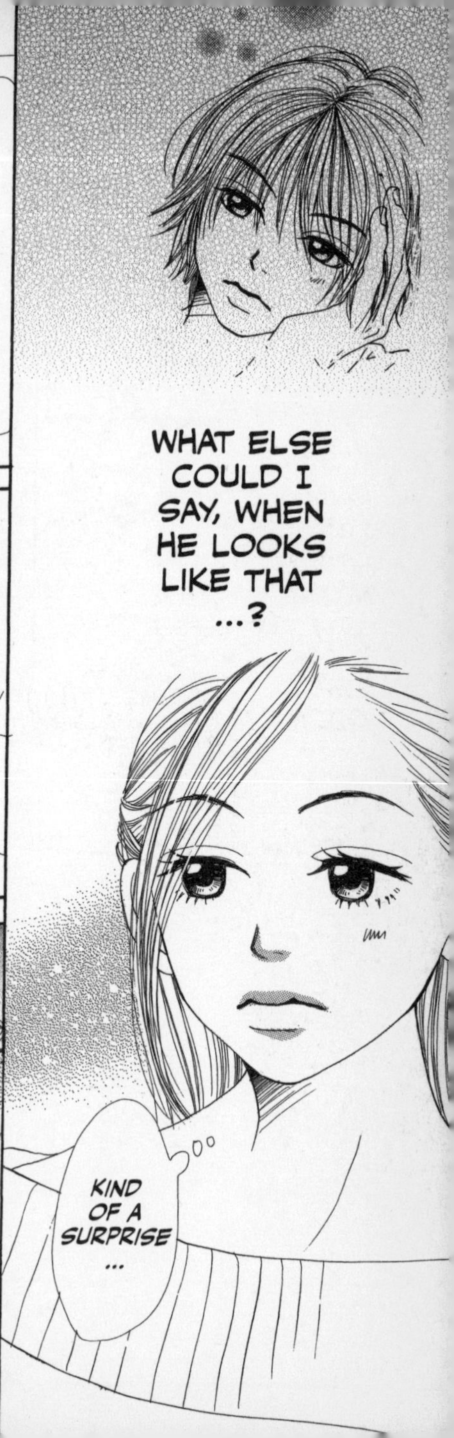
WHAT ELSE COULD I SAY, WHEN HE LOOKS LIKE THAT ...?
KIND OF A SURPRISE ...

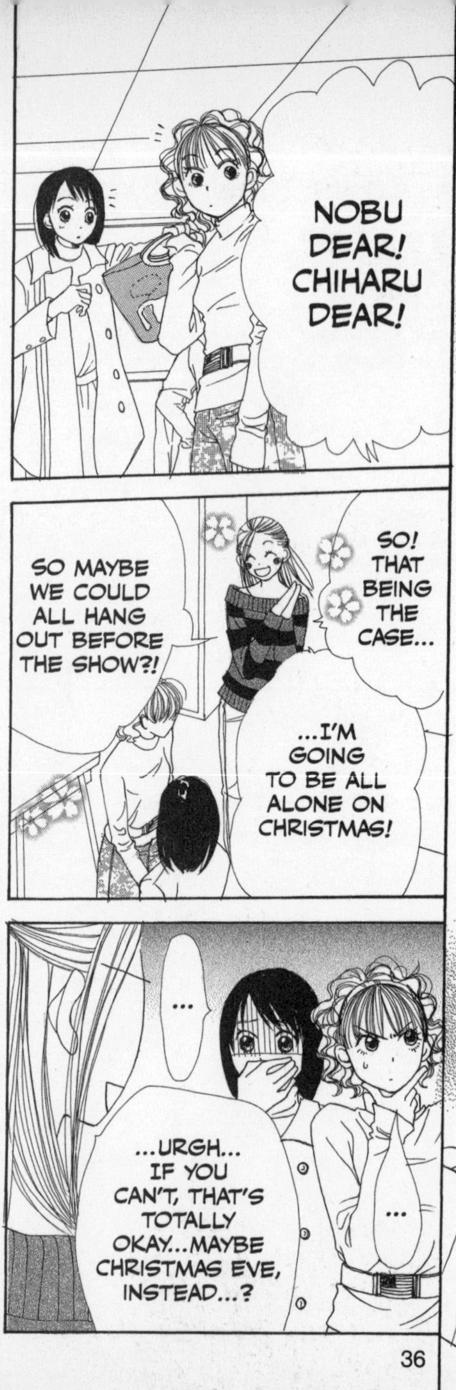
NOBU DEAR! CHIHARU DEAR!
SO! THAT BEING THE CASE...
...I'M GOING TO BE ALL ALONE ON CHRISTMAS!
SO MAYBE WE COULD ALL HANG OUT BEFORE THE SHOW?!
...
...
...URGH... IF YOU CAN'T, THAT'S TOTALLY OKAY...MAYBE CHRISTMAS EVE, INSTEAD...?

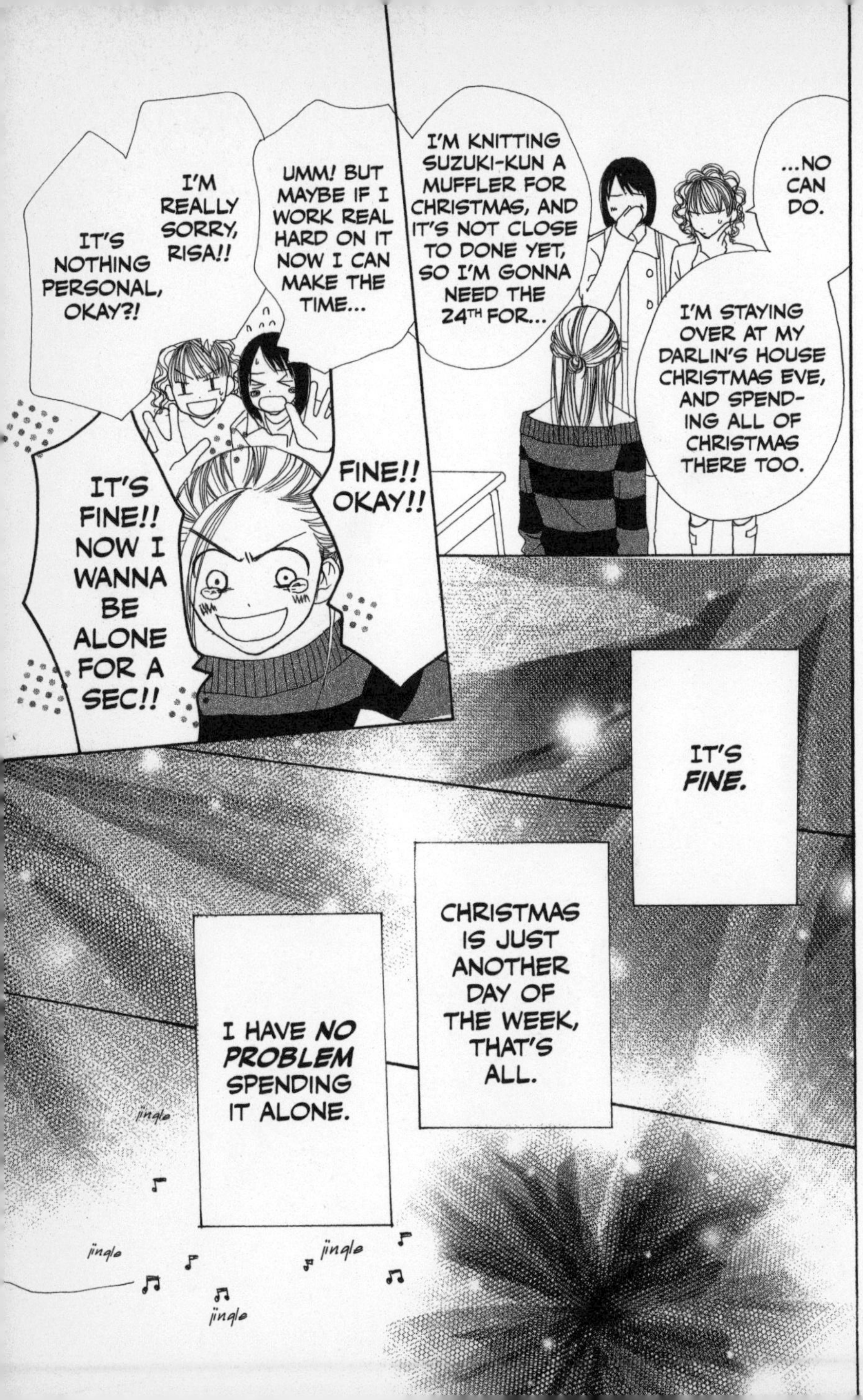
...NO CAN DO.
I'M STAYING OVER AT MY DARLIN'S HOUSE CHRISTMAS EVE, AND SPEND-ING ALL OF CHRISTMAS THERE TOO.
I'M KNITTING SUZUKI-KUN A MUFFLER FOR CHRISTMAS, AND IT'S NOT CLOSE TO DONE YET, SO I'M GONNA NEED THE 24TH FOR...
UMM! BUT MAYBE IF I WORK REAL HARD ON IT NOW I CAN MAKE THE TIME...
I'M REALLY SORRY, RISA!!
IT'S NOTHING PERSONAL, OKAY?!
FINE!! OKAY!!
IT'S FINE!! NOW I WANNA BE ALONE FOR A SEC!!
IT'S *FINE.*
CHRISTMAS IS JUST ANOTHER DAY OF THE WEEK, THAT'S ALL.
I HAVE *NO PROBLEM* SPENDING IT ALONE.
jingle
jingle
jingle
jingle

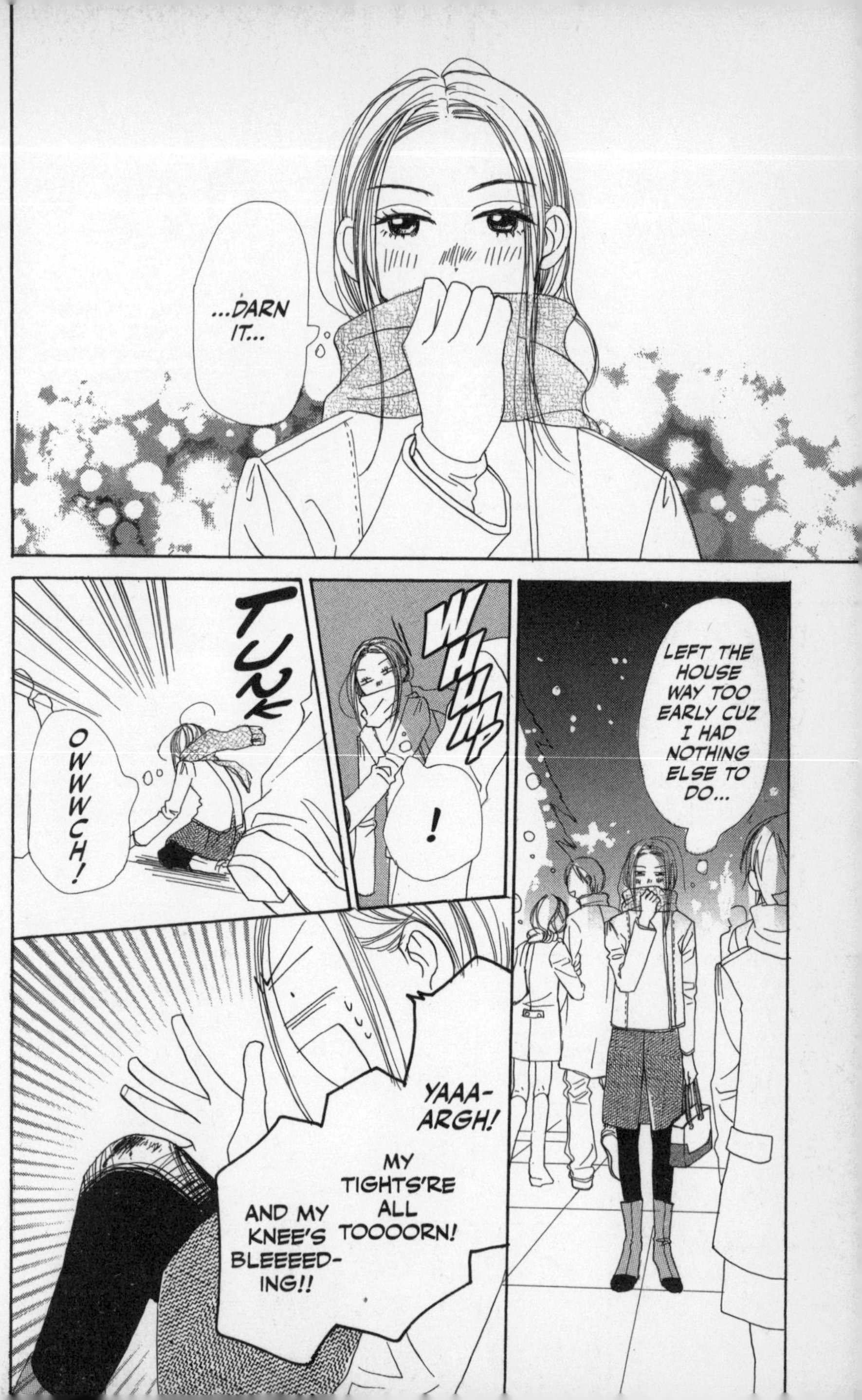
...DARN IT...
LEFT THE HOUSE WAY TOO EARLY CUZ I HAD NOTHING ELSE TO DO...
WHUMP
!
TUNK
OWWWCH!
YAAA-ARGH!
MY TIGHTS'RE ALL TOOOORN!
AND MY KNEE'S BLEEEED-ING!!

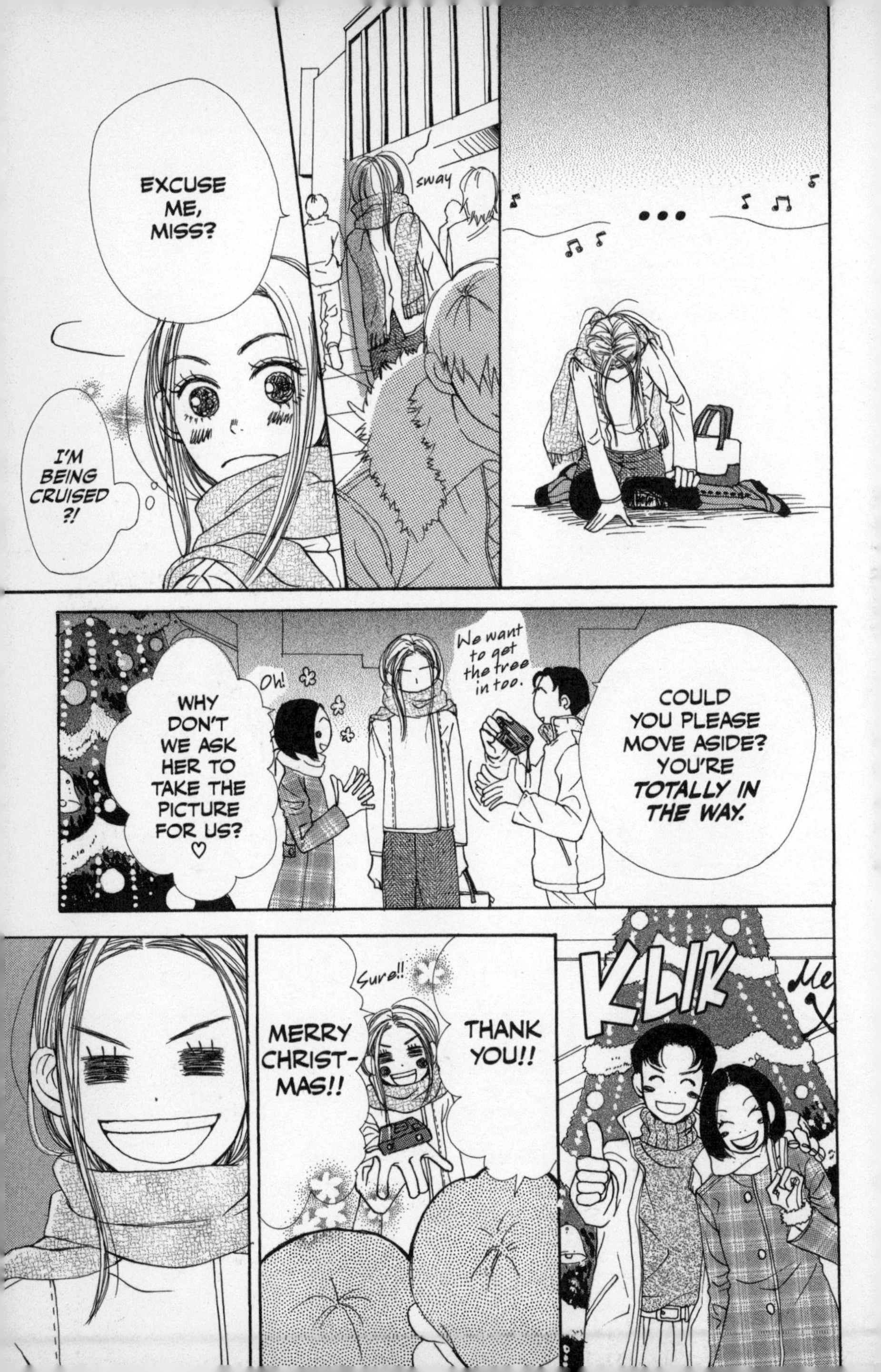
•••
sway
EXCUSE ME, MISS?
I'M BEING CRUISED ?!
COULD YOU PLEASE MOVE ASIDE? YOU'RE *TOTALLY IN THE WAY.*
We want to get the tree in too.
Oh!
WHY DON'T WE ASK HER TO TAKE THE PICTURE FOR US? ♡
KLIK
Me
THANK YOU!!
Sure!!
MERRY CHRIST-MAS!!

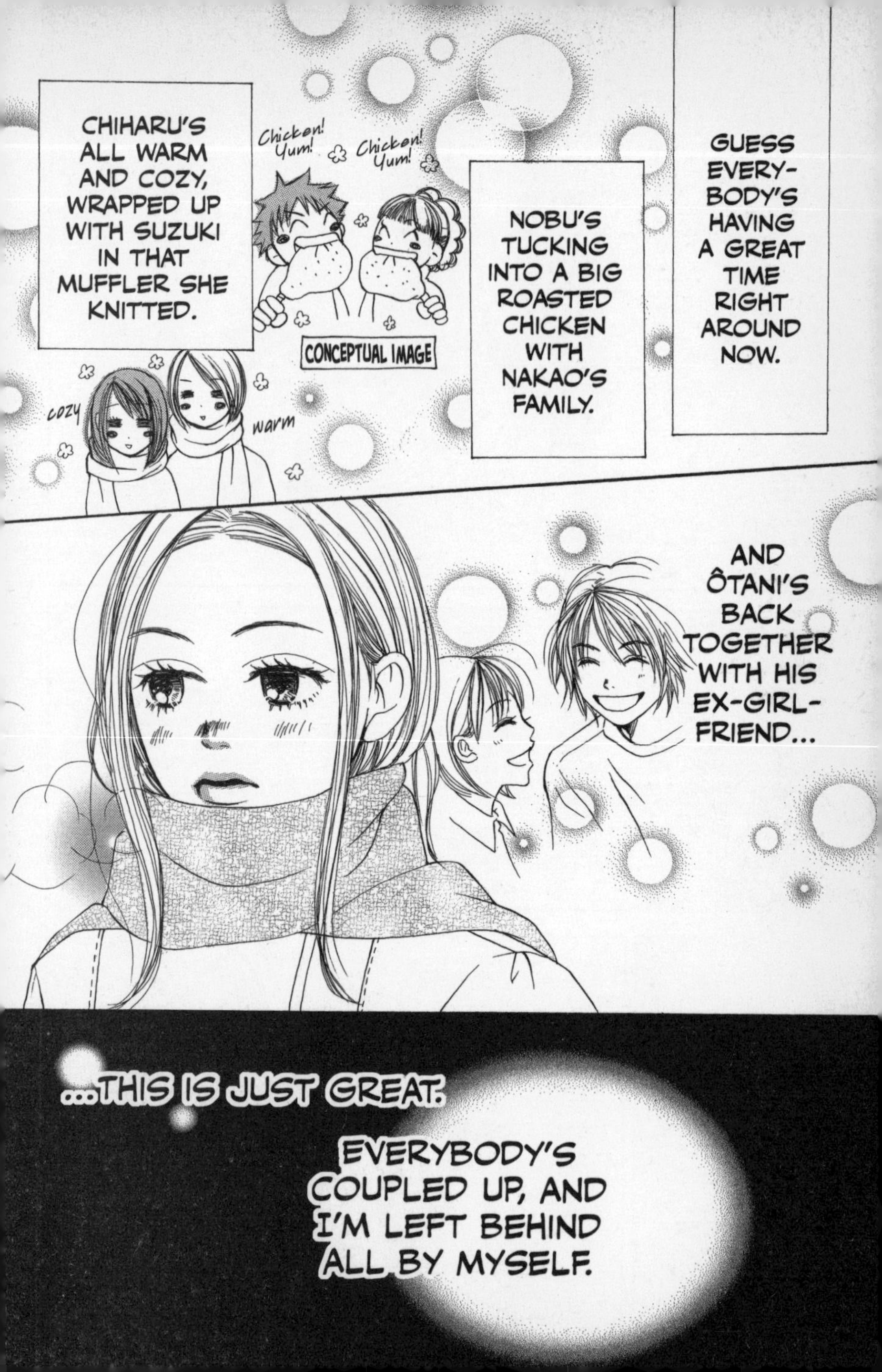
GUESS EVERYBODY'S HAVING A GREAT TIME RIGHT AROUND NOW.
NOBU'S TUCKING INTO A BIG ROASTED CHICKEN WITH NAKAO'S FAMILY.
Chicken! Yum!
Chicken! Yum!
CONCEPTUAL IMAGE
CHIHARU'S ALL WARM AND COZY, WRAPPED UP WITH SUZUKI IN THAT MUFFLER SHE KNITTED.
warm
cozy
AND ÔTANI'S BACK TOGETHER WITH HIS EX-GIRLFRIEND...
...THIS IS JUST GREAT.
EVERYBODY'S COUPLED UP, AND I'M LEFT BEHIND ALL BY MYSELF.

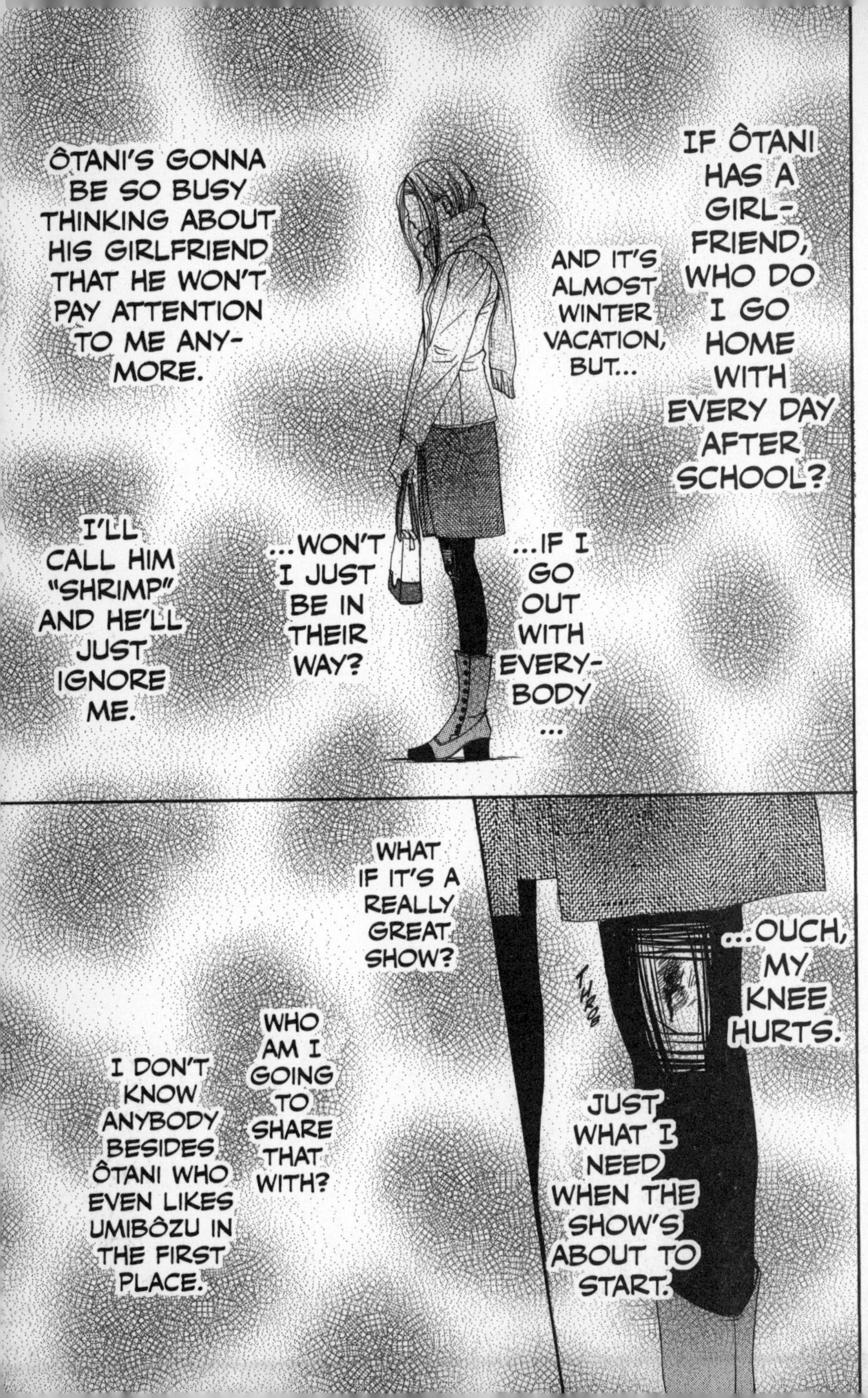
IF ÔTANI HAS A GIRL-FRIEND, WHO DO I GO HOME WITH EVERY DAY AFTER SCHOOL?
AND IT'S ALMOST WINTER VACATION, BUT...
ÔTANI'S GONNA BE SO BUSY THINKING ABOUT HIS GIRLFRIEND THAT HE WON'T PAY ATTENTION TO ME ANY-MORE.
...IF I GO OUT WITH EVERY-BODY ...
...WON'T I JUST BE IN THEIR WAY?
I'LL CALL HIM "SHRIMP" AND HE'LL JUST IGNORE ME.
...OUCH, MY KNEE HURTS.
JUST WHAT I NEED WHEN THE SHOW'S ABOUT TO START.
WHAT IF IT'S A REALLY GREAT SHOW?
WHO AM I GOING TO SHARE THAT WITH?
I DON'T KNOW ANYBODY BESIDES ÔTANI WHO EVEN LIKES UMIBÔZU IN THE FIRST PLACE.

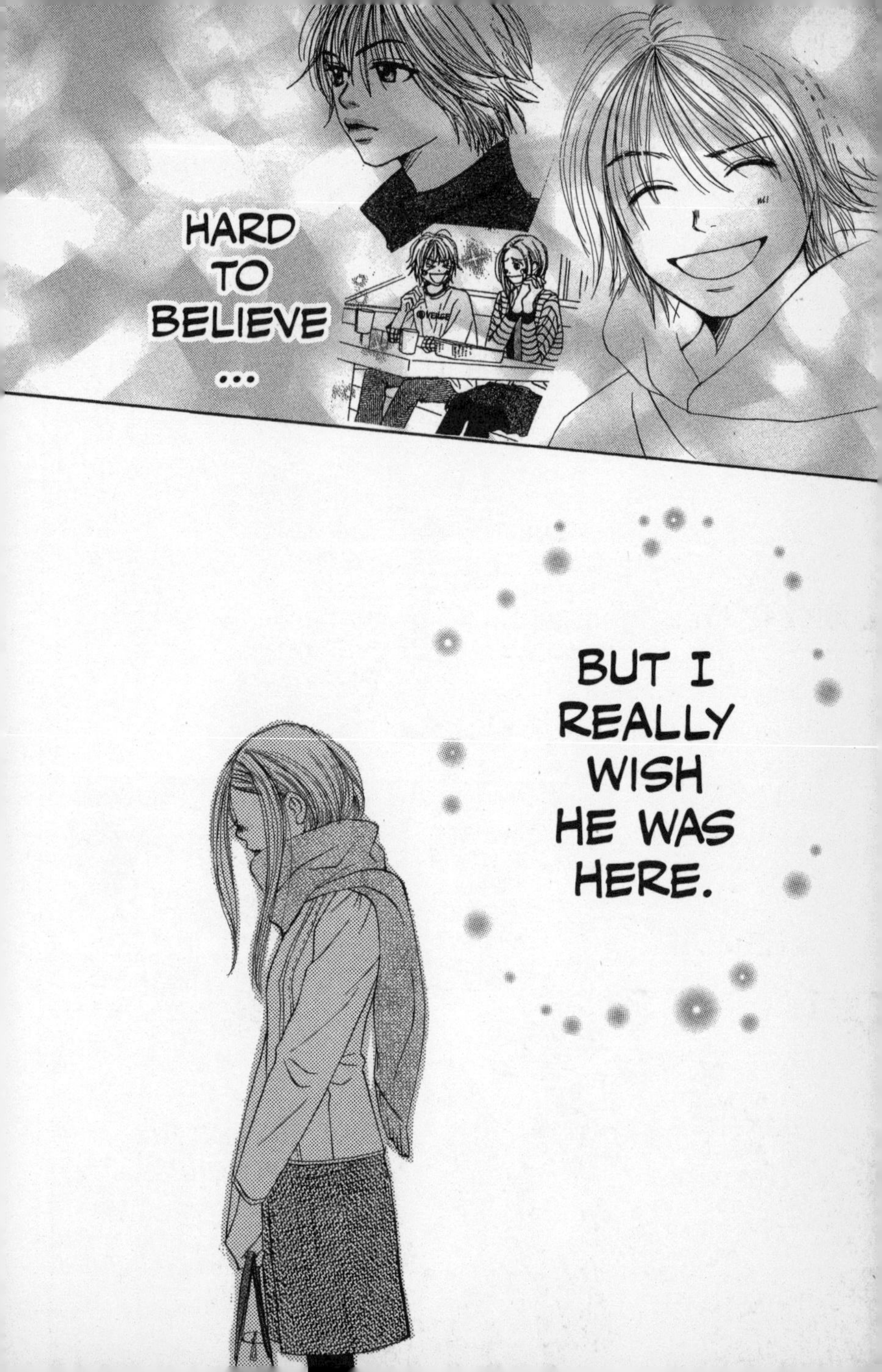
HARD TO BELIEVE ...
BUT I REALLY WISH HE WAS HERE.

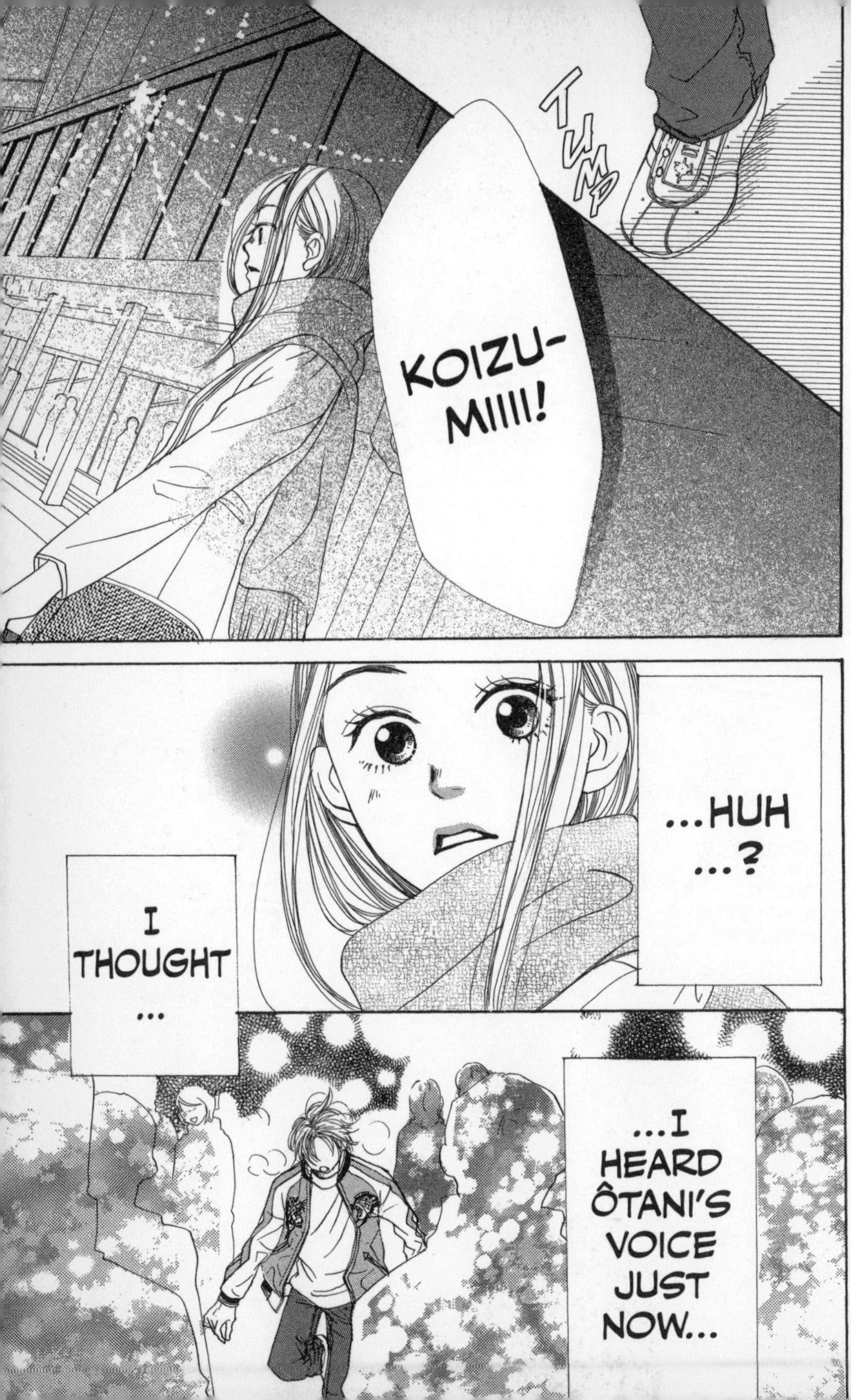
TUMP
KOIZU-MIIII!
...HUH ...?
I THOUGHT ...
...I HEARD ÔTANI'S VOICE JUST NOW...

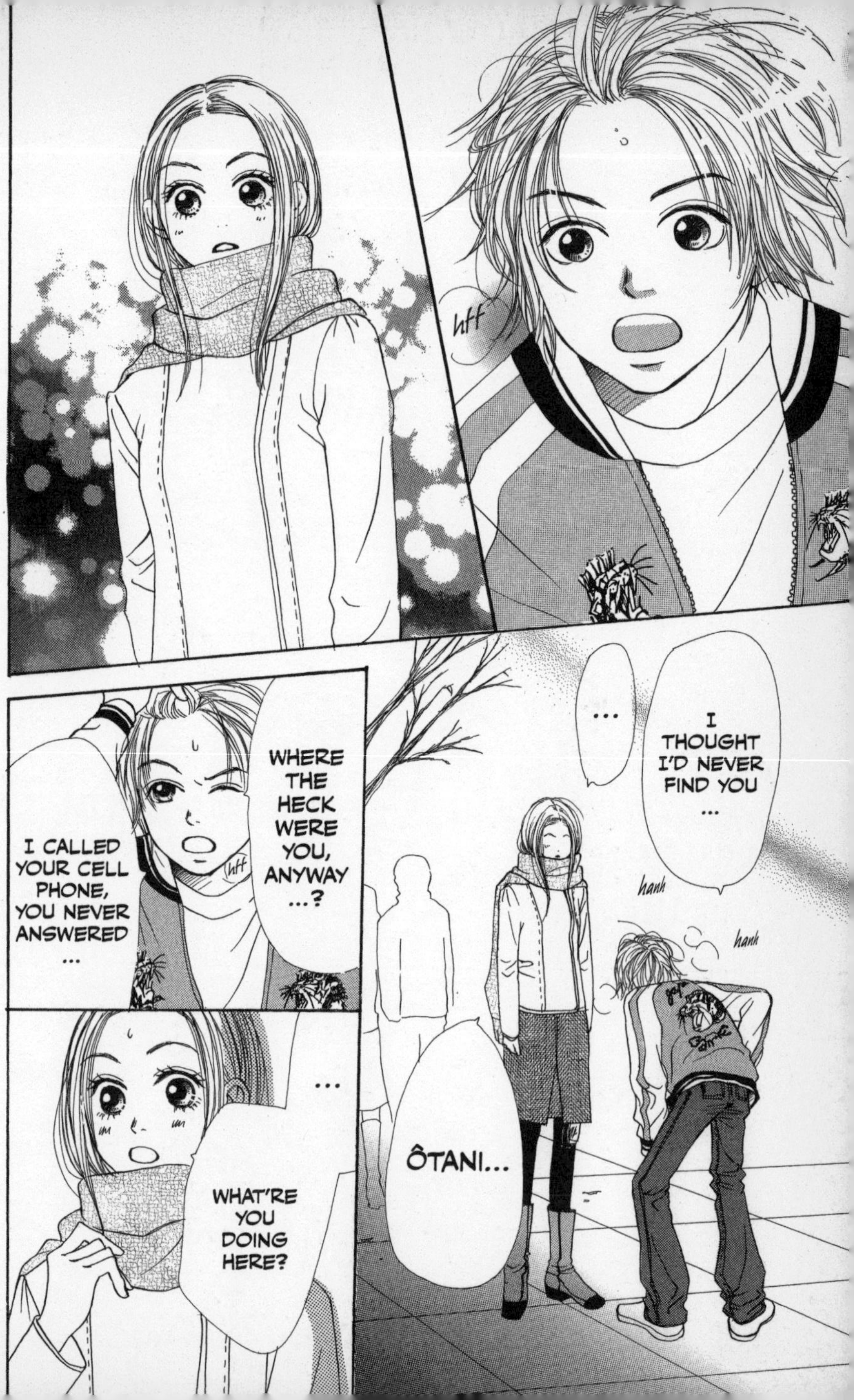
hff
I THOUGHT I'D NEVER FIND YOU ...
...
hanh
hanh
ÔTANI...
WHERE THE HECK WERE YOU, ANYWAY ...?
hff
I CALLED YOUR CELL PHONE, YOU NEVER ANSWERED ...
...
WHAT'RE YOU DOING HERE?

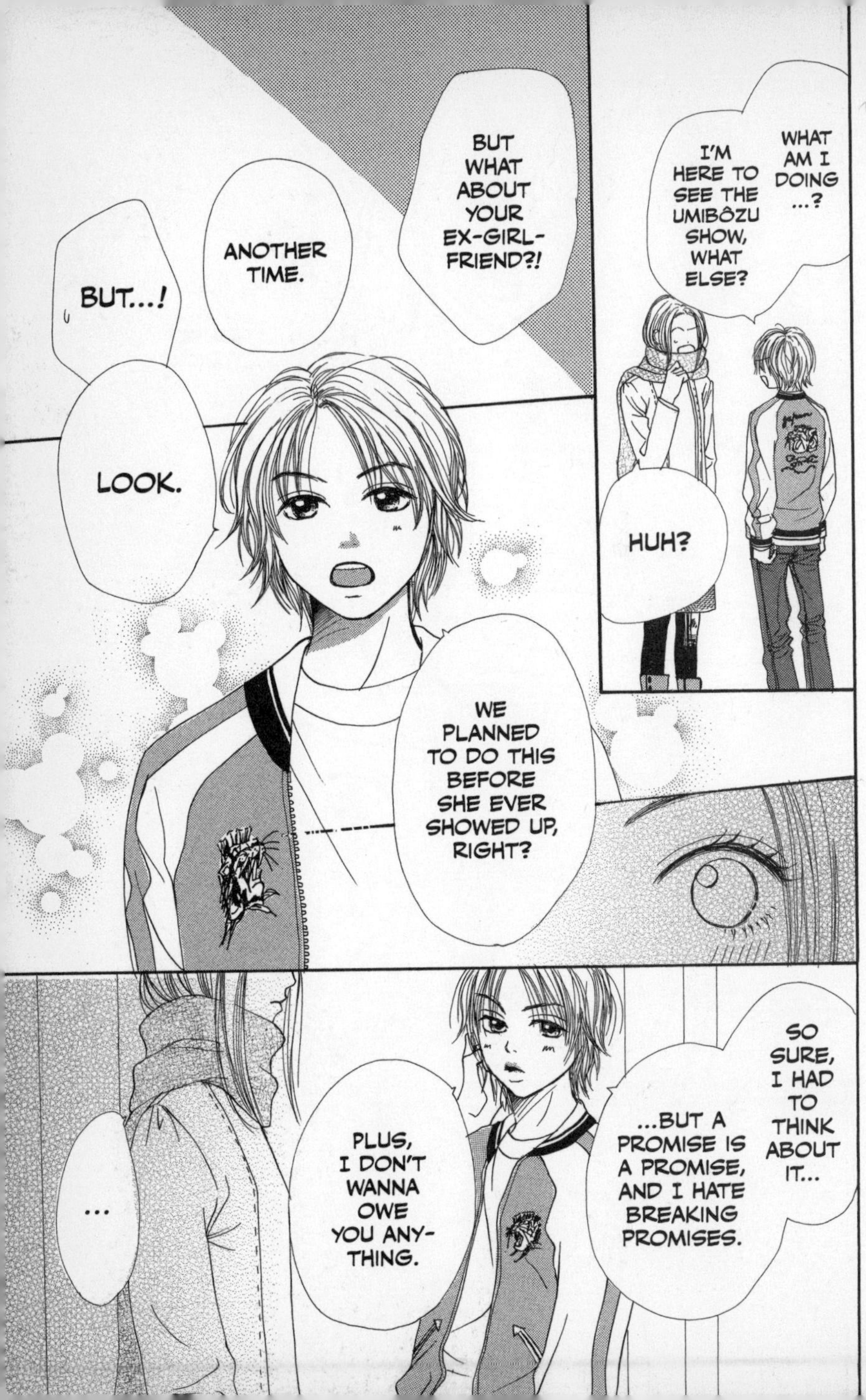
WHAT AM I DOING ...?
I'M HERE TO SEE THE UMIBÔZU SHOW, WHAT ELSE?
HUH?
BUT WHAT ABOUT YOUR EX-GIRL-FRIEND?!
ANOTHER TIME.
BUT...!
LOOK.
WE PLANNED TO DO THIS BEFORE SHE EVER SHOWED UP, RIGHT?
SO SURE, I HAD TO THINK ABOUT IT...
...BUT A PROMISE IS A PROMISE, AND I HATE BREAKING PROMISES.
PLUS, I DON'T WANNA OWE YOU ANY-THING.
...

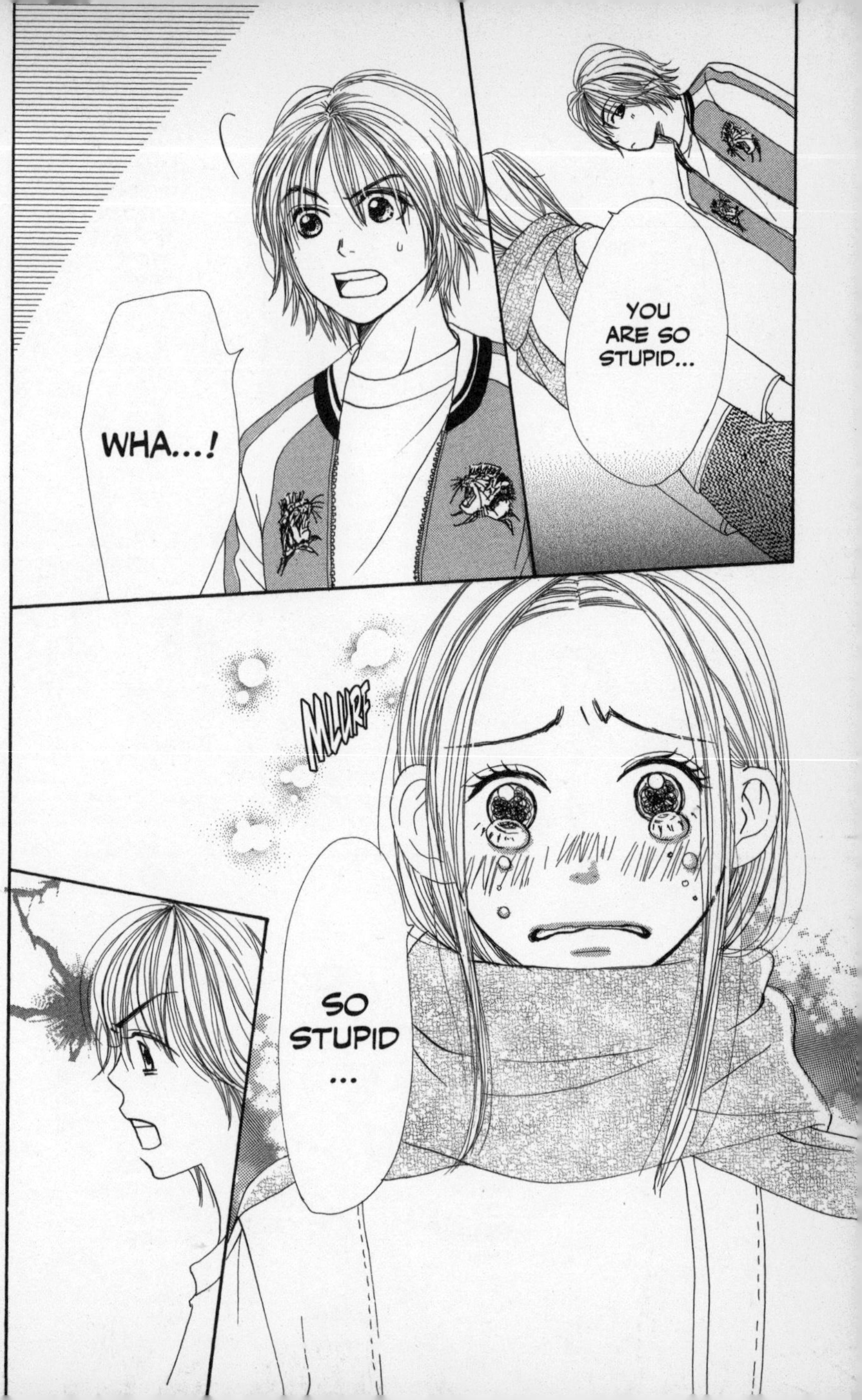
YOU ARE SO STUPID...
WHA...!
MLURF
SO STUPID ...

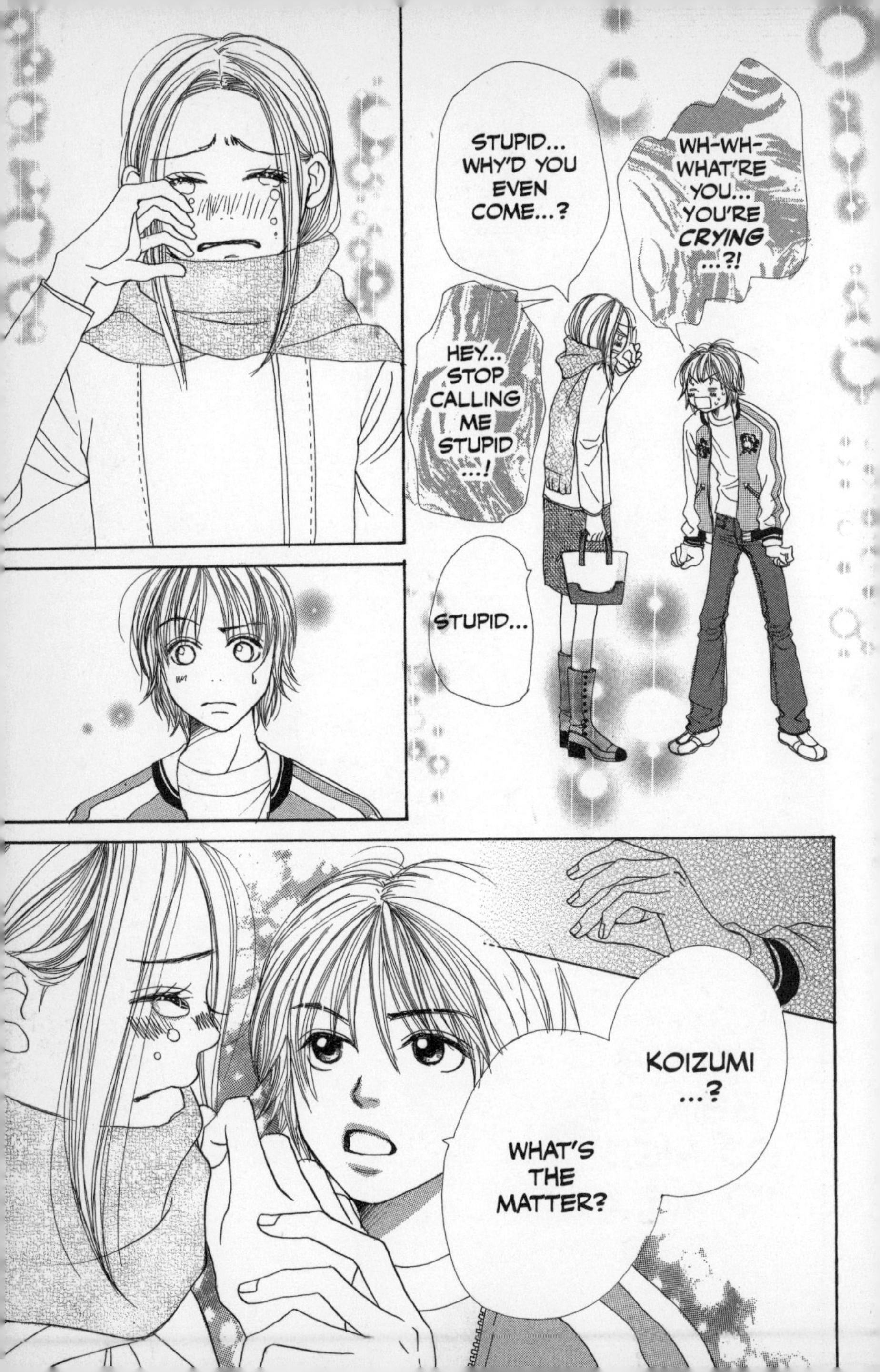
WH-WH-WHAT'RE YOU... YOU'RE *CRYING*...?!
STUPID... WHY'D YOU EVEN COME...?
HEY... STOP CALLING ME STUPID...!
STUPID...
KOIZUMI...?
WHAT'S THE MATTER?

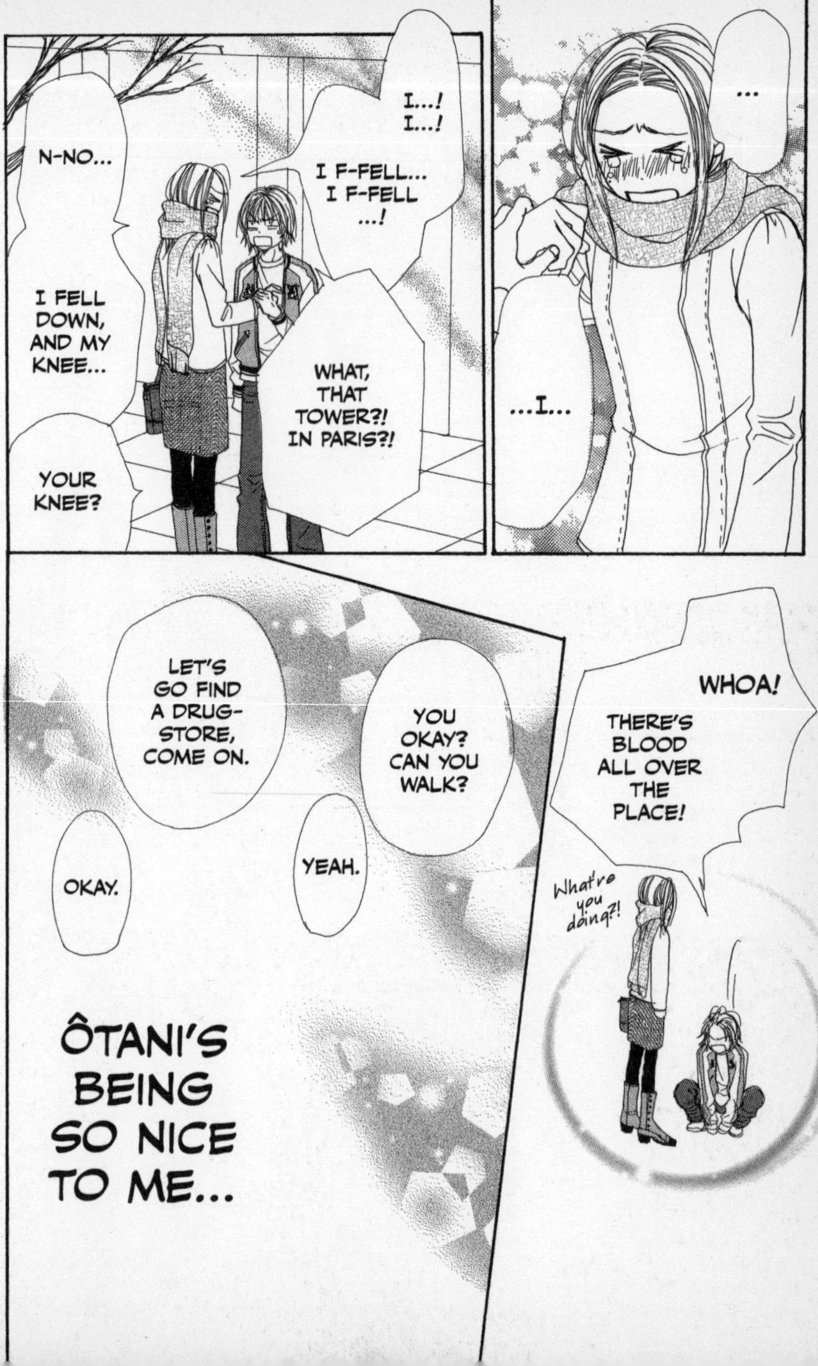
...
...I...
I...! I...!
I F-FELL... I F-FELL ...!
N-NO...
WHAT, THAT TOWER?! IN PARIS?!
I FELL DOWN, AND MY KNEE...
YOUR KNEE?
WHOA!
THERE'S BLOOD ALL OVER THE PLACE!
What're you doing?!
YOU OKAY? CAN YOU WALK?
LET'S GO FIND A DRUG-STORE, COME ON.
YEAH.
OKAY.
ÔTANI'S BEING SO NICE TO ME...

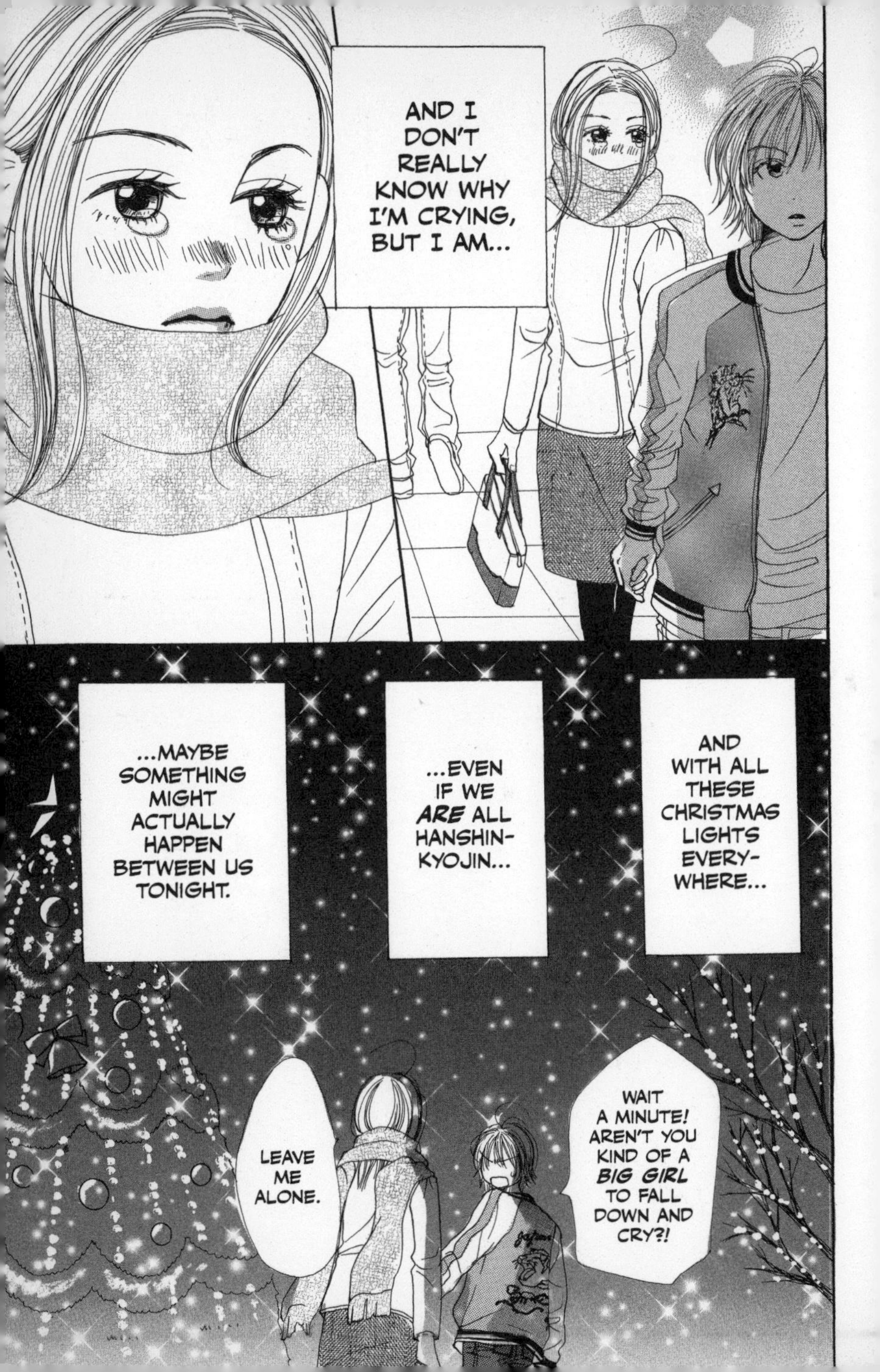
AND I DON'T REALLY KNOW WHY I'M CRYING, BUT I AM...
AND WITH ALL THESE CHRISTMAS LIGHTS EVERY-WHERE...
...EVEN IF WE *ARE* ALL HANSHIN-KYOJIN...
...MAYBE SOMETHING MIGHT ACTUALLY HAPPEN BETWEEN US TONIGHT.
WAIT A MINUTE! AREN'T YOU KIND OF A *BIG GIRL* TO FALL DOWN AND CRY?!
LEAVE ME ALONE.

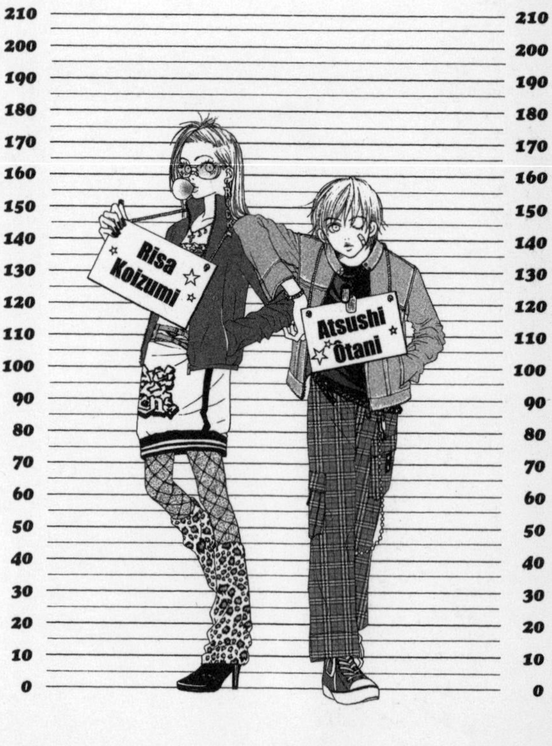
Atsushi Ôtani
Risa Koizumi

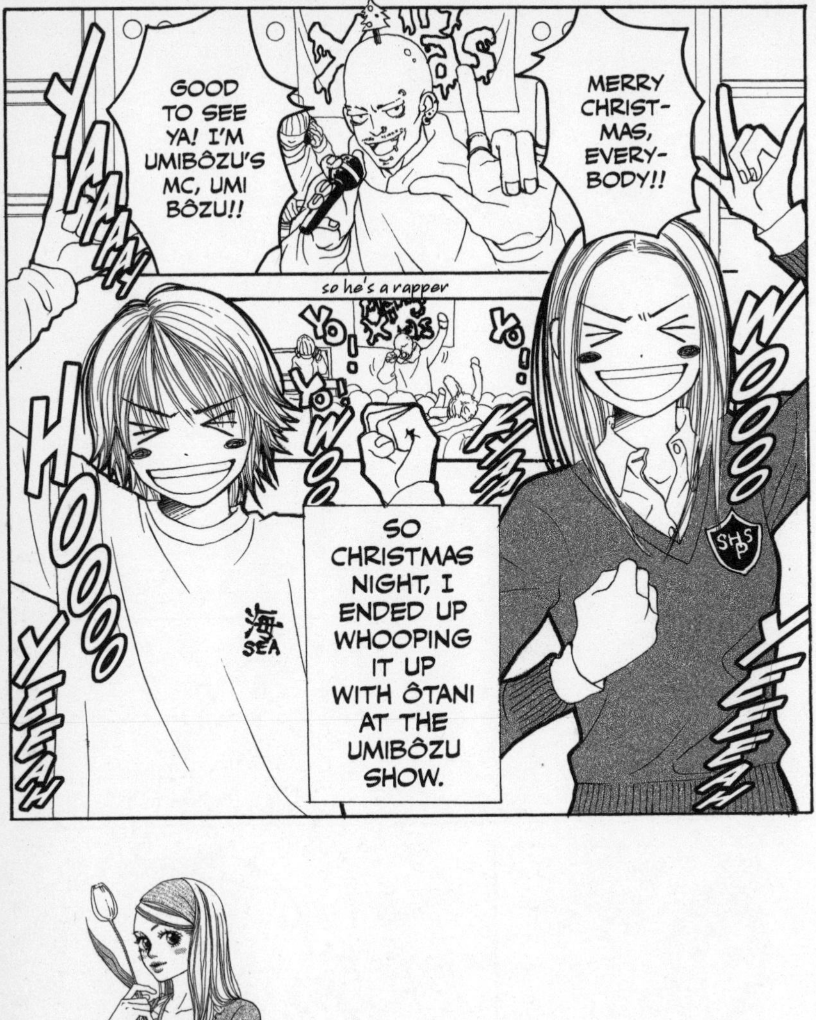
MERRY CHRISTMAS, EVERYBODY!!
GOOD TO SEE YA! I'M UMIBÔZU'S MC, UMI BÔZU!!
YAAAAH
WOOOOO
YO!
YO!
YO!
so he's a rapper
SO CHRISTMAS NIGHT, I ENDED UP WHOOPING IT UP WITH ÔTANI AT THE UMIBÔZU SHOW.
YEEEEAH
HOOOOO
YEEEAH
海 SEA

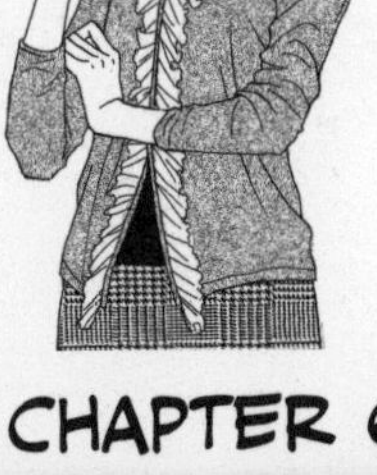

CHAPTER 6

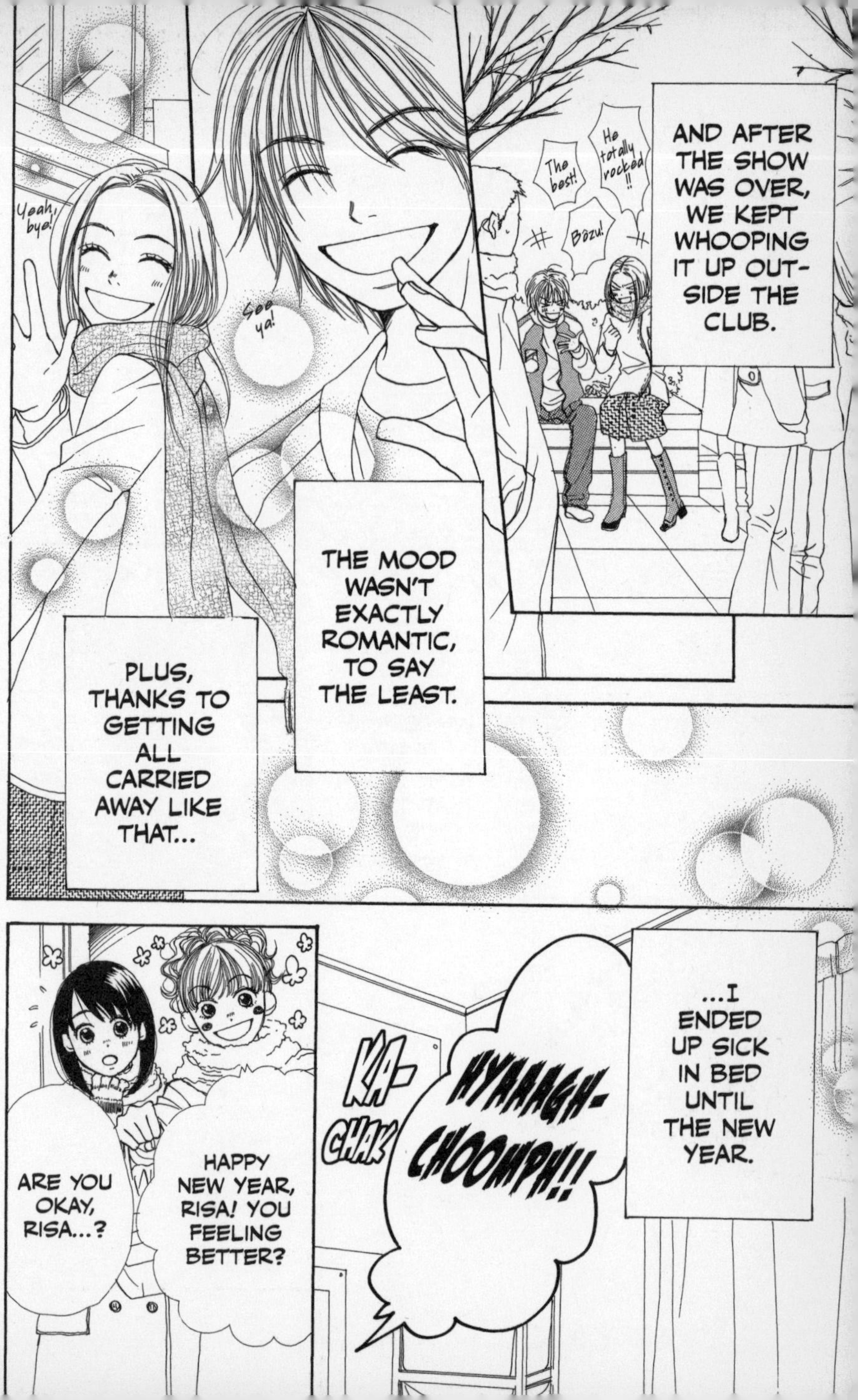
AND AFTER THE SHOW WAS OVER, WE KEPT WHOOPING IT UP OUT-SIDE THE CLUB.
He totally rocked!!
The best!
Bôzu!
See ya!
THE MOOD WASN'T EXACTLY ROMANTIC, TO SAY THE LEAST.
Yeah, bye!
PLUS, THANKS TO GETTING ALL CARRIED AWAY LIKE THAT...
...I ENDED UP SICK IN BED UNTIL THE NEW YEAR.
HYAAAGH-CHOOMPH!!
KA-CHAK
HAPPY NEW YEAR, RISA! YOU FEELING BETTER?
ARE YOU OKAY, RISA...?

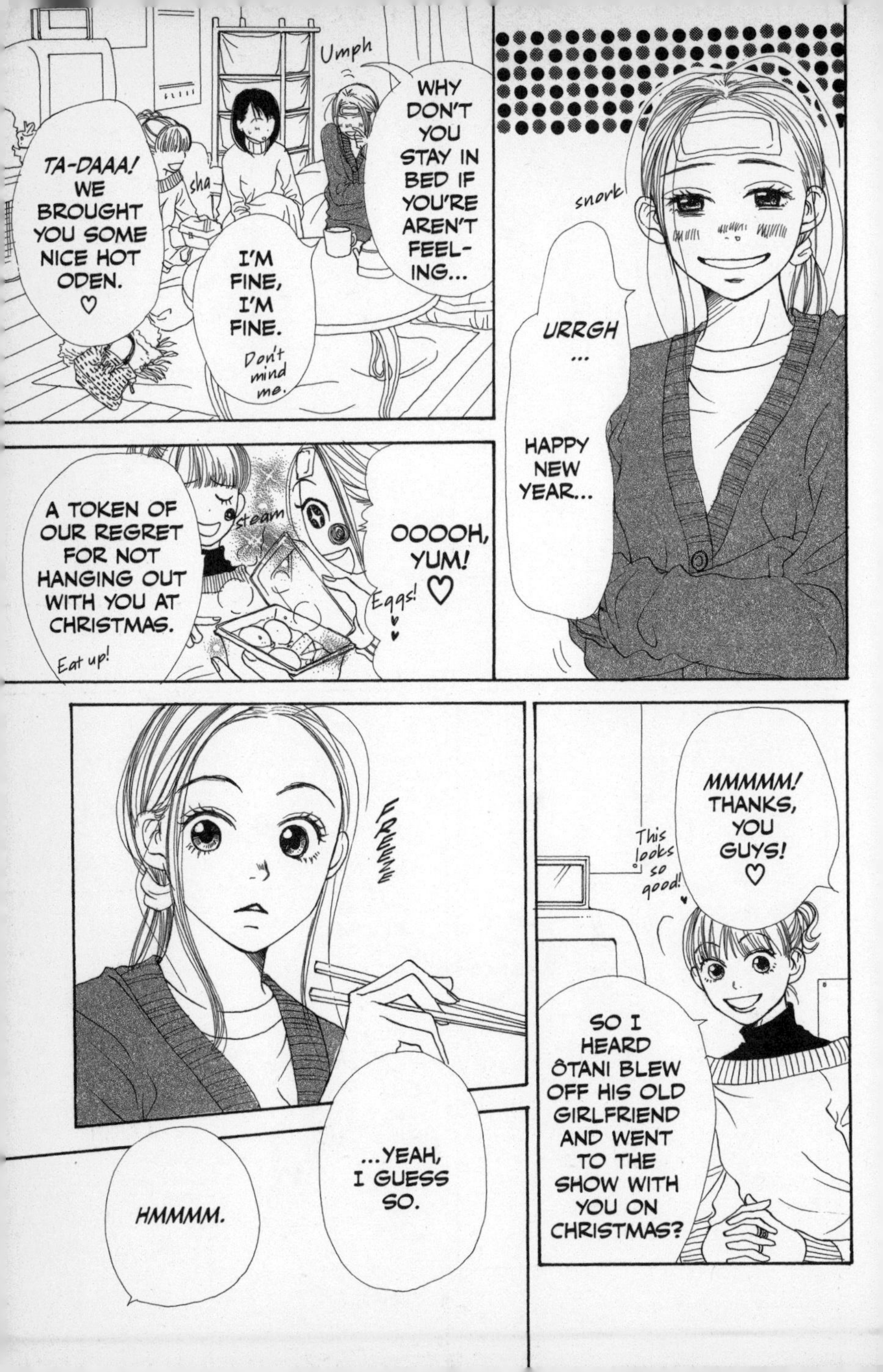
snork
URRGH...
HAPPY NEW YEAR...
Umph
WHY DON'T YOU STAY IN BED IF YOU'RE AREN'T FEEL-ING...
TA-DAAA! WE BROUGHT YOU SOME NICE HOT ODEN. ♡
sha
I'M FINE, I'M FINE.
Don't mind me.
OOOOH, YUM! ♡
Eggs! ♥
steam
A TOKEN OF OUR REGRET FOR NOT HANGING OUT WITH YOU AT CHRISTMAS.
Eat up!
MMMMM! THANKS, YOU GUYS! ♡
This looks so good! ♥
SO I HEARD ŌTANI BLEW OFF HIS OLD GIRLFRIEND AND WENT TO THE SHOW WITH YOU ON CHRISTMAS?
FREEZE
...YEAH, I GUESS SO.
HMMMM.

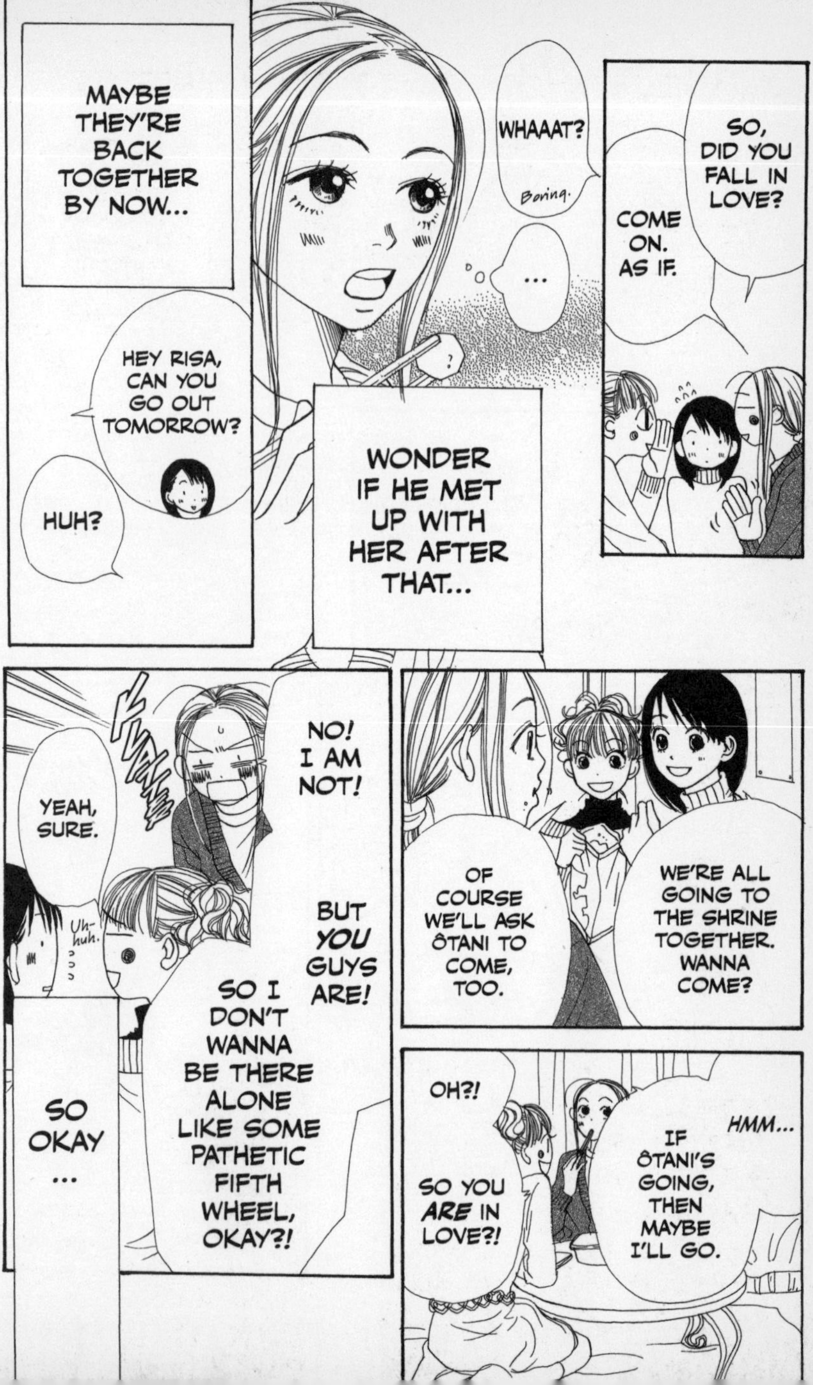
SO, DID YOU FALL IN LOVE?
COME ON. AS IF.
WHAAAT?
Boring.
...
WONDER IF HE MET UP WITH HER AFTER THAT...
MAYBE THEY'RE BACK TOGETHER BY NOW...
HEY RISA, CAN YOU GO OUT TOMORROW?
HUH?
WE'RE ALL GOING TO THE SHRINE TOGETHER. WANNA COME?
OF COURSE WE'LL ASK ŌTANI TO COME, TOO.
HMM...
IF ŌTANI'S GOING, THEN MAYBE I'LL GO.
OH?!
SO YOU *ARE* IN LOVE?!
NO! I AM NOT!
YEAH, SURE.
BUT *YOU* GUYS ARE!
SO I DON'T WANNA BE THERE ALONE LIKE SOME PATHETIC FIFTH WHEEL, OKAY?!
Uh-huh.
SO OKAY...

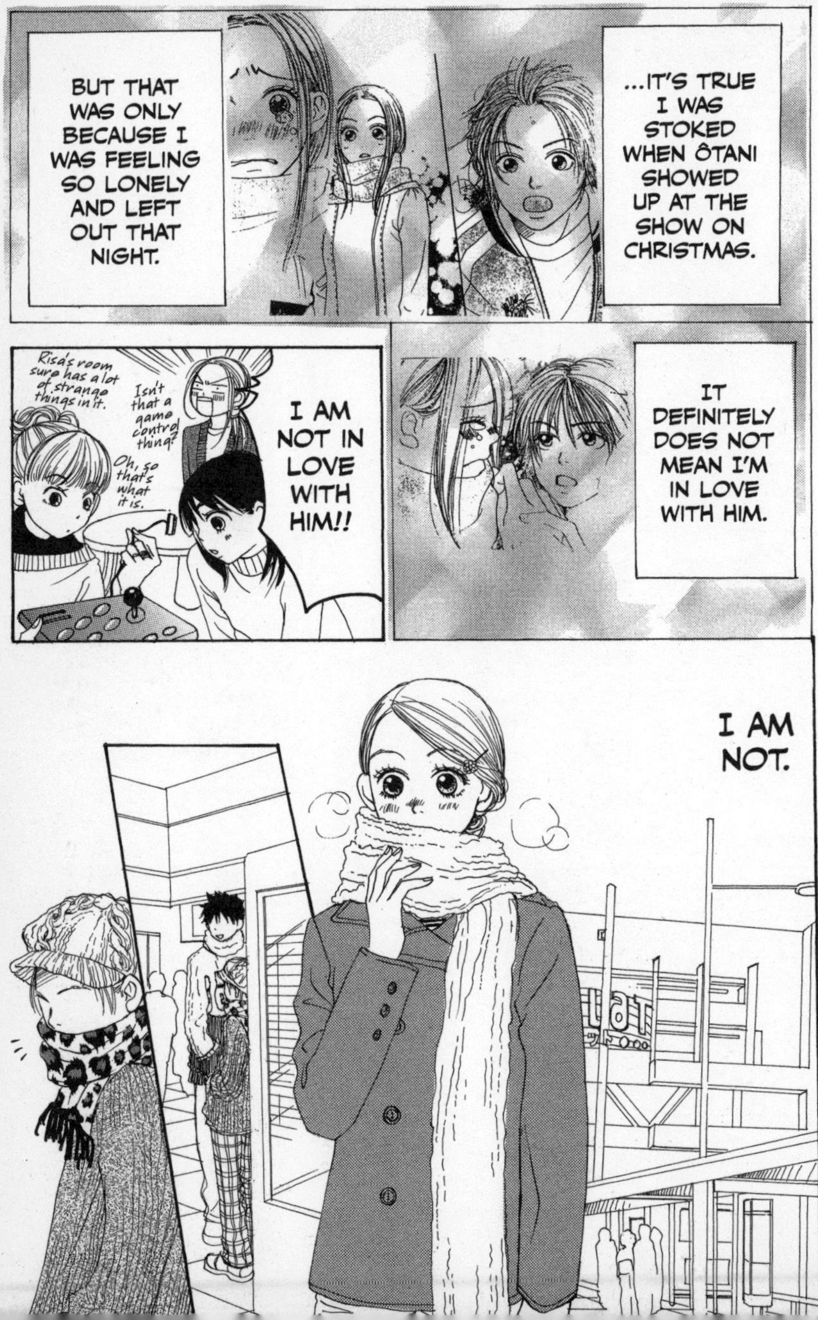
...IT'S TRUE I WAS STOKED WHEN ÔTANI SHOWED UP AT THE SHOW ON CHRISTMAS.
BUT THAT WAS ONLY BECAUSE I WAS FEELING SO LONELY AND LEFT OUT THAT NIGHT.
IT DEFINITELY DOES NOT MEAN I'M IN LOVE WITH HIM.
I AM NOT IN LOVE WITH HIM!!
Isn't that a game control thing?
Risa's room sure has a lot of strange things in it.
Oh, so that's what it is.
I AM NOT.

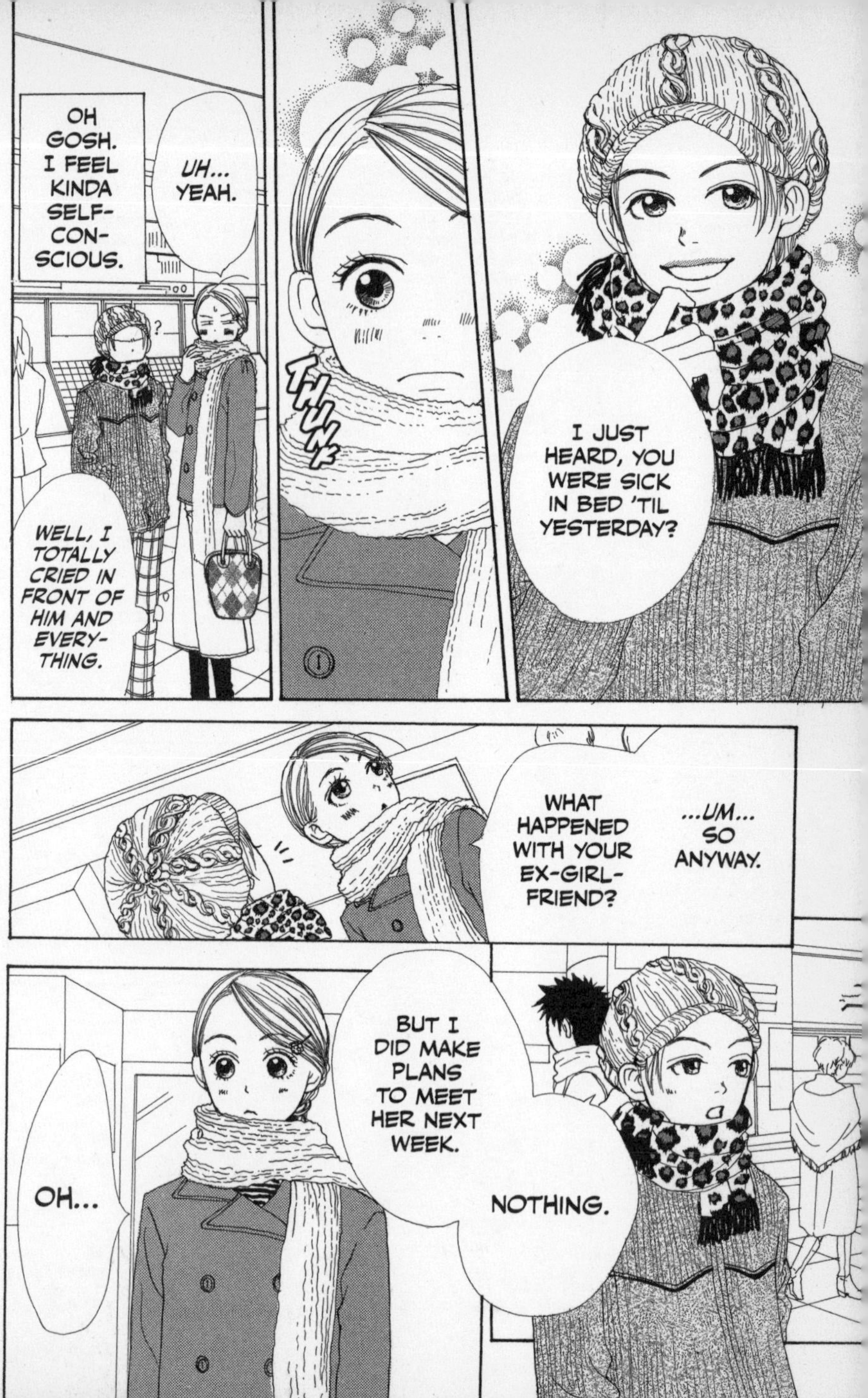
I JUST HEARD, YOU WERE SICK IN BED 'TIL YESTERDAY?
THUNK
UH... YEAH.
OH GOSH. I FEEL KINDA SELF-CONSCIOUS.
WELL, I TOTALLY CRIED IN FRONT OF HIM AND EVERYTHING.
...UM... SO ANYWAY.
WHAT HAPPENED WITH YOUR EX-GIRLFRIEND?
NOTHING.
BUT I DID MAKE PLANS TO MEET HER NEXT WEEK.
OH...

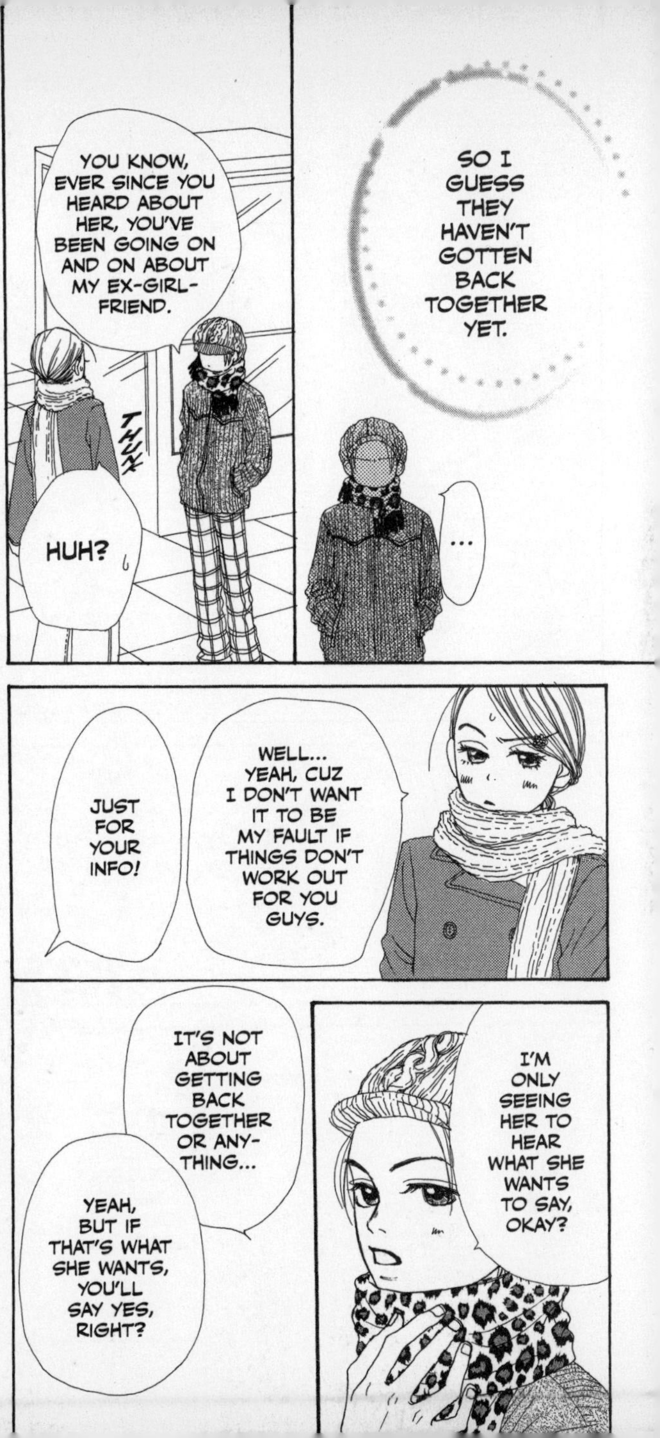
SO I GUESS THEY HAVEN'T GOTTEN BACK TOGETHER YET.
...
YOU KNOW, EVER SINCE YOU HEARD ABOUT HER, YOU'VE BEEN GOING ON AND ON ABOUT MY EX-GIRL-FRIEND.
THUNK
HUH?
WELL... YEAH, CUZ I DON'T WANT IT TO BE MY FAULT IF THINGS DON'T WORK OUT FOR YOU GUYS.
JUST FOR YOUR INFO!
I'M ONLY SEEING HER TO HEAR WHAT SHE WANTS TO SAY, OKAY?
IT'S NOT ABOUT GETTING BACK TOGETHER OR ANY-THING...
YEAH, BUT IF THAT'S WHAT SHE WANTS, YOU'LL SAY YES, RIGHT?

2.

Although this has nothing to do with anything...

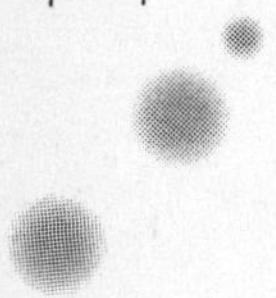

↑

My name for this screen tone here, which I occasionally use, is "nipple tone." If you paste it onto nipples, they get very nipple-like. Very realistic, no?

What am I writing...? If I have nothing to write about, I ought to think a little harder to come up with something better than this.

But anyway, "nipple tone" it is.

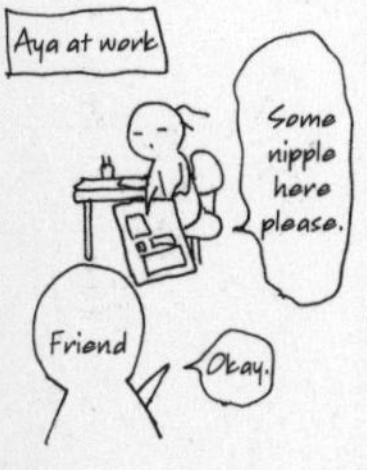
Aya at work
Some nipple here please.
Friend
Okay.

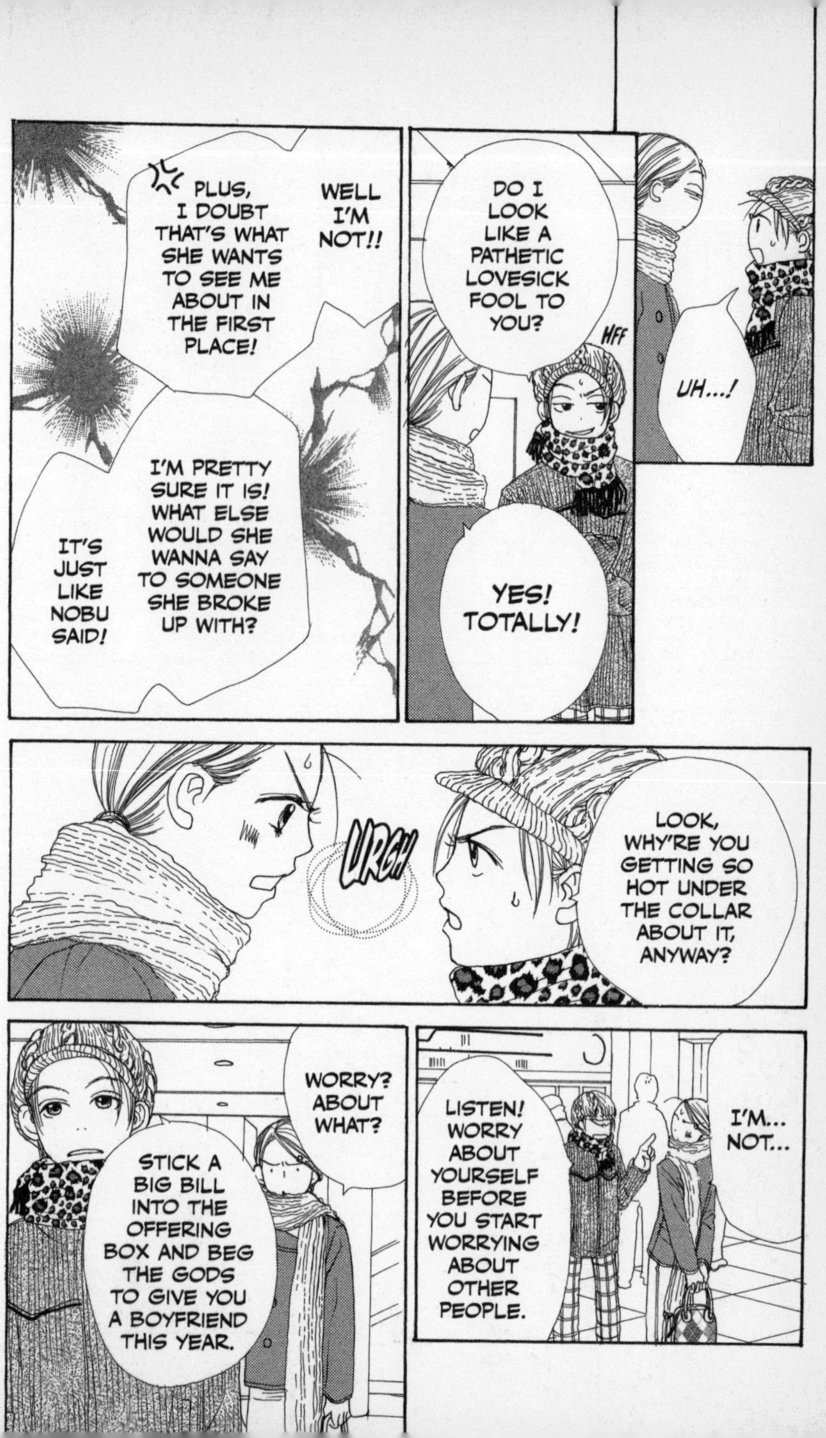
UH...!
DO I LOOK LIKE A PATHETIC LOVESICK FOOL TO YOU?
HFF
YES! TOTALLY!
WELL I'M NOT!!
PLUS, I DOUBT THAT'S WHAT SHE WANTS TO SEE ME ABOUT IN THE FIRST PLACE!
I'M PRETTY SURE IT IS! WHAT ELSE WOULD SHE WANNA SAY TO SOMEONE SHE BROKE UP WITH?
IT'S JUST LIKE NOBU SAID!
LOOK, WHY'RE YOU GETTING SO HOT UNDER THE COLLAR ABOUT IT, ANYWAY?
URGH
I'M... NOT...
LISTEN! WORRY ABOUT YOURSELF BEFORE YOU START WORRYING ABOUT OTHER PEOPLE.
WORRY? ABOUT WHAT?
STICK A BIG BILL INTO THE OFFERING BOX AND BEG THE GODS TO GIVE YOU A BOYFRIEND THIS YEAR.

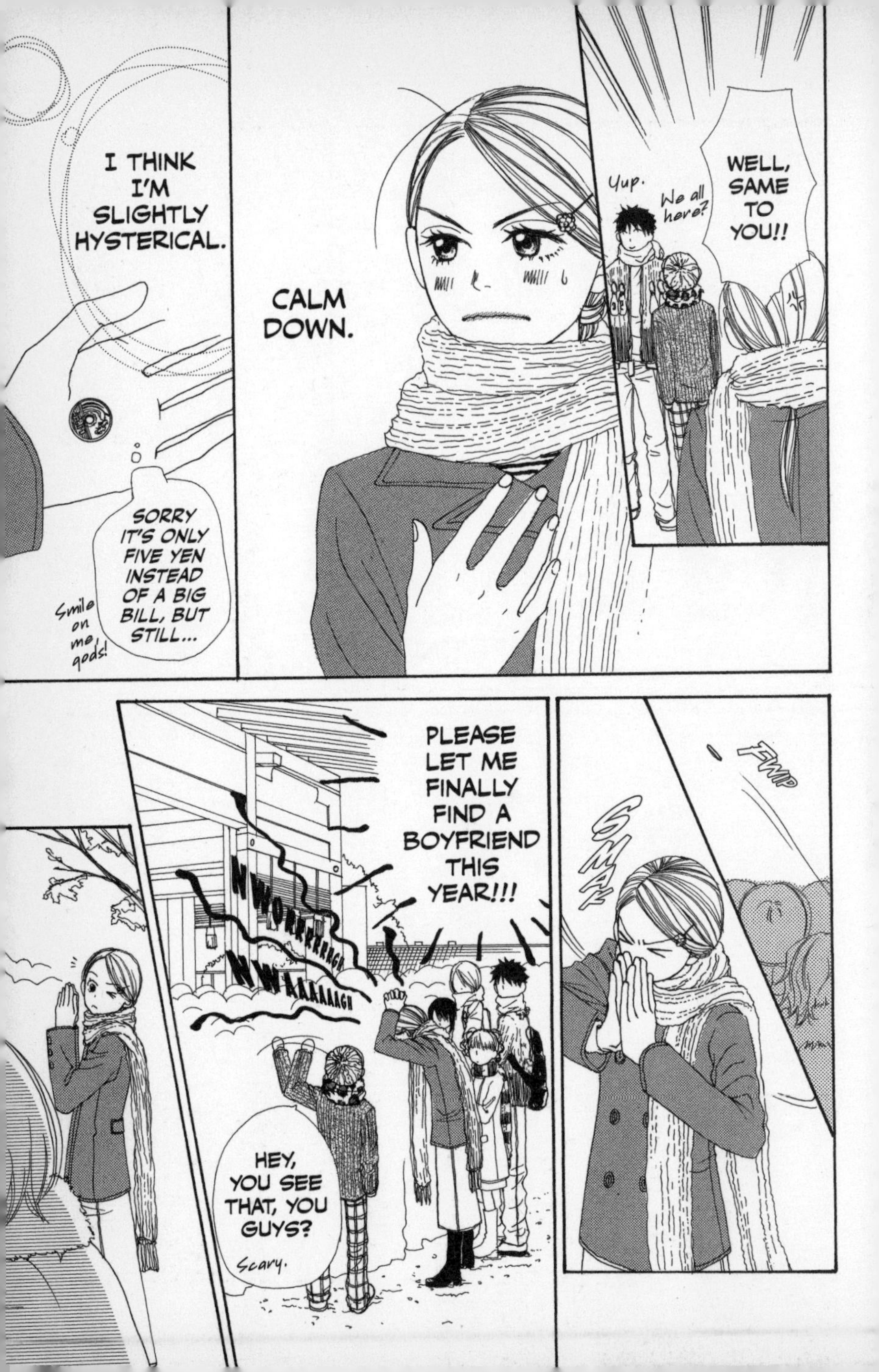
WELL, SAME TO YOU!!
We all here?
Yup.
CALM DOWN.
I THINK I'M SLIGHTLY HYSTERICAL.
SORRY IT'S ONLY FIVE YEN INSTEAD OF A BIG BILL, BUT STILL...
Smile on me, gods!
FWIP
PLEASE LET ME FINALLY FIND A BOYFRIEND THIS YEAR!!!
HEY, YOU SEE THAT, YOU GUYS?
Scary.

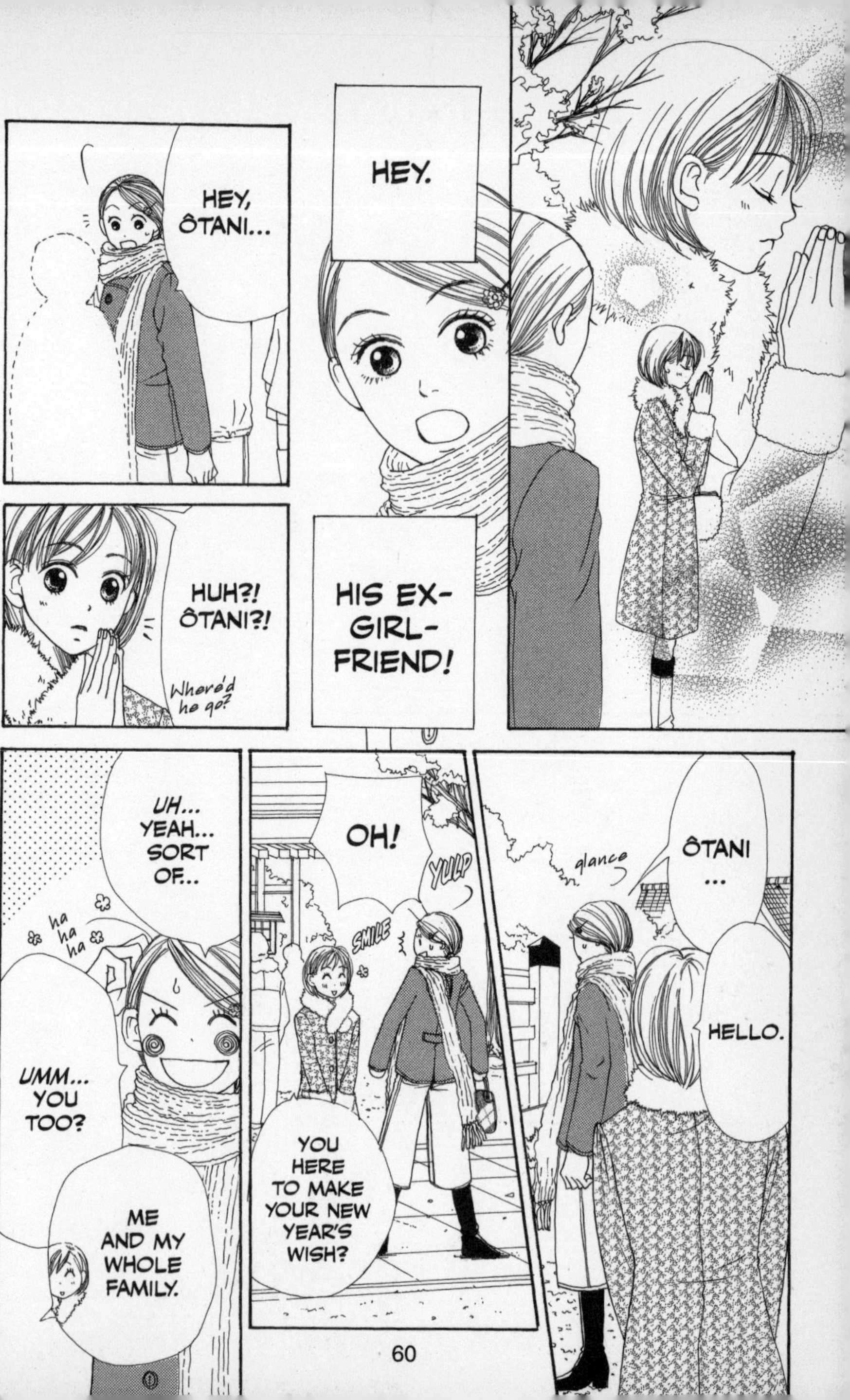
HEY.
HIS EX-GIRLFRIEND!
HEY, ÔTANI...
HUH?! ÔTANI?!
Where'd he go?
glance
ÔTANI ...
HELLO.
OH!
YULP
SMILE
YOU HERE TO MAKE YOUR NEW YEAR'S WISH?
UH... YEAH... SORT OF...
ha ha ha
UMM... YOU TOO?
ME AND MY WHOLE FAMILY.

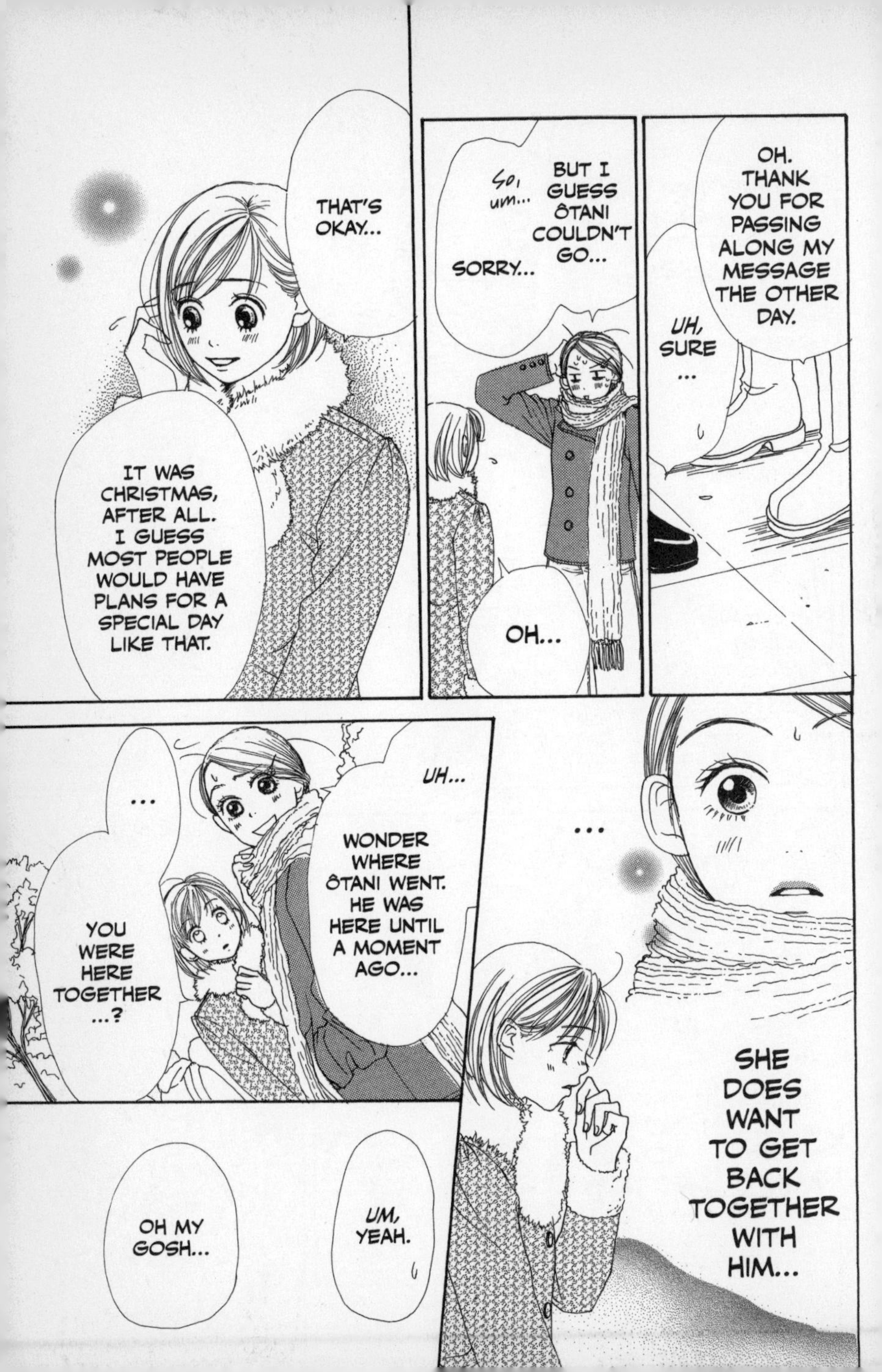
OH. THANK YOU FOR PASSING ALONG MY MESSAGE THE OTHER DAY.
UH, SURE ...
BUT I GUESS ŌTANI COULDN'T GO...
So, um...
SORRY...
OH...
THAT'S OKAY...
IT WAS CHRISTMAS, AFTER ALL. I GUESS MOST PEOPLE WOULD HAVE PLANS FOR A SPECIAL DAY LIKE THAT.
...
SHE DOES WANT TO GET BACK TOGETHER WITH HIM...
UH...
WONDER WHERE ŌTANI WENT. HE WAS HERE UNTIL A MOMENT AGO...
...
YOU WERE HERE TOGETHER ...?
UM, YEAH.
OH MY GOSH...

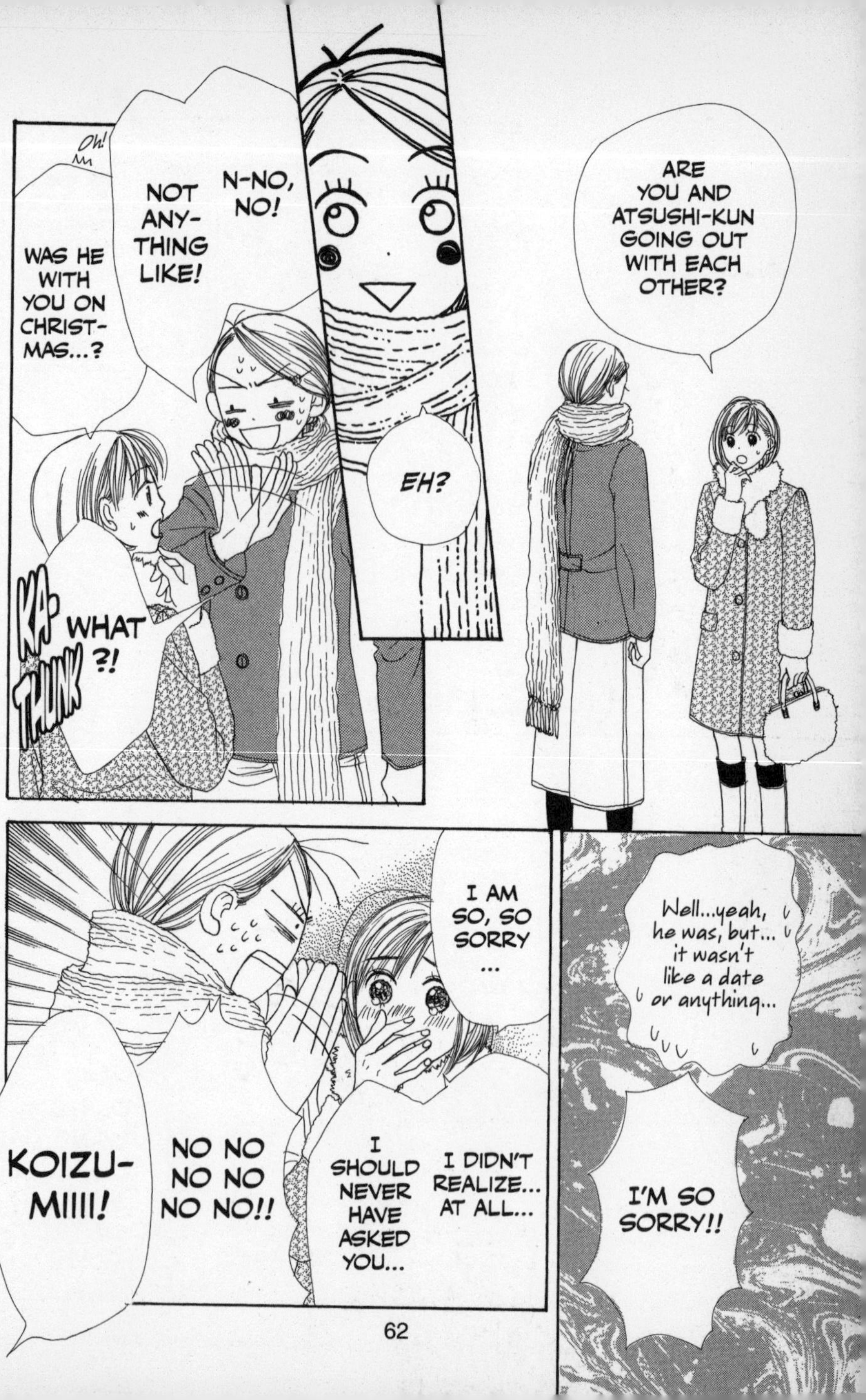
ARE YOU AND ATSUSHI-KUN GOING OUT WITH EACH OTHER?
EH?
N-NO, NO!
NOT ANY-THING LIKE!
Oh!
WAS HE WITH YOU ON CHRIST-MAS...?
KA-THUNK
WHAT?!
Well...yeah, he was, but... it wasn't like a date or anything...
I'M SO SORRY!!
I AM SO, SO SORRY ...
I DIDN'T REALIZE... AT ALL...
I SHOULD NEVER HAVE ASKED YOU...
NO NO NO NO NO NO!!
KOIZU-MIIII!

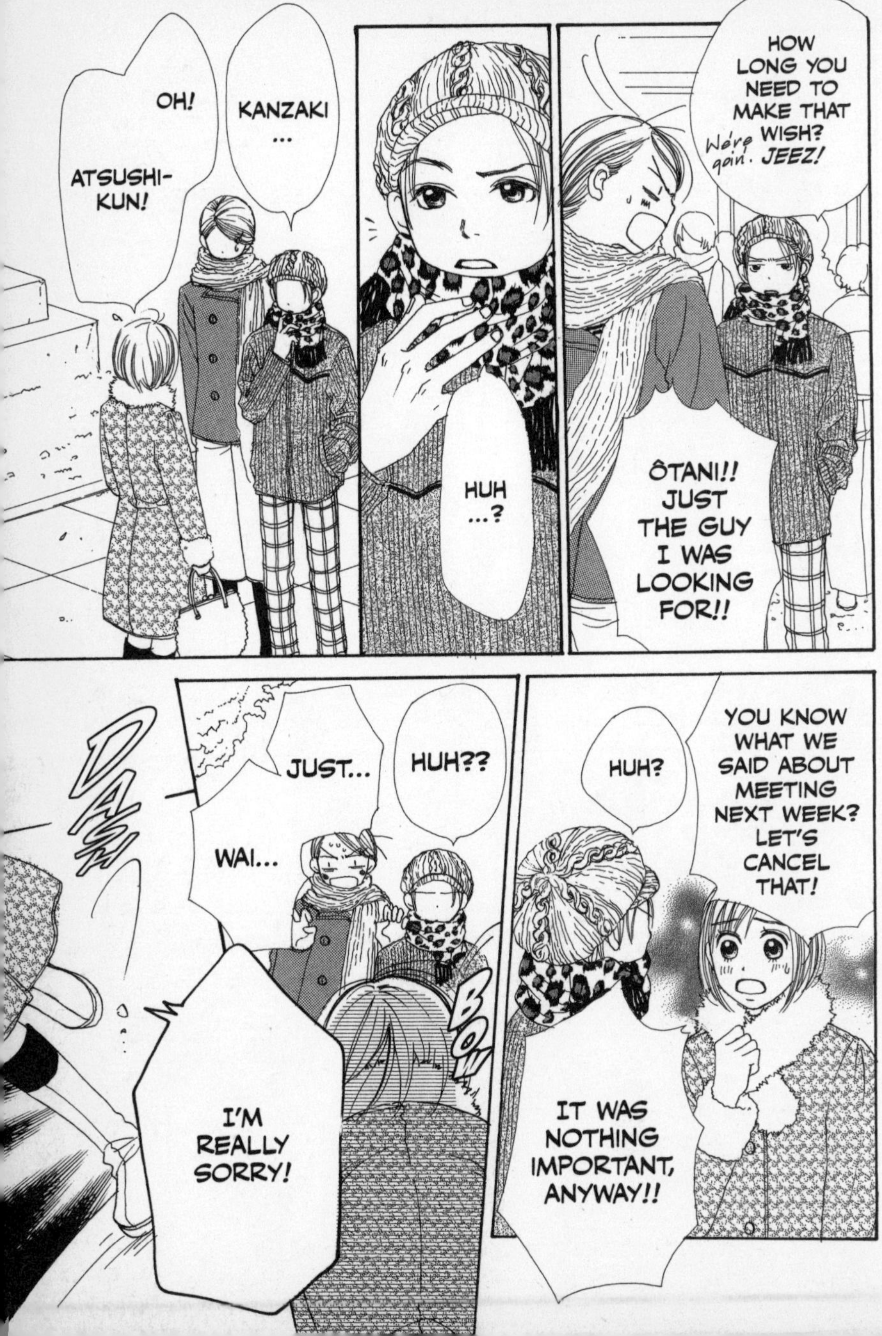
HOW LONG YOU NEED TO MAKE THAT WISH? JEEZ!
We're goin.
ÔTANI!! JUST THE GUY I WAS LOOKING FOR!!
HUH ...?
KANZAKI ...
OH!
ATSUSHI-KUN!
YOU KNOW WHAT WE SAID ABOUT MEETING NEXT WEEK? LET'S CANCEL THAT!
HUH?
IT WAS NOTHING IMPORTANT, ANYWAY!!
HUH??
JUST...
WAI...
BOW
I'M REALLY SORRY!
DASH

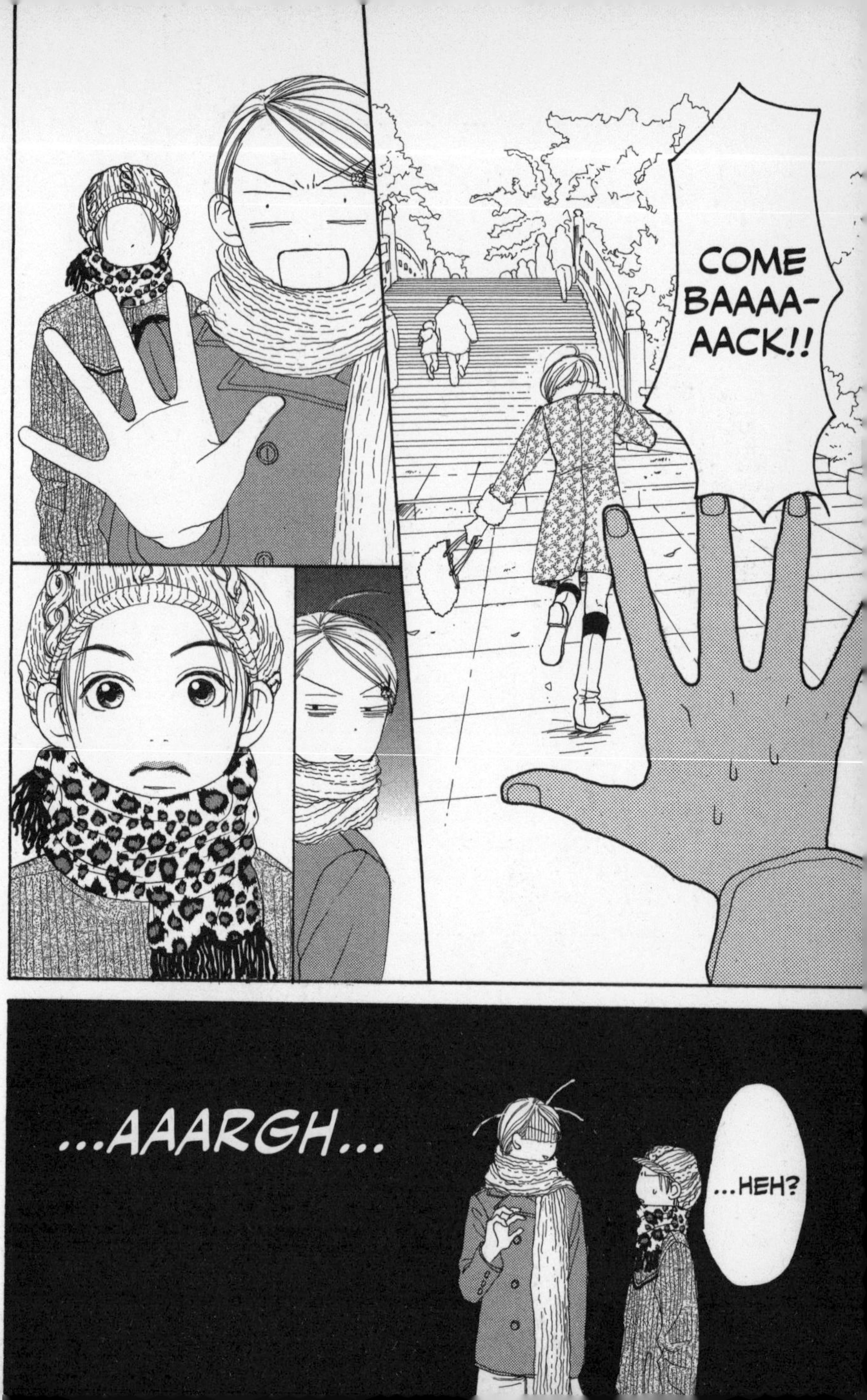
COME BAAAA-AACK!!
...AAARGH...
...HEH?

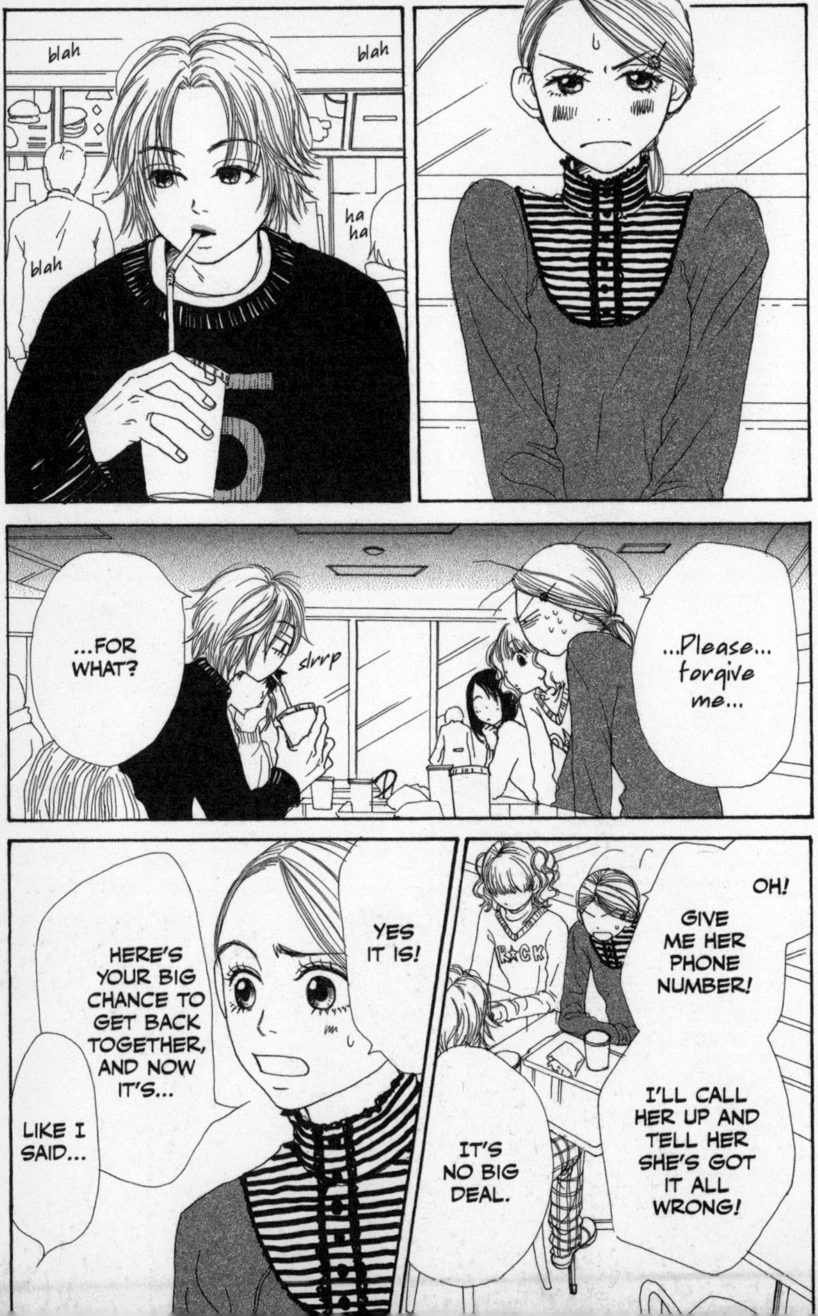
blah
blah
ha ha
blah
...Please... forgive me...
slrrp
...FOR WHAT?
OH!
GIVE ME HER PHONE NUMBER!
I'LL CALL HER UP AND TELL HER SHE'S GOT IT ALL WRONG!
IT'S NO BIG DEAL.
YES IT IS!
HERE'S YOUR BIG CHANCE TO GET BACK TOGETHER, AND NOW IT'S...
LIKE I SAID...

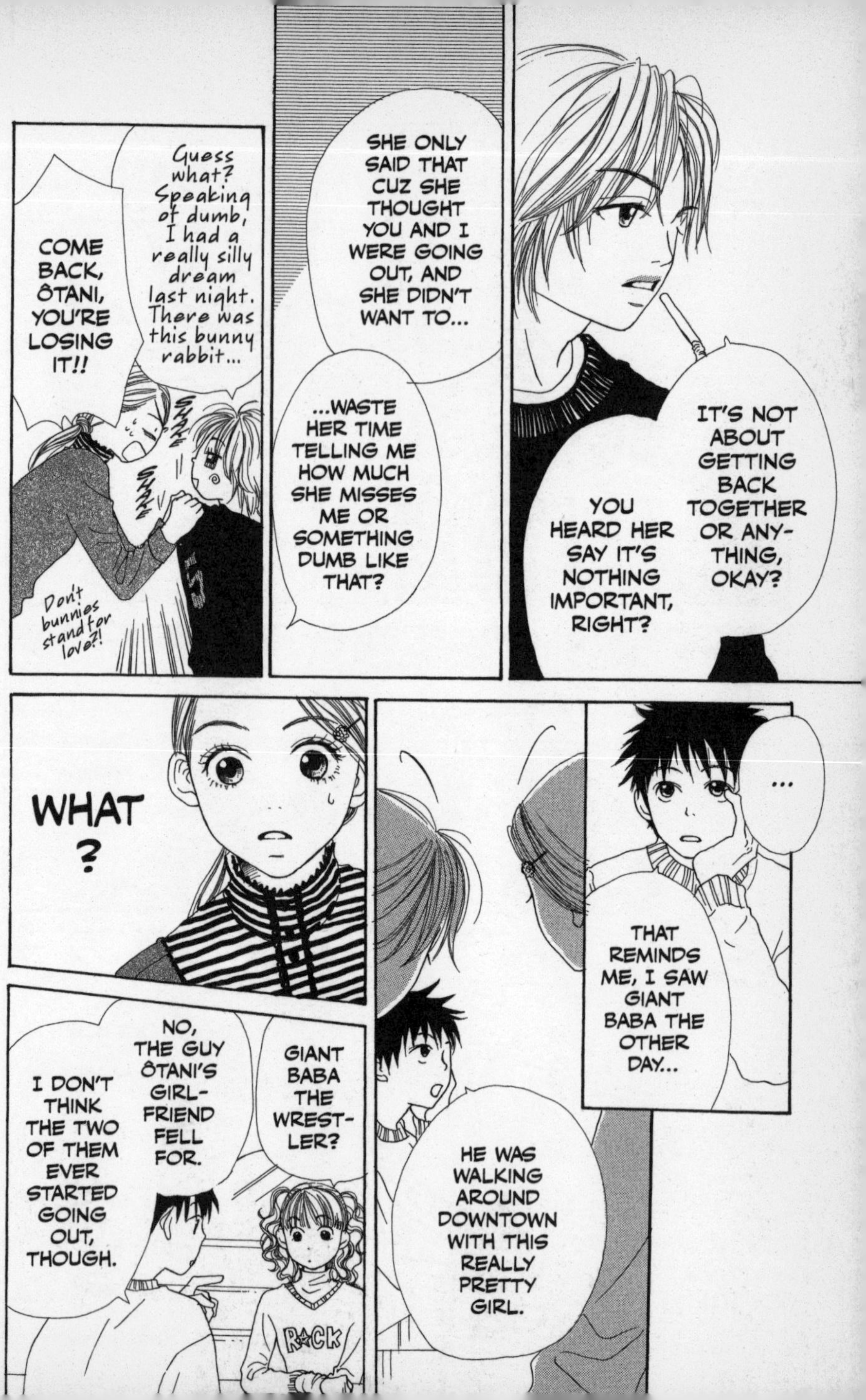
IT'S NOT ABOUT GETTING BACK TOGETHER OR ANY-THING, OKAY?
YOU HEARD HER SAY IT'S NOTHING IMPORTANT, RIGHT?
SHE ONLY SAID THAT CUZ SHE THOUGHT YOU AND I WERE GOING OUT, AND SHE DIDN'T WANT TO...
...WASTE HER TIME TELLING ME HOW MUCH SHE MISSES ME OR SOMETHING DUMB LIKE THAT?
Guess what? Speaking of dumb, I had a really silly dream last night. There was this bunny rabbit...
COME BACK, ŌTANI, YOU'RE LOSING IT!!
SHAKE
SHAKE
Don't bunnies stand for love?!
...
THAT REMINDS ME, I SAW GIANT BABA THE OTHER DAY...
HE WAS WALKING AROUND DOWNTOWN WITH THIS REALLY PRETTY GIRL.
WHAT?
GIANT BABA THE WREST-LER?
NO, THE GUY ŌTANI'S GIRL-FRIEND FELL FOR.
I DON'T THINK THE TWO OF THEM EVER STARTED GOING OUT, THOUGH.
R★CK

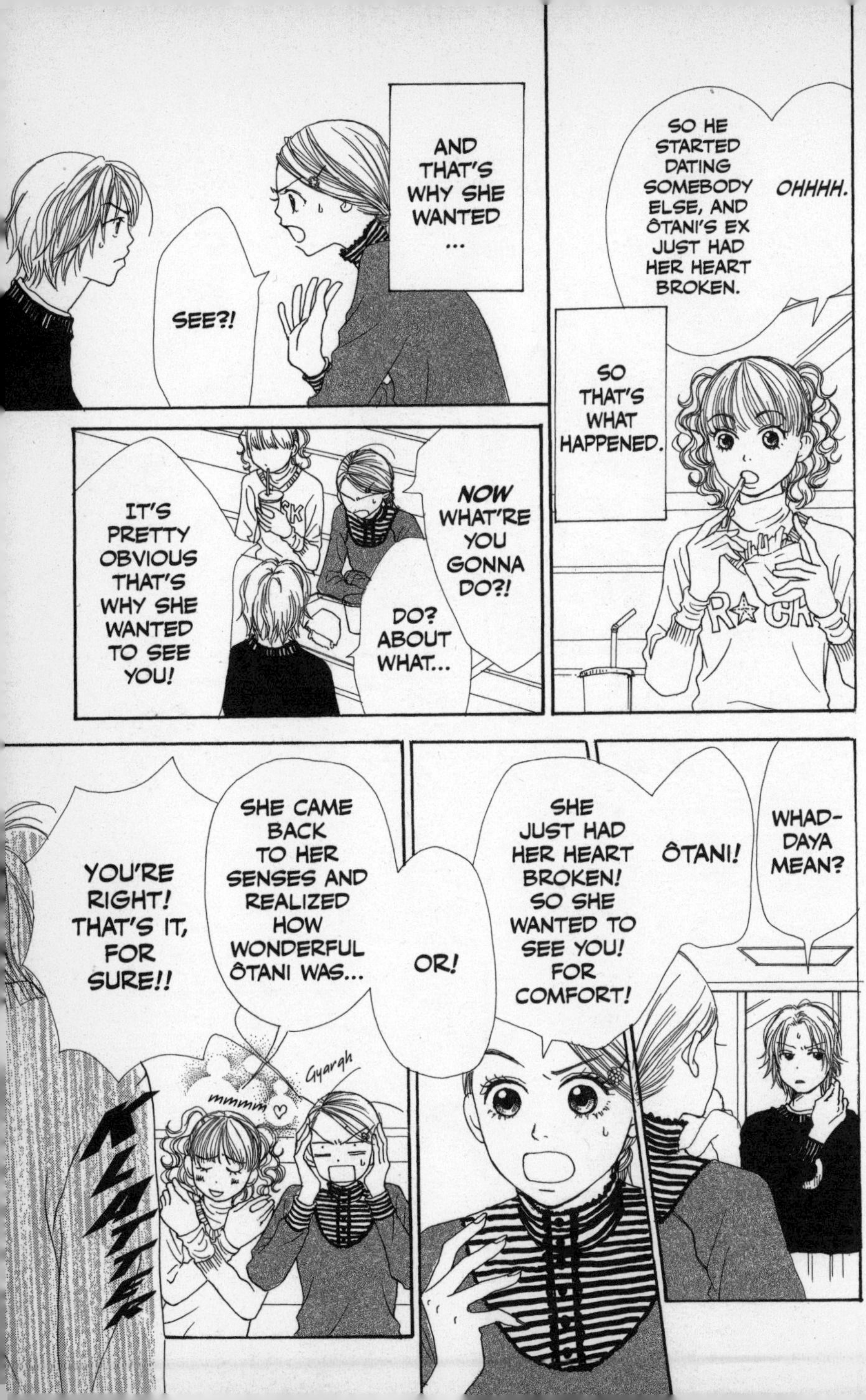
SO HE STARTED DATING SOMEBODY ELSE, AND ÔTANI'S EX JUST HAD HER HEART BROKEN.
OHHHH.
SO THAT'S WHAT HAPPENED.
AND THAT'S WHY SHE WANTED ...
SEE?!
NOW WHAT'RE YOU GONNA DO?!
DO? ABOUT WHAT...
IT'S PRETTY OBVIOUS THAT'S WHY SHE WANTED TO SEE YOU!
WHAD-DAYA MEAN?
ÔTANI!
SHE JUST HAD HER HEART BROKEN! SO SHE WANTED TO SEE YOU! FOR COMFORT!
OR!
SHE CAME BACK TO HER SENSES AND REALIZED HOW WONDERFUL ÔTANI WAS...
Gyargh
mmmm ♡
YOU'RE RIGHT! THAT'S IT, FOR SURE!!
KLATTER

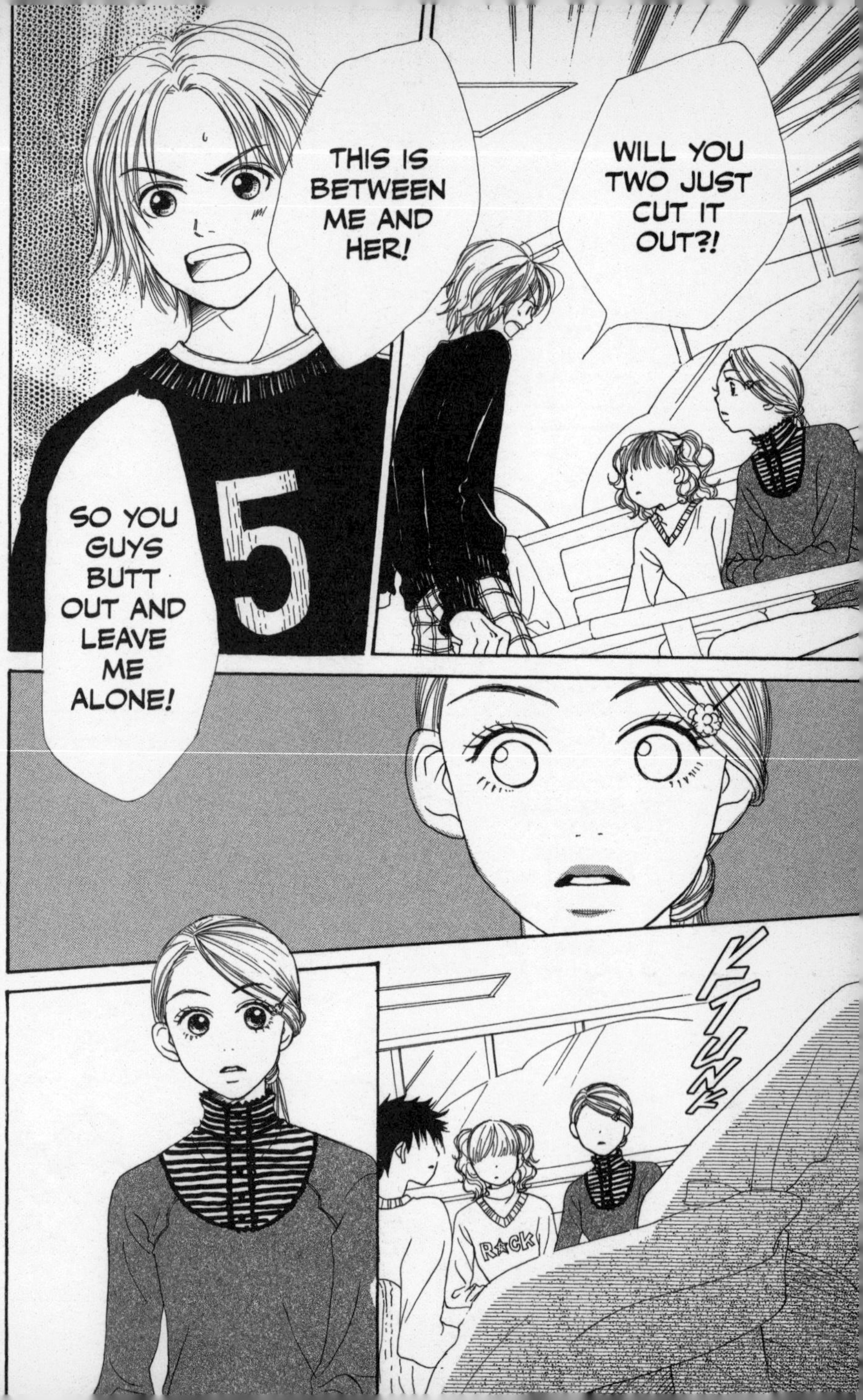
WILL YOU TWO JUST CUT IT OUT?!
THIS IS BETWEEN ME AND HER!
SO YOU GUYS BUTT OUT AND LEAVE ME ALONE!
KYUNK
R★CK

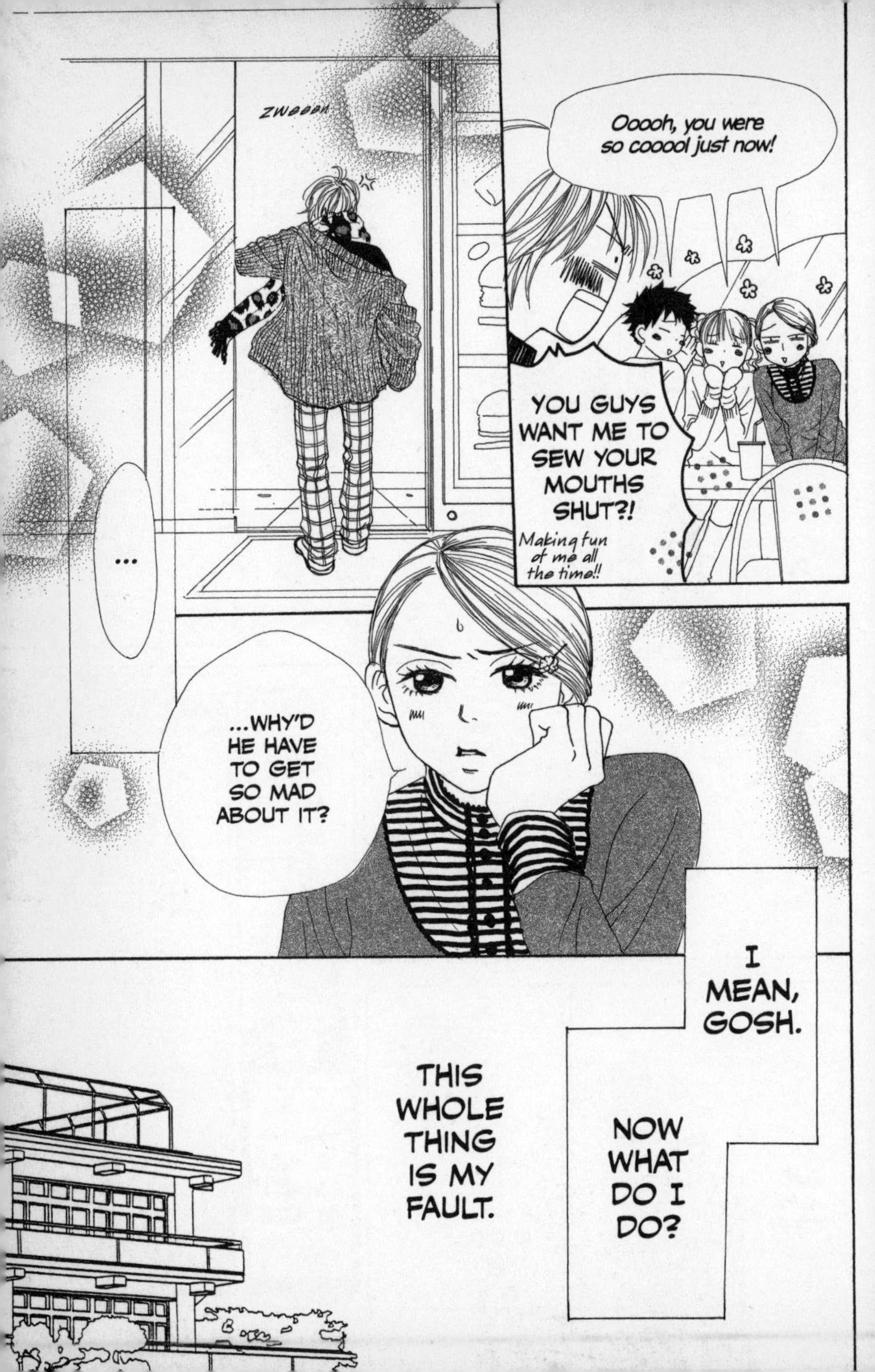
Ooooh, you were so cooool just now!
YOU GUYS WANT ME TO SEW YOUR MOUTHS SHUT?!
Making fun of me all the time!!
ZWEEEN
...
...WHY'D HE HAVE TO GET SO MAD ABOUT IT?
I MEAN, GOSH.
NOW WHAT DO I DO?
THIS WHOLE THING IS MY FAULT.

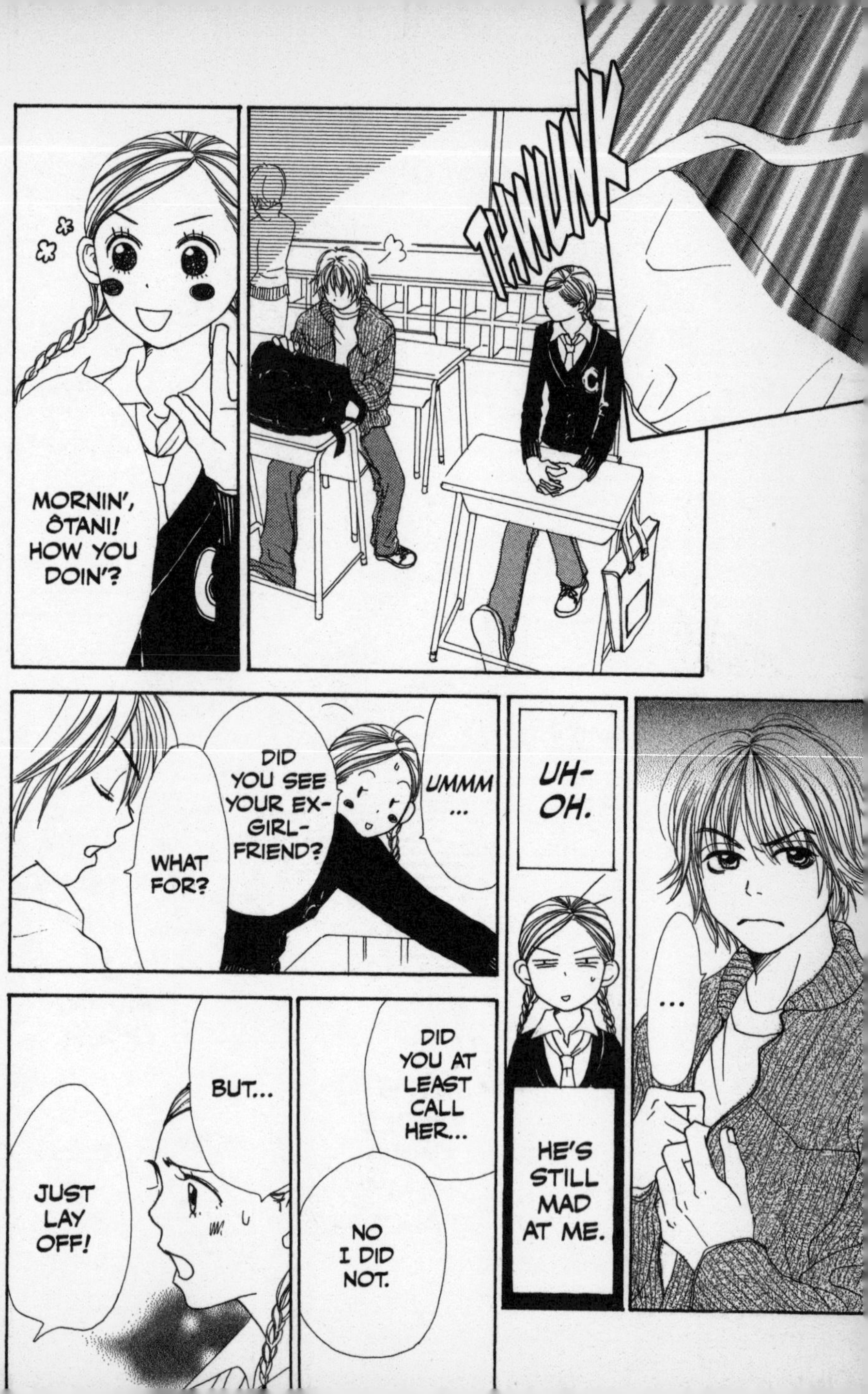
THWUNK
MORNIN', ŌTANI! HOW YOU DOIN'?
...
UH-OH.
HE'S STILL MAD AT ME.
UMMM ...
DID YOU SEE YOUR EX-GIRL-FRIEND?
WHAT FOR?
DID YOU AT LEAST CALL HER...
NO I DID NOT.
BUT...
JUST LAY OFF!

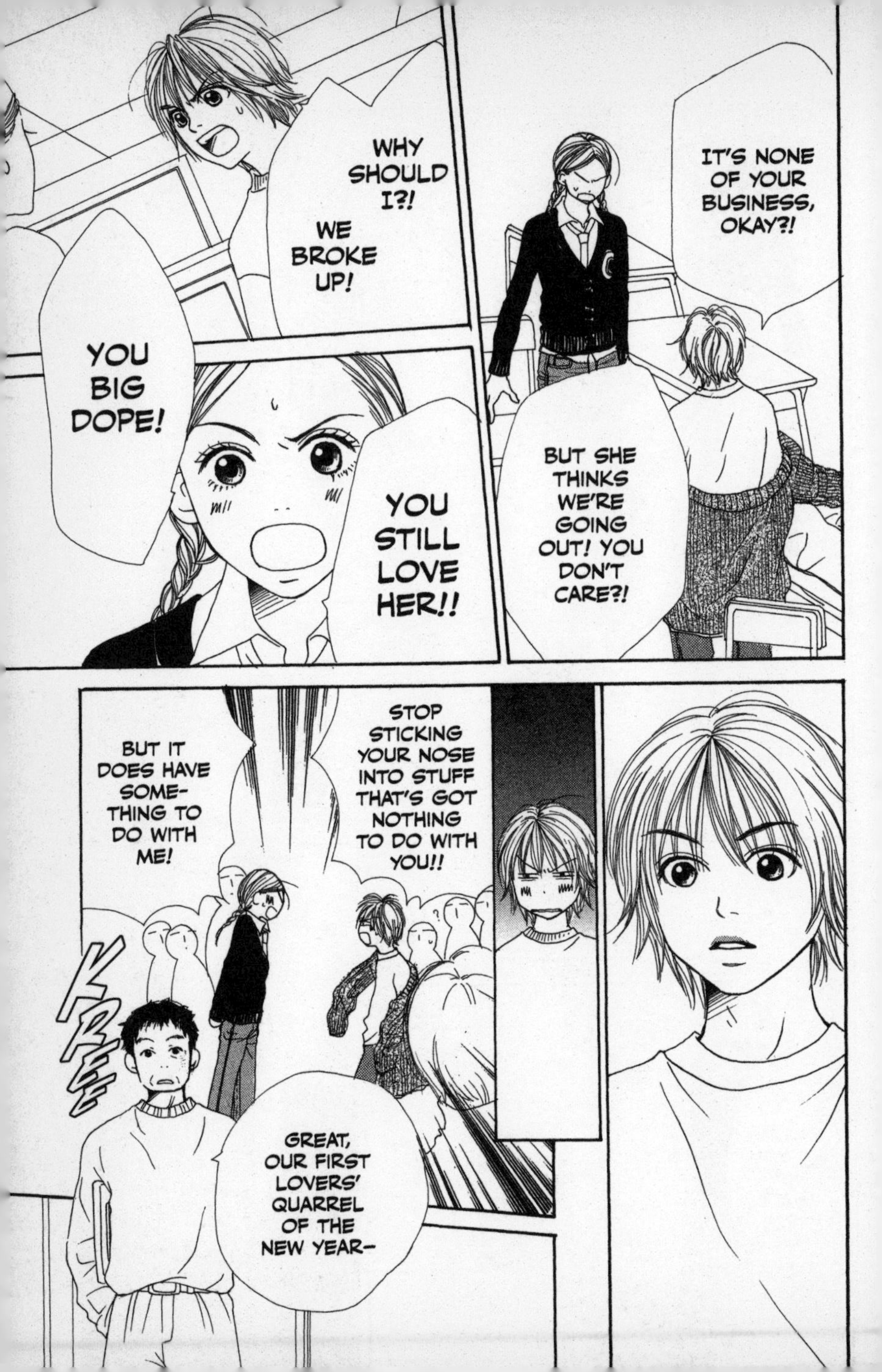
IT'S NONE OF YOUR BUSINESS, OKAY?!
BUT SHE THINKS WE'RE GOING OUT! YOU DON'T CARE?!
WHY SHOULD I?!
WE BROKE UP!
YOU STILL LOVE HER!!
YOU BIG DOPE!
STOP STICKING YOUR NOSE INTO STUFF THAT'S GOT NOTHING TO DO WITH YOU!!
BUT IT DOES HAVE SOME-THING TO DO WITH ME!
GREAT, OUR FIRST LOVERS' QUARREL OF THE NEW YEAR-

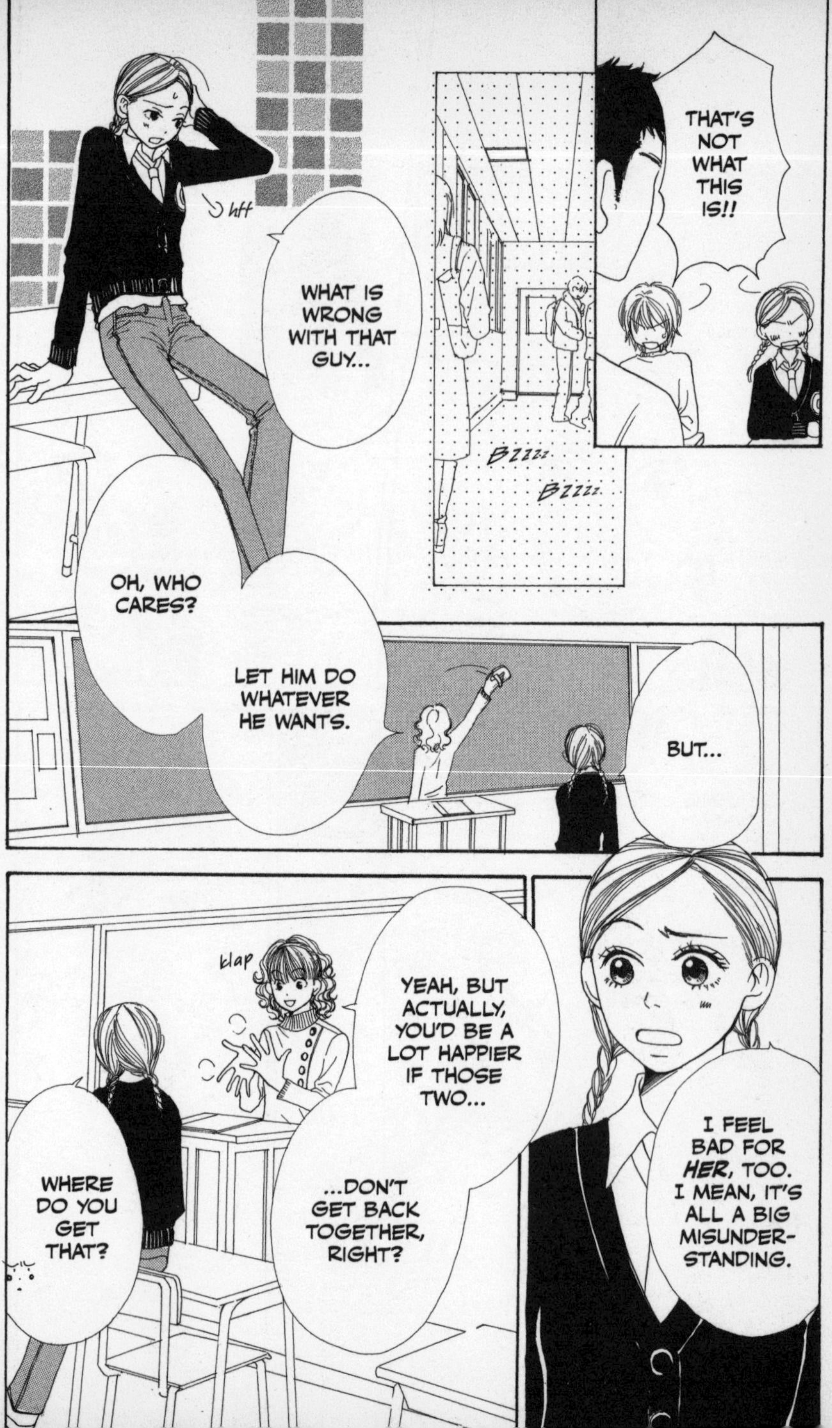
THAT'S NOT WHAT THIS IS!!
Bzzzz
Bzzzz.
hff
WHAT IS WRONG WITH THAT GUY...
OH, WHO CARES?
LET HIM DO WHATEVER HE WANTS.
BUT...
I FEEL BAD FOR *HER*, TOO. I MEAN, IT'S ALL A BIG MISUNDER-STANDING.
klap
YEAH, BUT ACTUALLY, YOU'D BE A LOT HAPPIER IF THOSE TWO...
...DON'T GET BACK TOGETHER, RIGHT?
WHERE DO YOU GET THAT?

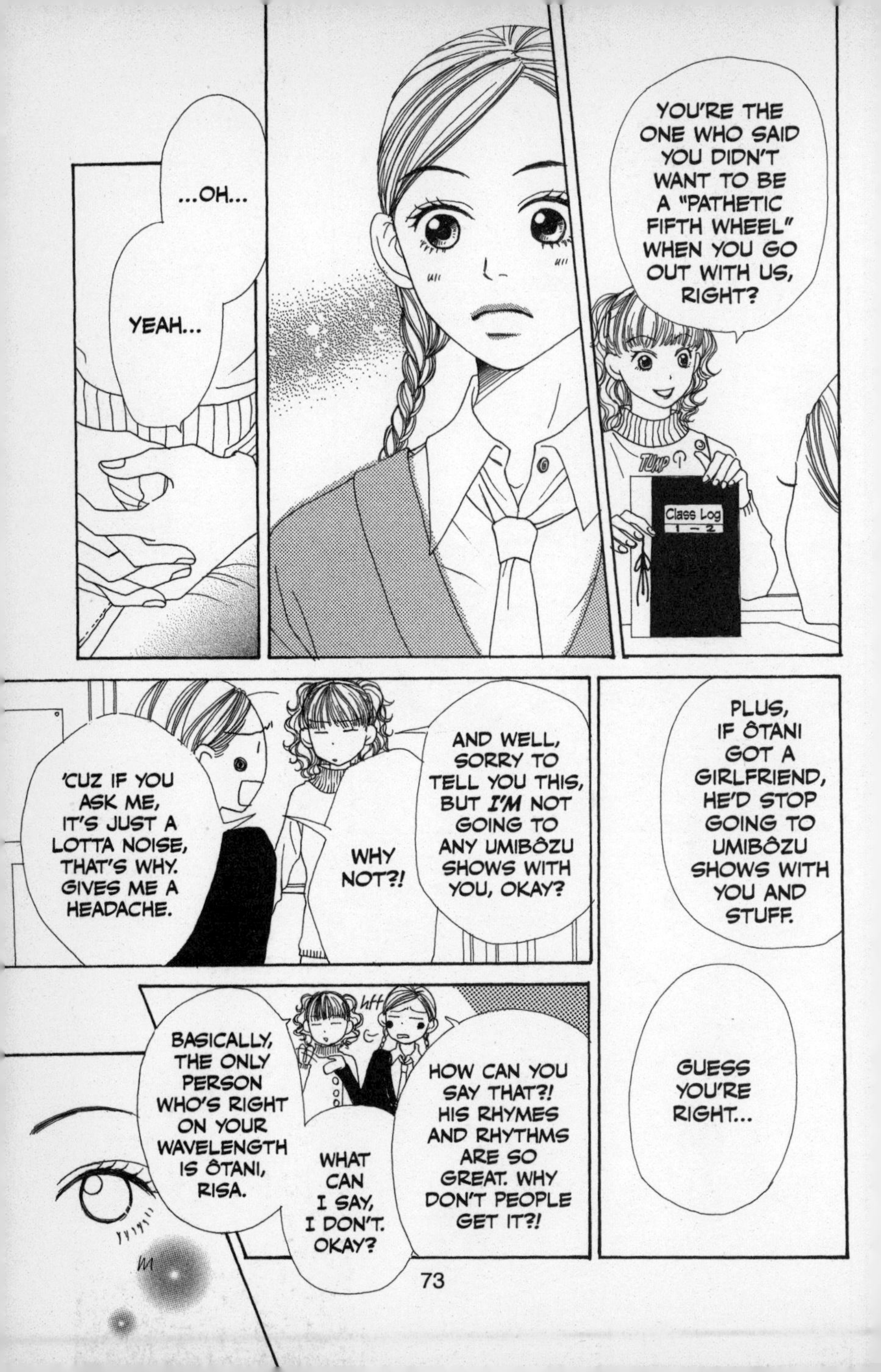

YOU'RE THE ONE WHO SAID YOU DIDN'T WANT TO BE A "PATHETIC FIFTH WHEEL" WHEN YOU GO OUT WITH US, RIGHT?
Class Log 1 – 2
...OH...
YEAH...
PLUS, IF ÔTANI GOT A GIRLFRIEND, HE'D STOP GOING TO UMIBÔZU SHOWS WITH YOU AND STUFF.
AND WELL, SORRY TO TELL YOU THIS, BUT *I'M* NOT GOING TO ANY UMIBÔZU SHOWS WITH YOU, OKAY?
WHY NOT?!
'CUZ IF YOU ASK ME, IT'S JUST A LOTTA NOISE, THAT'S WHY. GIVES ME A HEADACHE.
GUESS YOU'RE RIGHT...
HOW CAN YOU SAY THAT?! HIS RHYMES AND RHYTHMS ARE SO GREAT. WHY DON'T PEOPLE GET IT?!
WHAT CAN I SAY, I DON'T. OKAY?
BASICALLY, THE ONLY PERSON WHO'S RIGHT ON YOUR WAVELENGTH IS ÔTANI, RISA.

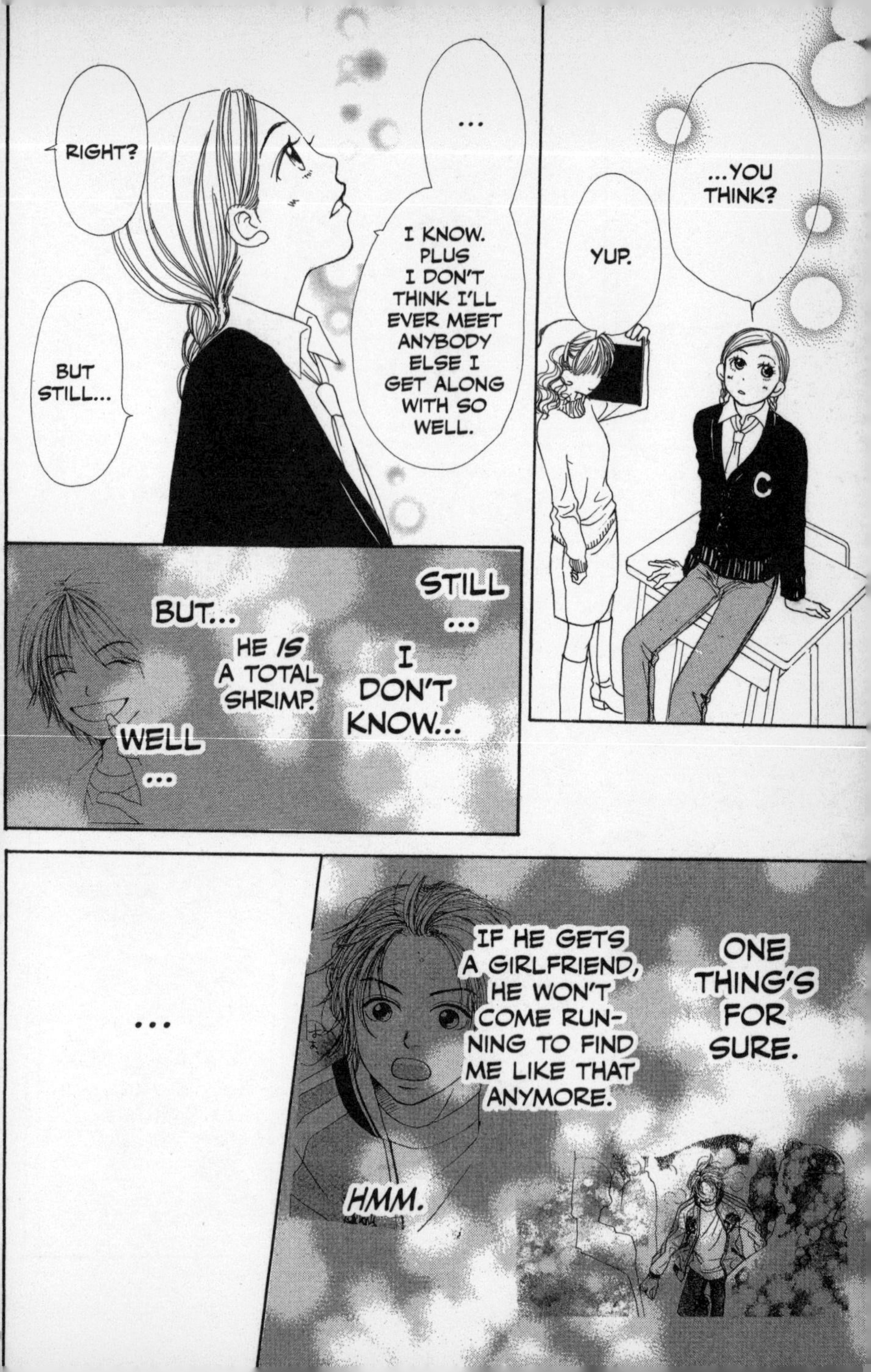
...YOU THINK?
YUP.
...
I KNOW. PLUS I DON'T THINK I'LL EVER MEET ANYBODY ELSE I GET ALONG WITH SO WELL.
RIGHT?
BUT STILL...
STILL ...
I DON'T KNOW...
HE *IS* A TOTAL SHRIMP.
BUT...
WELL ...
ONE THING'S FOR SURE.
IF HE GETS A GIRLFRIEND, HE WON'T COME RUN-NING TO FIND ME LIKE THAT ANYMORE.
HMM.
...

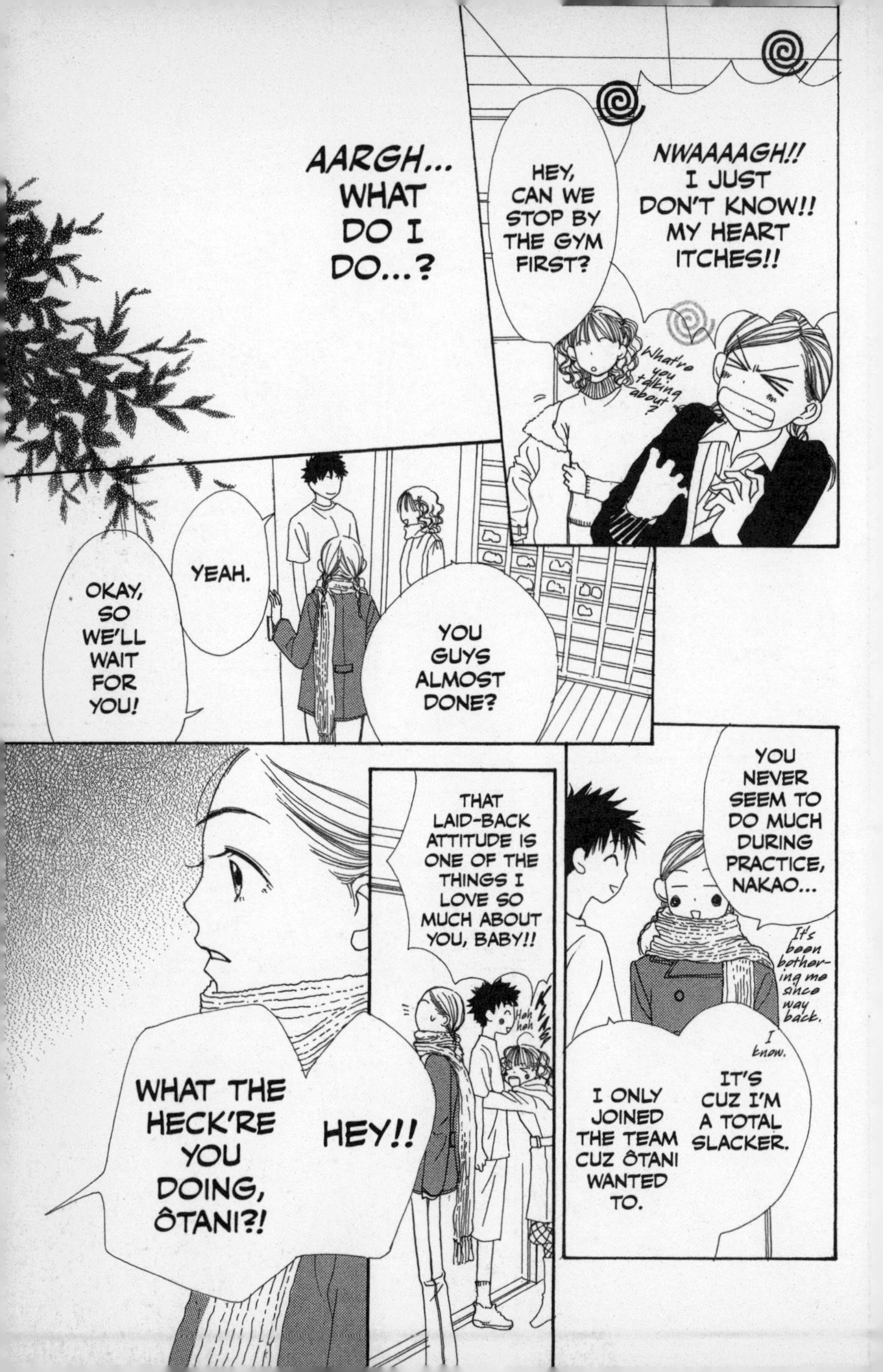
NWAAAAGH!! I JUST DON'T KNOW!! MY HEART ITCHES!!
HEY, CAN WE STOP BY THE GYM FIRST?
What're you talking about?
AARGH... WHAT DO I DO...?
YOU GUYS ALMOST DONE?
YEAH.
OKAY, SO WE'LL WAIT FOR YOU!
YOU NEVER SEEM TO DO MUCH DURING PRACTICE, NAKAO...
It's been bothering me since way back.
I know.
IT'S CUZ I'M A TOTAL SLACKER.
I ONLY JOINED THE TEAM CUZ ÔTANI WANTED TO.
THAT LAID-BACK ATTITUDE IS ONE OF THE THINGS I LOVE SO MUCH ABOUT YOU, BABY!!
Heh heh
HEY!!
WHAT THE HECK'RE YOU DOING, ÔTANI?!

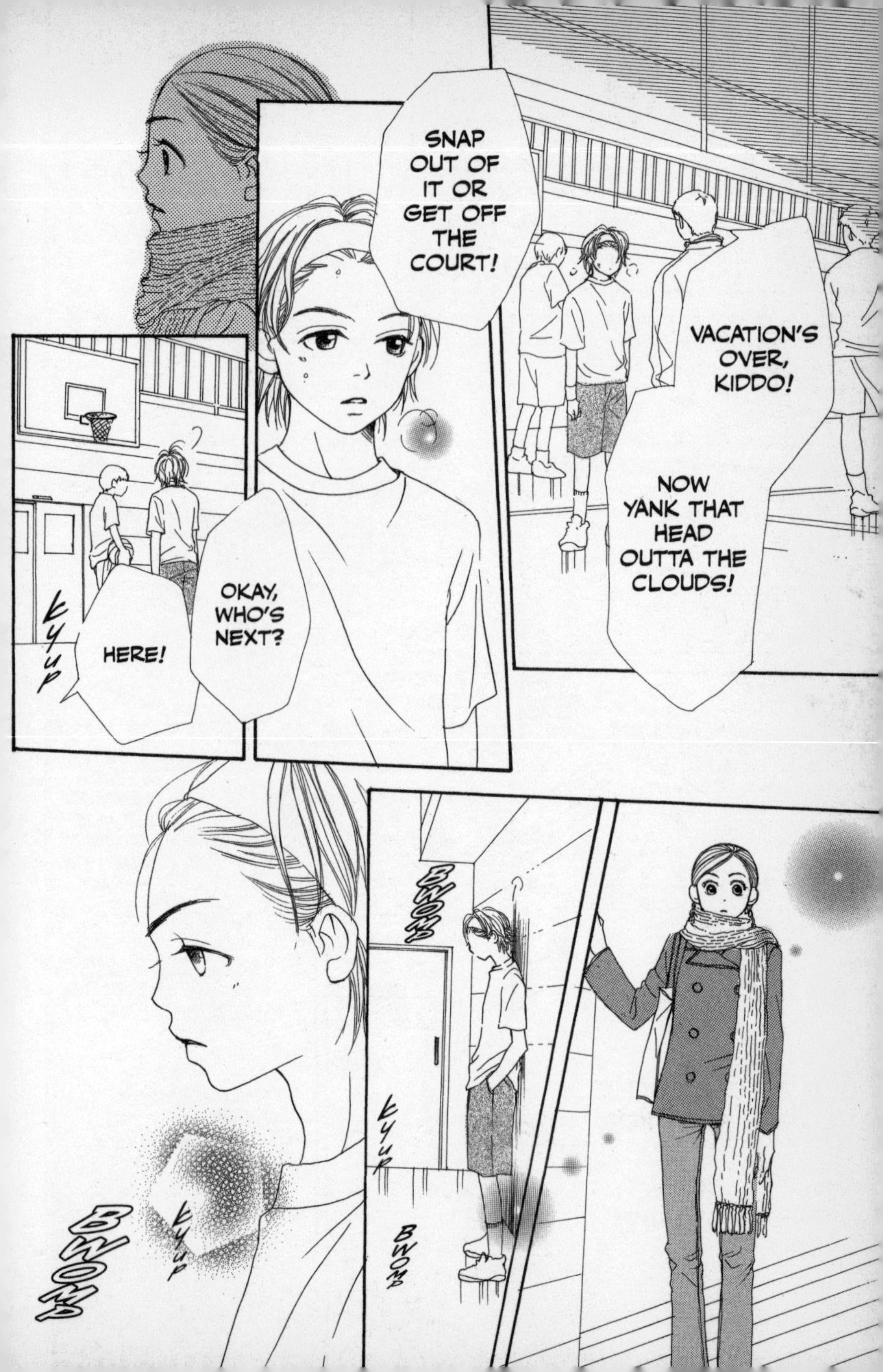
SNAP OUT OF IT OR GET OFF THE COURT!
VACATION'S OVER, KIDDO!
NOW YANK THAT HEAD OUTTA THE CLOUDS!
OKAY, WHO'S NEXT?
HERE!
KYUP
BWOMP
KYUP
BWOMP
KYUP
BWOMP

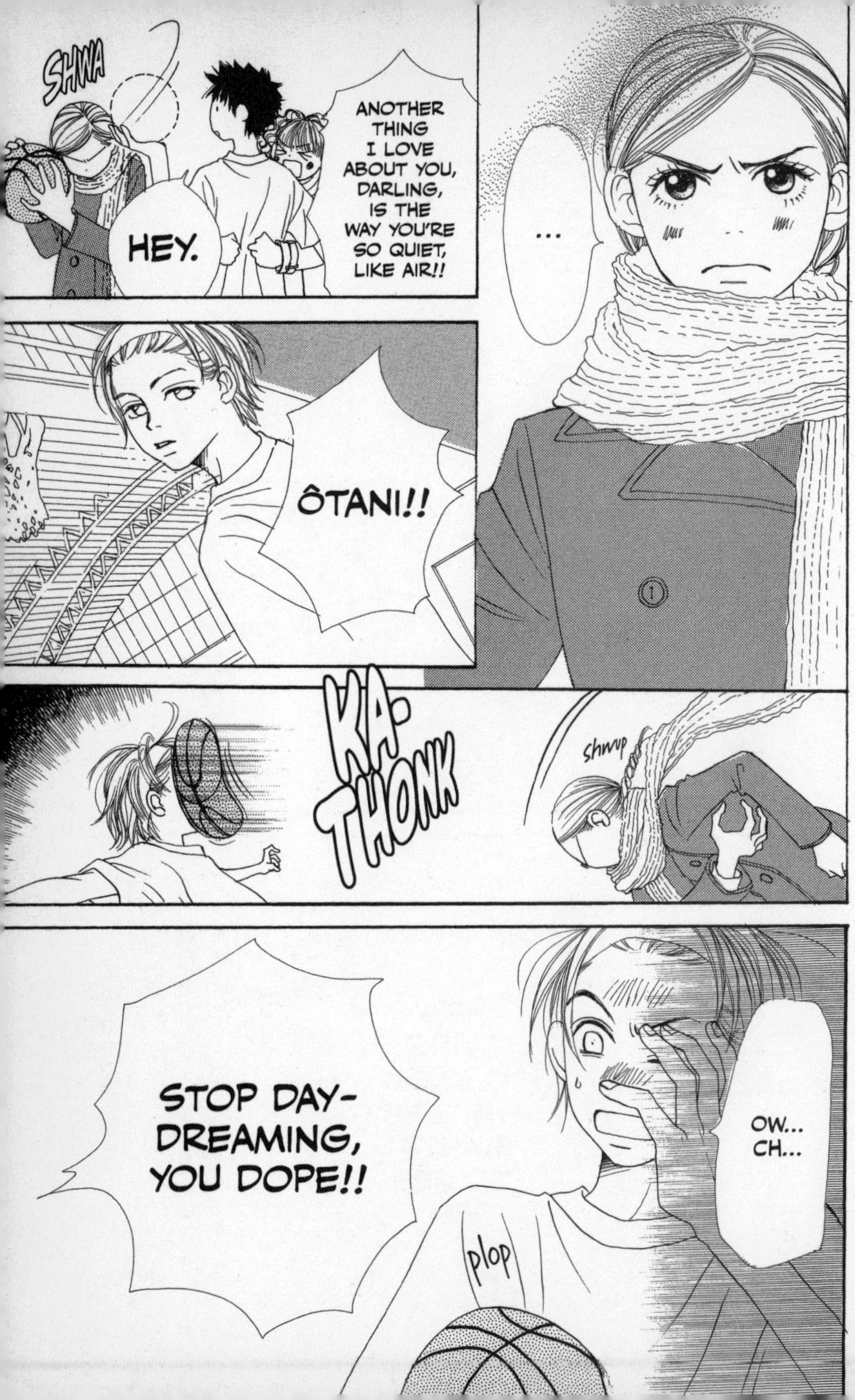
...
ANOTHER THING I LOVE ABOUT YOU, DARLING, IS THE WAY YOU'RE SO QUIET, LIKE AIR!!
SHWA
HEY.
ÔTANI!!
shwup
KA-THONK
OW... CH...
plop
STOP DAY-DREAMING, YOU DOPE!!

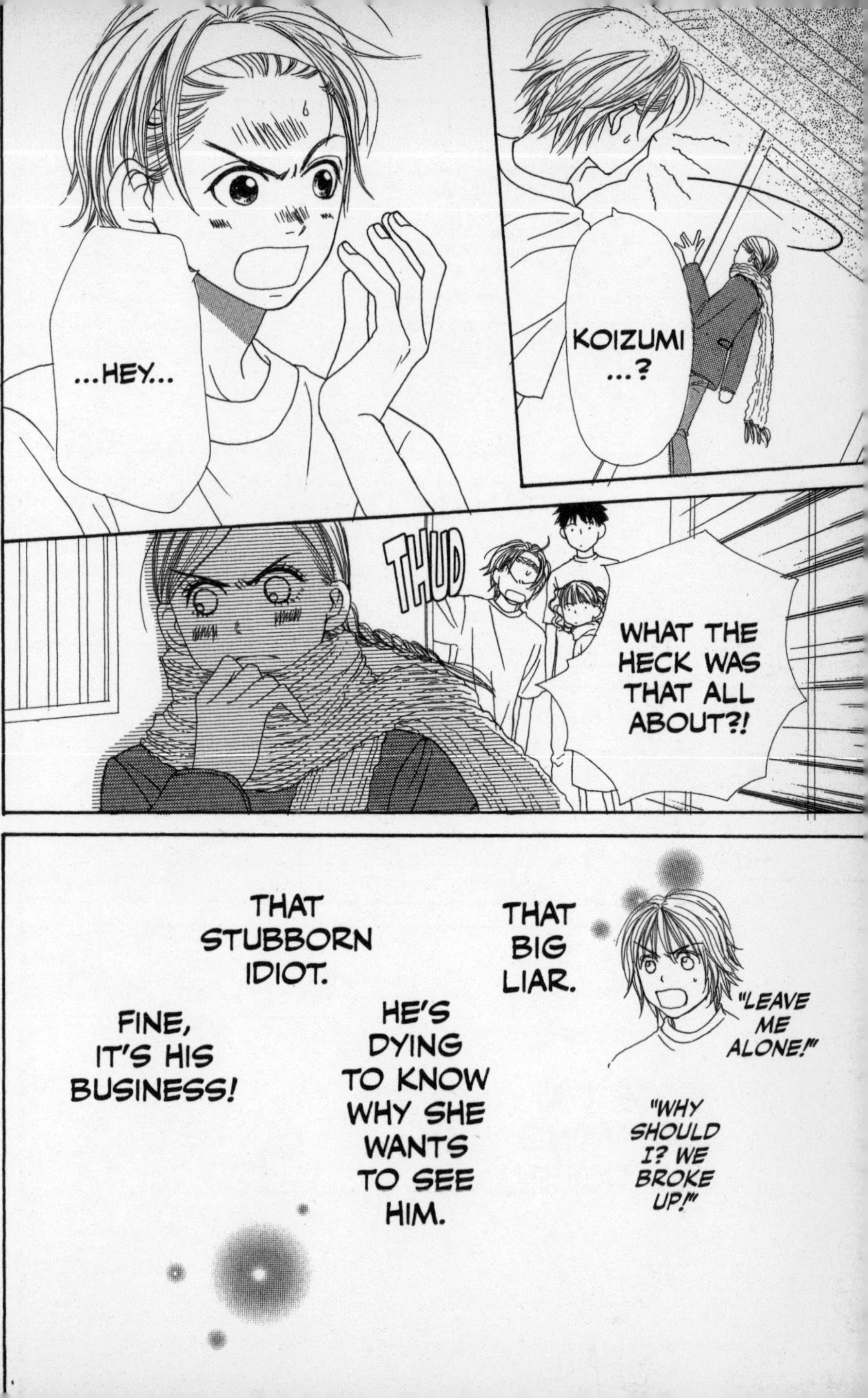
KOIZUMI ...?
...HEY...
THUD
WHAT THE HECK WAS THAT ALL ABOUT?!
"LEAVE ME ALONE!"
"WHY SHOULD I? WE BROKE UP!"
THAT BIG LIAR.
THAT STUBBORN IDIOT.
HE'S DYING TO KNOW WHY SHE WANTS TO SEE HIM.
FINE, IT'S HIS BUSINESS!

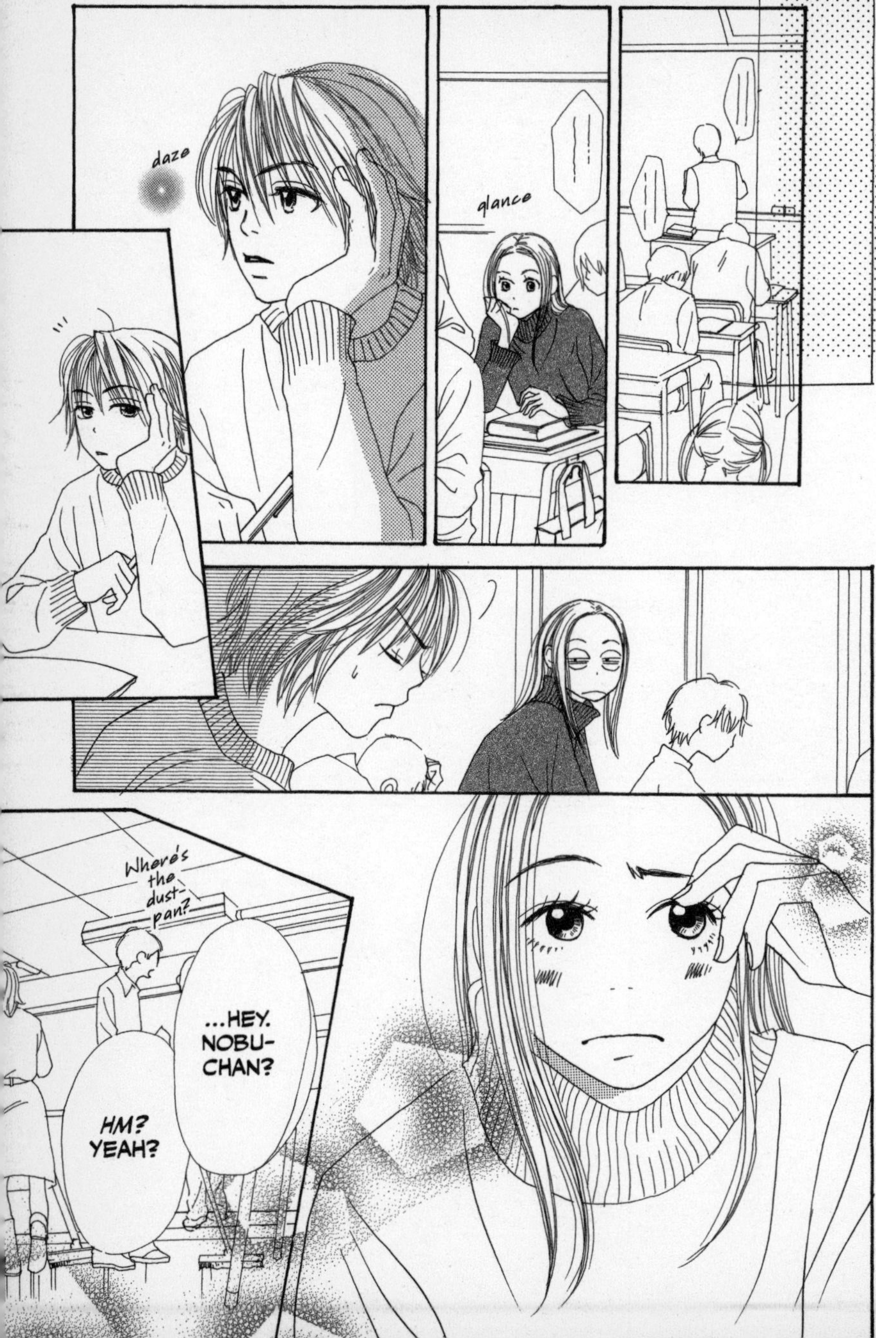
glance
daze
...HEY. NOBU-CHAN?
HM? YEAH?
Where's the dust-pan?

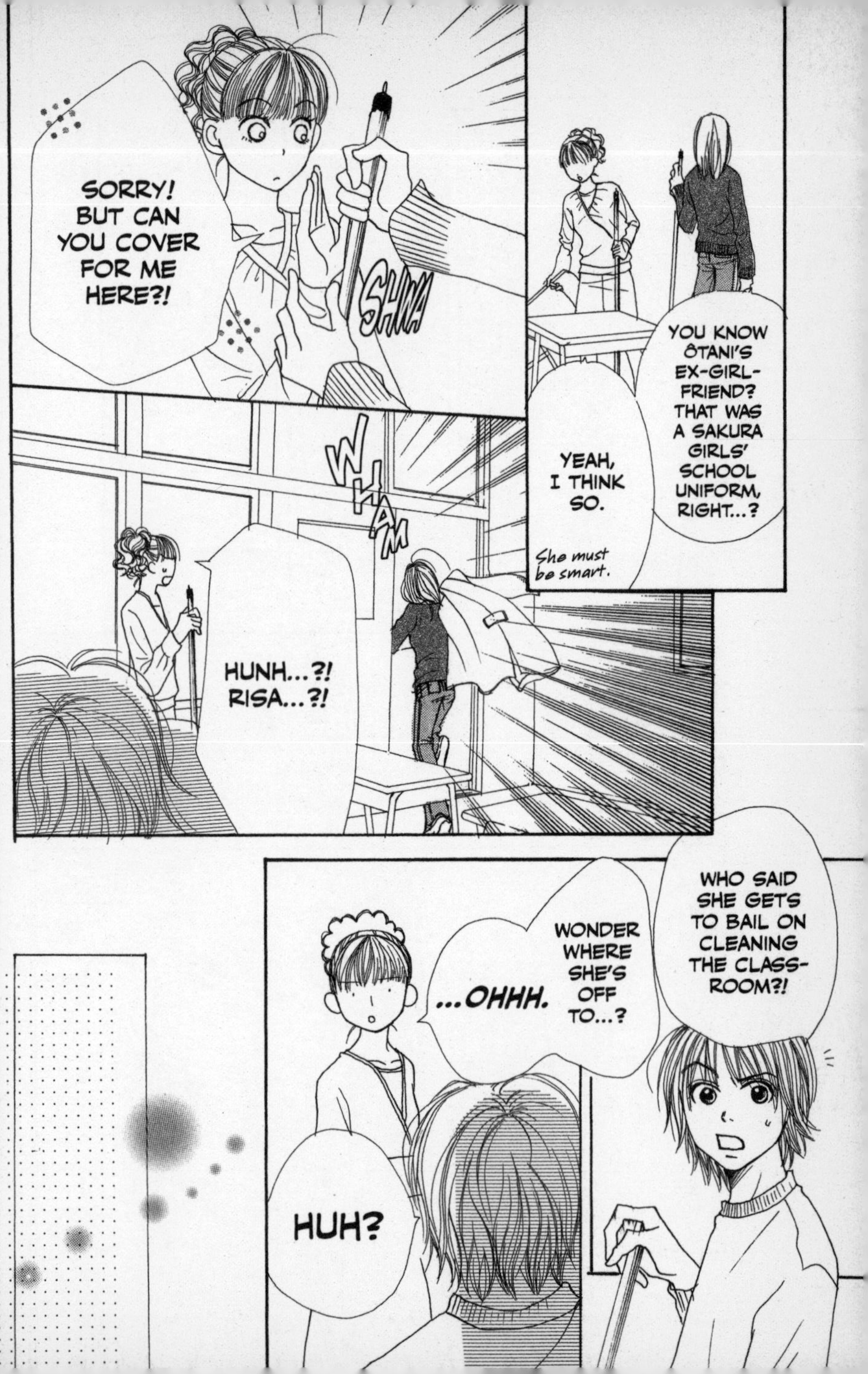

YOU KNOW ŌTANI'S EX-GIRL-FRIEND? THAT WAS A SAKURA GIRLS' SCHOOL UNIFORM, RIGHT...?
YEAH, I THINK SO.
She must be smart.
SORRY! BUT CAN YOU COVER FOR ME HERE?!
SHWA
WHAM
HUNH...?! RISA...?!
WHO SAID SHE GETS TO BAIL ON CLEANING THE CLASS-ROOM?!
WONDER WHERE SHE'S OFF TO...?
...OHHH.
HUH?

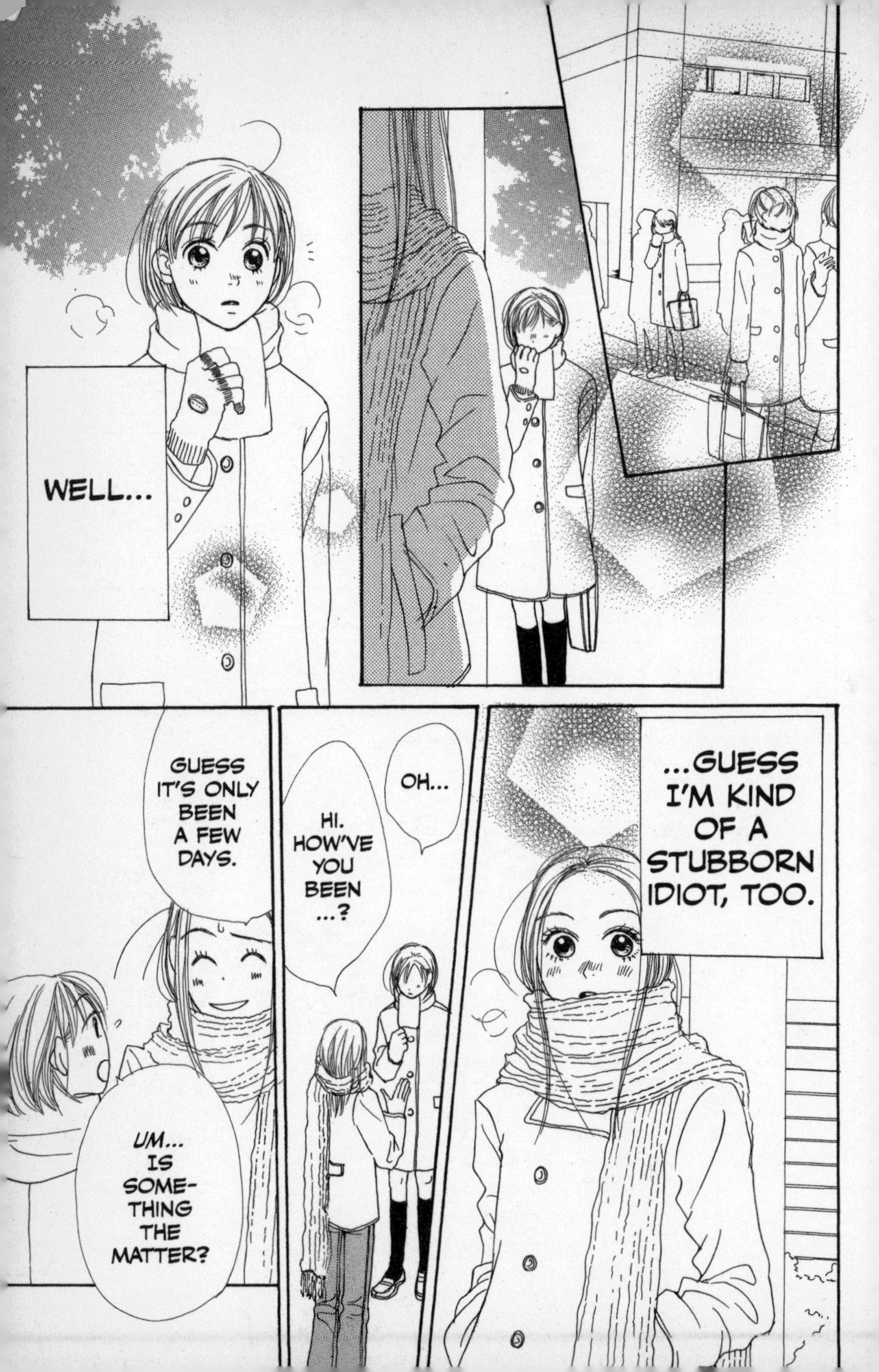
WELL...
...GUESS I'M KIND OF A STUBBORN IDIOT, TOO.
OH...
HI. HOW'VE YOU BEEN ...?
GUESS IT'S ONLY BEEN A FEW DAYS.
UM... IS SOME-THING THE MATTER?

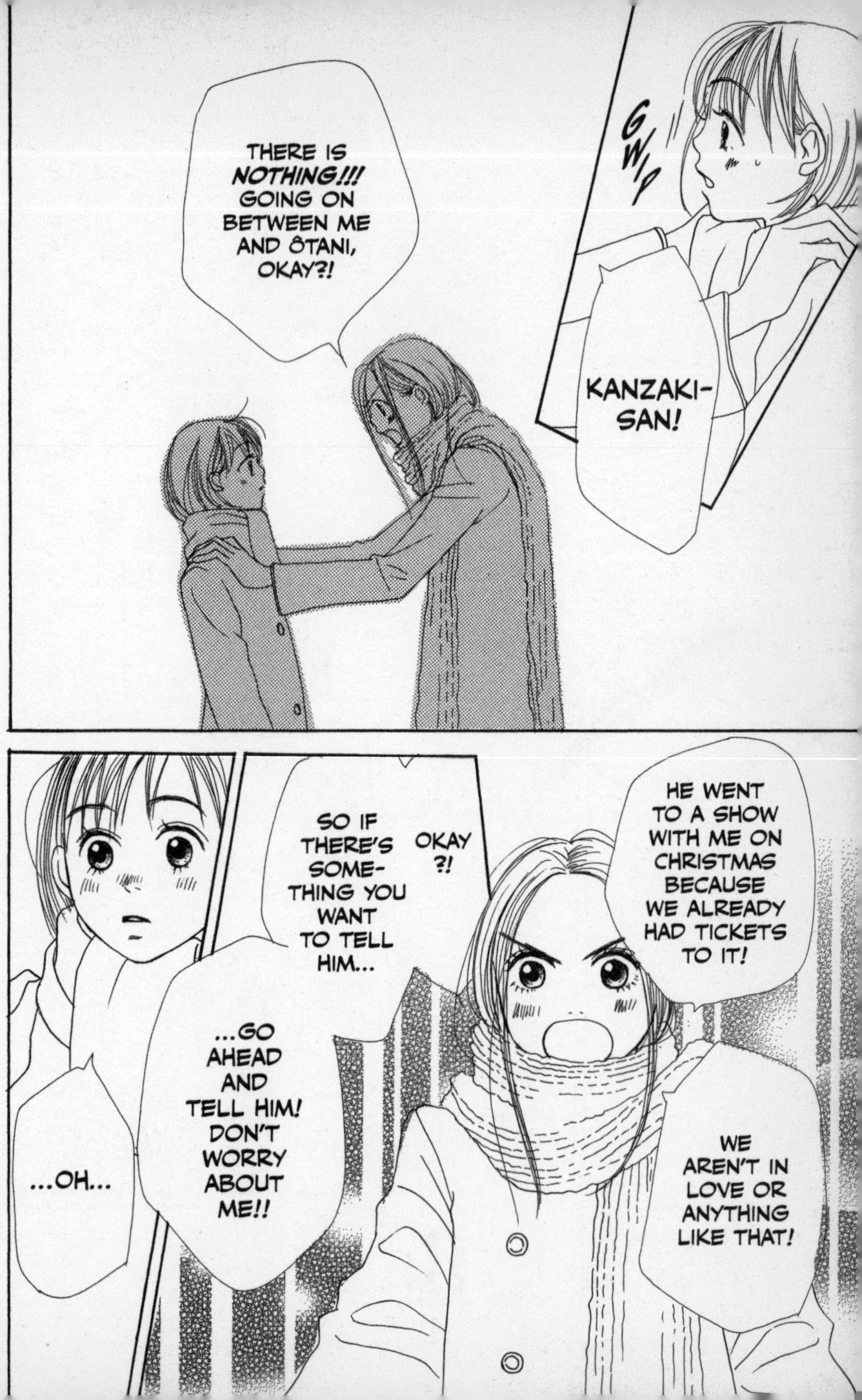
GWA
KANZAKI-SAN!
THERE IS ***NOTHING!!!*** GOING ON BETWEEN ME AND ŌTANI, OKAY?!
HE WENT TO A SHOW WITH ME ON CHRISTMAS BECAUSE WE ALREADY HAD TICKETS TO IT!
WE AREN'T IN LOVE OR ANYTHING LIKE THAT!
SO IF THERE'S SOMETHING YOU WANT TO TELL HIM...
OKAY?!
...GO AHEAD AND TELL HIM! DON'T WORRY ABOUT ME!!
...OH...

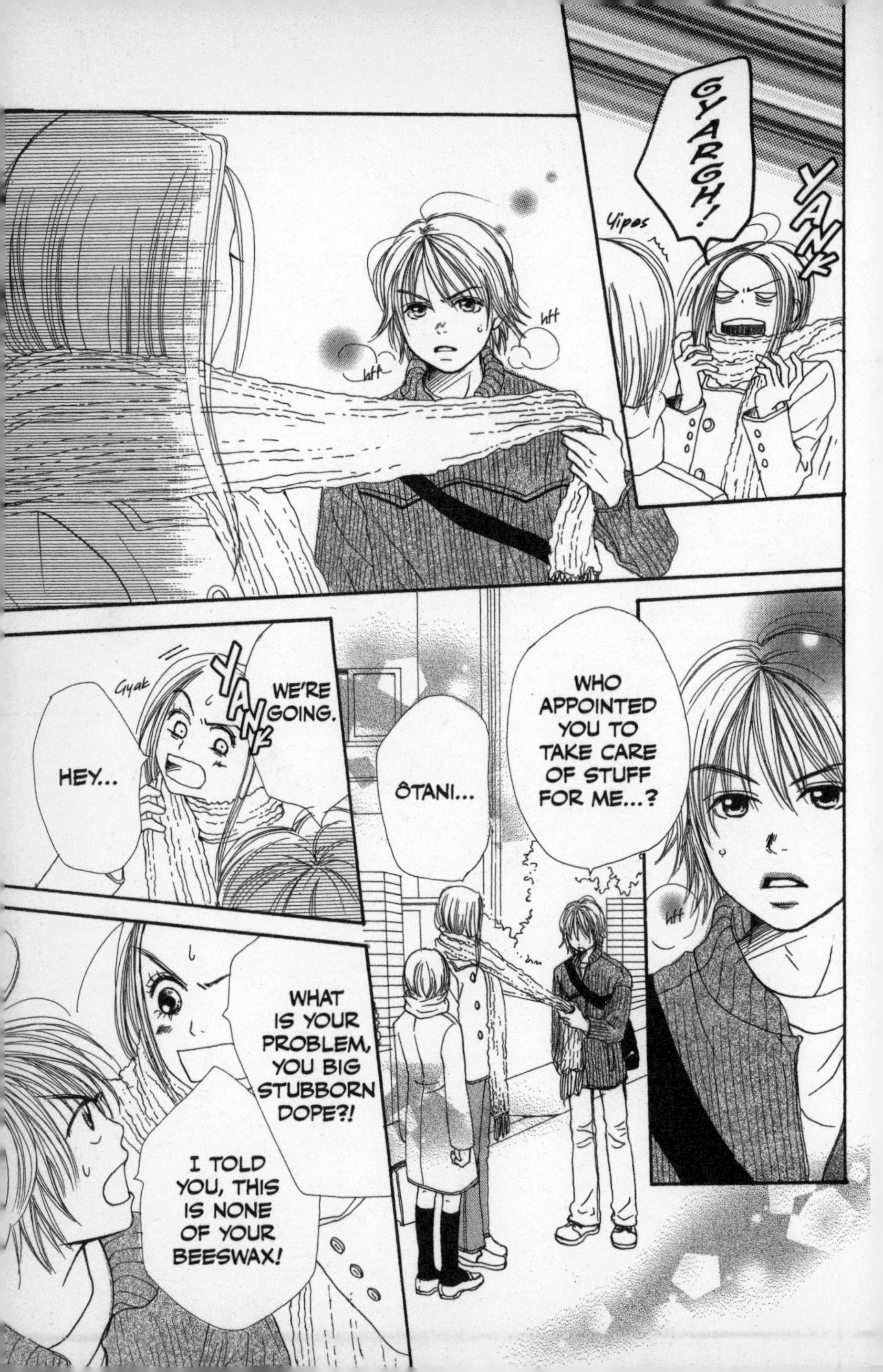

GYARGH!
YANK
Yipes
hff
hff
WHO APPOINTED YOU TO TAKE CARE OF STUFF FOR ME...?
hff
ÔTANI...
WE'RE GOING.
YANK
Gyak
HEY...
WHAT IS YOUR PROBLEM, YOU BIG STUBBORN DOPE?!
I TOLD YOU, THIS IS NONE OF YOUR BEESWAX!

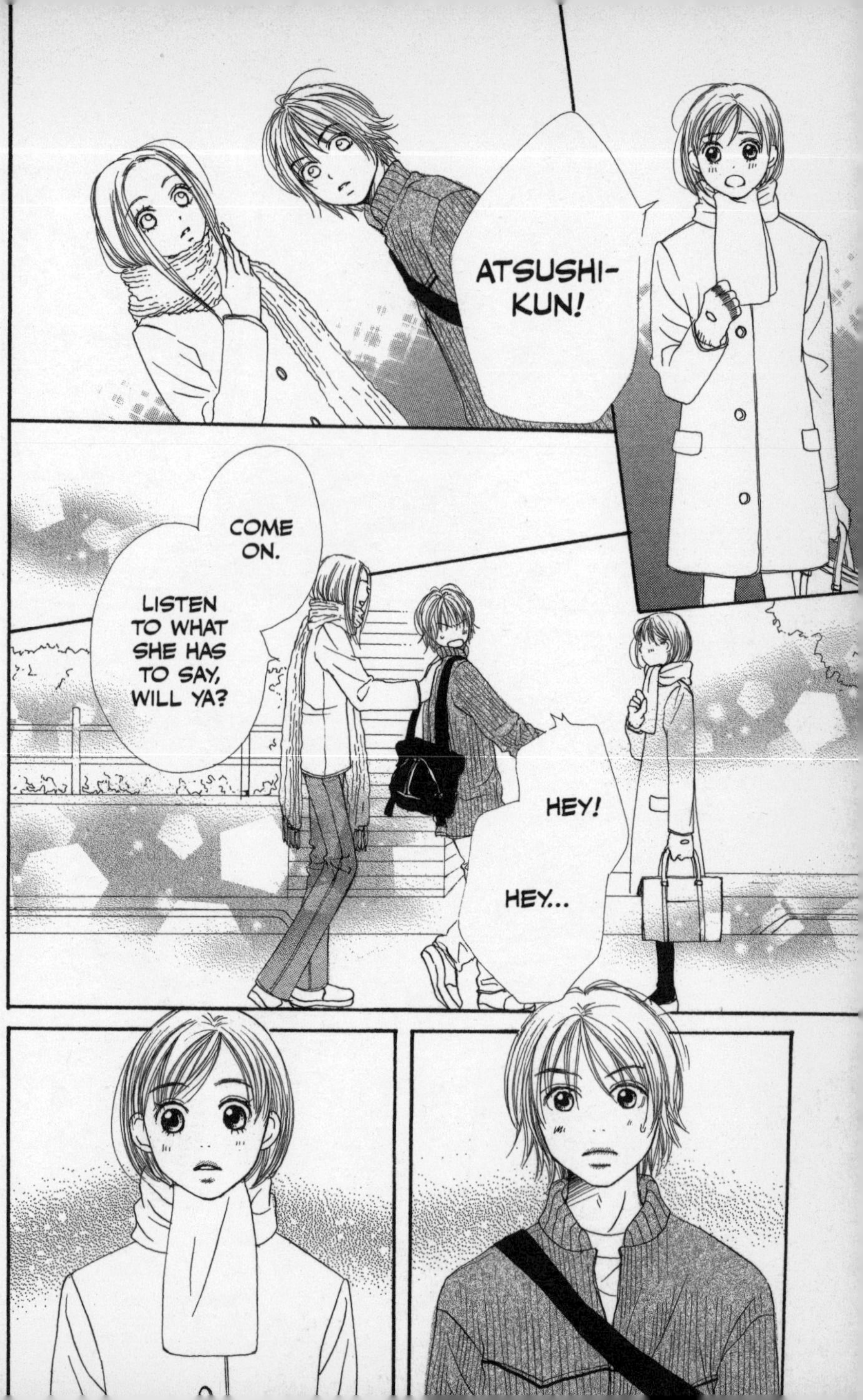
ATSUSHI-KUN!
HEY!
HEY...
COME ON.
LISTEN TO WHAT SHE HAS TO SAY, WILL YA?

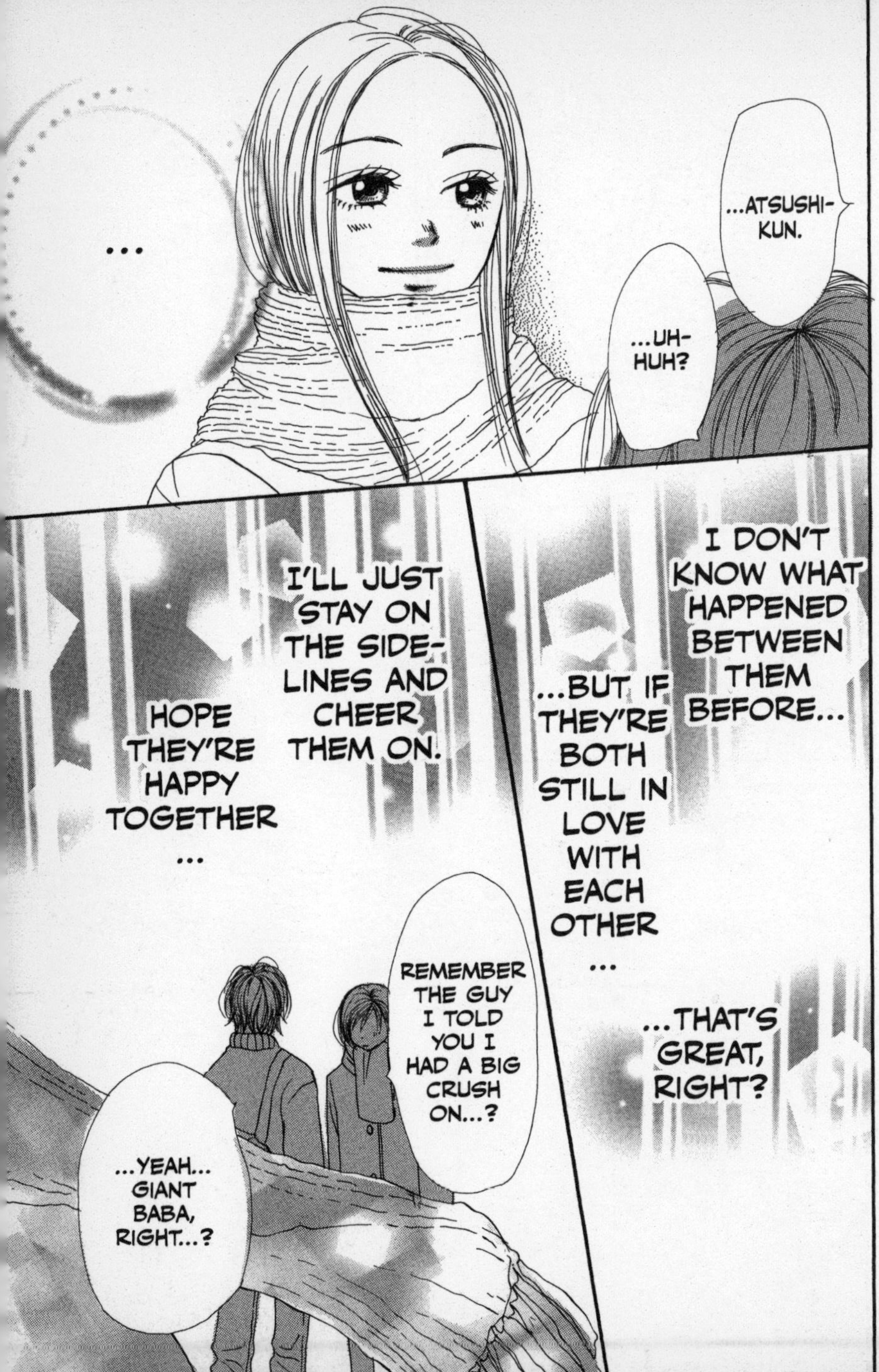
...ATSUSHI-KUN.
...UH-HUH?
...
I DON'T KNOW WHAT HAPPENED BETWEEN THEM BEFORE...
...BUT IF THEY'RE BOTH STILL IN LOVE WITH EACH OTHER...
...THAT'S GREAT, RIGHT?
I'LL JUST STAY ON THE SIDE-LINES AND CHEER THEM ON.
HOPE THEY'RE HAPPY TOGETHER...
REMEMBER THE GUY I TOLD YOU I HAD A BIG CRUSH ON...?
...YEAH... GIANT BABA, RIGHT...?

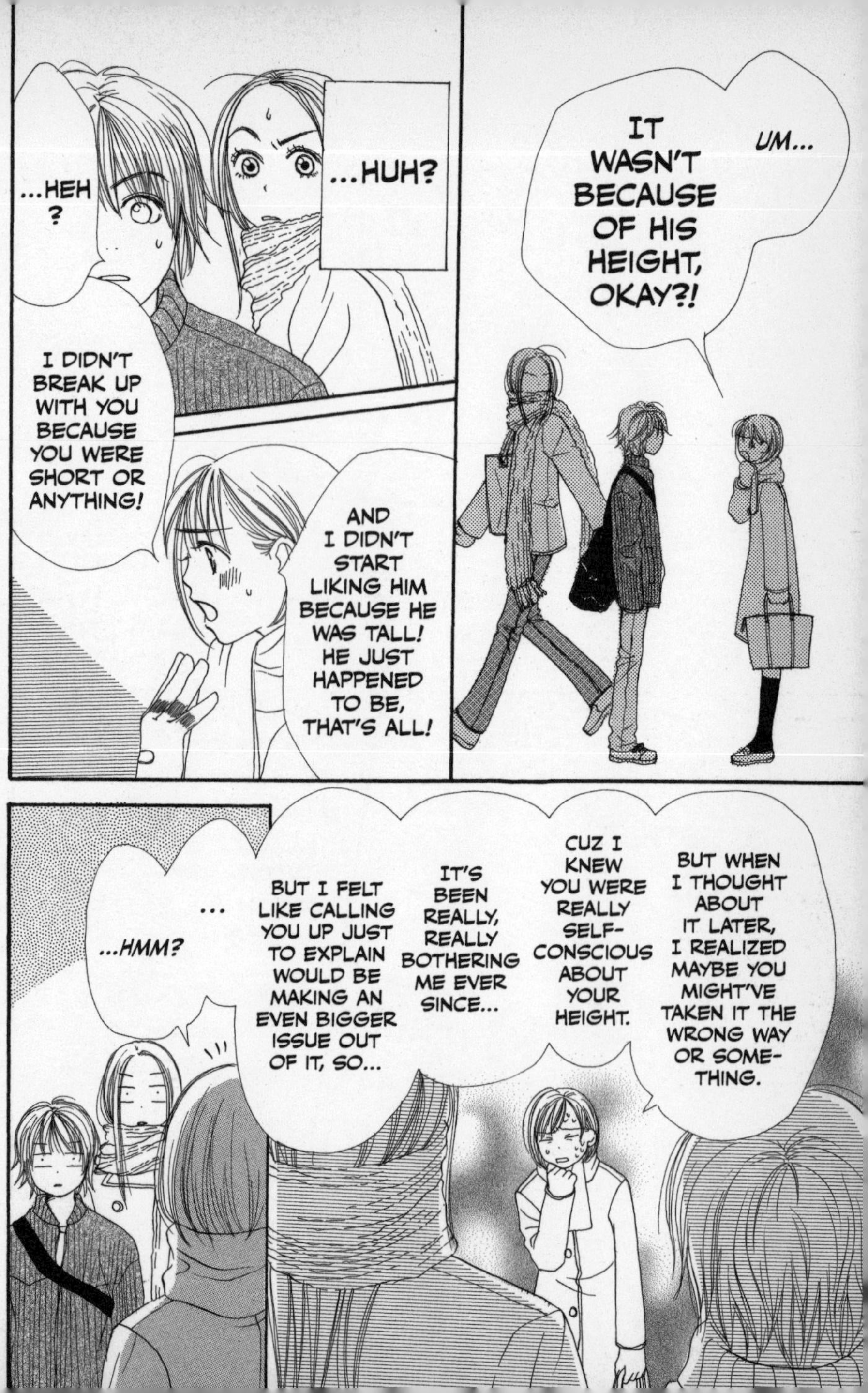
UM...
IT WASN'T BECAUSE OF HIS HEIGHT, OKAY?!
...HUH?
...HEH ?
I DIDN'T BREAK UP WITH YOU BECAUSE YOU WERE SHORT OR ANYTHING!
AND I DIDN'T START LIKING HIM BECAUSE HE WAS TALL! HE JUST HAPPENED TO BE, THAT'S ALL!
BUT WHEN I THOUGHT ABOUT IT LATER, I REALIZED MAYBE YOU MIGHT'VE TAKEN IT THE WRONG WAY OR SOME-THING.
CUZ I KNEW YOU WERE REALLY SELF-CONSCIOUS ABOUT YOUR HEIGHT.
IT'S BEEN REALLY, REALLY BOTHERING ME EVER SINCE...
BUT I FELT LIKE CALLING YOU UP JUST TO EXPLAIN WOULD BE MAKING AN EVEN BIGGER ISSUE OUT OF IT, SO...
...
...HMM?

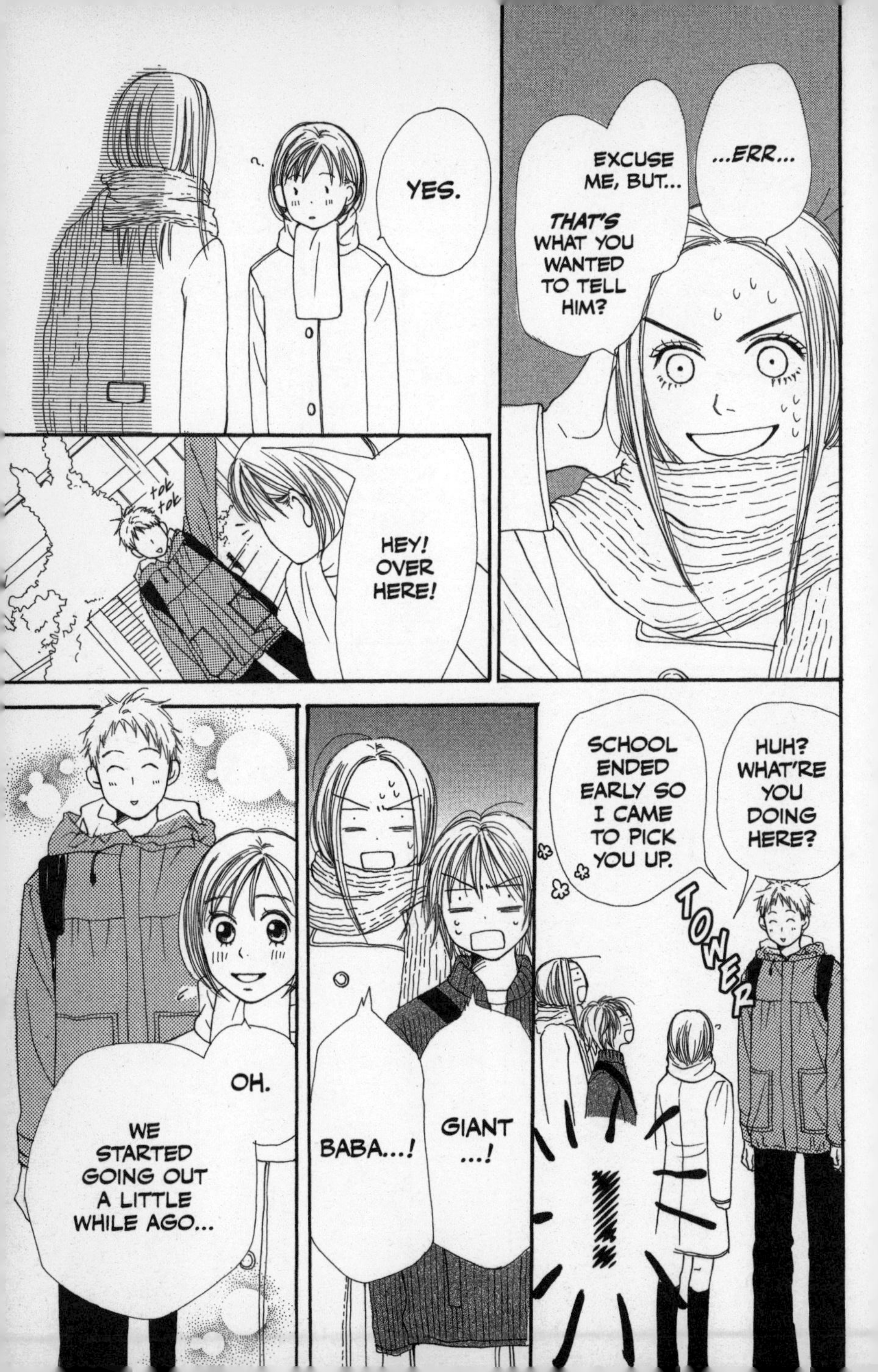
...ERR...
EXCUSE ME, BUT... *THAT'S* WHAT YOU WANTED TO TELL HIM?
YES.
HEY! OVER HERE!
tok tok
HUH? WHAT'RE YOU DOING HERE?
SCHOOL ENDED EARLY SO I CAME TO PICK YOU UP.
TOWER
GIANT ...!
BABA...!
OH.
WE STARTED GOING OUT A LITTLE WHILE AGO...

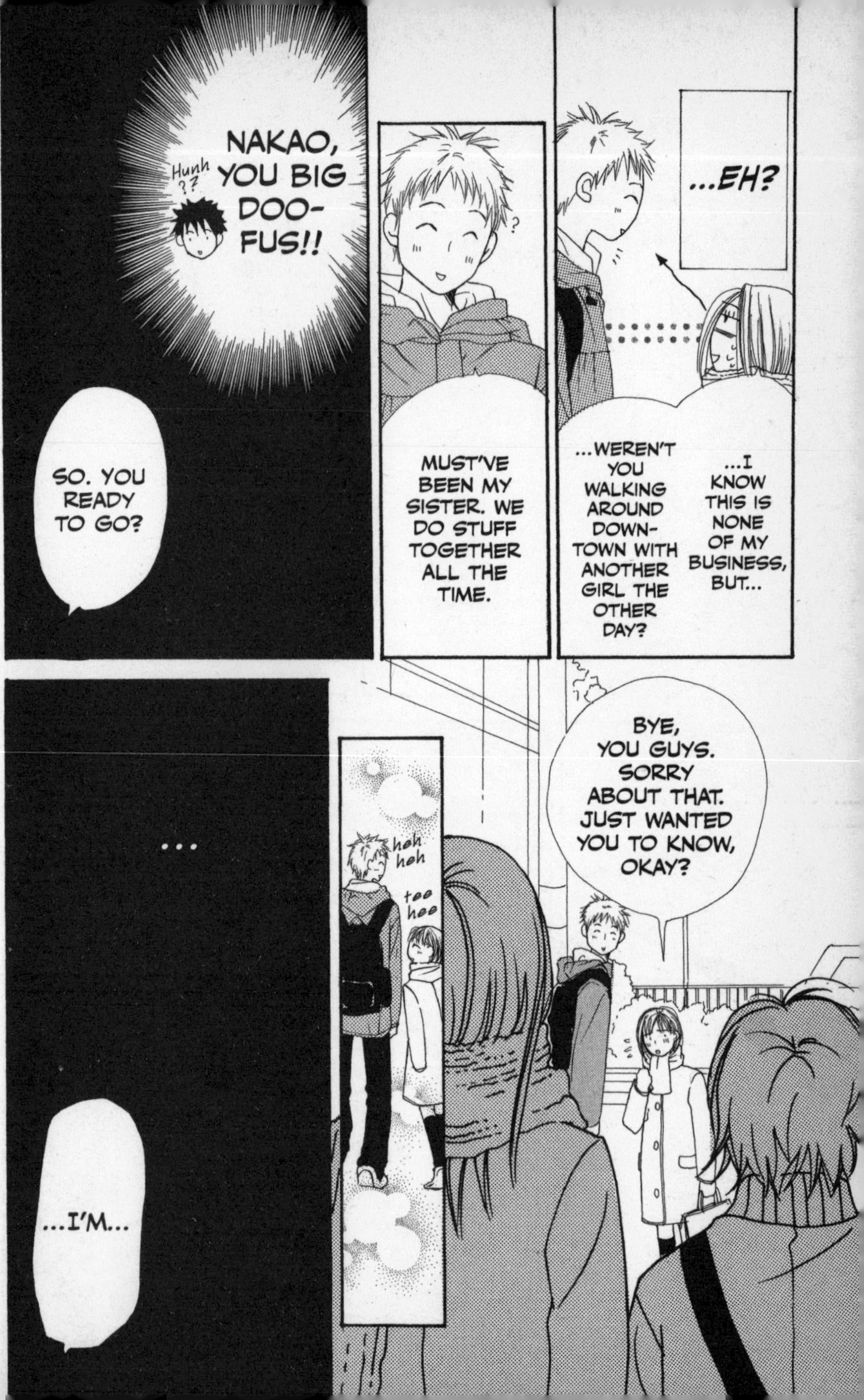
...EH?
...I KNOW THIS IS NONE OF MY BUSINESS, BUT...
...WEREN'T YOU WALKING AROUND DOWNTOWN WITH ANOTHER GIRL THE OTHER DAY?
MUST'VE BEEN MY SISTER. WE DO STUFF TOGETHER ALL THE TIME.
NAKAO, YOU BIG DOO-FUS!!
Hunh ??
SO. YOU READY TO GO?
BYE, YOU GUYS. SORRY ABOUT THAT. JUST WANTED YOU TO KNOW, OKAY?
heh heh
tee hee
...
...I'M...

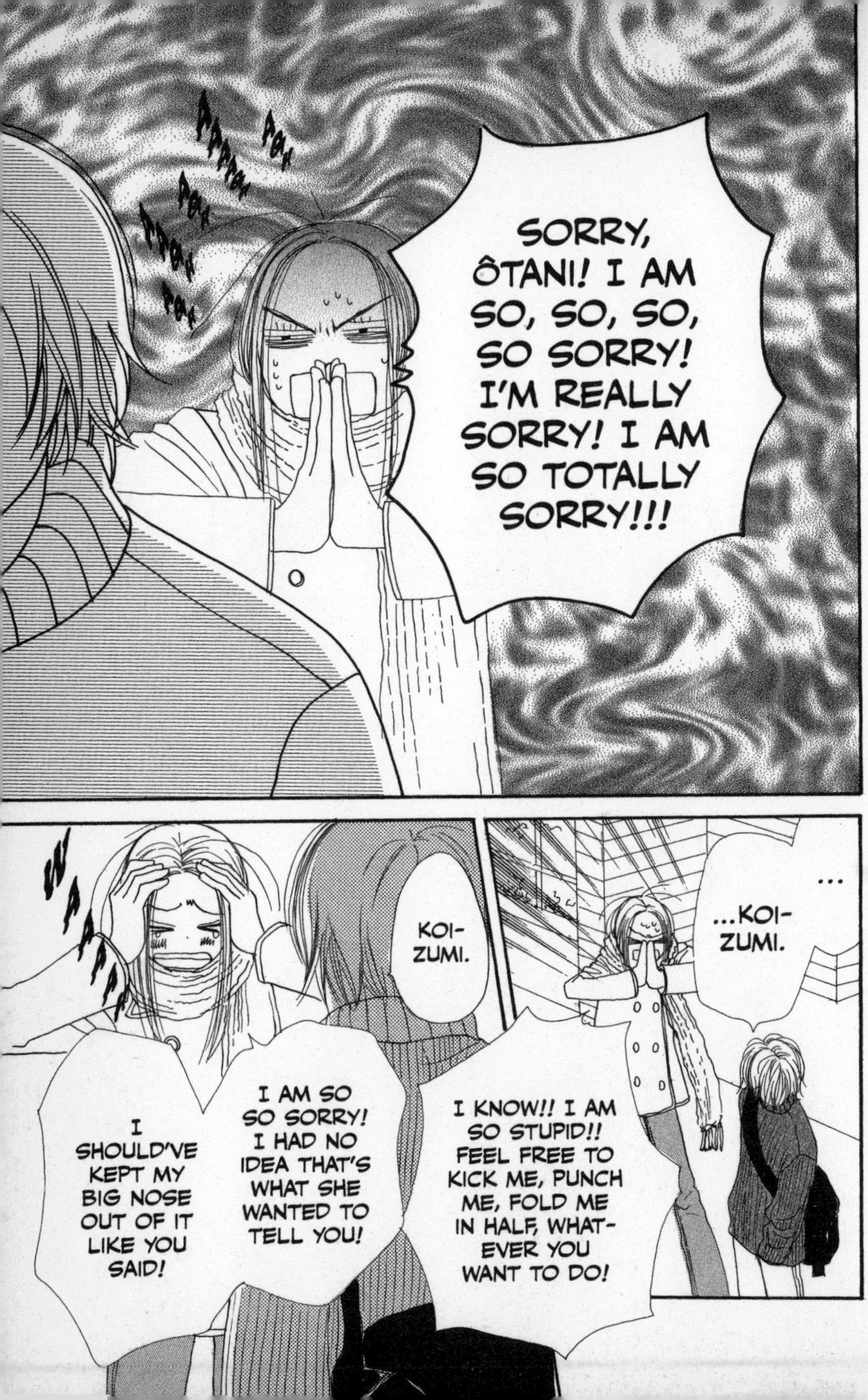
SORRY, ÔTANI! I AM SO, SO, SO, SO SORRY! I'M REALLY SORRY! I AM SO TOTALLY SORRY!!!
...
...KOI-ZUMI.
KOI-ZUMI.
I KNOW!! I AM SO STUPID!! FEEL FREE TO KICK ME, PUNCH ME, FOLD ME IN HALF, WHAT-EVER YOU WANT TO DO!
I AM SO SO SORRY! I HAD NO IDEA THAT'S WHAT SHE WANTED TO TELL YOU!
I SHOULD'VE KEPT MY BIG NOSE OUT OF IT LIKE YOU SAID!

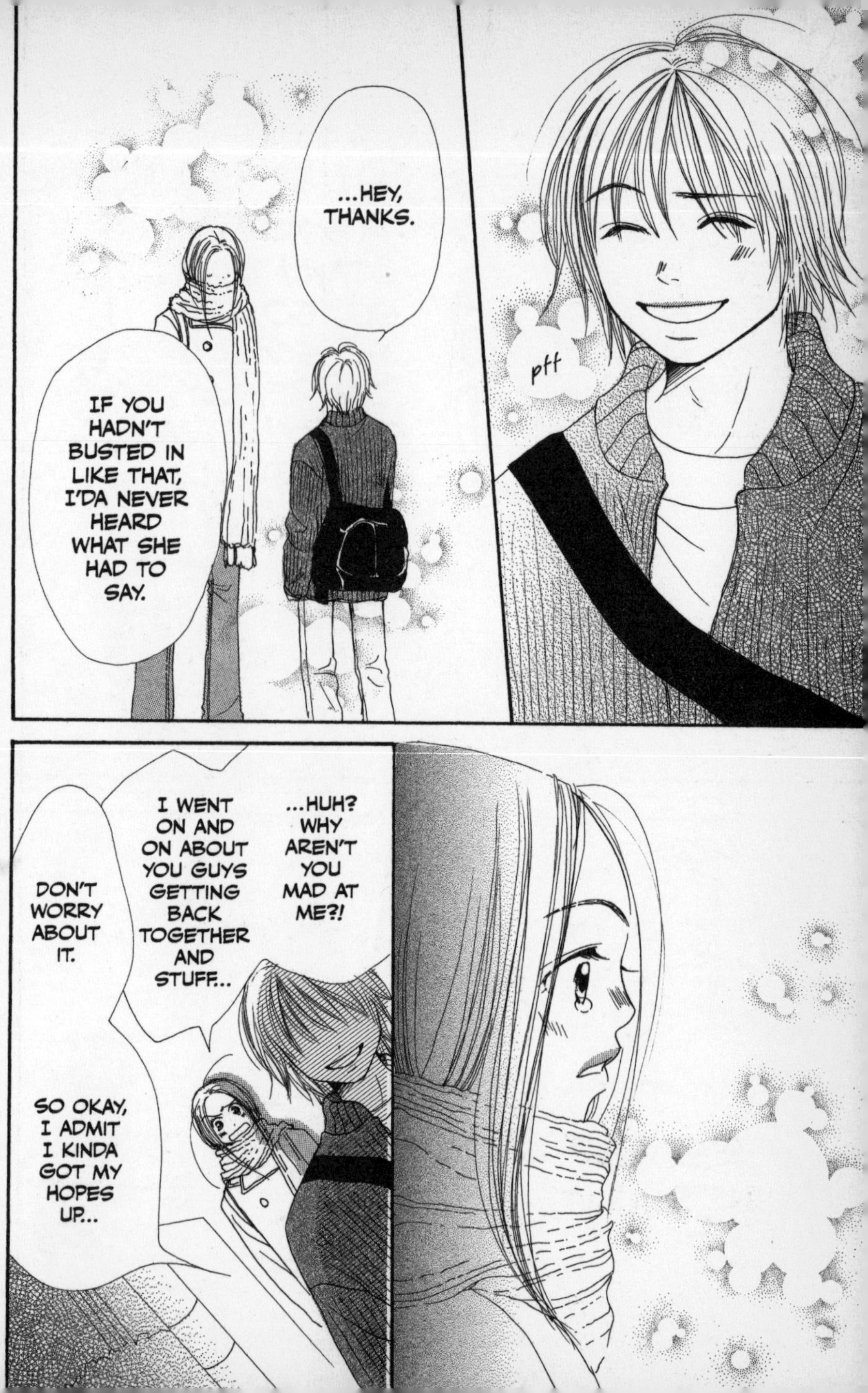
pff
...HEY, THANKS.
IF YOU HADN'T BUSTED IN LIKE THAT, I'DA NEVER HEARD WHAT SHE HAD TO SAY.
...HUH? WHY AREN'T YOU MAD AT ME?!
I WENT ON AND ON ABOUT YOU GUYS GETTING BACK TOGETHER AND STUFF...
DON'T WORRY ABOUT IT.
SO OKAY, I ADMIT I KINDA GOT MY HOPES UP...

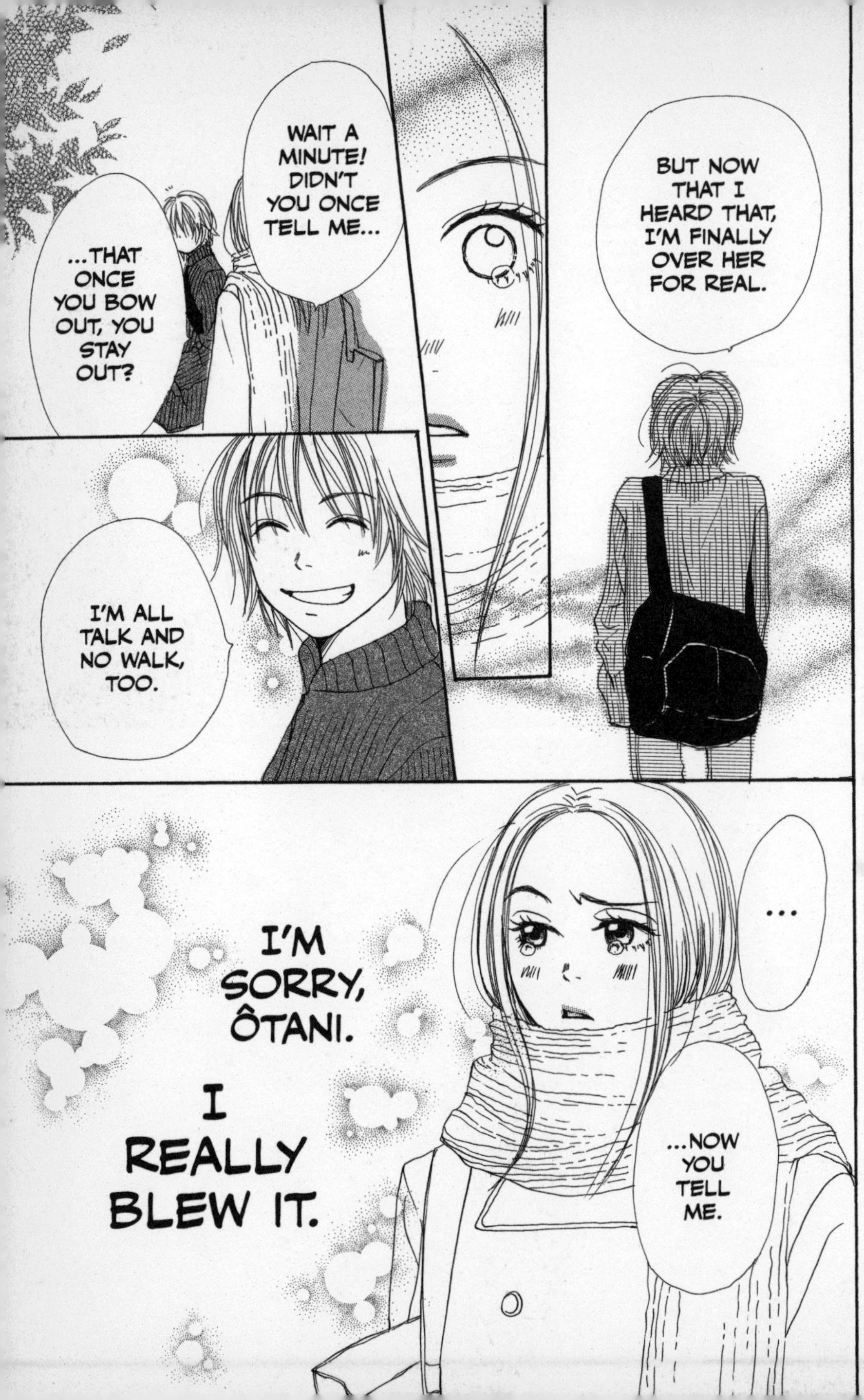
BUT NOW THAT I HEARD THAT, I'M FINALLY OVER HER FOR REAL.
WAIT A MINUTE! DIDN'T YOU ONCE TELL ME...
...THAT ONCE YOU BOW OUT, YOU STAY OUT?
I'M ALL TALK AND NO WALK, TOO.
...
...NOW YOU TELL ME.
I'M SORRY, ÔTANI.
I REALLY BLEW IT.

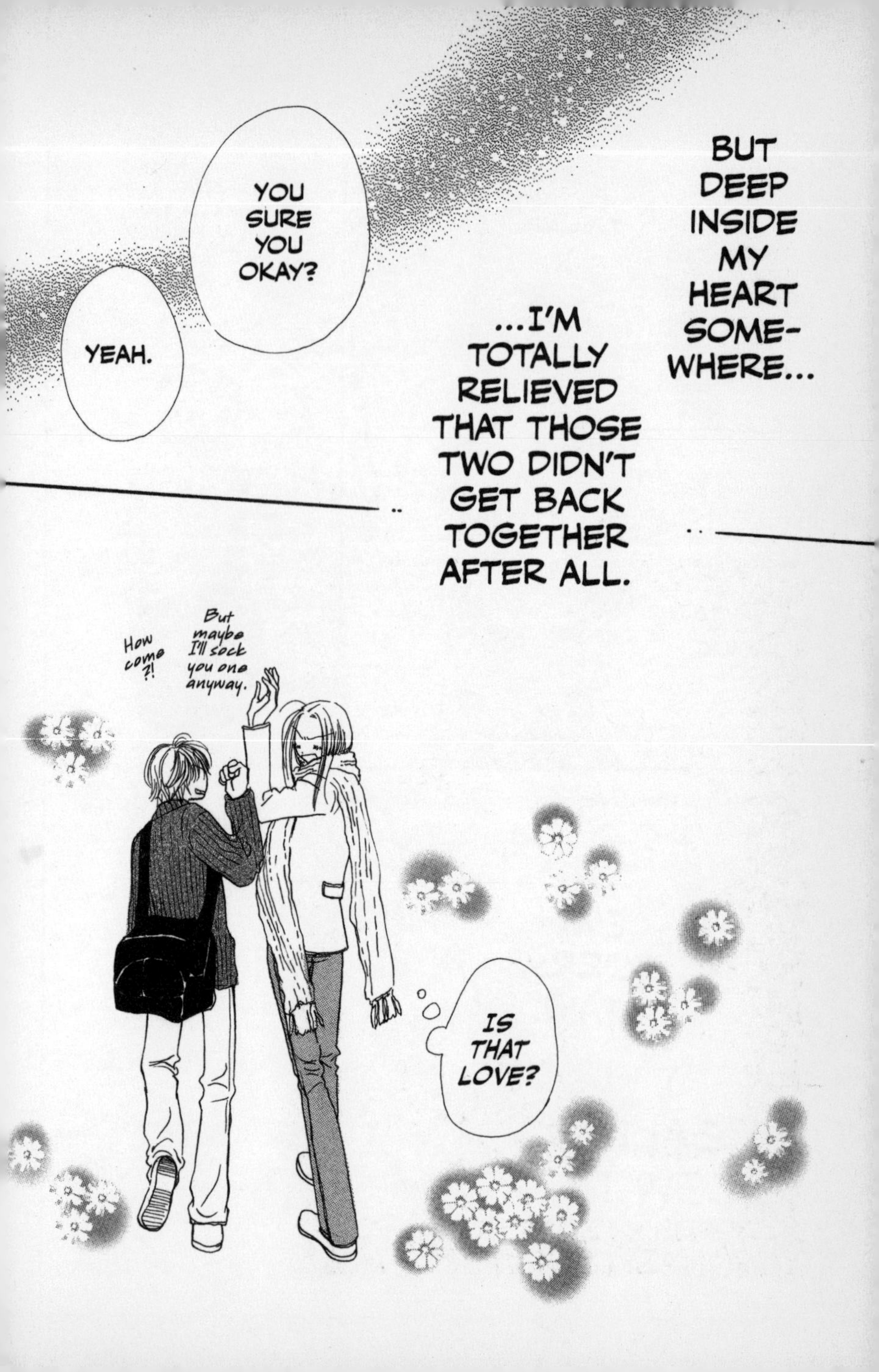
BUT DEEP INSIDE MY HEART SOME-WHERE...
YOU SURE YOU OKAY?
YEAH.
...I'M TOTALLY RELIEVED THAT THOSE TWO DIDN'T GET BACK TOGETHER AFTER ALL.
IS THAT LOVE?
But maybe I'll sock you one anyway.
How come?!

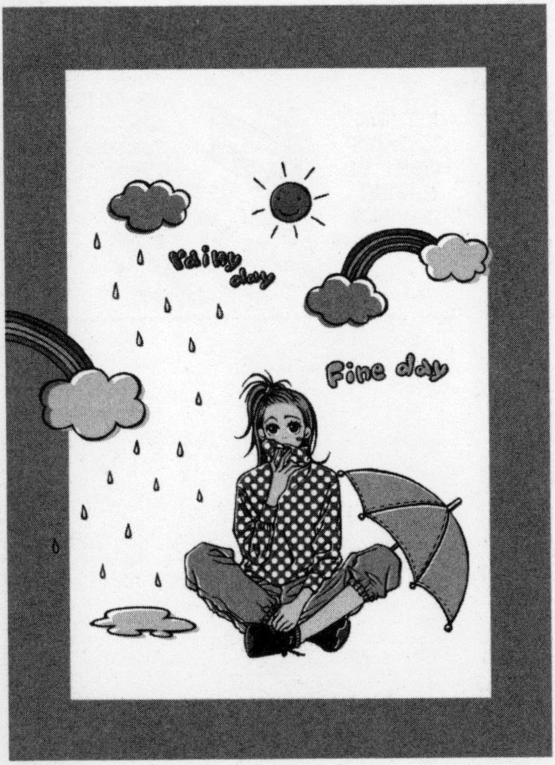
rainy day
Fine day

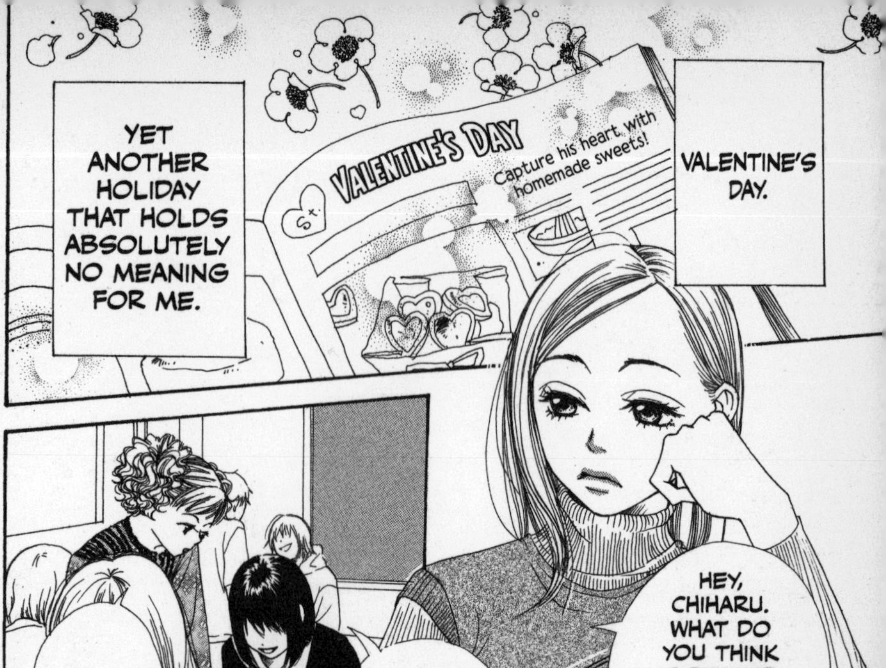
VALENTINE'S DAY.
VALENTINE'S DAY
Capture his heart with homemade sweets!
YET ANOTHER HOLIDAY THAT HOLDS ABSOLUTELY NO MEANING FOR ME.
HEY, CHIHARU. WHAT DO YOU THINK IS BETTER, CHOCOLATE COOKIES OR CHOCOLATE CAKE?
I THINK COOKIES MIGHT BE EASIER TO MAKE, DON'T YOU?
Here, like these.
THAT'S TRUE.
hmmmm

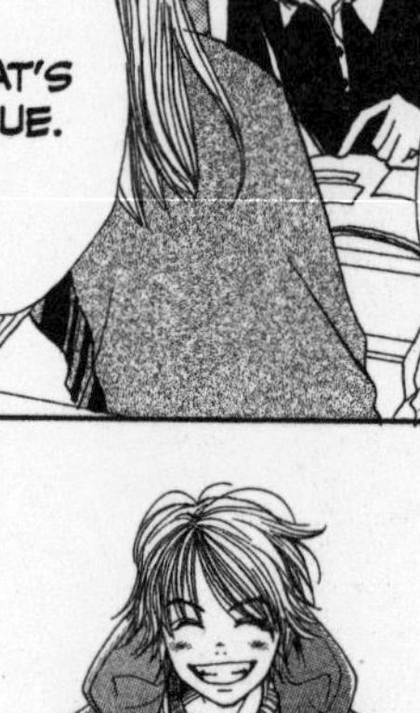

CHAPTER 7

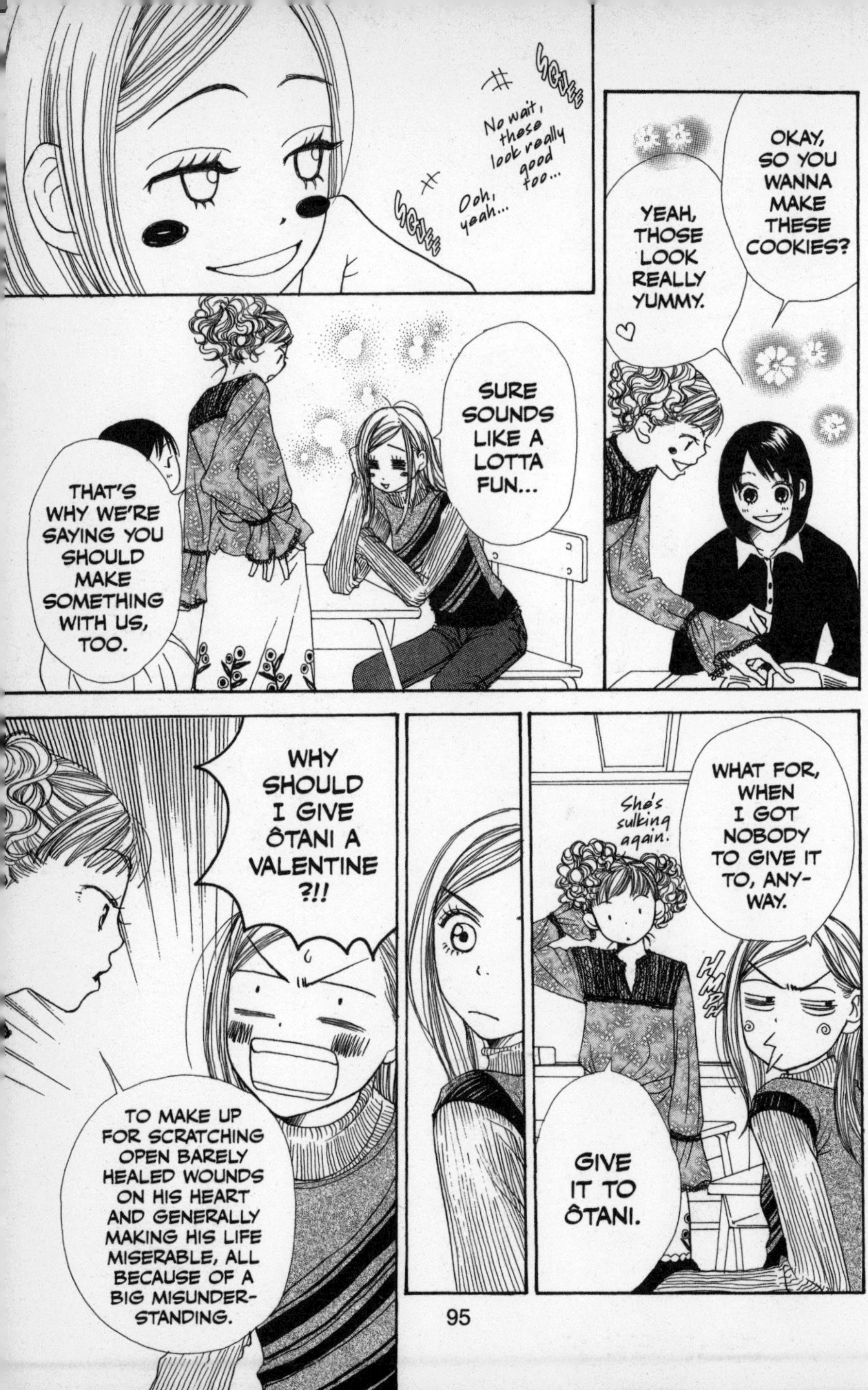
OKAY, SO YOU WANNA MAKE THESE COOKIES?
YEAH, THOSE LOOK REALLY YUMMY.
No wait, these look really good too...
Ooh, yeah...
SURE SOUNDS LIKE A LOTTA FUN...
THAT'S WHY WE'RE SAYING YOU SHOULD MAKE SOMETHING WITH US, TOO.
WHAT FOR, WHEN I GOT NOBODY TO GIVE IT TO, ANYWAY.
HMPH
She's sulking again.
GIVE IT TO ŌTANI.
WHY SHOULD I GIVE ŌTANI A VALENTINE ?!!
TO MAKE UP FOR SCRATCHING OPEN BARELY HEALED WOUNDS ON HIS HEART AND GENERALLY MAKING HIS LIFE MISERABLE, ALL BECAUSE OF A BIG MISUNDERSTANDING.

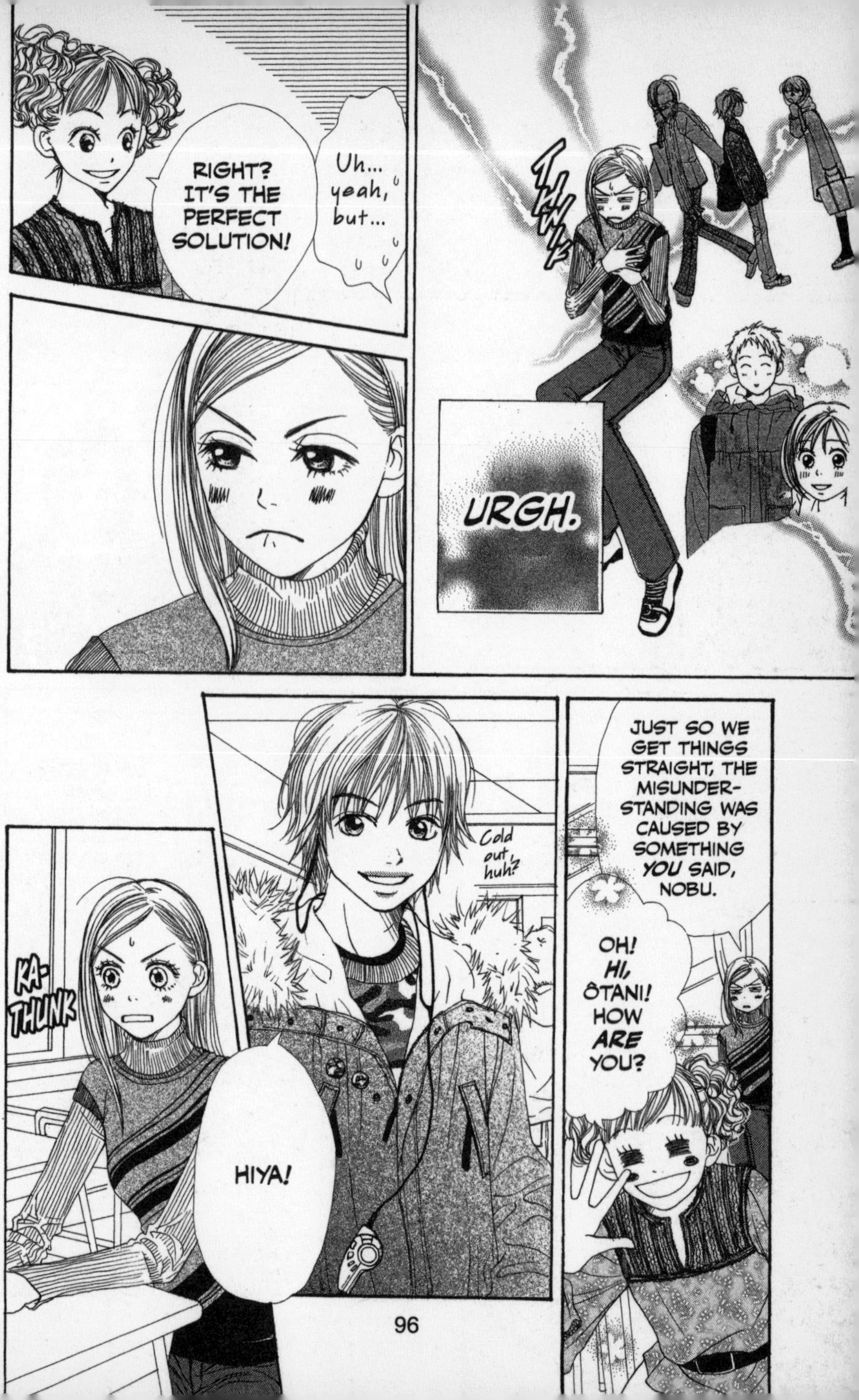
URGH.
Uh... yeah, but...
RIGHT? IT'S THE PERFECT SOLUTION!
JUST SO WE GET THINGS STRAIGHT, THE MISUNDER-STANDING WAS CAUSED BY SOMETHING *YOU* SAID, NOBU.
OH! *HI*, ŌTANI! HOW *ARE* YOU?
Cold out, huh?
HIYA!
KA-THUNK

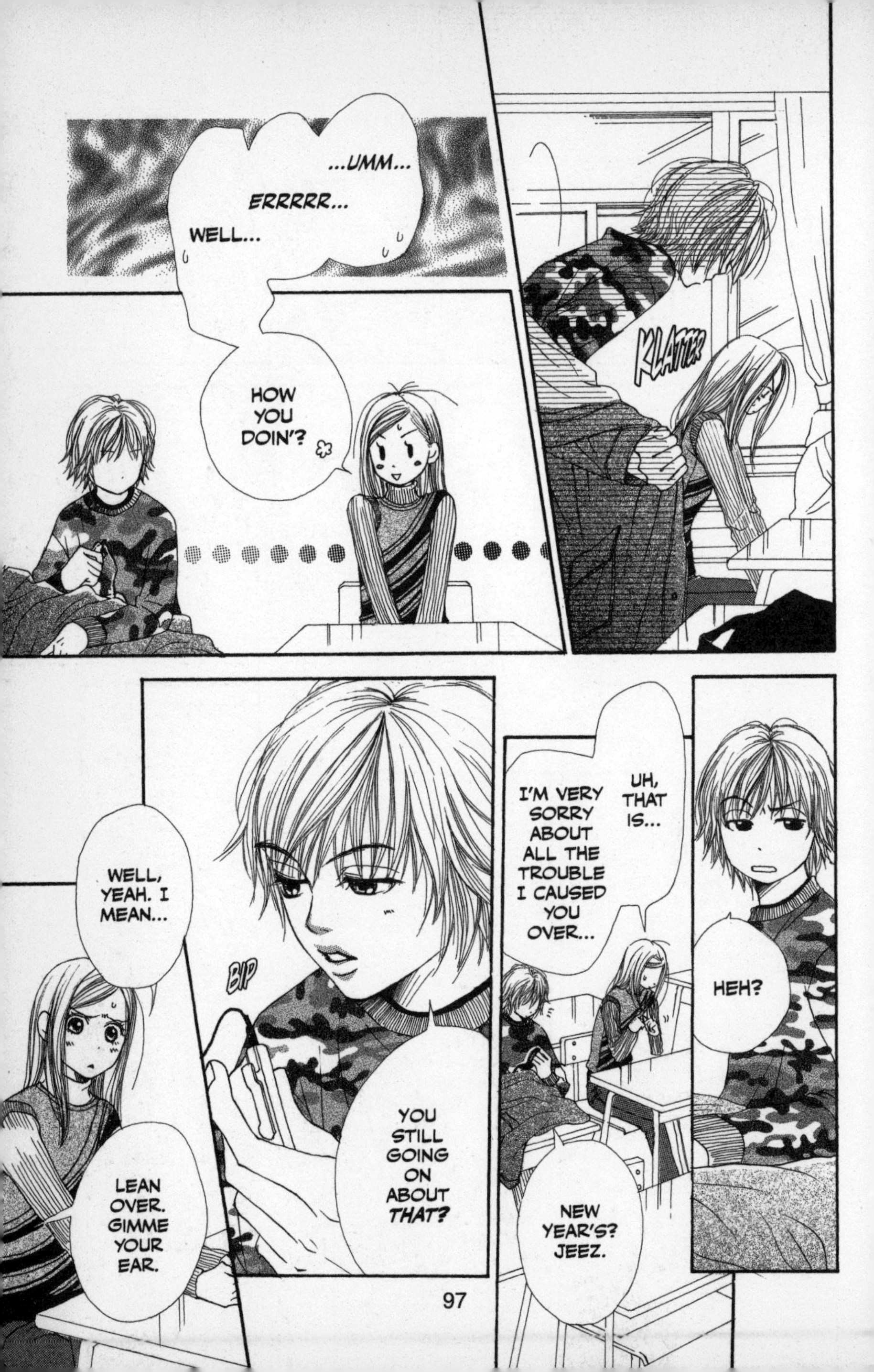
KLATTER
...UMM...
ERRRRR...
WELL...
HOW YOU DOIN'?
HEH?
UH, THAT IS...
I'M VERY SORRY ABOUT ALL THE TROUBLE I CAUSED YOU OVER...
NEW YEAR'S? JEEZ.
YOU STILL GOING ON ABOUT *THAT?*
BIP
WELL, YEAH. I MEAN...
LEAN OVER. GIMME YOUR EAR.

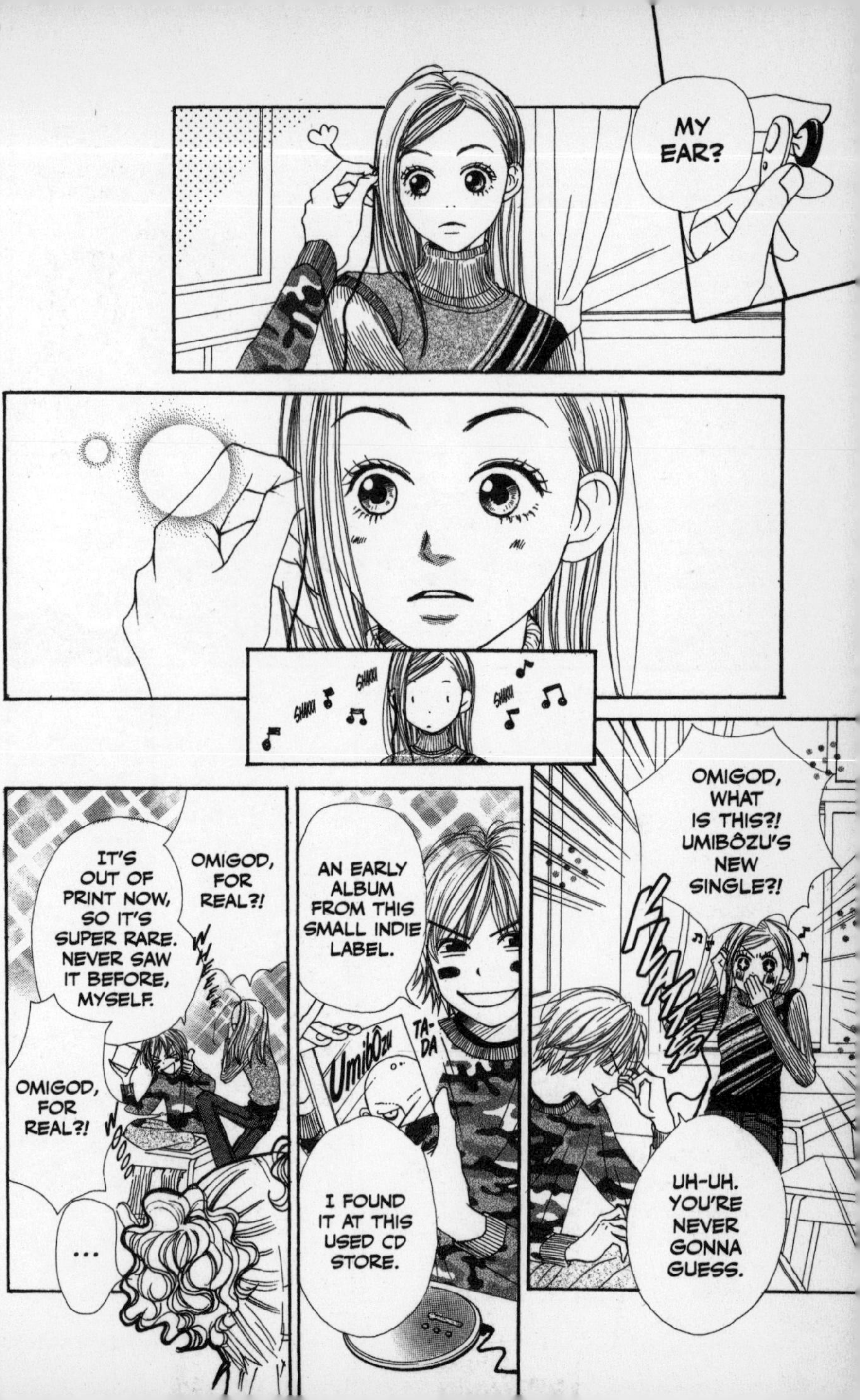
MY EAR?
OMIGOD, WHAT IS THIS?! UMIBÔZU'S NEW SINGLE?!
UH-UH. YOU'RE NEVER GONNA GUESS.
AN EARLY ALBUM FROM THIS SMALL INDIE LABEL.
TA-DA
Umibôzu
I FOUND IT AT THIS USED CD STORE.
OMIGOD, FOR REAL?!
IT'S OUT OF PRINT NOW, SO IT'S SUPER RARE. NEVER SAW IT BEFORE, MYSELF.
OMIGOD, FOR REAL?!
...

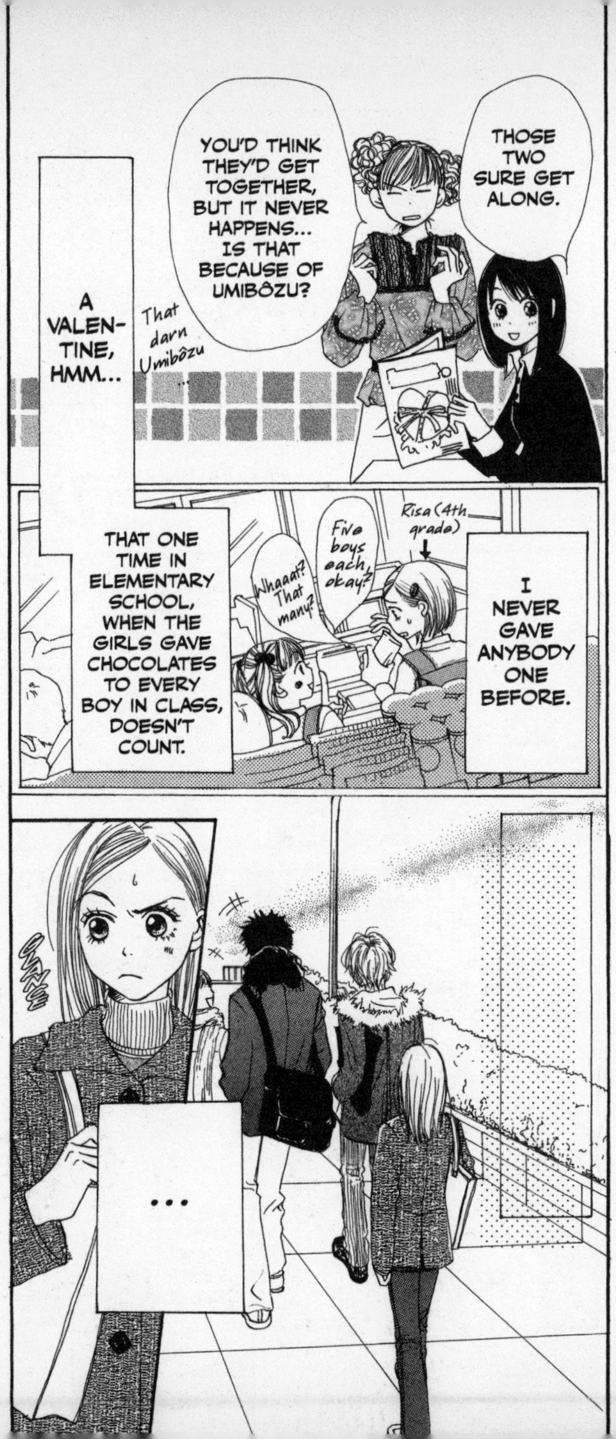
THOSE TWO SURE GET ALONG.
YOU'D THINK THEY'D GET TOGETHER, BUT IT NEVER HAPPENS... IS THAT BECAUSE OF UMIBÔZU?
That darn Umibôzu...
A VALENTINE, HMM...
I NEVER GAVE ANYBODY ONE BEFORE.
Risa (4th grade)
Five boys each, okay?
Whaaat? That many?
THAT ONE TIME IN ELEMENTARY SCHOOL, WHEN THE GIRLS GAVE CHOCOLATES TO EVERY BOY IN CLASS, DOESN'T COUNT.
...

3.

Errr...
so let's leave the hard, complicated political discussion at that for now...

Oh, come on. You were talking about nipples. No! Please don't say that! I am now consumed with mortification for what I wrote before. I think I must've been half-asleep.
Errr...
so let's leave the hard, complicated nipples at that for now...

ha ha ha ha ha

Too, too stupid for words! What is this space for, anyway?! Oh! Speaking of space... Sega's "Space Channel 5" is really cute. In fact, it's so cute you can't really concentrate on playing the game, which makes it kinda hard.
I cry at the end of Part 2 no matter how many times I do it. Ulala is so cute... Stay on that channel!

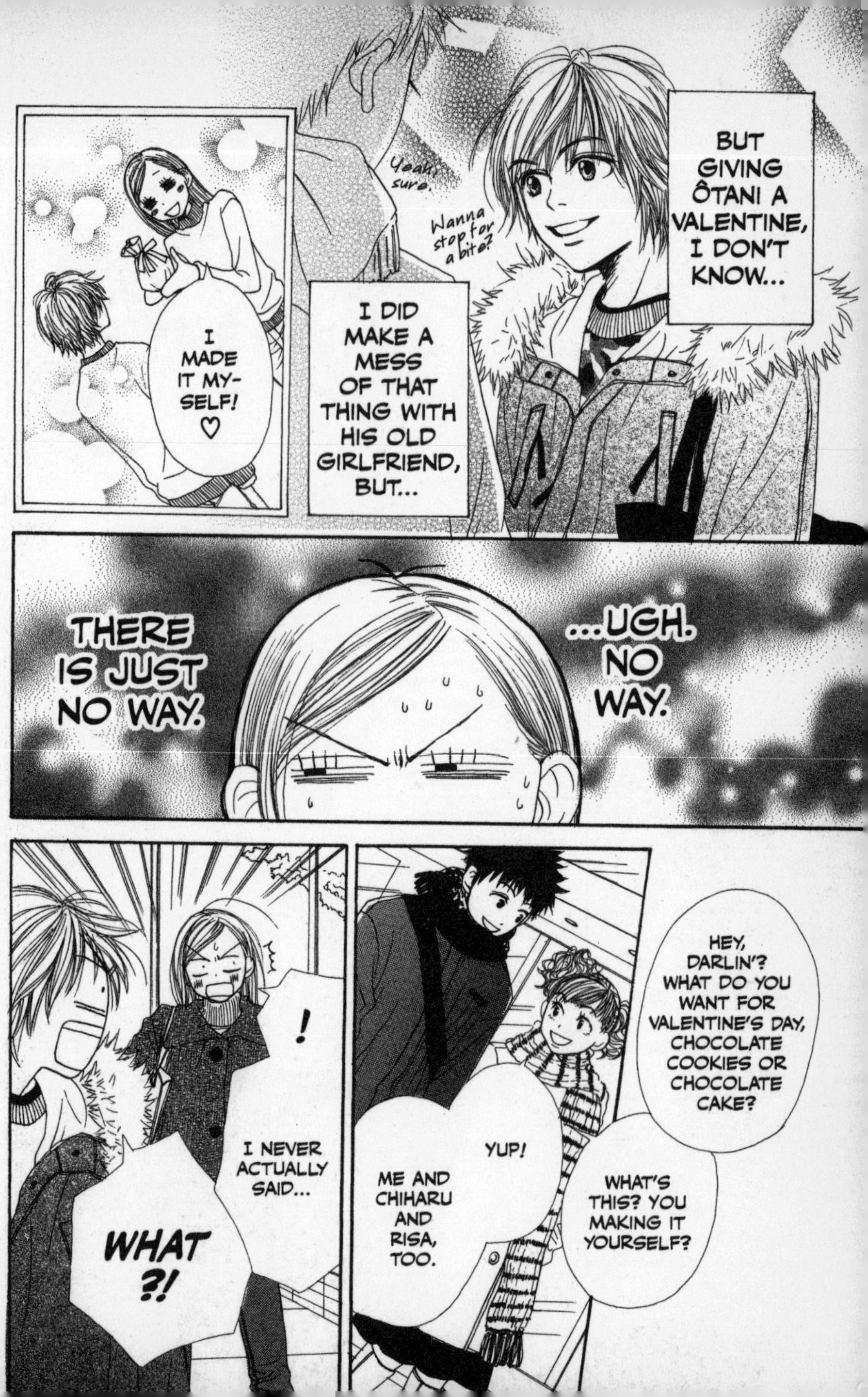
BUT GIVING ÔTANI A VALENTINE, I DON'T KNOW...
Yeah, sure.
Wanna stop for a bite?
I DID MAKE A MESS OF THAT THING WITH HIS OLD GIRLFRIEND, BUT...
I MADE IT MY-SELF! ♡
...UGH. NO WAY.
THERE IS JUST NO WAY.
HEY, DARLIN'? WHAT DO YOU WANT FOR VALENTINE'S DAY, CHOCOLATE COOKIES OR CHOCOLATE CAKE?
WHAT'S THIS? YOU MAKING IT YOURSELF?
YUP!
ME AND CHIHARU AND RISA, TOO.
!
I NEVER ACTUALLY SAID...
WHAT?!

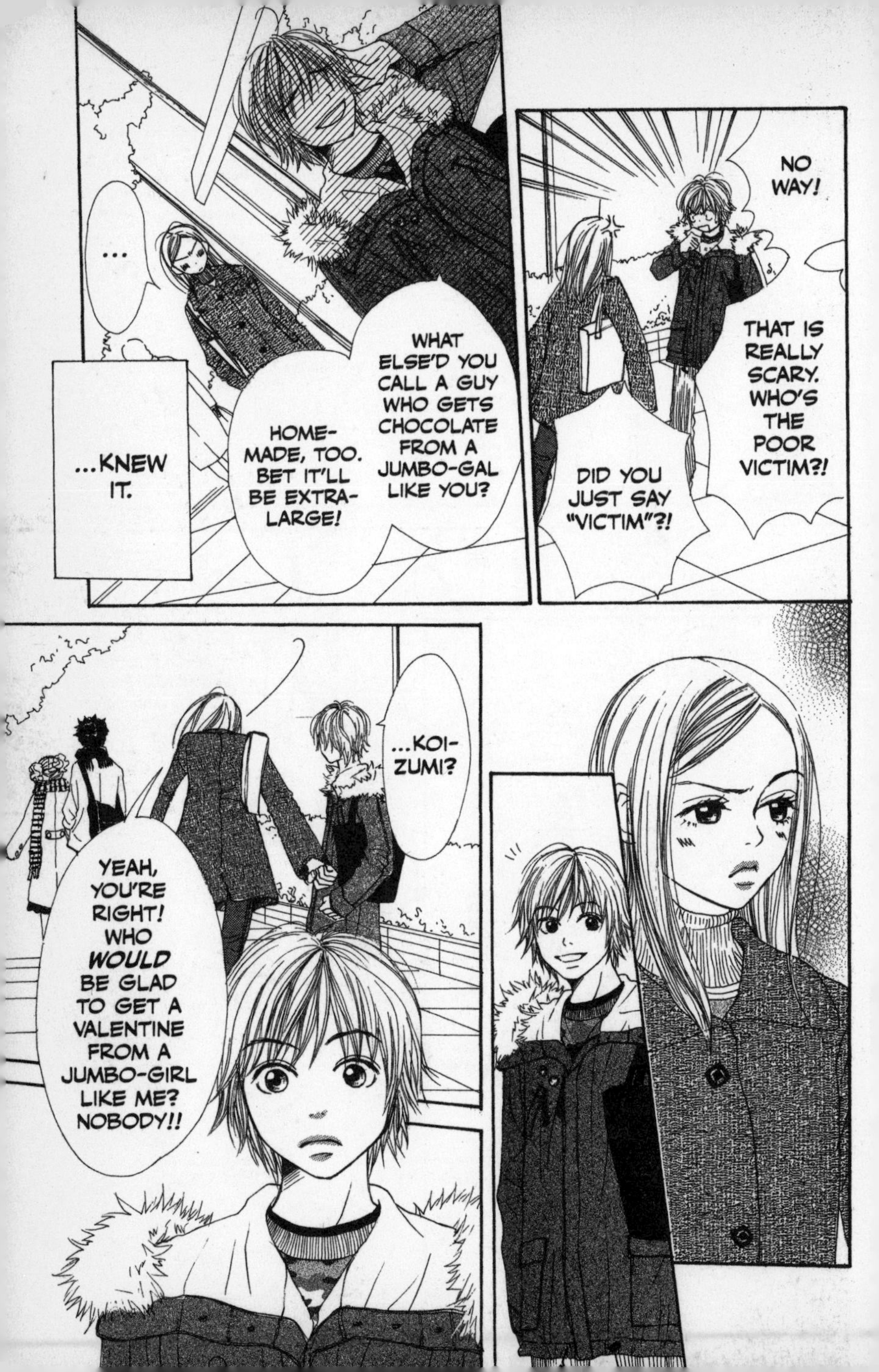
NO WAY!
THAT IS REALLY SCARY. WHO'S THE POOR VICTIM?!
DID YOU JUST SAY "VICTIM"?!
WHAT ELSE'D YOU CALL A GUY WHO GETS CHOCOLATE FROM A JUMBO-GAL LIKE YOU?
HOME-MADE, TOO. BET IT'LL BE EXTRA-LARGE!
...
...KNEW IT.
...KOI-ZUMI?
YEAH, YOU'RE RIGHT! WHO *WOULD* BE GLAD TO GET A VALENTINE FROM A JUMBO-GIRL LIKE ME? NOBODY!!

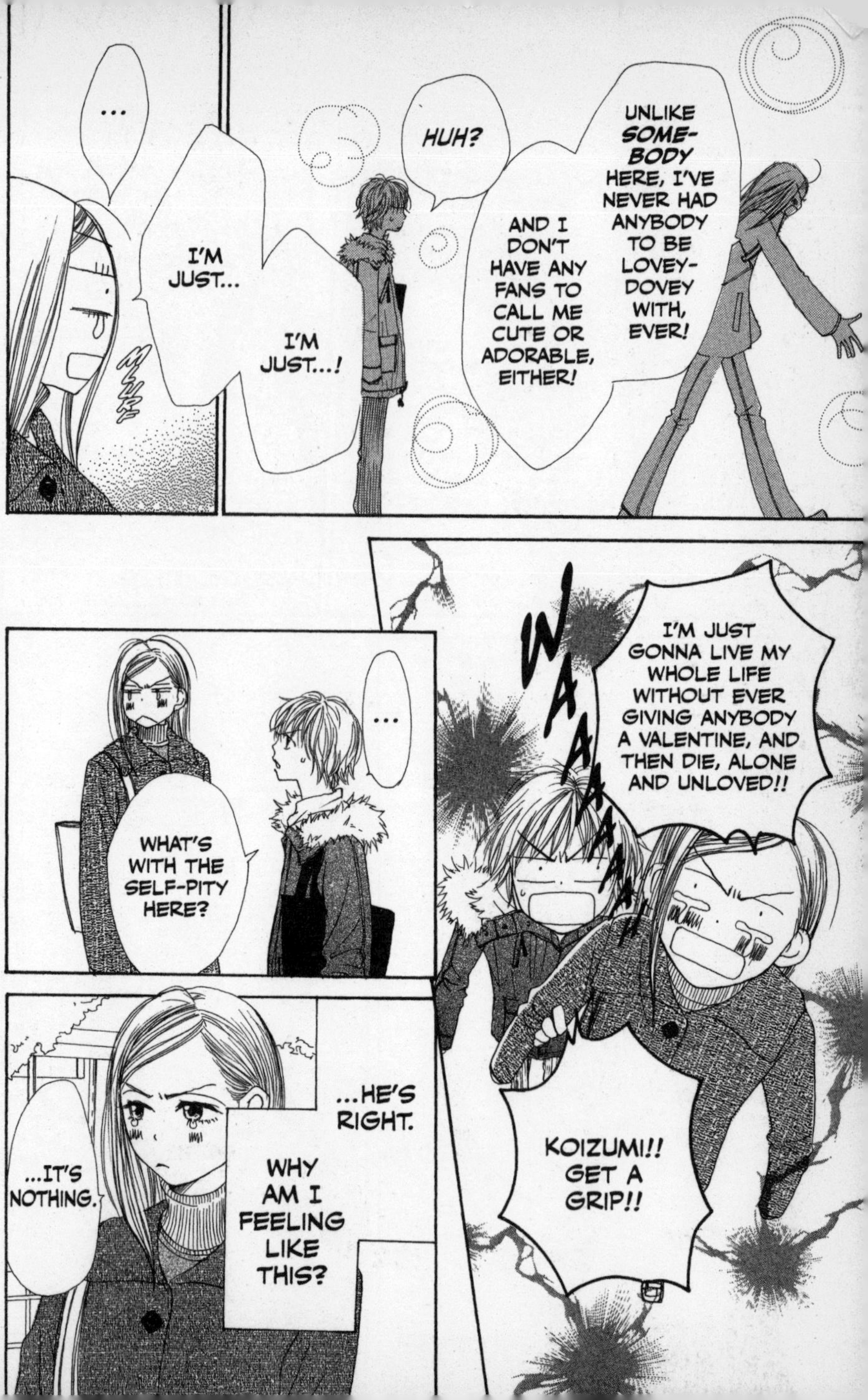
UNLIKE SOMEBODY HERE, I'VE NEVER HAD ANYBODY TO BE LOVEY-DOVEY WITH, EVER!
AND I DON'T HAVE ANY FANS TO CALL ME CUTE OR ADORABLE, EITHER!
HUH?
...
I'M JUST...
I'M JUST...!
I'M JUST GONNA LIVE MY WHOLE LIFE WITHOUT EVER GIVING ANYBODY A VALENTINE, AND THEN DIE, ALONE AND UNLOVED!!
KOIZUMI!! GET A GRIP!!
...
WHAT'S WITH THE SELF-PITY HERE?
...HE'S RIGHT.
WHY AM I FEELING LIKE THIS?
...IT'S NOTHING.

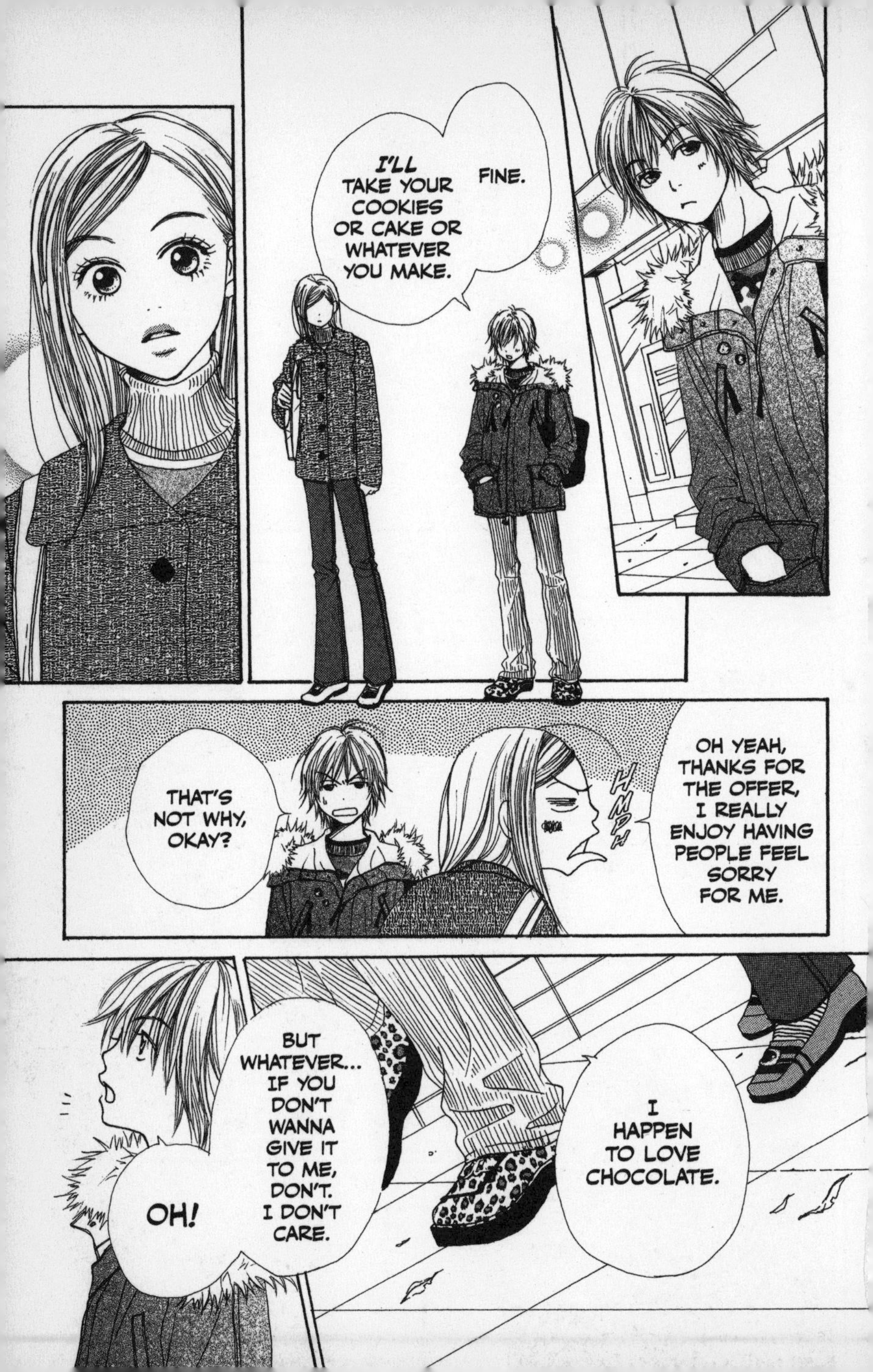
FINE.
I'LL TAKE YOUR COOKIES OR CAKE OR WHATEVER YOU MAKE.
OH YEAH, THANKS FOR THE OFFER, I REALLY ENJOY HAVING PEOPLE FEEL SORRY FOR ME.
HMPH
THAT'S NOT WHY, OKAY?
I HAPPEN TO LOVE CHOCOLATE.
BUT WHATEVER... IF YOU DON'T WANNA GIVE IT TO ME, DON'T. I DON'T CARE.
OH!

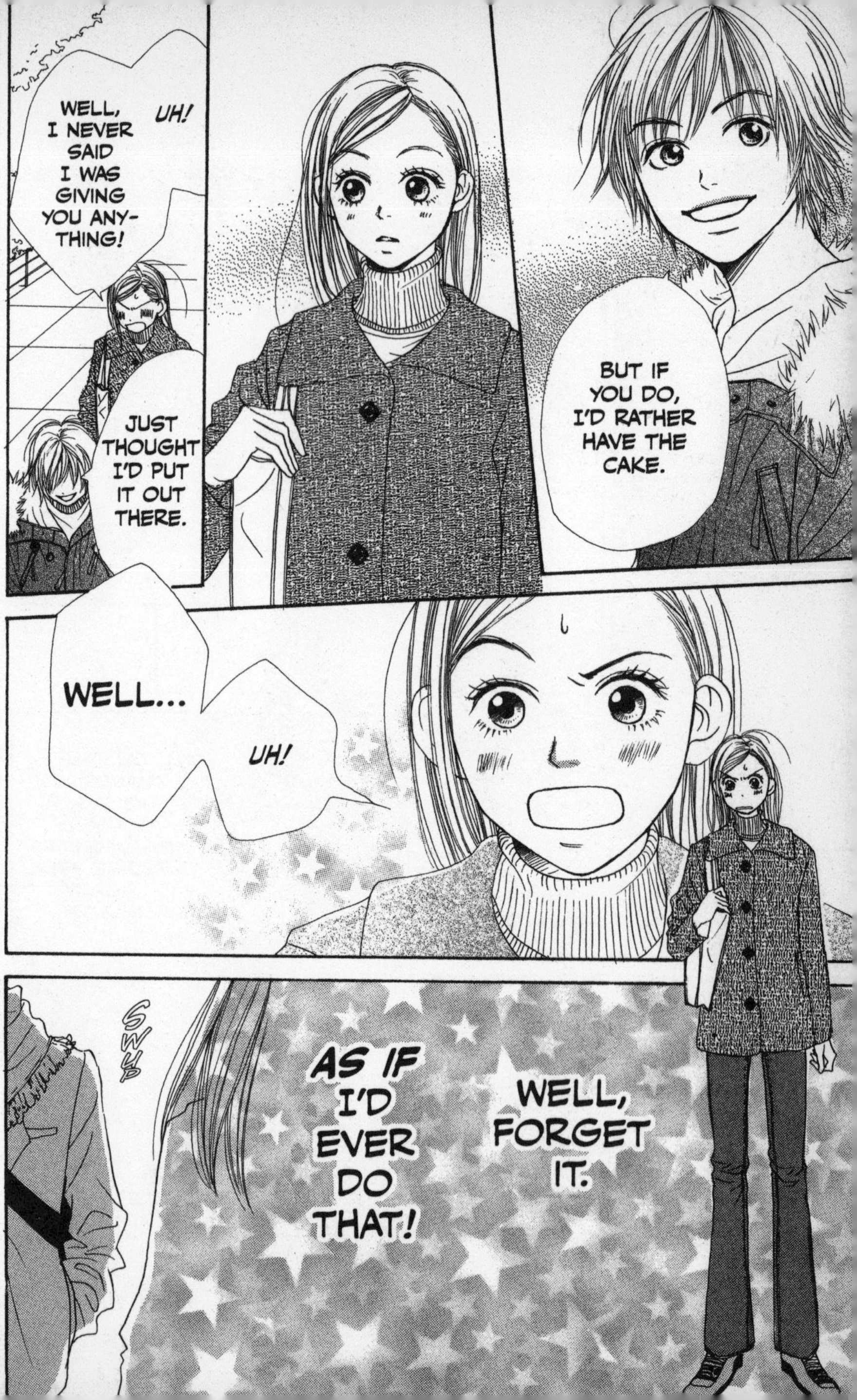
BUT IF YOU DO, I'D RATHER HAVE THE CAKE.
UH!
WELL, I NEVER SAID I WAS GIVING YOU ANYTHING!
JUST THOUGHT I'D PUT IT OUT THERE.
WELL...
UH!
WELL, FORGET IT.
AS IF I'D EVER DO THAT!
SWUP

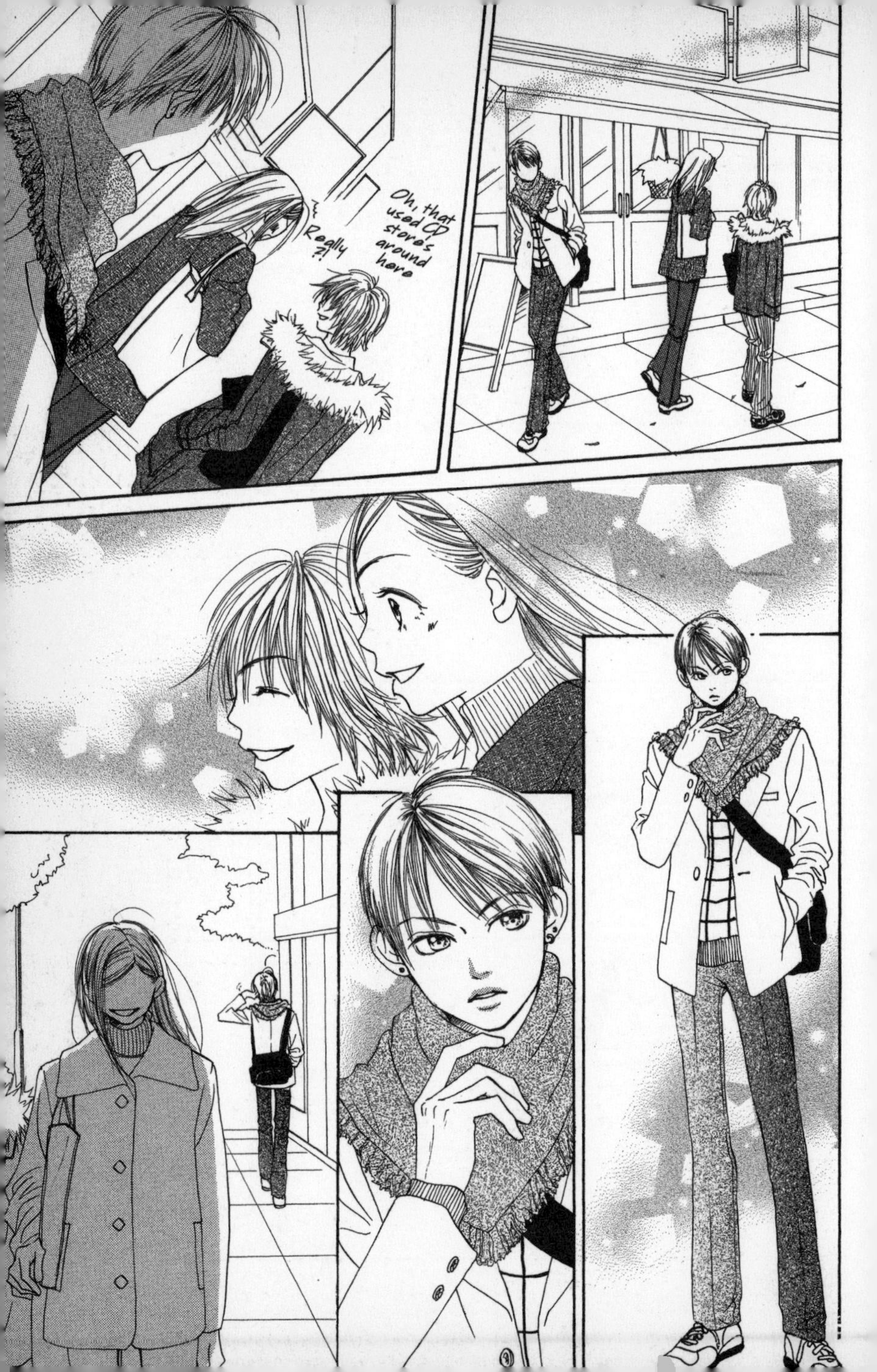
Oh, that used CD store's around here
Really ?!

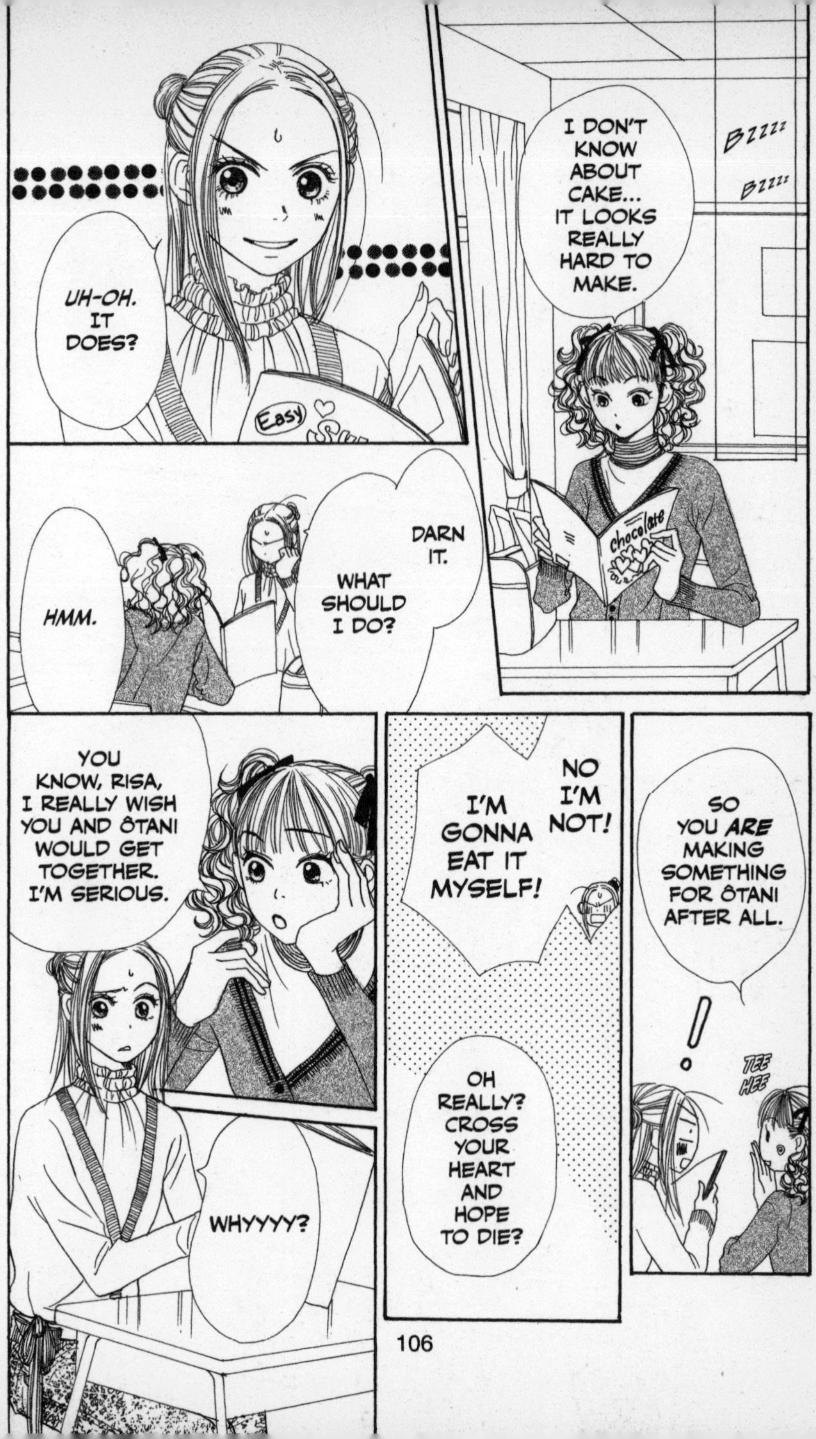
I DON'T KNOW ABOUT CAKE... IT LOOKS REALLY HARD TO MAKE.
BZZZZ
BZZZZ
chocolate
UH-OH. IT DOES?
Easy
DARN IT.
WHAT SHOULD I DO?
HMM.
SO YOU ARE MAKING SOMETHING FOR ŌTANI AFTER ALL.
!
TEE HEE
NO I'M NOT!
I'M GONNA EAT IT MYSELF!
OH REALLY? CROSS YOUR HEART AND HOPE TO DIE?
YOU KNOW, RISA, I REALLY WISH YOU AND ŌTANI WOULD GET TOGETHER. I'M SERIOUS.
WHYYYY?

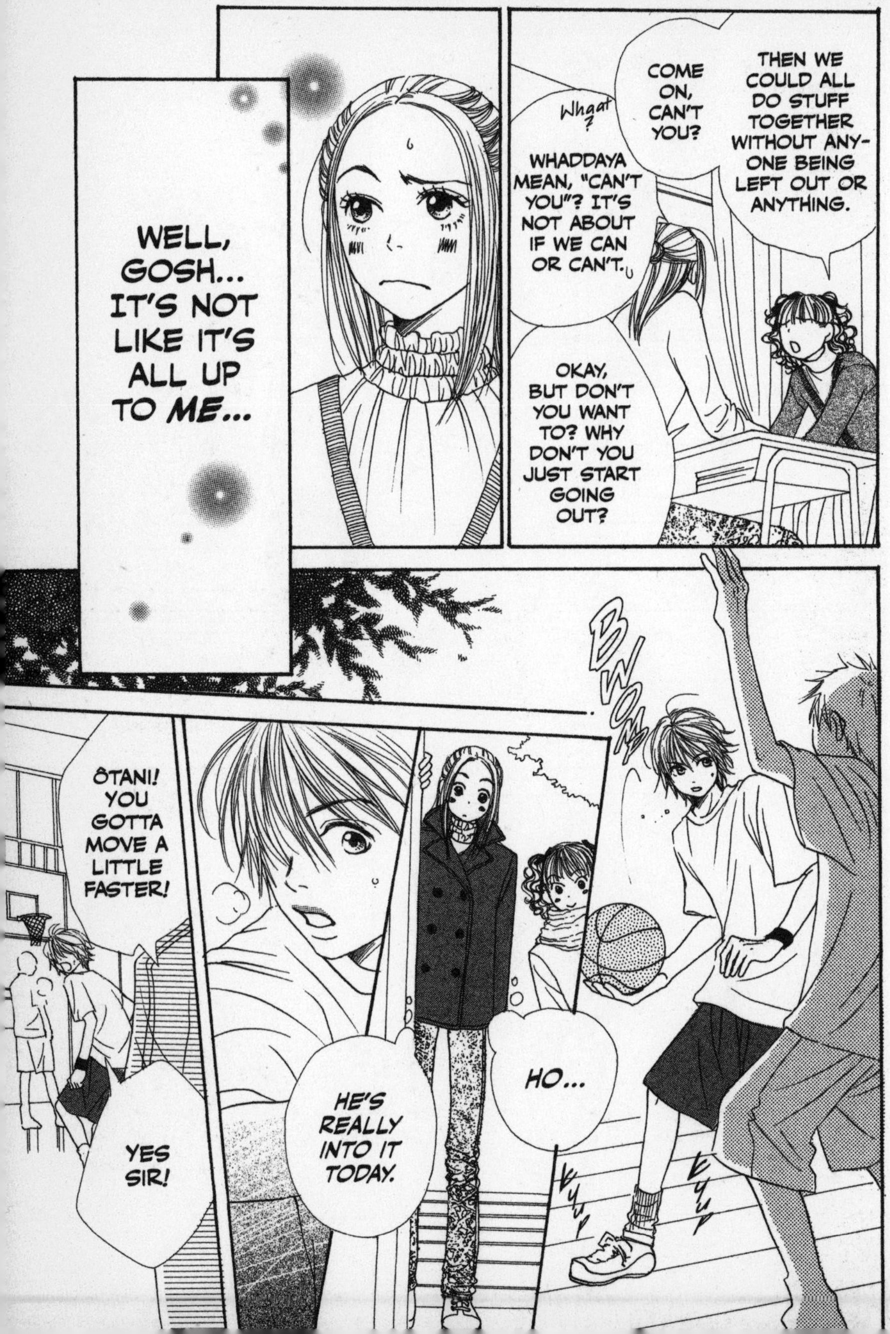
THEN WE COULD ALL DO STUFF TOGETHER WITHOUT ANYONE BEING LEFT OUT OR ANYTHING.
COME ON, CAN'T YOU?
Whaat?
WHADDAYA MEAN, "CAN'T YOU"? IT'S NOT ABOUT IF WE CAN OR CAN'T.
OKAY, BUT DON'T YOU WANT TO? WHY DON'T YOU JUST START GOING OUT?
WELL, GOSH... IT'S NOT LIKE IT'S ALL UP TO *ME*...
BWOM
HO...
HE'S REALLY INTO IT TODAY.
ŌTANI! YOU GOTTA MOVE A LITTLE FASTER!
YES SIR!

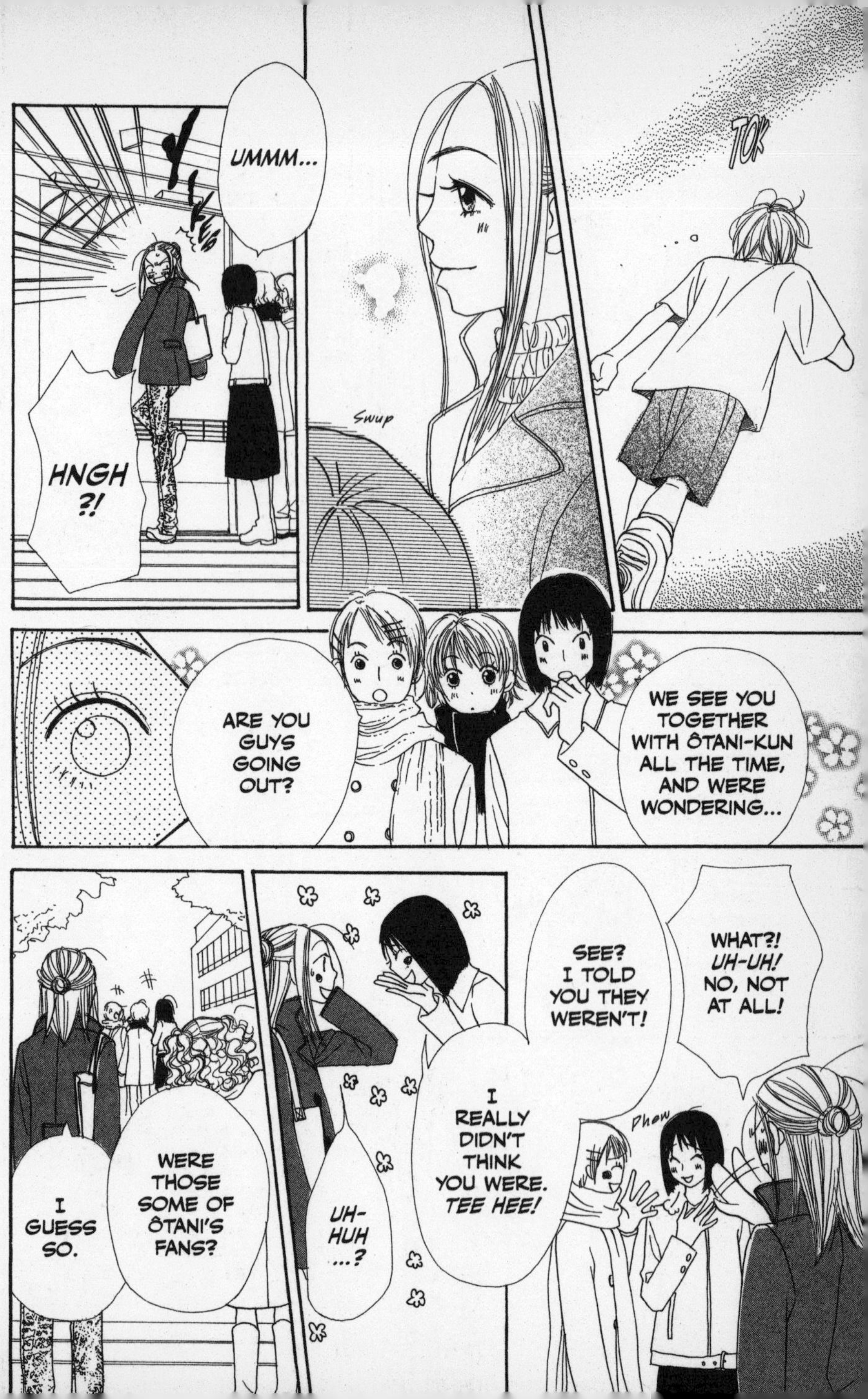

TOK
. . .
Swup
UMMM...
HNGH ?!
WE SEE YOU TOGETHER WITH ŌTANI-KUN ALL THE TIME, AND WERE WONDERING...
ARE YOU GUYS GOING OUT?
WHAT?! UH-UH! NO, NOT AT ALL!
SEE? I TOLD YOU THEY WEREN'T!
Phew
I REALLY DIDN'T THINK YOU WERE. TEE HEE!
UH-HUH ...?
WERE THOSE SOME OF ŌTANI'S FANS?
I GUESS SO.

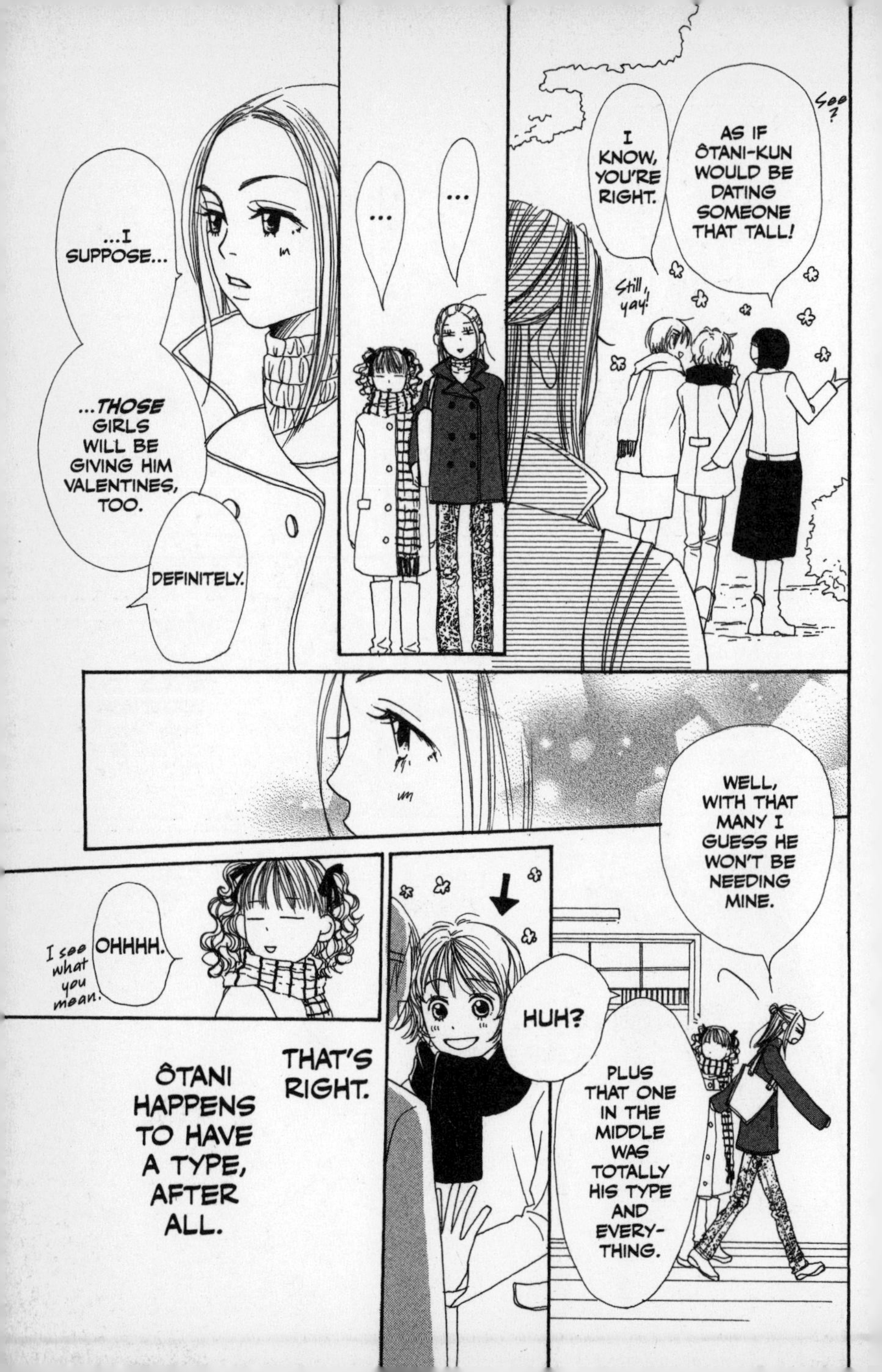
See?
AS IF ÔTANI-KUN WOULD BE DATING SOMEONE THAT TALL!
I KNOW, YOU'RE RIGHT.
Still, yay!
...
...
...I SUPPOSE...
...THOSE GIRLS WILL BE GIVING HIM VALENTINES, TOO.
DEFINITELY.
WELL, WITH THAT MANY I GUESS HE WON'T BE NEEDING MINE.
PLUS THAT ONE IN THE MIDDLE WAS TOTALLY HIS TYPE AND EVERY-THING.
OHHHH.
I see what you mean.
HUH?
THAT'S RIGHT.
ÔTANI HAPPENS TO HAVE A TYPE, AFTER ALL.

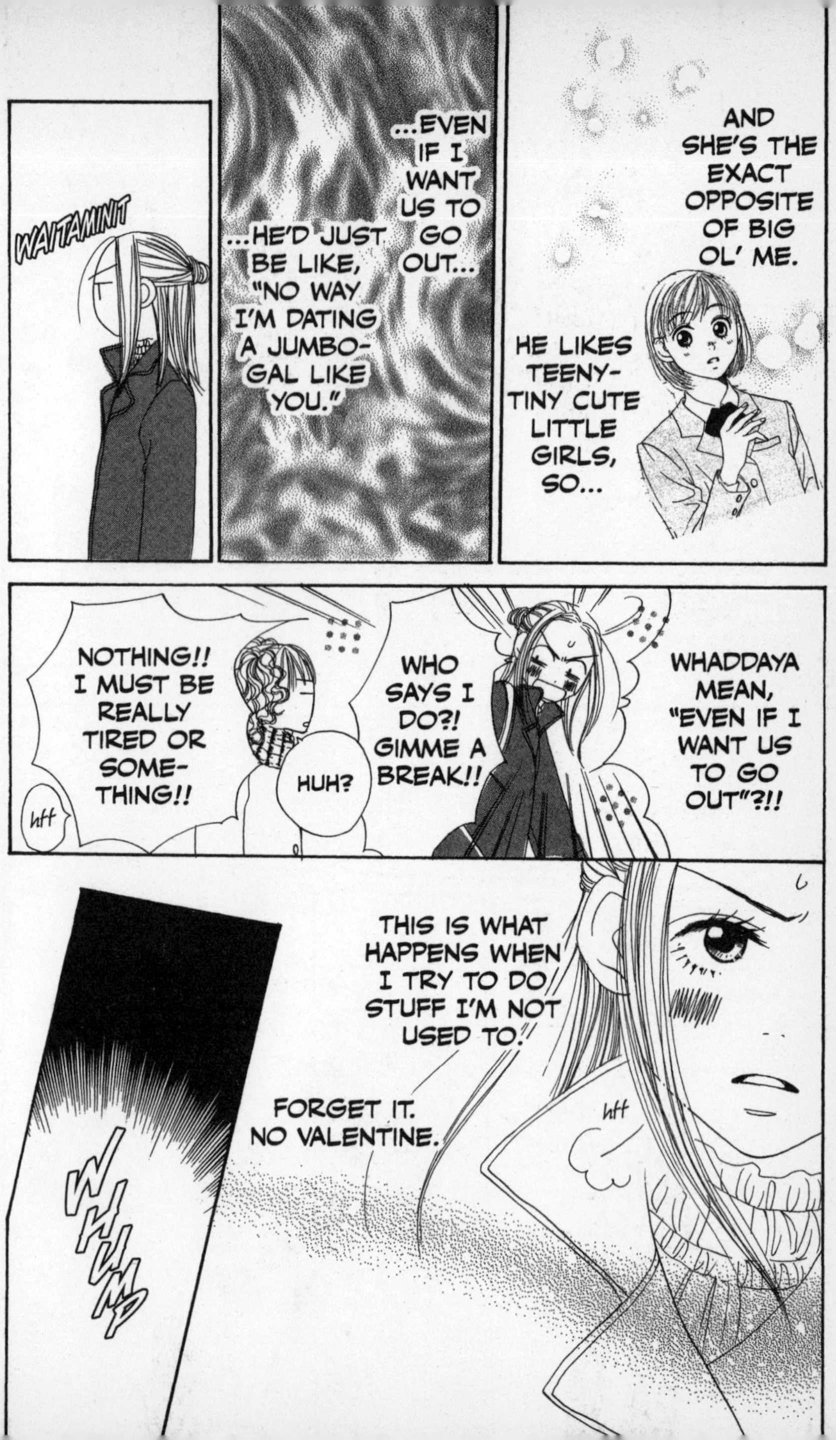
AND SHE'S THE EXACT OPPOSITE OF BIG OL' ME.
HE LIKES TEENY-TINY CUTE LITTLE GIRLS, SO...
...EVEN IF I WANT US TO GO OUT...
...HE'D JUST BE LIKE, "NO WAY I'M DATING A JUMBO-GAL LIKE YOU."
WAITAMINIT
WHADDAYA MEAN, "EVEN IF I WANT US TO GO OUT"?!!
WHO SAYS I DO?! GIMME A BREAK!!
HUH?
NOTHING!! I MUST BE REALLY TIRED OR SOME-THING!!
hff
THIS IS WHAT HAPPENS WHEN I TRY TO DO STUFF I'M NOT USED TO.
hff
FORGET IT. NO VALENTINE.
WHUMP

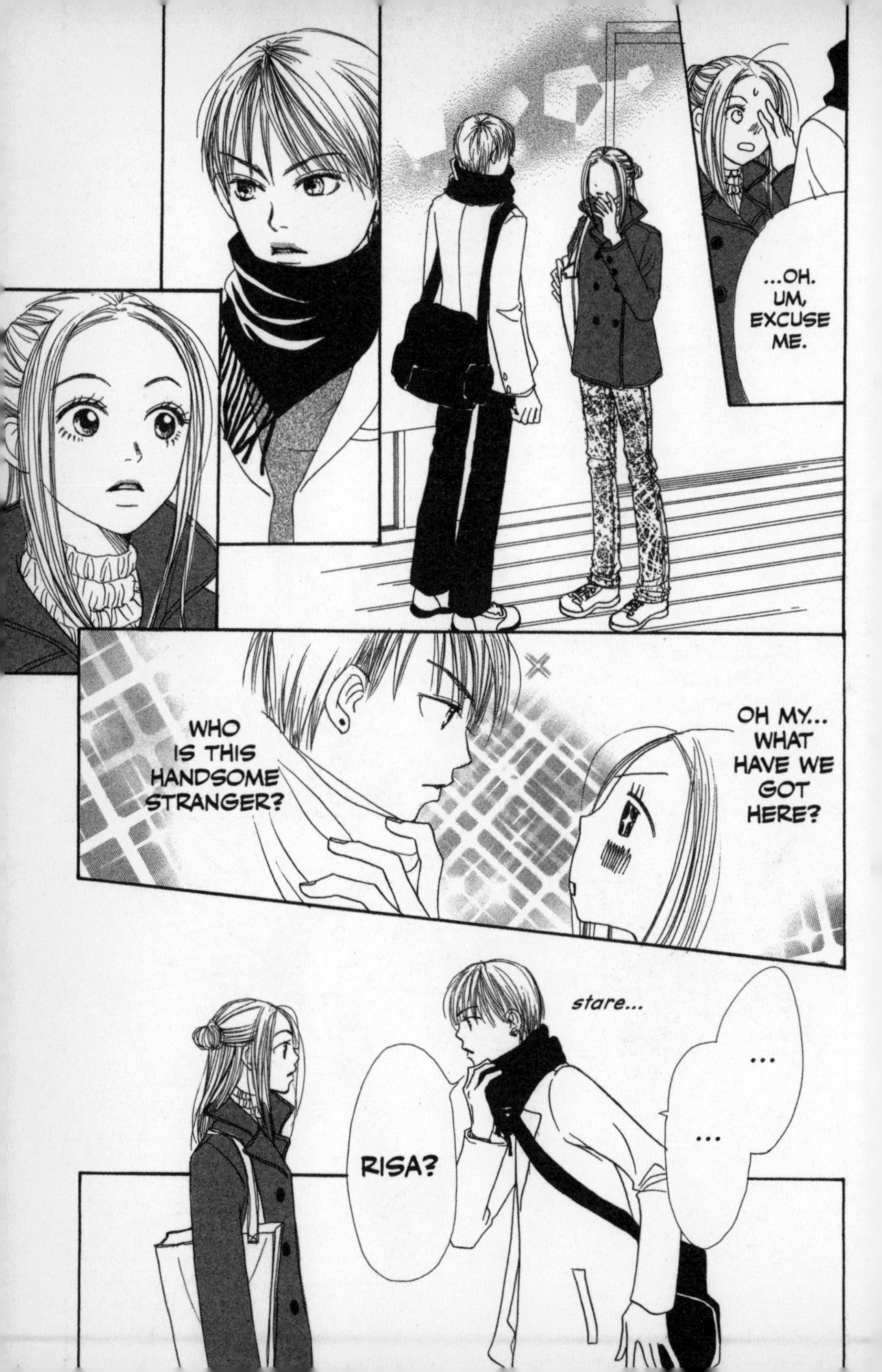
...OH. UM, EXCUSE ME.
OH MY... WHAT HAVE WE GOT HERE?
WHO IS THIS HANDSOME STRANGER?
...
...
stare...
RISA?

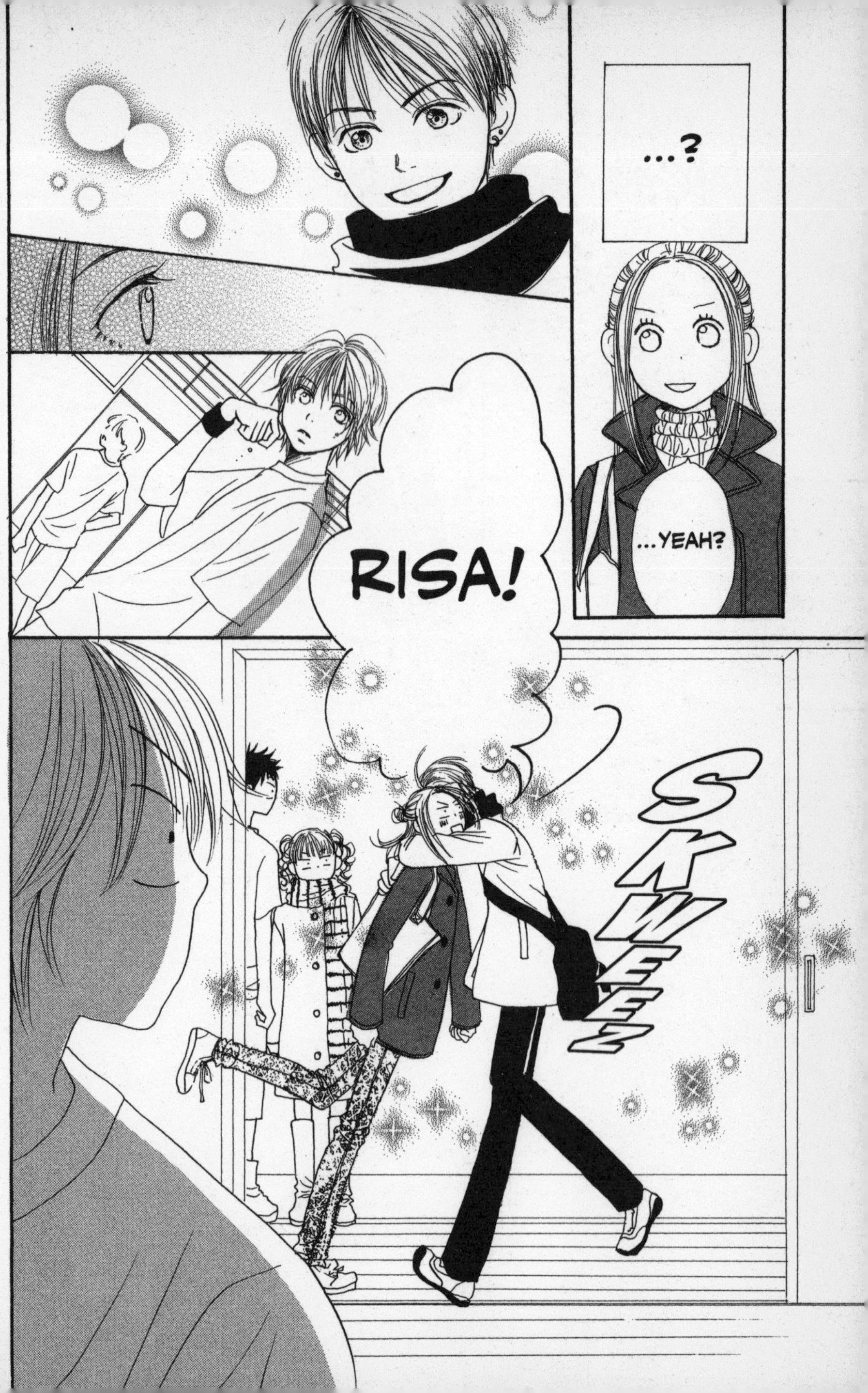
...?
...YEAH?
RISA!
SKWEEZ

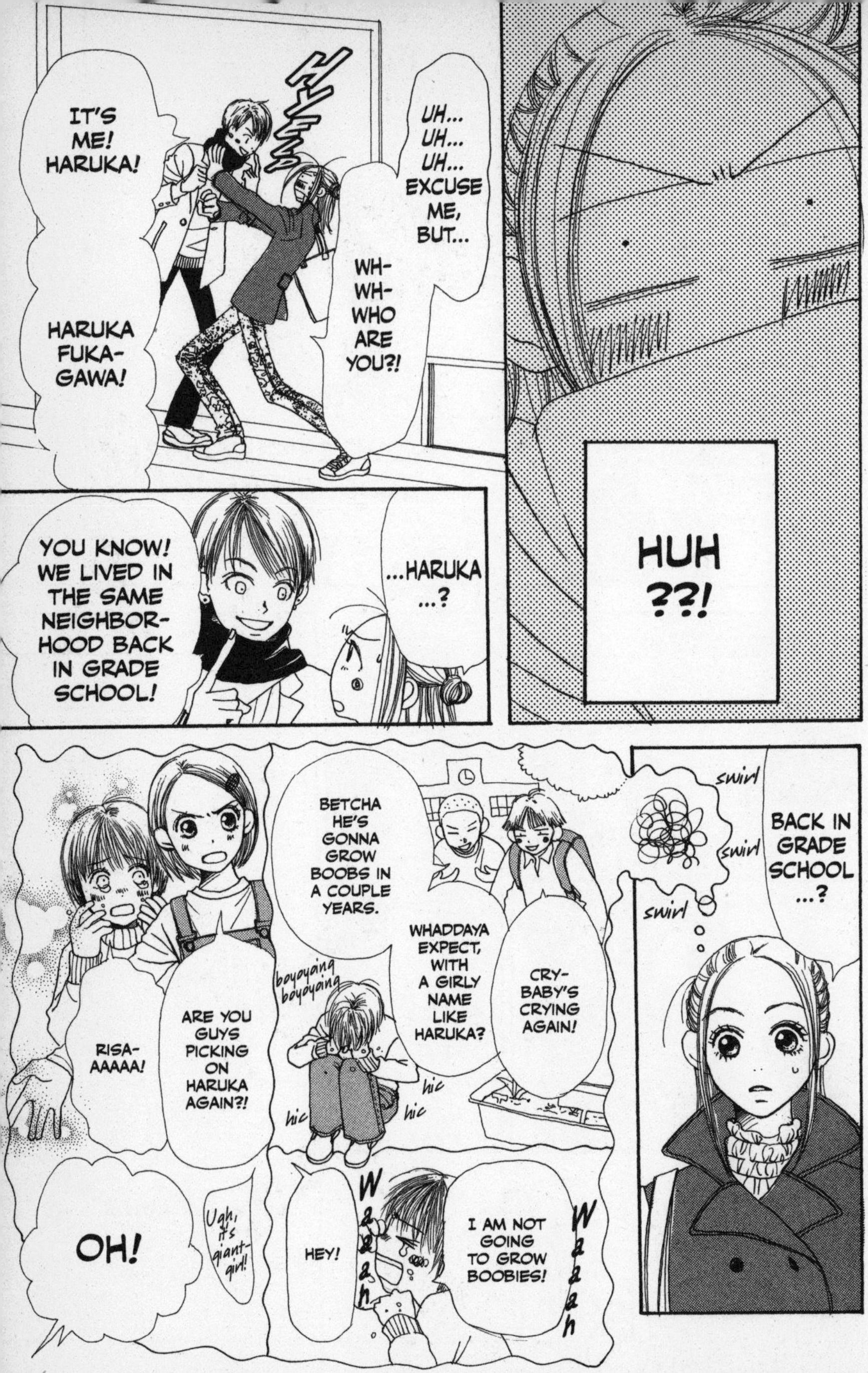
HUH ??!
UH... UH... UH... EXCUSE ME, BUT...
WH-WH-WHO ARE YOU?!
IT'S ME! HARUKA!
HARUKA FUKA-GAWA!
...HARUKA ...?
YOU KNOW! WE LIVED IN THE SAME NEIGHBOR-HOOD BACK IN GRADE SCHOOL!
BACK IN GRADE SCHOOL ...?
swirl swirl swirl
CRY-BABY'S CRYING AGAIN!
WHADDAYA EXPECT, WITH A GIRLY NAME LIKE HARUKA?
BETCHA HE'S GONNA GROW BOOBS IN A COUPLE YEARS.
boyoyaing boyoyaing
hic hic hic
ARE YOU GUYS PICKING ON HARUKA AGAIN?!
RISA-AAAAA!
Waaah
I AM NOT GOING TO GROW BOOBIES!
Waaah
HEY!
Ugh, it's giant-girl!
OH!

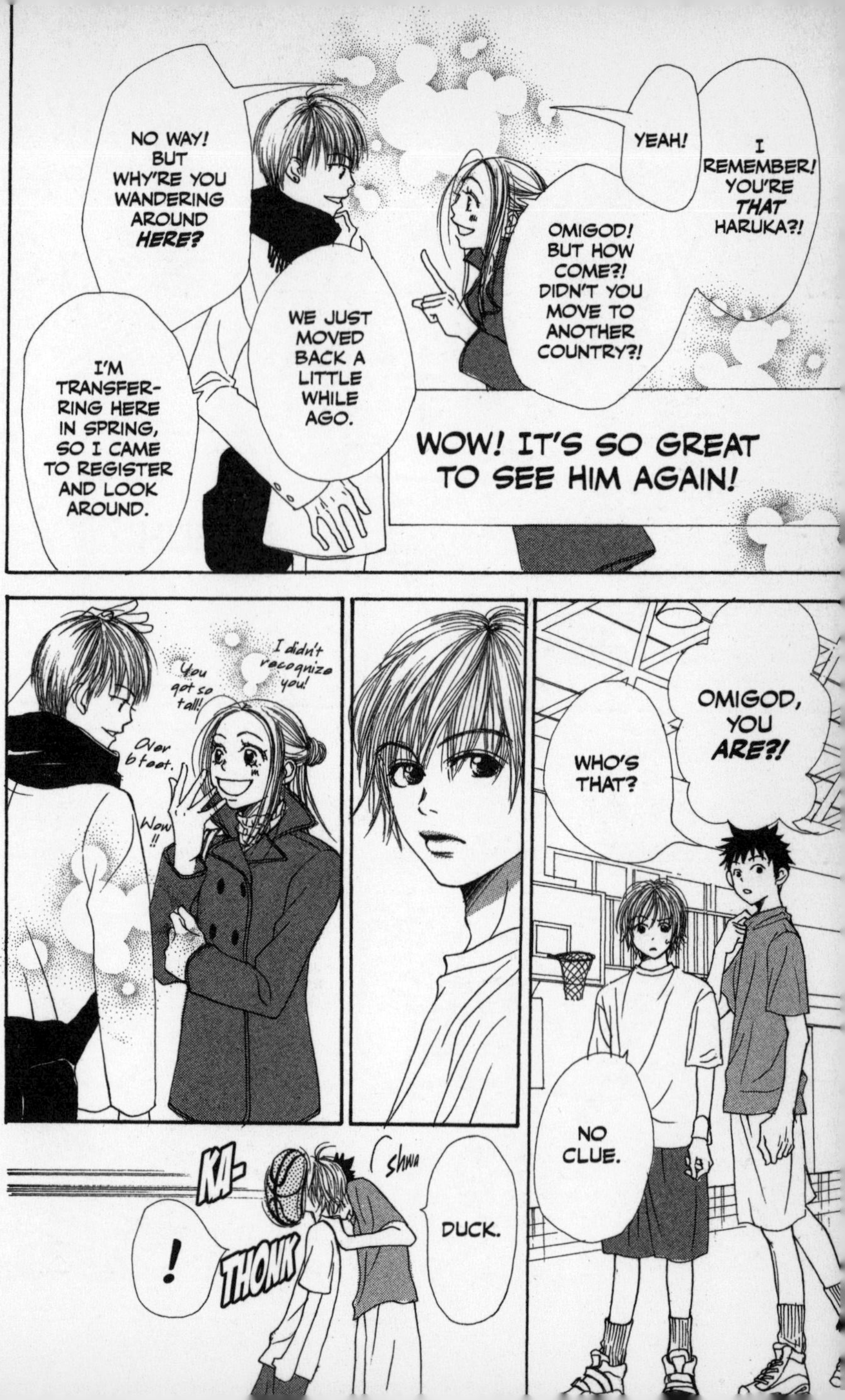

I REMEMBER! YOU'RE *THAT* HARUKA?!
YEAH!
OMIGOD! BUT HOW COME?! DIDN'T YOU MOVE TO ANOTHER COUNTRY?!
NO WAY! BUT WHY'RE YOU WANDERING AROUND *HERE?*
WE JUST MOVED BACK A LITTLE WHILE AGO.
I'M TRANSFERRING HERE IN SPRING, SO I CAME TO REGISTER AND LOOK AROUND.
WOW! IT'S SO GREAT TO SEE HIM AGAIN!
OMIGOD, YOU *ARE?!*
WHO'S THAT?
NO CLUE.
I didn't recognize you!
You got so tall!
Over 6 feet.
Wow!!
shwa
DUCK.
KA-
THONK
!

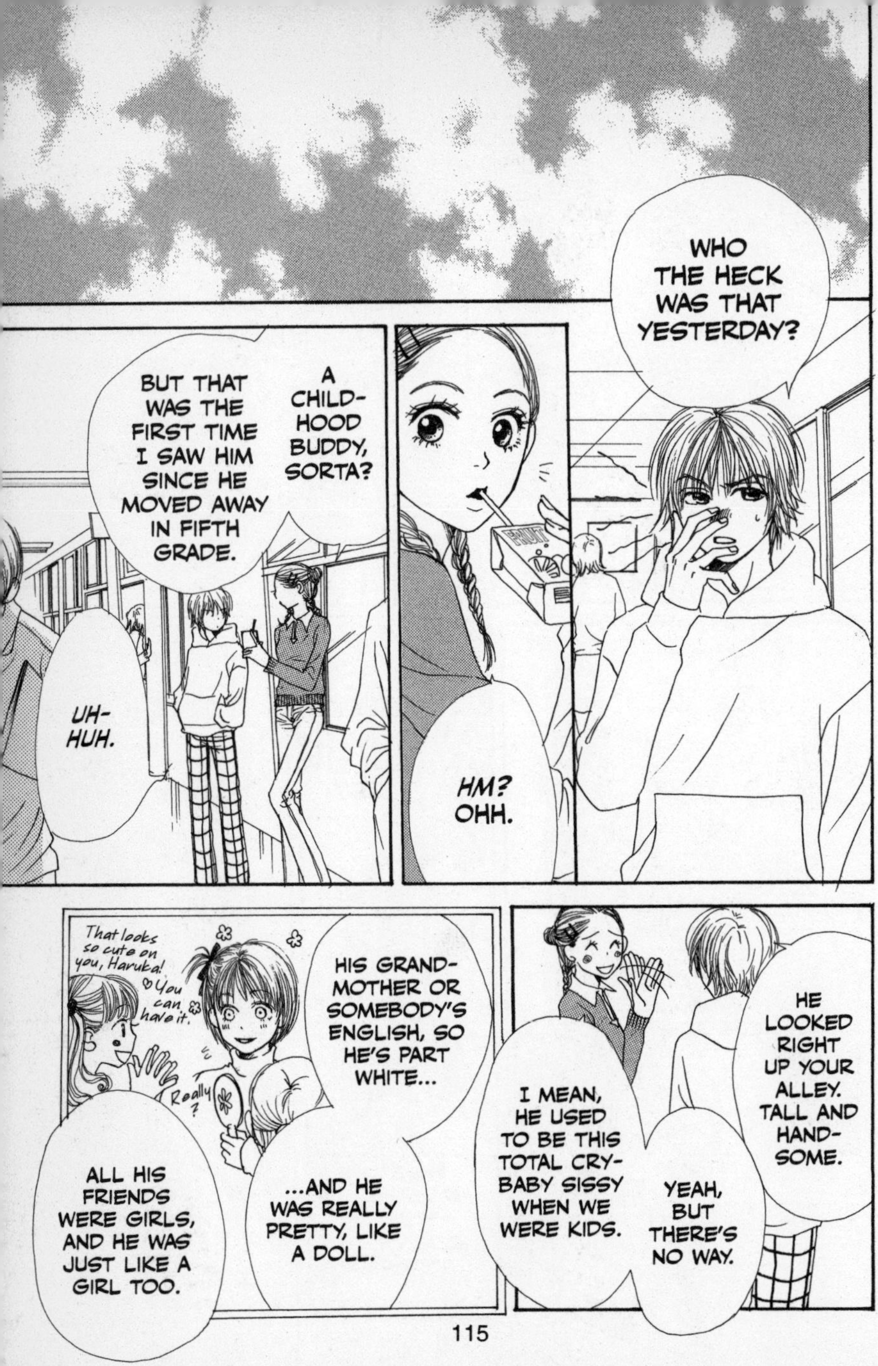
WHO THE HECK WAS THAT YESTERDAY?
HM? OHH.
A CHILDHOOD BUDDY, SORTA?
BUT THAT WAS THE FIRST TIME I SAW HIM SINCE HE MOVED AWAY IN FIFTH GRADE.
UH-HUH.
HE LOOKED RIGHT UP YOUR ALLEY. TALL AND HANDSOME.
YEAH, BUT THERE'S NO WAY.
I MEAN, HE USED TO BE THIS TOTAL CRY-BABY SISSY WHEN WE WERE KIDS.
HIS GRANDMOTHER OR SOMEBODY'S ENGLISH, SO HE'S PART WHITE...
That looks so cute on you, Haruka!
You can have it.
Really?
...AND HE WAS REALLY PRETTY, LIKE A DOLL.
ALL HIS FRIENDS WERE GIRLS, AND HE WAS JUST LIKE A GIRL TOO.

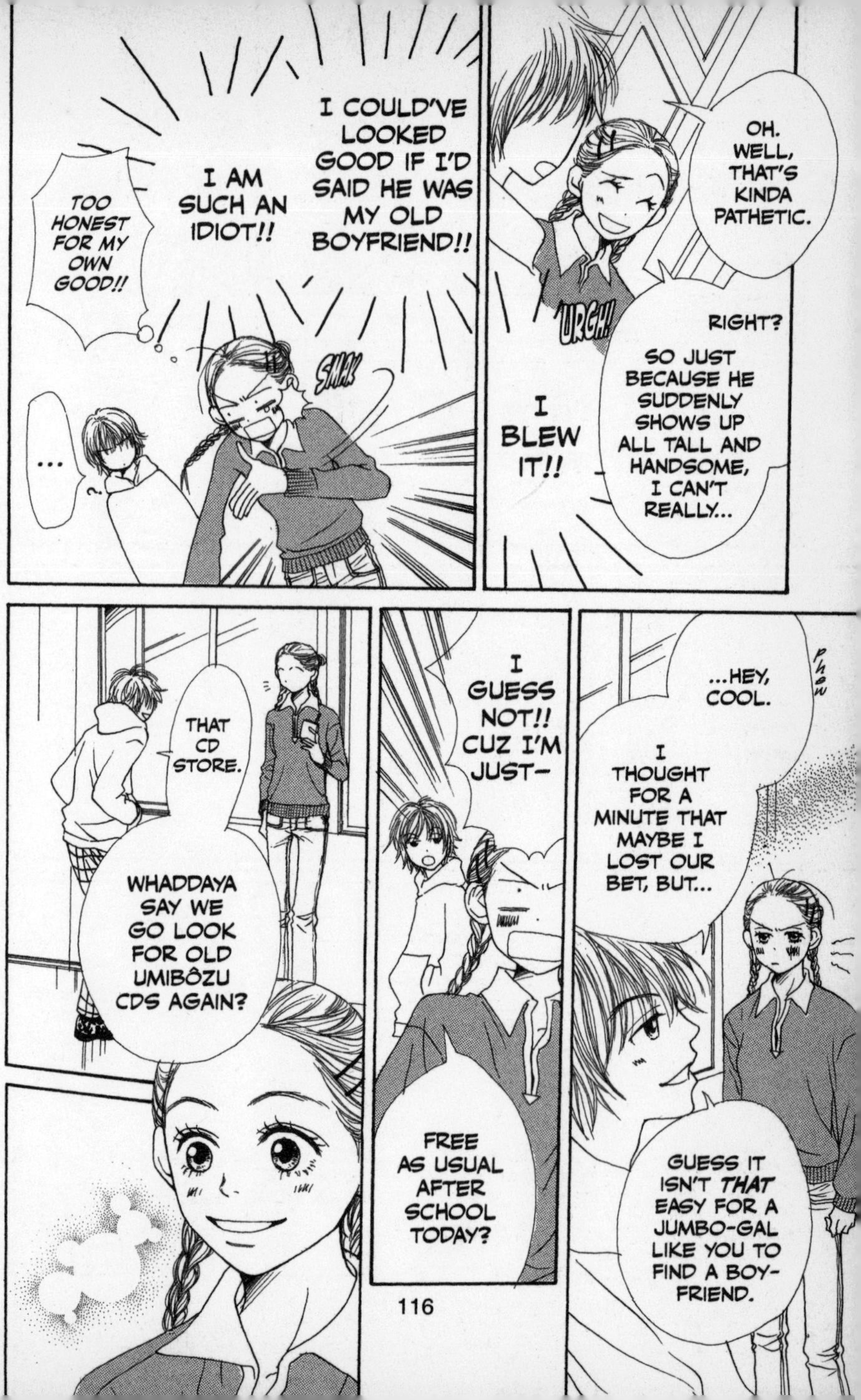
OH. WELL, THAT'S KINDA PATHETIC.
RIGHT?
SO JUST BECAUSE HE SUDDENLY SHOWS UP ALL TALL AND HANDSOME, I CAN'T REALLY...
URGH!
I BLEW IT!!
I COULD'VE LOOKED GOOD IF I'D SAID HE WAS MY OLD BOYFRIEND!!
I AM SUCH AN IDIOT!!
TOO HONEST FOR MY OWN GOOD!!
SMAK!
...
phew
...HEY, COOL.
I THOUGHT FOR A MINUTE THAT MAYBE I LOST OUR BET, BUT...
GUESS IT ISN'T *THAT* EASY FOR A JUMBO-GAL LIKE YOU TO FIND A BOY-FRIEND.
I GUESS NOT!! CUZ I'M JUST-
FREE AS USUAL AFTER SCHOOL TODAY?
THAT CD STORE.
WHADDAYA SAY WE GO LOOK FOR OLD UMIBÔZU CDS AGAIN?

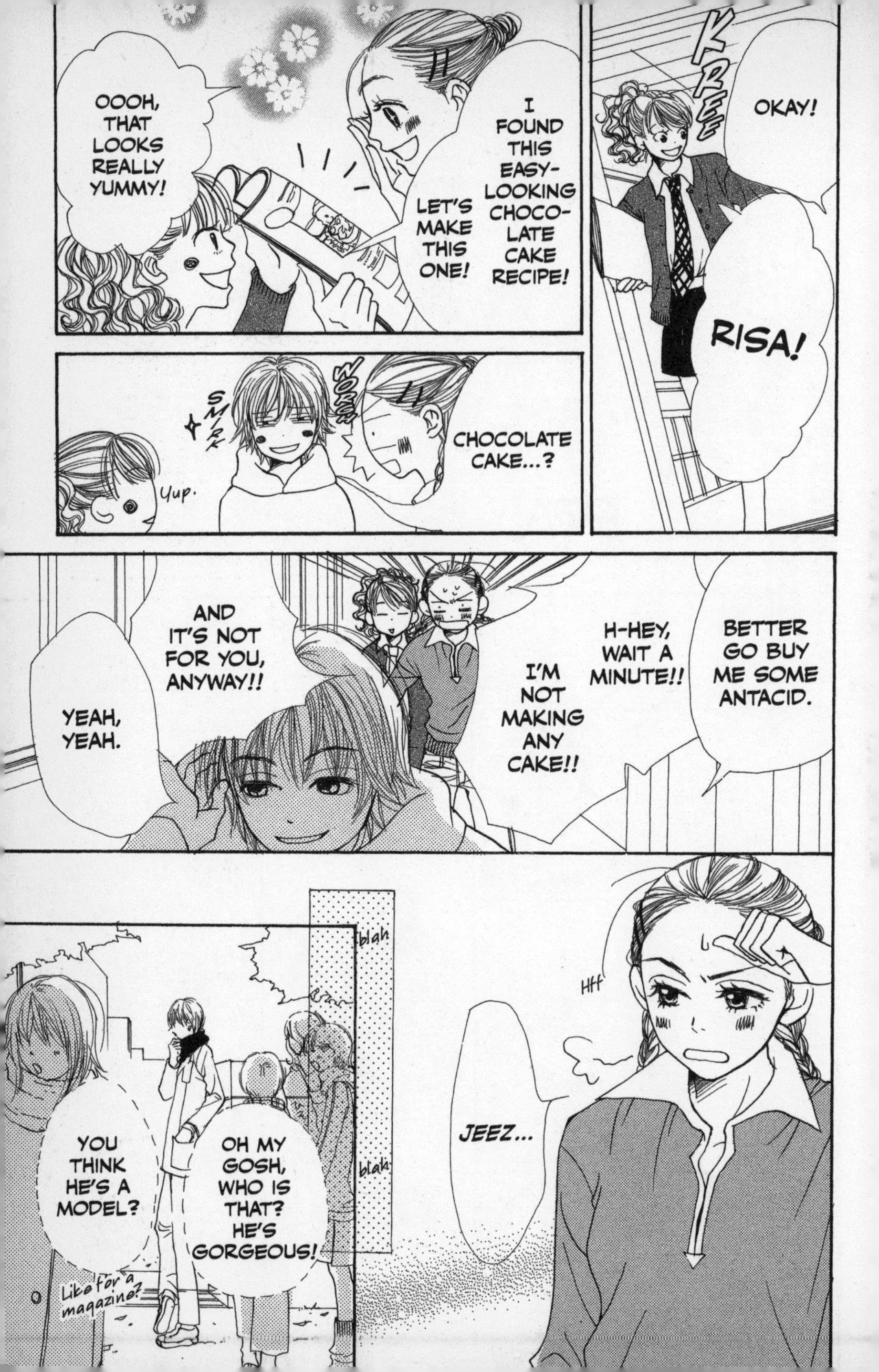
KREEE
OKAY!
RISA!
I FOUND THIS EASY-LOOKING CHOCOLATE CAKE RECIPE!
LET'S MAKE THIS ONE!
OOOH, THAT LOOKS REALLY YUMMY!
CHOCOLATE CAKE...?
WORCH
SMIRK
Yup.
BETTER GO BUY ME SOME ANTACID.
H-HEY, WAIT A MINUTE!!
I'M NOT MAKING ANY CAKE!!
AND IT'S NOT FOR YOU, ANYWAY!!
YEAH, YEAH.
Hff
JEEZ...
blah
blah
OH MY GOSH, WHO IS THAT? HE'S GORGEOUS!
YOU THINK HE'S A MODEL?
Like for a magazine?

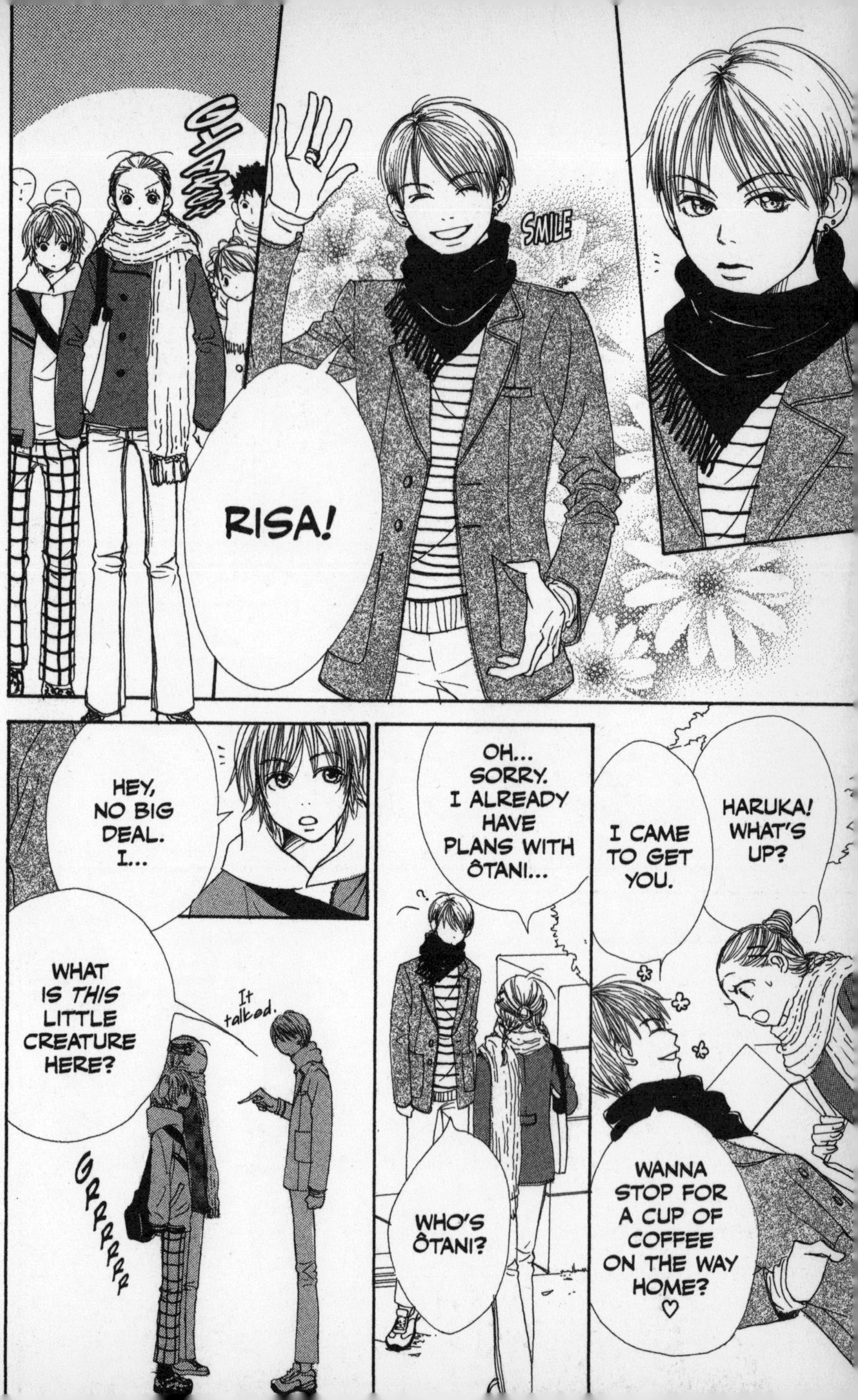
SMILE
RISA!
HARUKA! WHAT'S UP?
I CAME TO GET YOU.
WANNA STOP FOR A CUP OF COFFEE ON THE WAY HOME? ♡
OH... SORRY. I ALREADY HAVE PLANS WITH ÔTANI...
WHO'S ÔTANI?
HEY, NO BIG DEAL. I...
WHAT IS *THIS* LITTLE CREATURE HERE?
It talked.

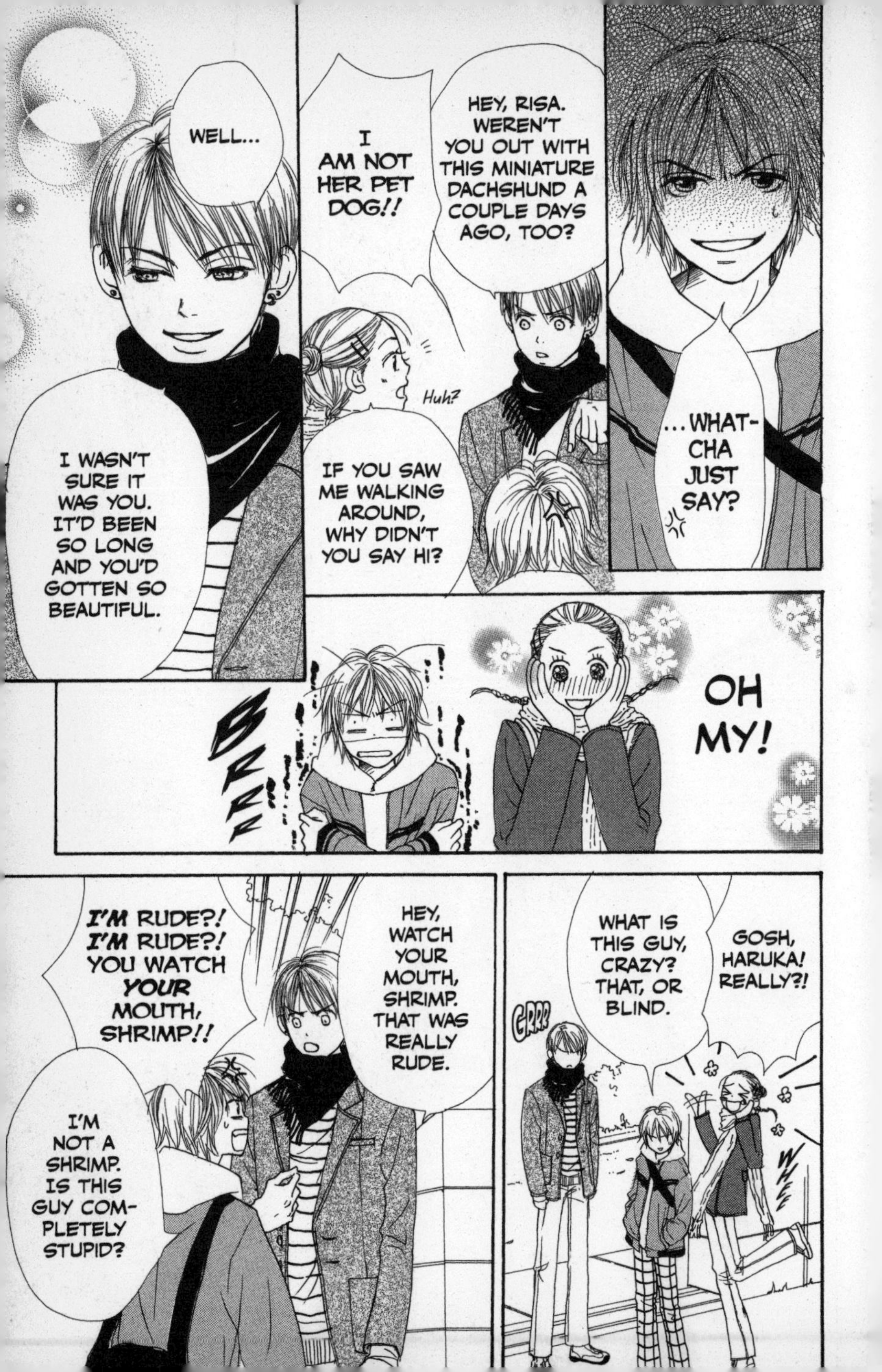
...WHAT-CHA JUST SAY?
HEY, RISA. WEREN'T YOU OUT WITH THIS MINIATURE DACHSHUND A COUPLE DAYS AGO, TOO?
I AM NOT HER PET DOG!!
Huh?
IF YOU SAW ME WALKING AROUND, WHY DIDN'T YOU SAY HI?
WELL...
I WASN'T SURE IT WAS YOU. IT'D BEEN SO LONG AND YOU'D GOTTEN SO BEAUTIFUL.
OH MY!
BRRRR
GOSH, HARUKA! REALLY?!
WHAT IS THIS GUY, CRAZY? THAT, OR BLIND.
GRRR
WHEE
HEY, WATCH YOUR MOUTH, SHRIMP. THAT WAS REALLY RUDE.
I'M RUDE?! I'M RUDE?! YOU WATCH YOUR MOUTH, SHRIMP!!
I'M NOT A SHRIMP. IS THIS GUY COMPLETELY STUPID?

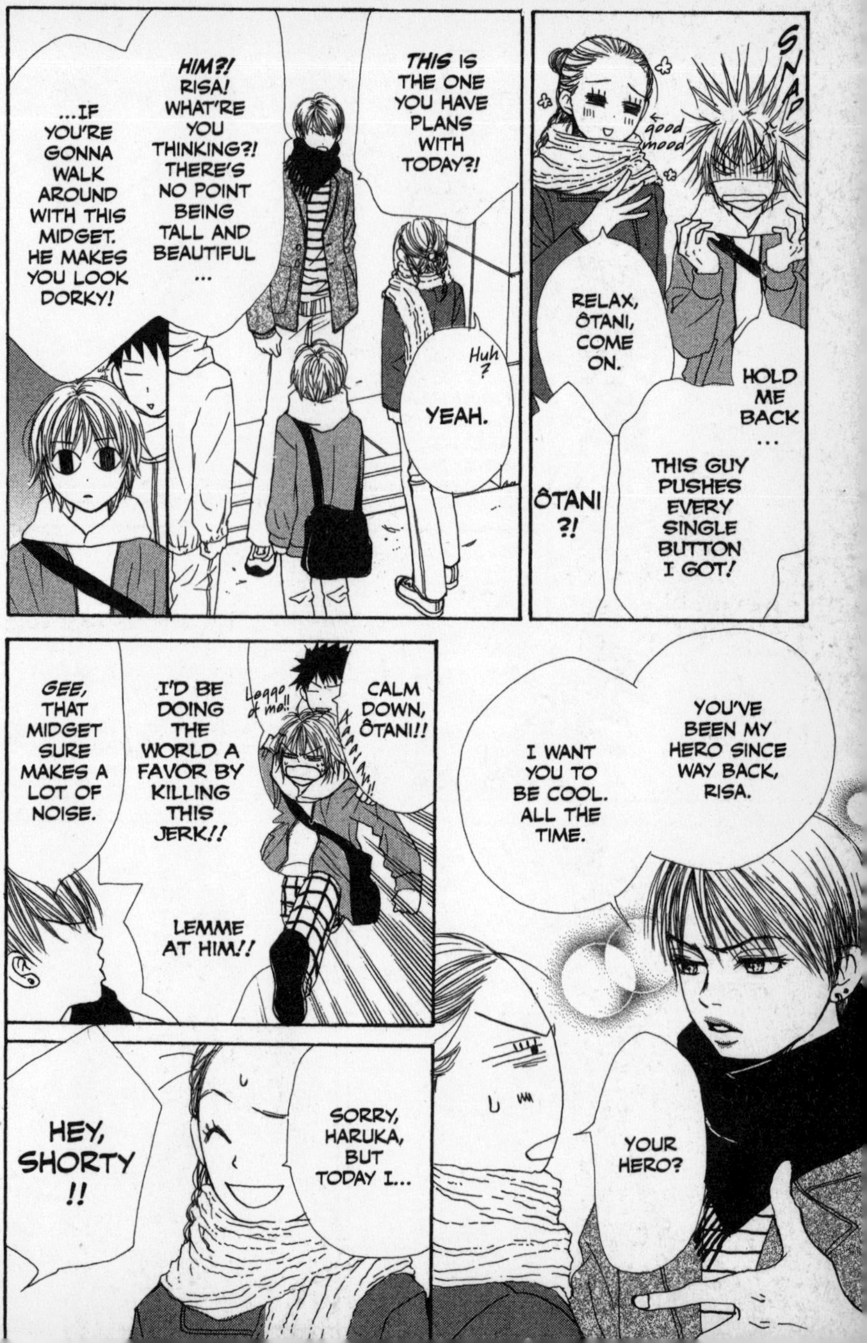
SNAP
good mood
RELAX, ÔTANI, COME ON.
HOLD ME BACK ...
THIS GUY PUSHES EVERY SINGLE BUTTON I GOT!
ÔTANI ?!
THIS IS THE ONE YOU HAVE PLANS WITH TODAY?!
Huh ?
YEAH.
HIM?! RISA! WHAT'RE YOU THINKING?! THERE'S NO POINT BEING TALL AND BEAUTIFUL ...
...IF YOU'RE GONNA WALK AROUND WITH THIS MIDGET. HE MAKES YOU LOOK DORKY!
YOU'VE BEEN MY HERO SINCE WAY BACK, RISA.
I WANT YOU TO BE COOL. ALL THE TIME.
YOUR HERO?
CALM DOWN, ÔTANI!!
Leggo of me!!
I'D BE DOING THE WORLD A FAVOR BY KILLING THIS JERK!!
GEE, THAT MIDGET SURE MAKES A LOT OF NOISE.
LEMME AT HIM!!
SORRY, HARUKA, BUT TODAY I...
HEY, SHORTY !!

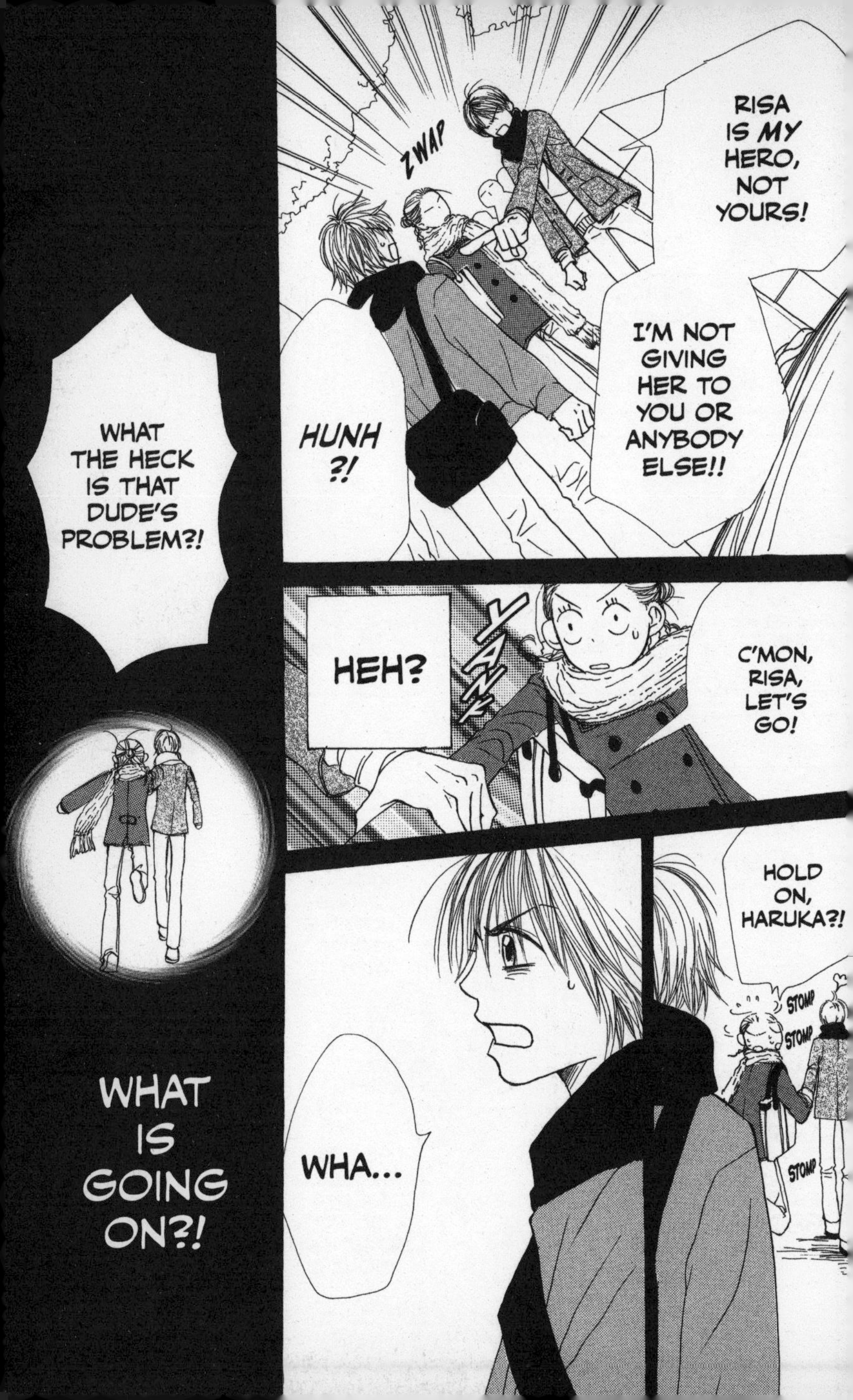
RISA IS MY HERO, NOT YOURS!
ZWAP
I'M NOT GIVING HER TO YOU OR ANYBODY ELSE!!
HUNH ?!
C'MON, RISA, LET'S GO!
YANK
HEH?
HOLD ON, HARUKA?!
STOMP
STOMP
STOMP
WHA...
WHAT THE HECK IS THAT DUDE'S PROBLEM?!
WHAT IS GOING ON?!

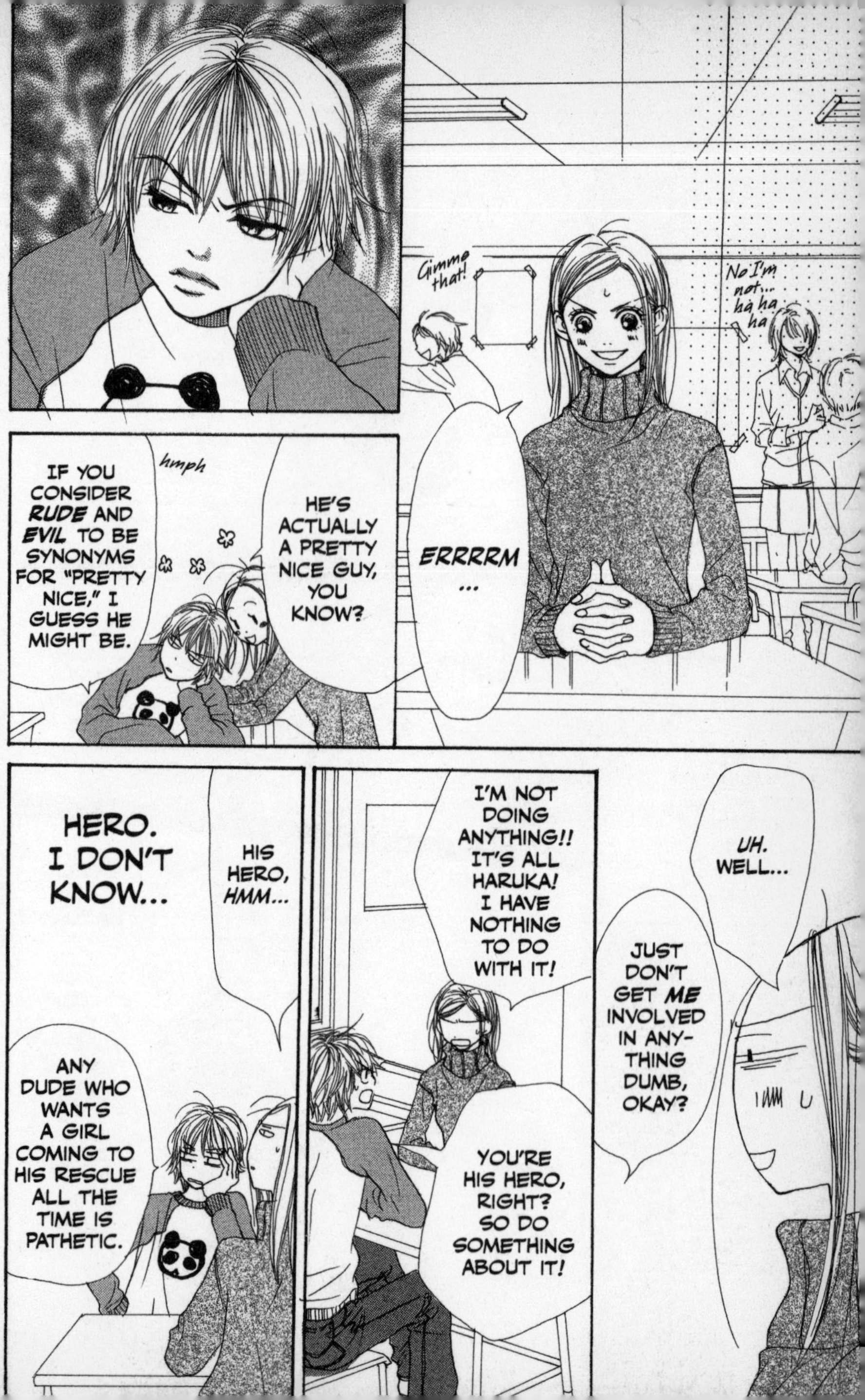
Gimme that!
No I'm not... ha ha ha
ERRRRM ...
HE'S ACTUALLY A PRETTY NICE GUY, YOU KNOW?
hmph
IF YOU CONSIDER ***RUDE*** AND ***EVIL*** TO BE SYNONYMS FOR "PRETTY NICE," I GUESS HE MIGHT BE.
UH. WELL...
I'M NOT DOING ANYTHING!! IT'S ALL HARUKA! I HAVE NOTHING TO DO WITH IT!
JUST DON'T GET ***ME*** INVOLVED IN ANY-THING DUMB, OKAY?
YOU'RE HIS HERO, RIGHT? SO DO SOMETHING ABOUT IT!
HIS HERO, *HMM...*
HERO. I DON'T KNOW...
ANY DUDE WHO WANTS A GIRL COMING TO HIS RESCUE ALL THE TIME IS PATHETIC.

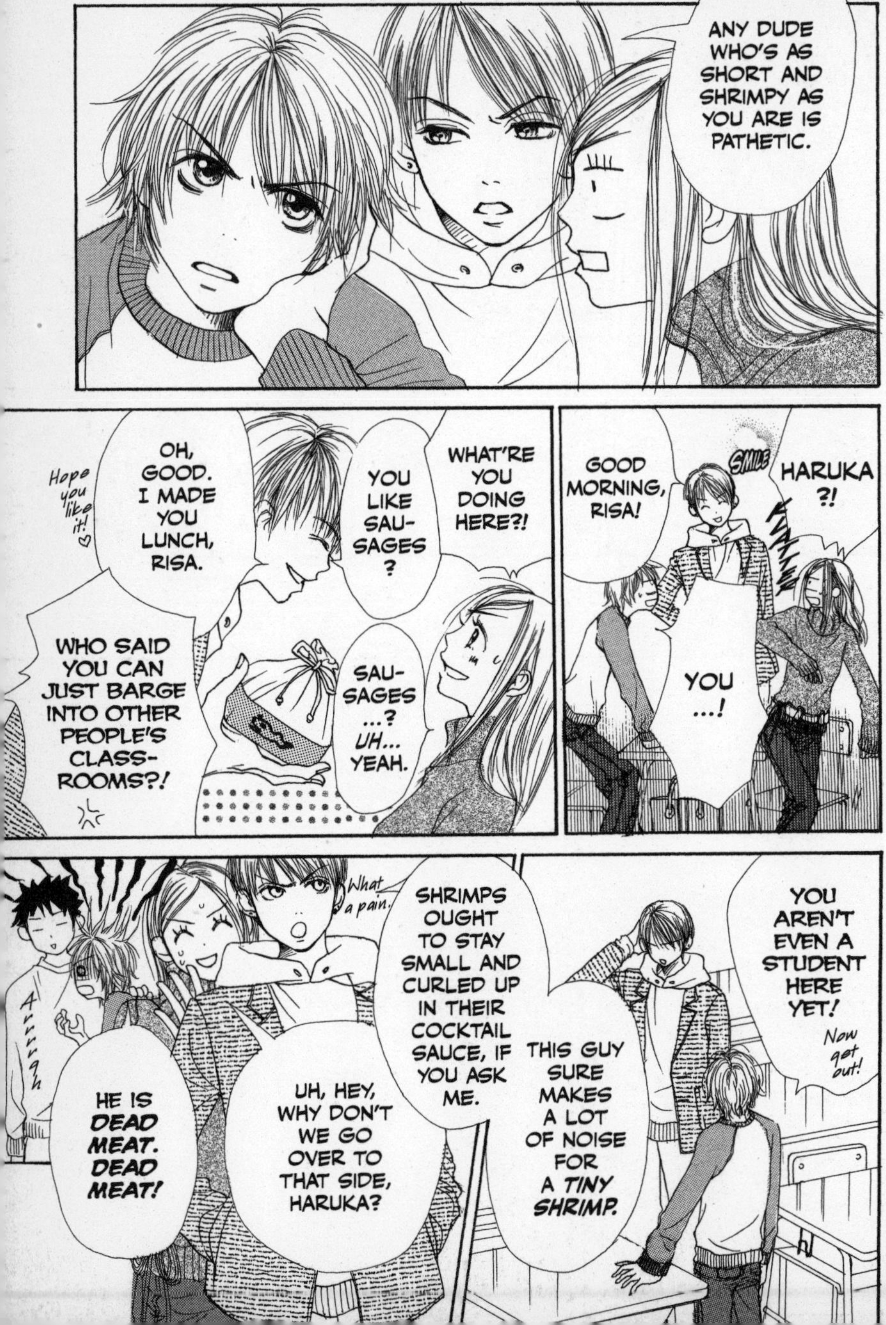
ANY DUDE WHO'S AS SHORT AND SHRIMPY AS YOU ARE IS PATHETIC.
HARUKA?!
SMILE
GOOD MORNING, RISA!
YOU ...!
WHAT'RE YOU DOING HERE?!
YOU LIKE SAUSAGES?
OH, GOOD. I MADE YOU LUNCH, RISA.
Hope you like it! ♡
SAUSAGES ...? UH... YEAH.
WHO SAID YOU CAN JUST BARGE INTO OTHER PEOPLE'S CLASSROOMS?!
YOU AREN'T EVEN A STUDENT HERE YET!
Now get out!
THIS GUY SURE MAKES A LOT OF NOISE FOR A *TINY SHRIMP*.
SHRIMPS OUGHT TO STAY SMALL AND CURLED UP IN THEIR COCKTAIL SAUCE, IF YOU ASK ME.
What a pain.
UH, HEY, WHY DON'T WE GO OVER TO THAT SIDE, HARUKA?
HE IS ***DEAD MEAT. DEAD MEAT!***
Arrrrgh

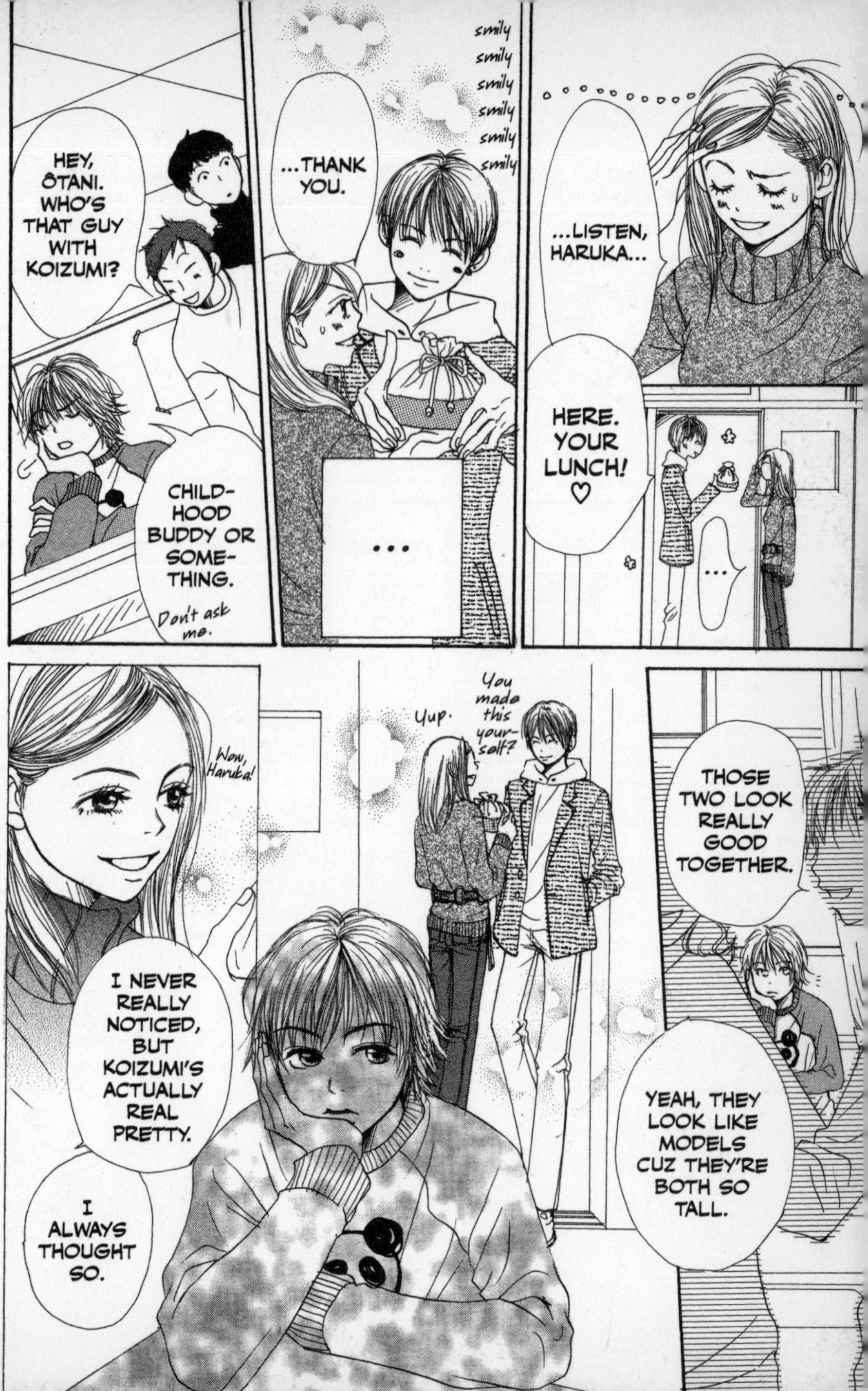
...LISTEN, HARUKA...
HERE. YOUR LUNCH! ♡
...
smily smily smily smily smily smily
...THANK YOU.
...
HEY, ŌTANI. WHO'S THAT GUY WITH KOIZUMI?
CHILD-HOOD BUDDY OR SOME-THING.
Don't ask me.
THOSE TWO LOOK REALLY GOOD TOGETHER.
YEAH, THEY LOOK LIKE MODELS CUZ THEY'RE BOTH SO TALL.
You made this your-self?
Yup.
Wow, Haruka!
I NEVER REALLY NOTICED, BUT KOIZUMI'S ACTUALLY REAL PRETTY.
I ALWAYS THOUGHT SO.

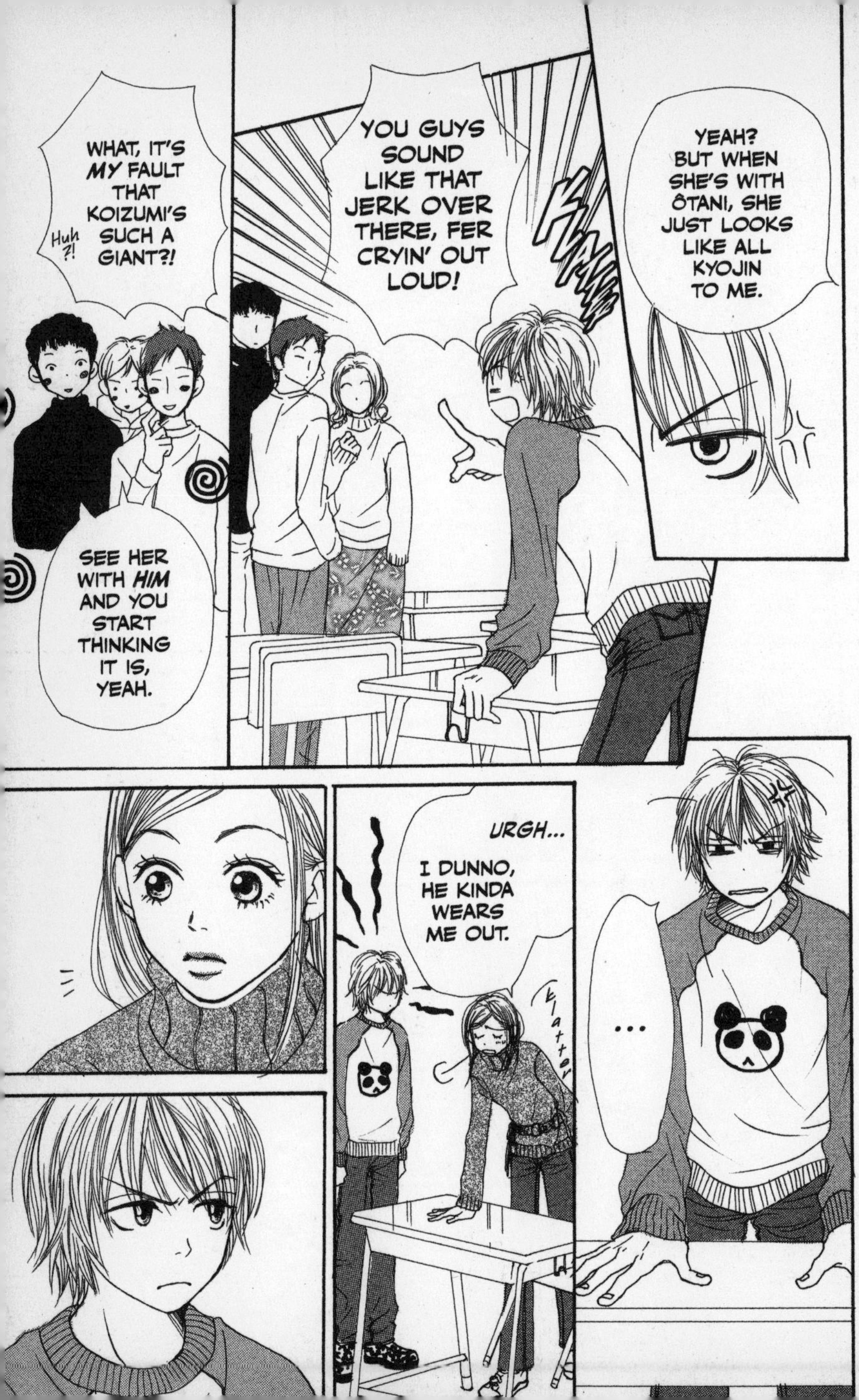
YEAH? BUT WHEN SHE'S WITH ÔTANI, SHE JUST LOOKS LIKE ALL KYOJIN TO ME.
YOU GUYS SOUND LIKE THAT JERK OVER THERE, FER CRYIN' OUT LOUD!
WHAT, IT'S MY FAULT THAT KOIZUMI'S SUCH A GIANT?!
Huh?!
SEE HER WITH HIM AND YOU START THINKING IT IS, YEAH.
...
URGH...
I DUNNO, HE KINDA WEARS ME OUT.
klatter

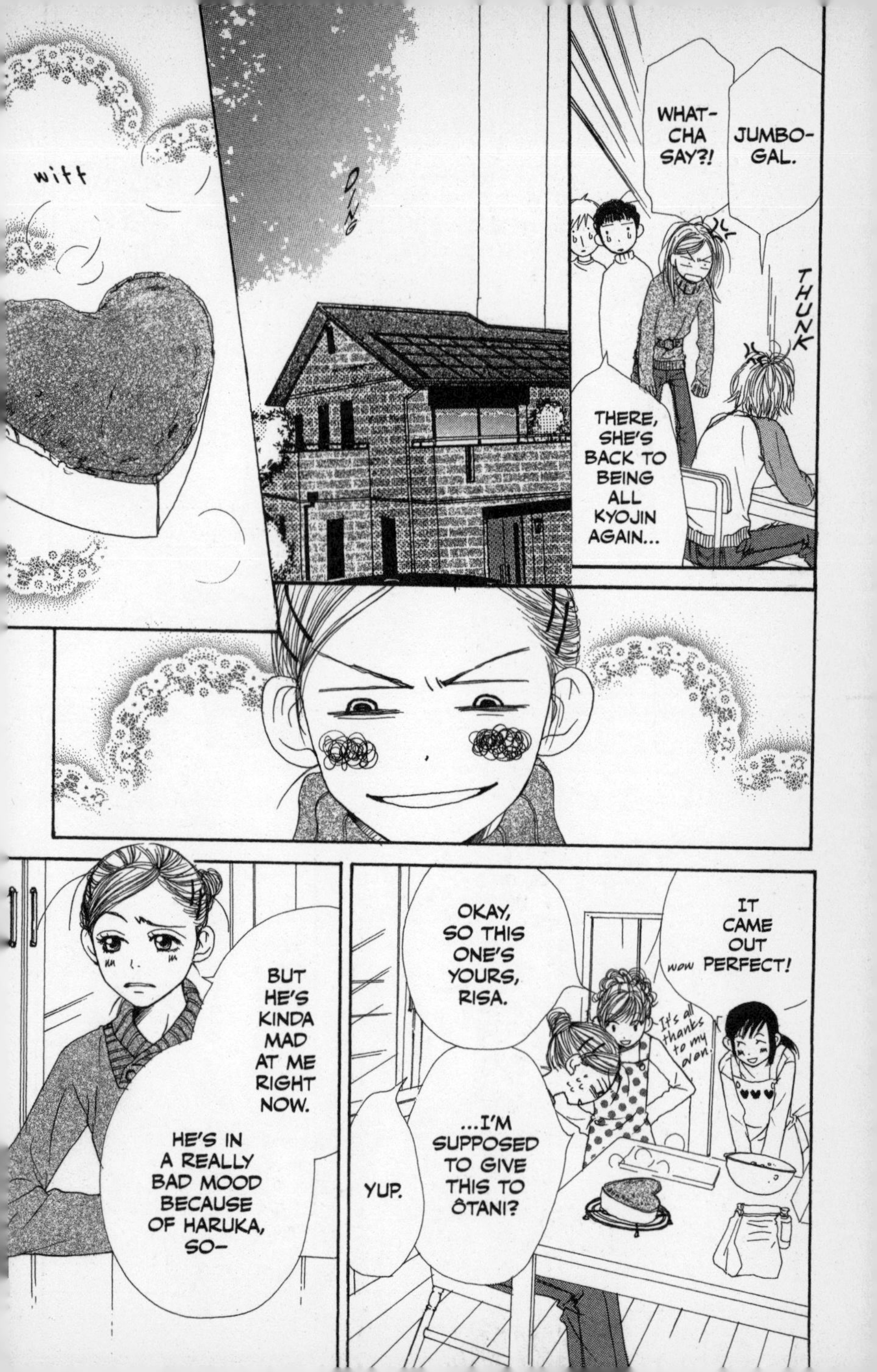
JUMBO-GAL.
WHAT-CHA SAY?!
THUNK
THERE, SHE'S BACK TO BEING ALL KYOJIN AGAIN...
DING
witt
IT CAME OUT PERFECT!
wow
It's all thanks to my oven.
OKAY, SO THIS ONE'S YOURS, RISA.
...I'M SUPPOSED TO GIVE THIS TO ÔTANI?
YUP.
BUT HE'S KINDA MAD AT ME RIGHT NOW.
HE'S IN A REALLY BAD MOOD BECAUSE OF HARUKA, SO–

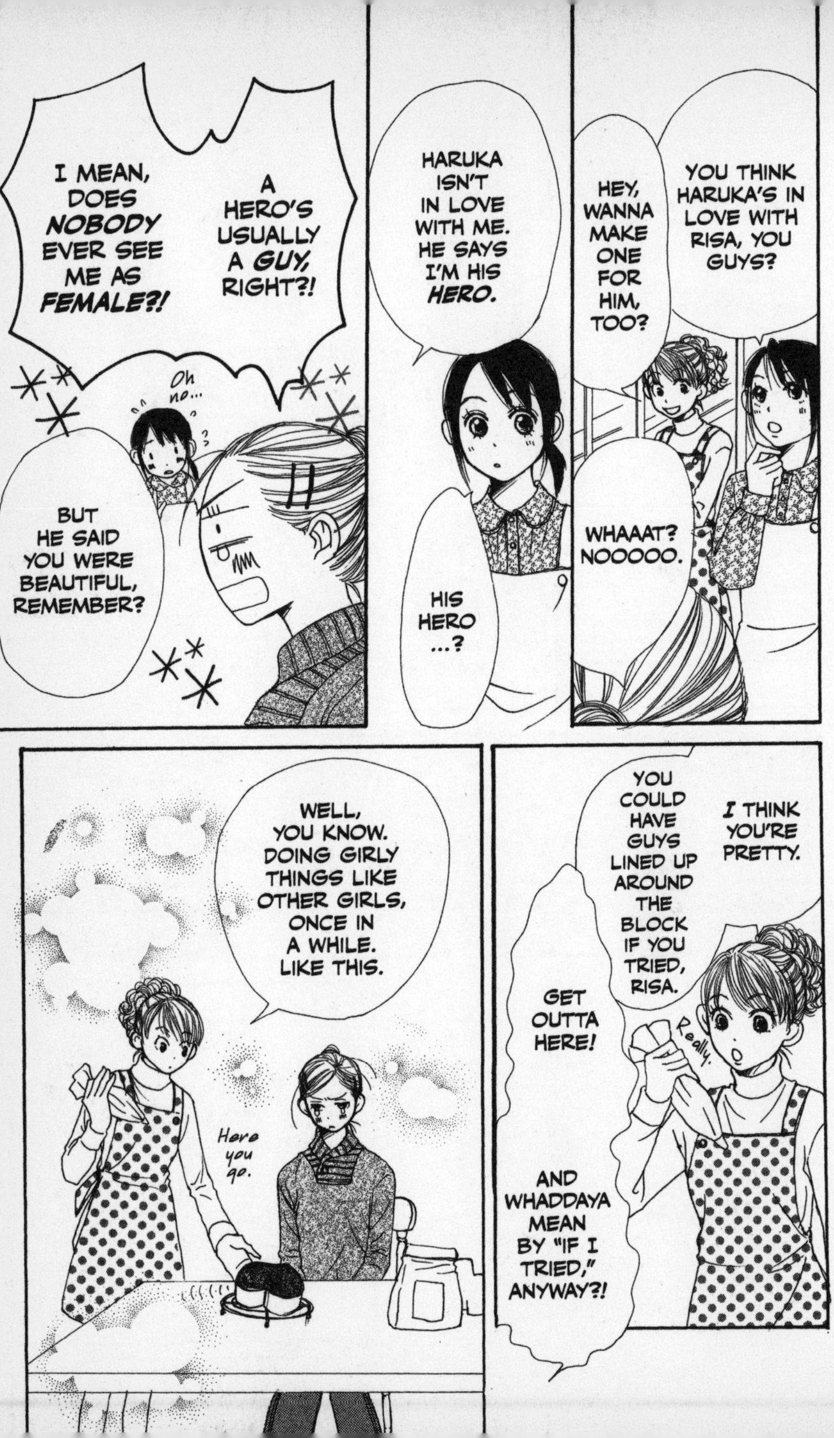
YOU THINK HARUKA'S IN LOVE WITH RISA, YOU GUYS?
HEY, WANNA MAKE ONE FOR HIM, TOO?
WHAAAT? NOOOOO.
HARUKA ISN'T IN LOVE WITH ME. HE SAYS I'M HIS *HERO.*
HIS HERO ...?
A HERO'S USUALLY A *GUY,* RIGHT?!
I MEAN, DOES *NOBODY* EVER SEE ME AS *FEMALE?!*
Oh no...
BUT HE SAID YOU WERE BEAUTIFUL, REMEMBER?
I THINK YOU'RE PRETTY.
YOU COULD HAVE GUYS LINED UP AROUND THE BLOCK IF YOU TRIED, RISA.
Really.
GET OUTTA HERE!
AND WHADDAYA MEAN BY "IF I TRIED," ANYWAY?!
WELL, YOU KNOW. DOING GIRLY THINGS LIKE OTHER GIRLS, ONCE IN A WHILE. LIKE THIS.
Here you go.

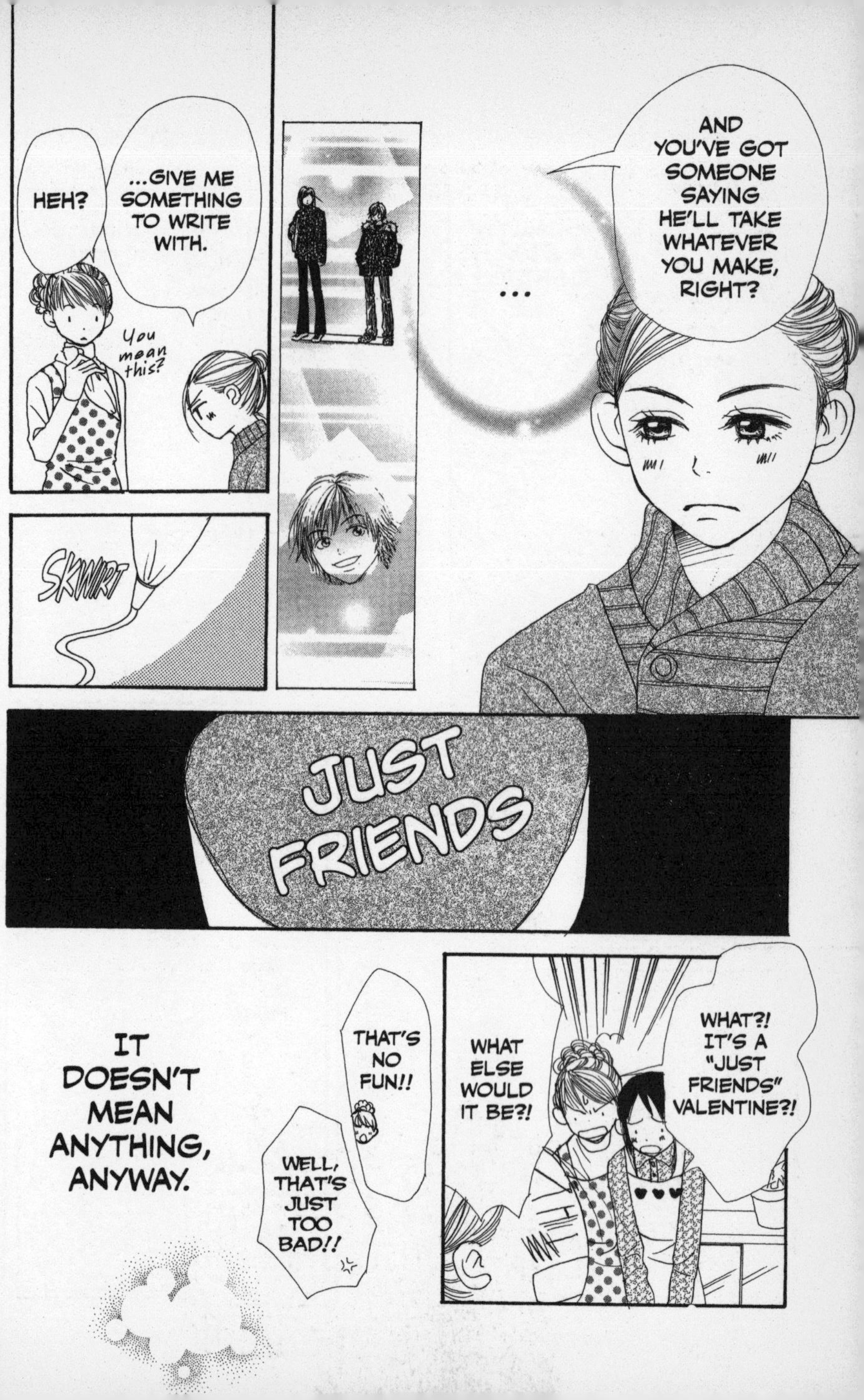
AND YOU'VE GOT SOMEONE SAYING HE'LL TAKE WHATEVER YOU MAKE, RIGHT?
...
...GIVE ME SOMETHING TO WRITE WITH.
HEH?
You mean this?
SKWIRT
JUST FRIENDS
WHAT?! IT'S A "JUST FRIENDS" VALENTINE?!
WHAT ELSE WOULD IT BE?!
THAT'S NO FUN!!
WELL, THAT'S JUST TOO BAD!!
IT DOESN'T MEAN ANYTHING, ANYWAY.

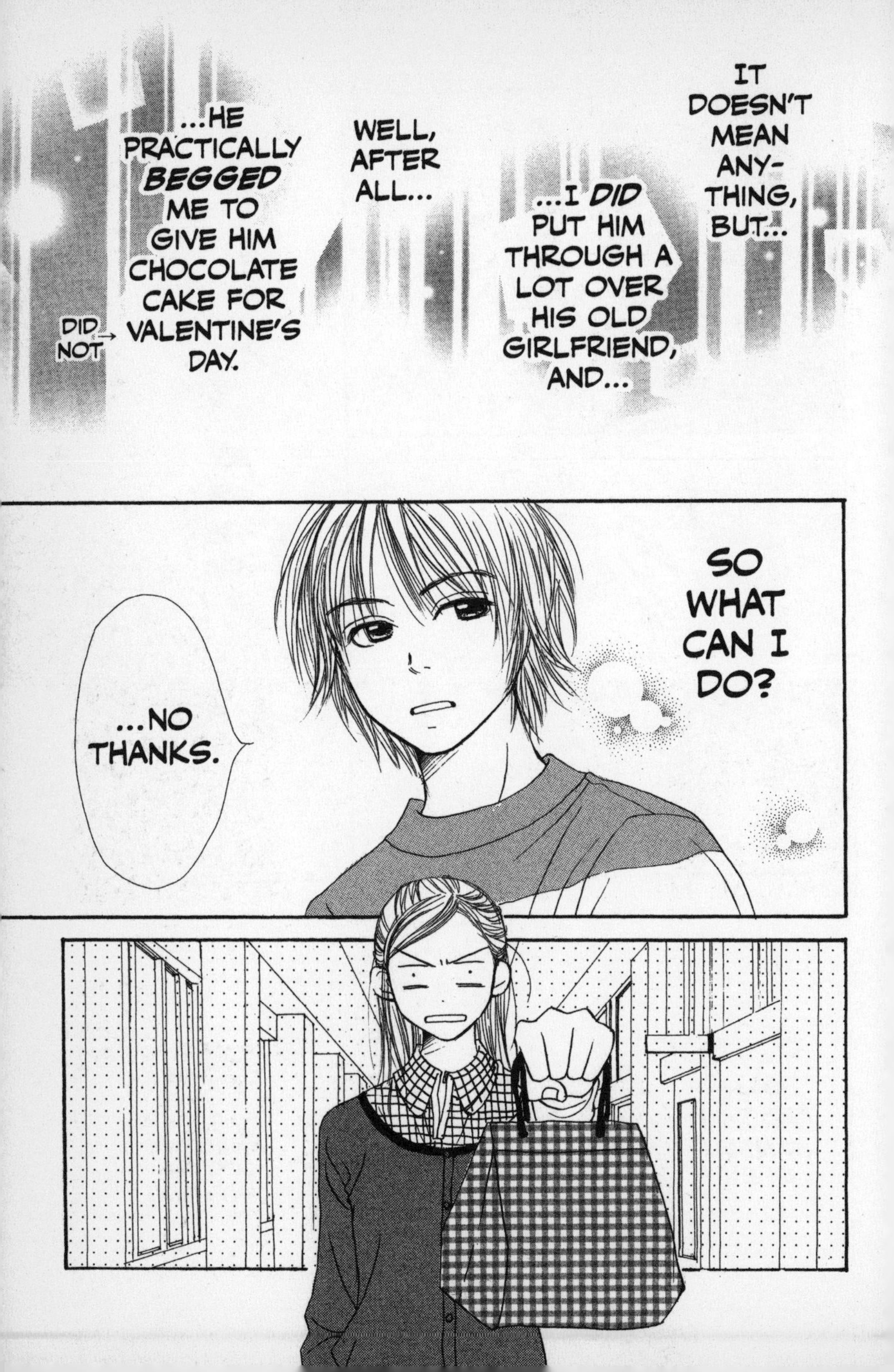
IT DOESN'T MEAN ANY-THING, BUT...
...I DID PUT HIM THROUGH A LOT OVER HIS OLD GIRLFRIEND, AND...
WELL, AFTER ALL...
...HE PRACTICALLY BEGGED ME TO GIVE HIM CHOCOLATE CAKE FOR VALENTINE'S DAY.
DID NOT
SO WHAT CAN I DO?
...NO THANKS.

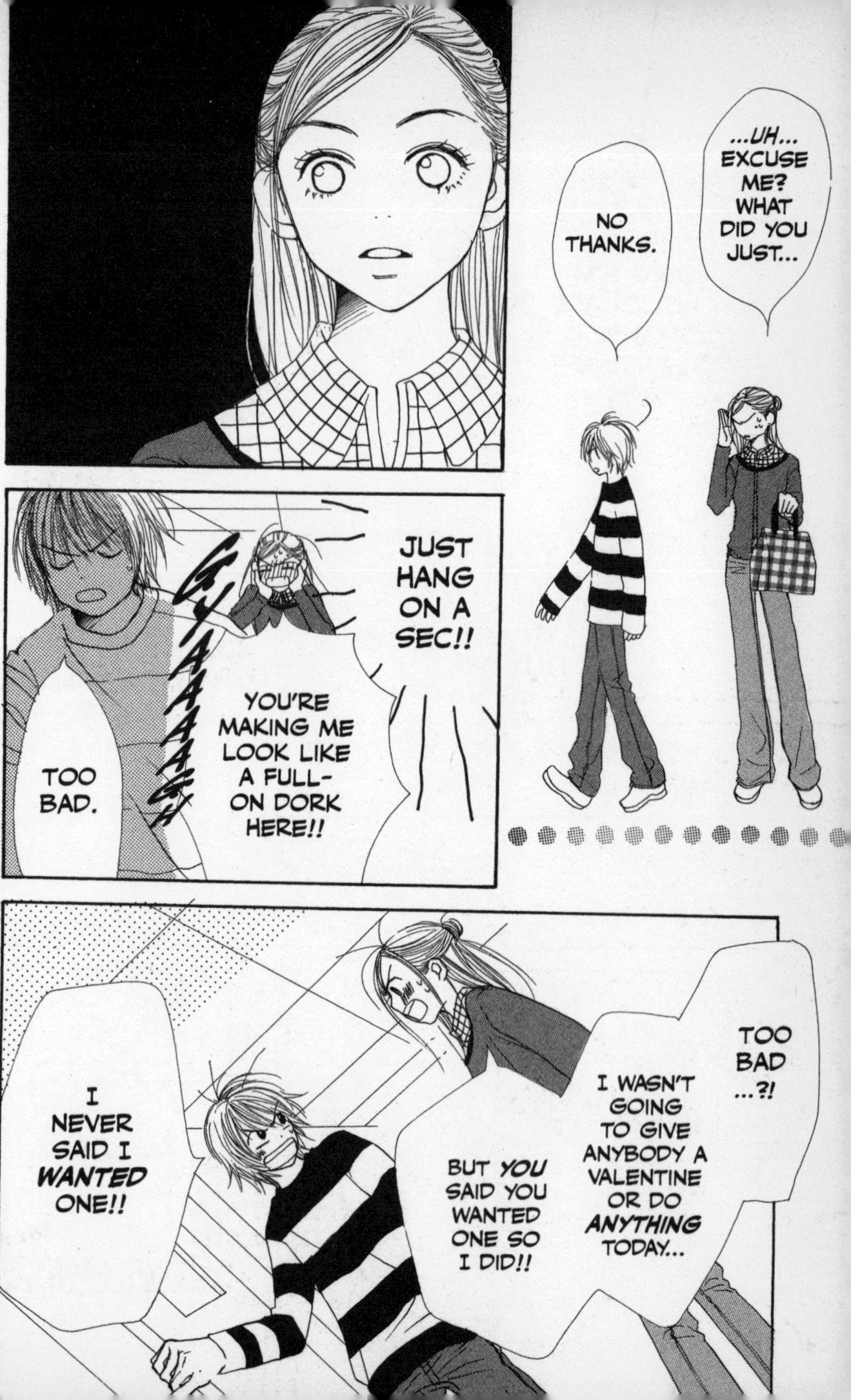
...UH... EXCUSE ME? WHAT DID YOU JUST...
NO THANKS.
JUST HANG ON A SEC!!
GYAAAAAAAGH
YOU'RE MAKING ME LOOK LIKE A FULL-ON DORK HERE!!
TOO BAD.
TOO BAD ...?!
I WASN'T GOING TO GIVE ANYBODY A VALENTINE OR DO ANYTHING TODAY...
BUT YOU SAID YOU WANTED ONE SO I DID!!
I NEVER SAID I WANTED ONE!!

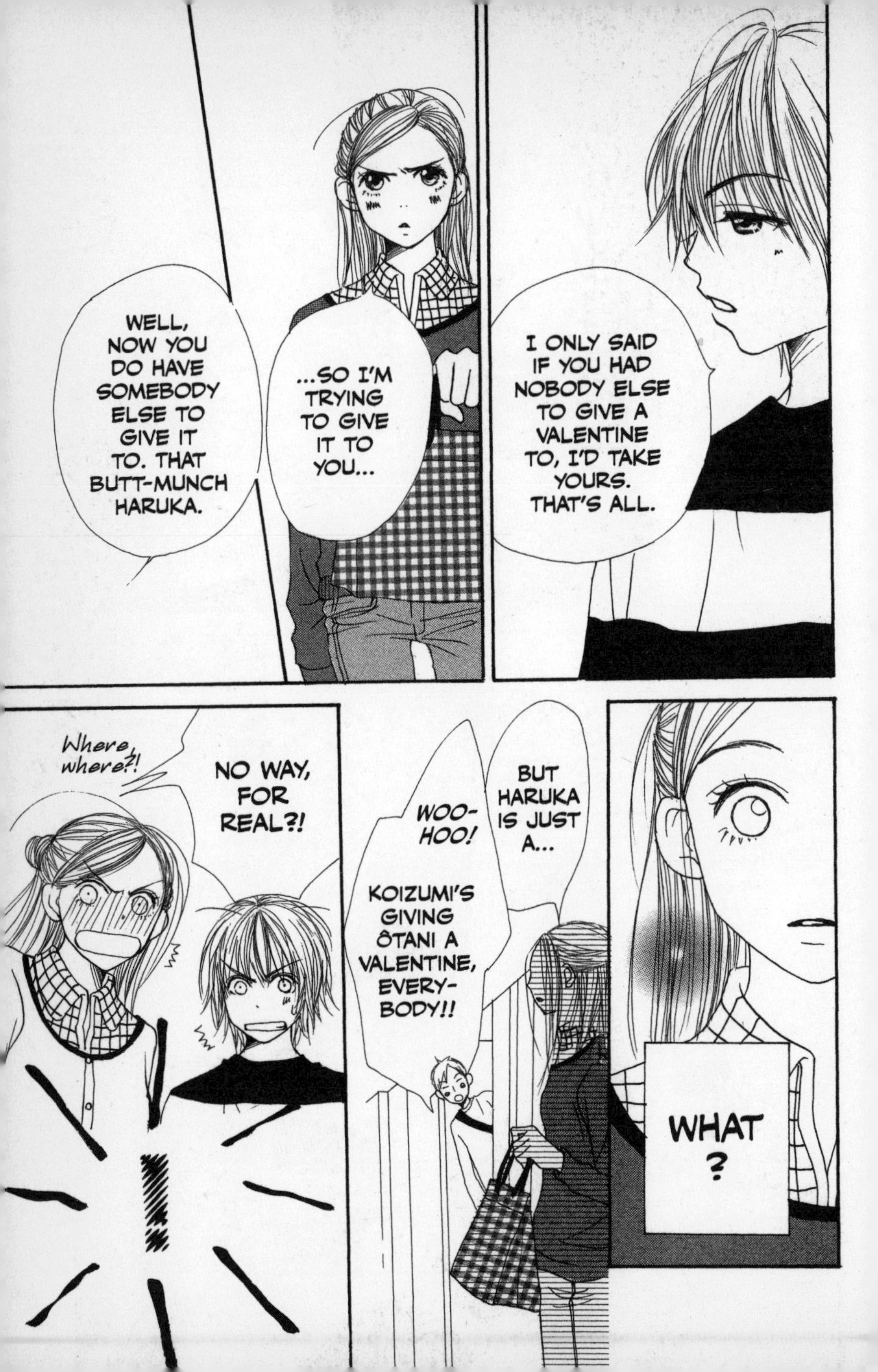
I ONLY SAID IF YOU HAD NOBODY ELSE TO GIVE A VALENTINE TO, I'D TAKE YOURS. THAT'S ALL.
...SO I'M TRYING TO GIVE IT TO YOU...
WELL, NOW YOU DO HAVE SOMEBODY ELSE TO GIVE IT TO. THAT BUTT-MUNCH HARUKA.
WHAT?
BUT HARUKA IS JUST A...
WOO-HOO!
KOIZUMI'S GIVING ŌTANI A VALENTINE, EVERYBODY!!
NO WAY, FOR REAL?!
Where, where?!

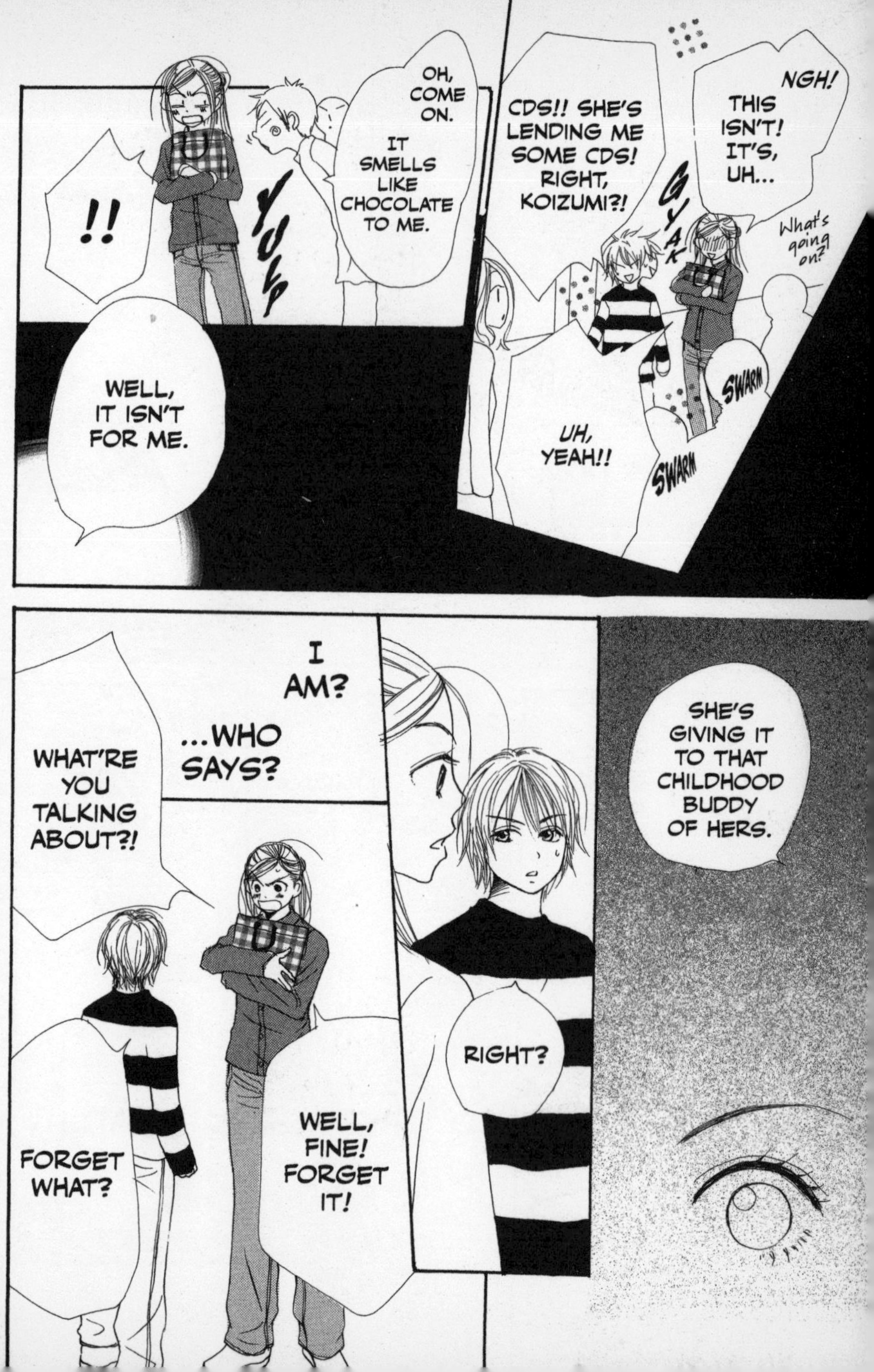
NGH! THIS ISN'T! IT'S, UH...
What's going on?
CDS!! SHE'S LENDING ME SOME CDS! RIGHT, KOIZUMI?!
GYAK
UH, YEAH!!
SWARM
SWARM
OH, COME ON.
IT SMELLS LIKE CHOCOLATE TO ME.
!!
WELL, IT ISN'T FOR ME.
SHE'S GIVING IT TO THAT CHILDHOOD BUDDY OF HERS.
RIGHT?
I AM?
...WHO SAYS?
WHAT'RE YOU TALKING ABOUT?!
WELL, FINE! FORGET IT!
FORGET WHAT?

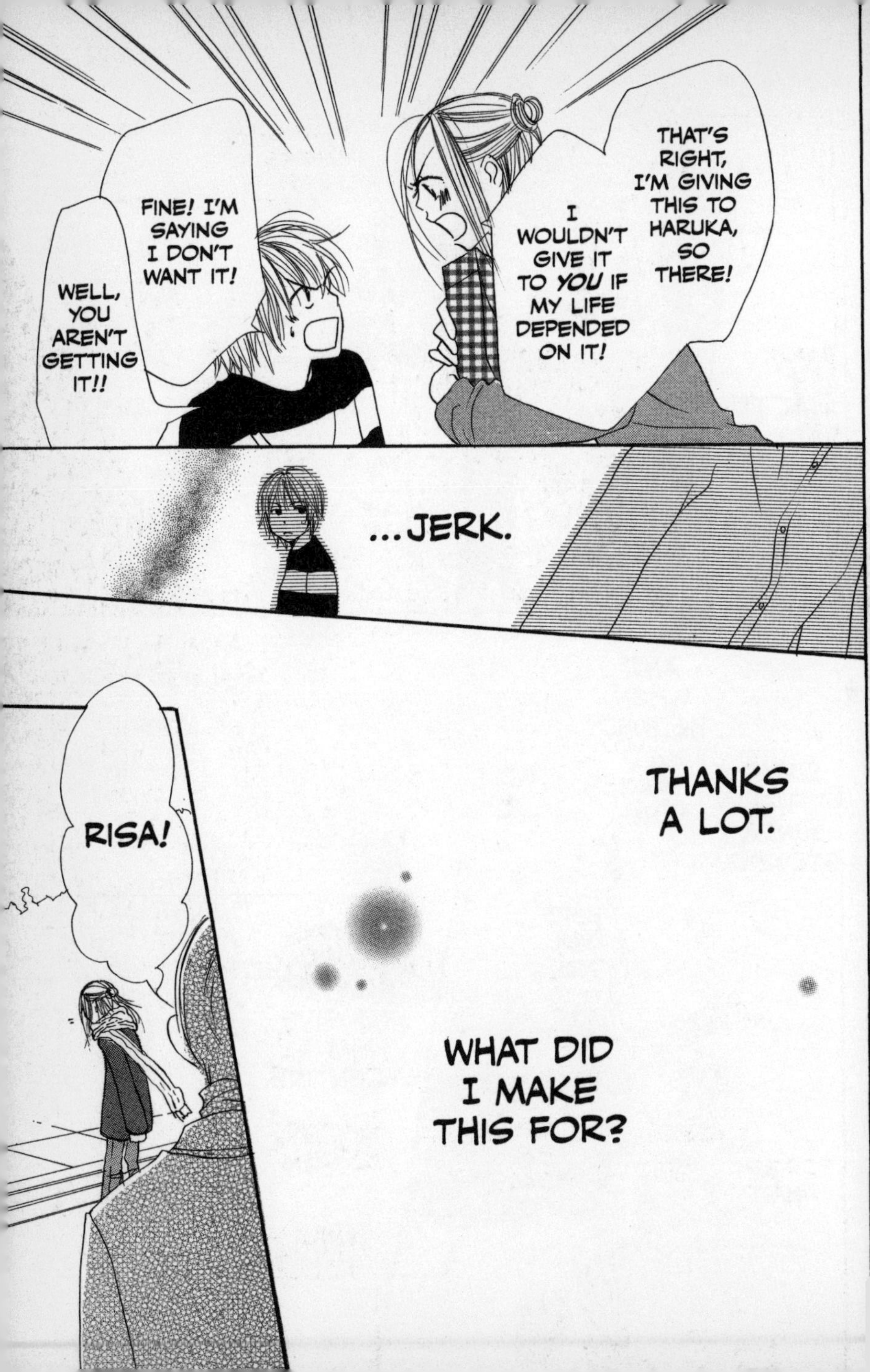
THAT'S RIGHT, I'M GIVING THIS TO HARUKA, SO THERE!
I WOULDN'T GIVE IT TO *YOU* IF MY LIFE DEPENDED ON IT!
FINE! I'M SAYING I DON'T WANT IT!
WELL, YOU AREN'T GETTING IT!!
...JERK.
THANKS A LOT.
RISA!
WHAT DID I MAKE THIS FOR?

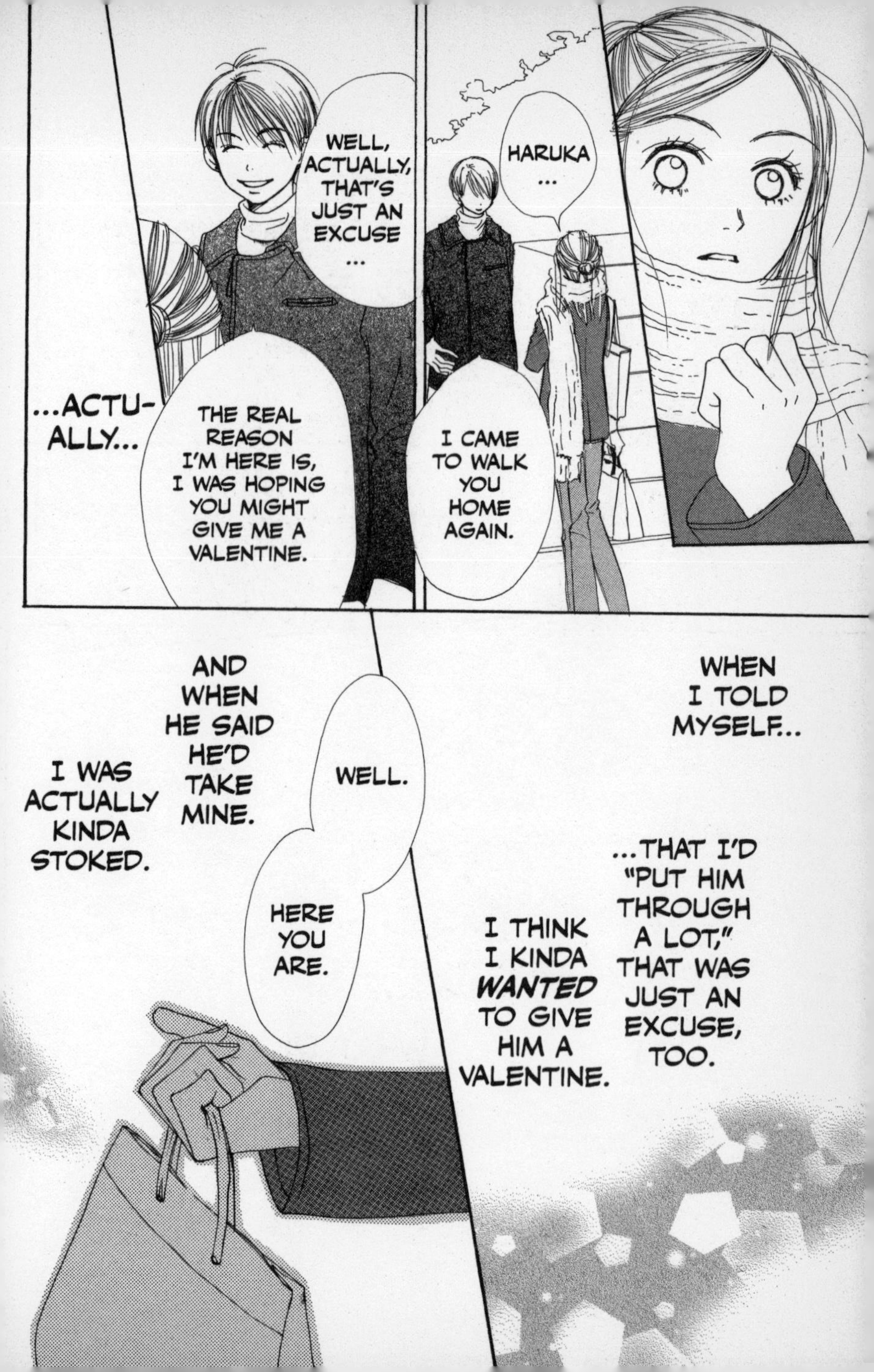
HARUKA ...
I CAME TO WALK YOU HOME AGAIN.
WELL, ACTUALLY, THAT'S JUST AN EXCUSE ...
...ACTU-ALLY...
THE REAL REASON I'M HERE IS, I WAS HOPING YOU MIGHT GIVE ME A VALENTINE.
WHEN I TOLD MYSELF...
...THAT I'D "PUT HIM THROUGH A LOT," THAT WAS JUST AN EXCUSE, TOO.
I THINK I KINDA *WANTED* TO GIVE HIM A VALENTINE.
WELL.
HERE YOU ARE.
AND WHEN HE SAID HE'D TAKE MINE.
I WAS ACTUALLY KINDA STOKED.

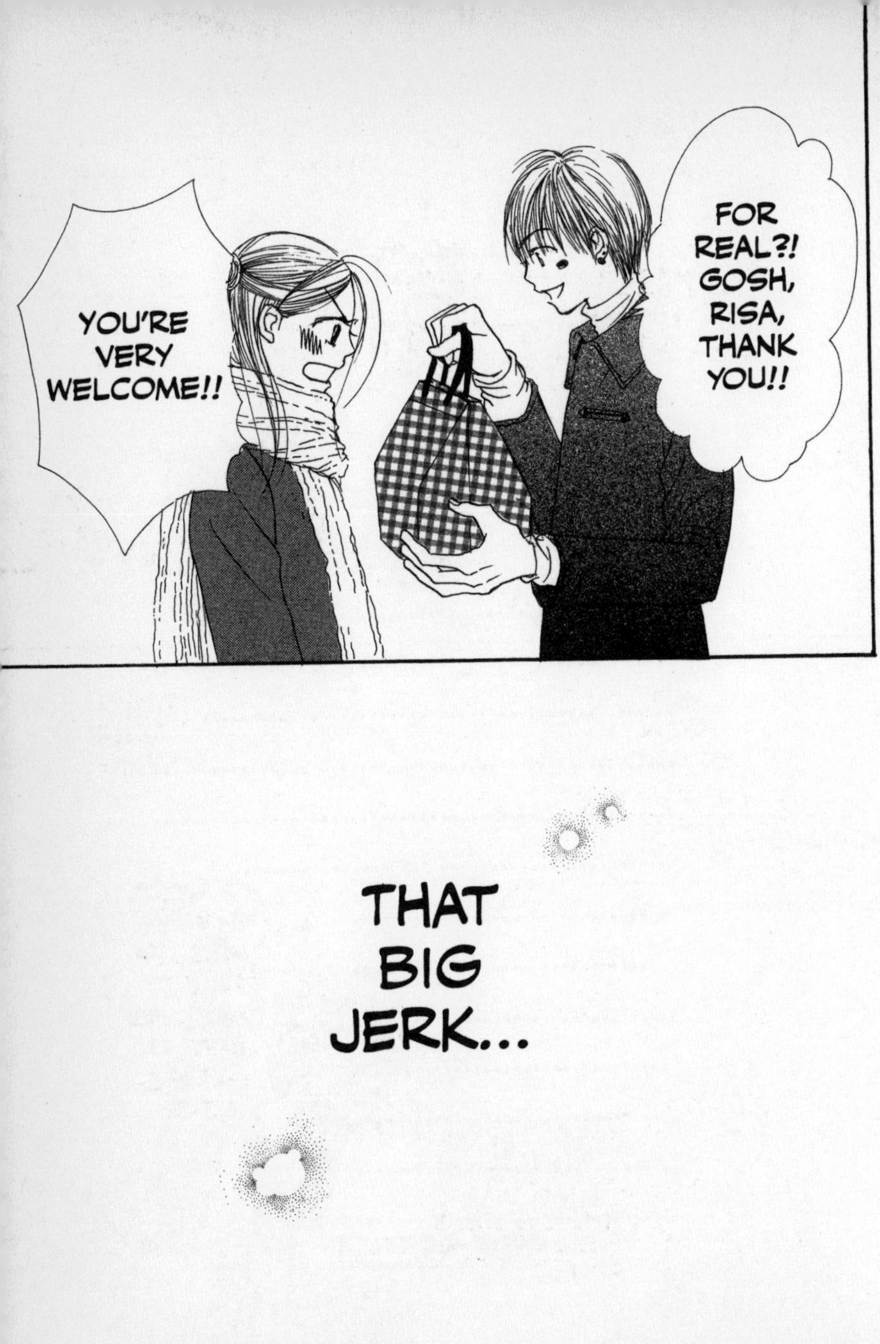
FOR REAL?! GOSH, RISA, THANK YOU!!
YOU'RE VERY WELCOME!!
THAT BIG JERK...

How about some stationery?
Use a copier to make as many sheets as you want.
What a pain in the butt!!
Uh-oh... maybe you don't want it...after all...?

NO.

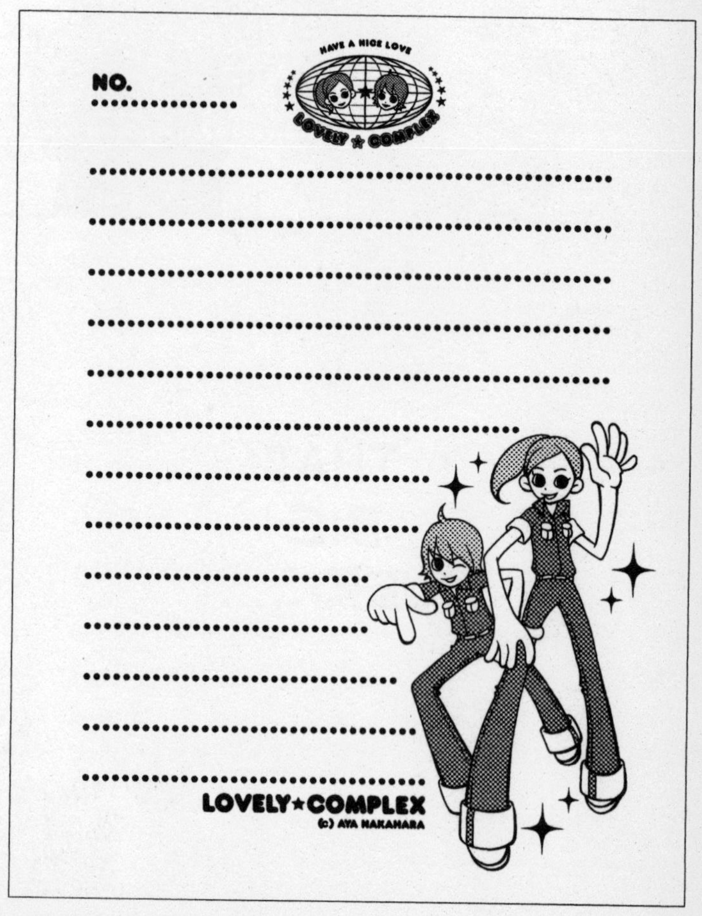

LOVELY★COMPLEX
(c) AYA NAKAHARA

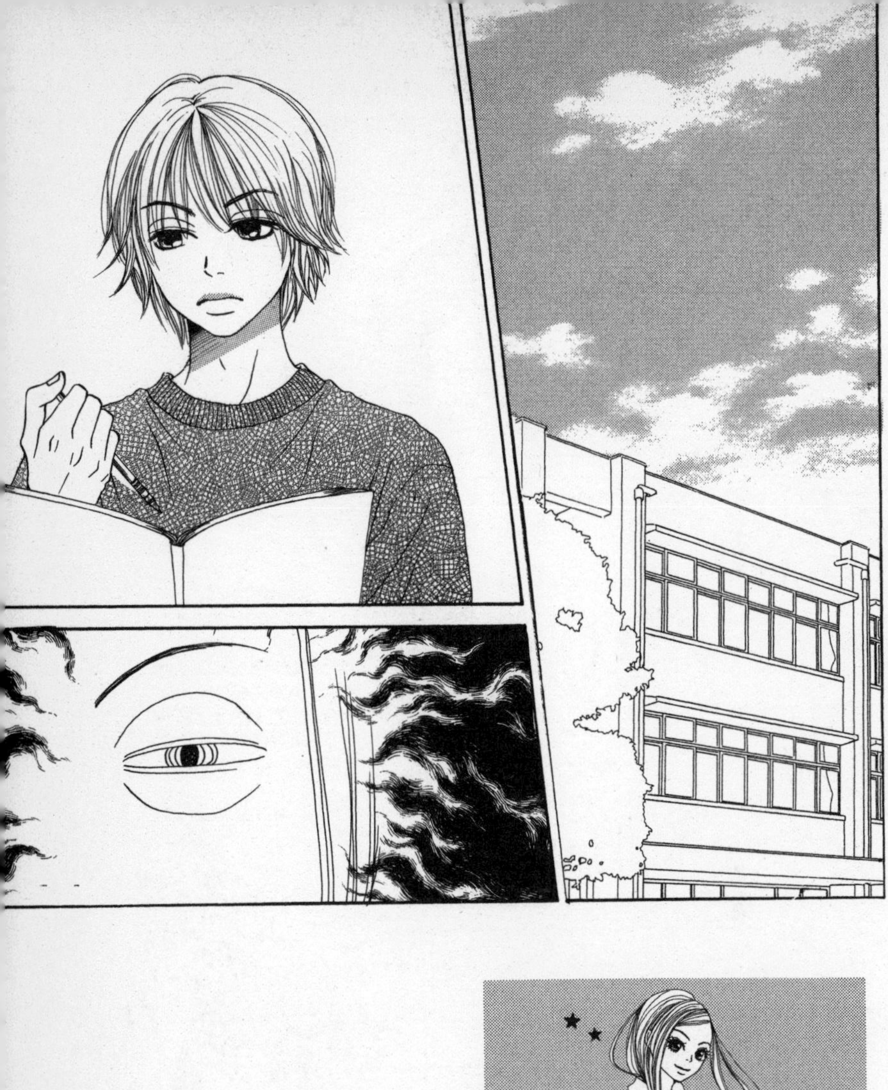

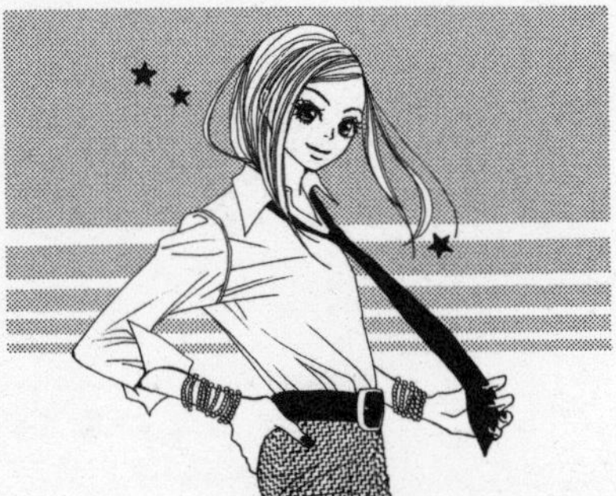

CHAPTER 8

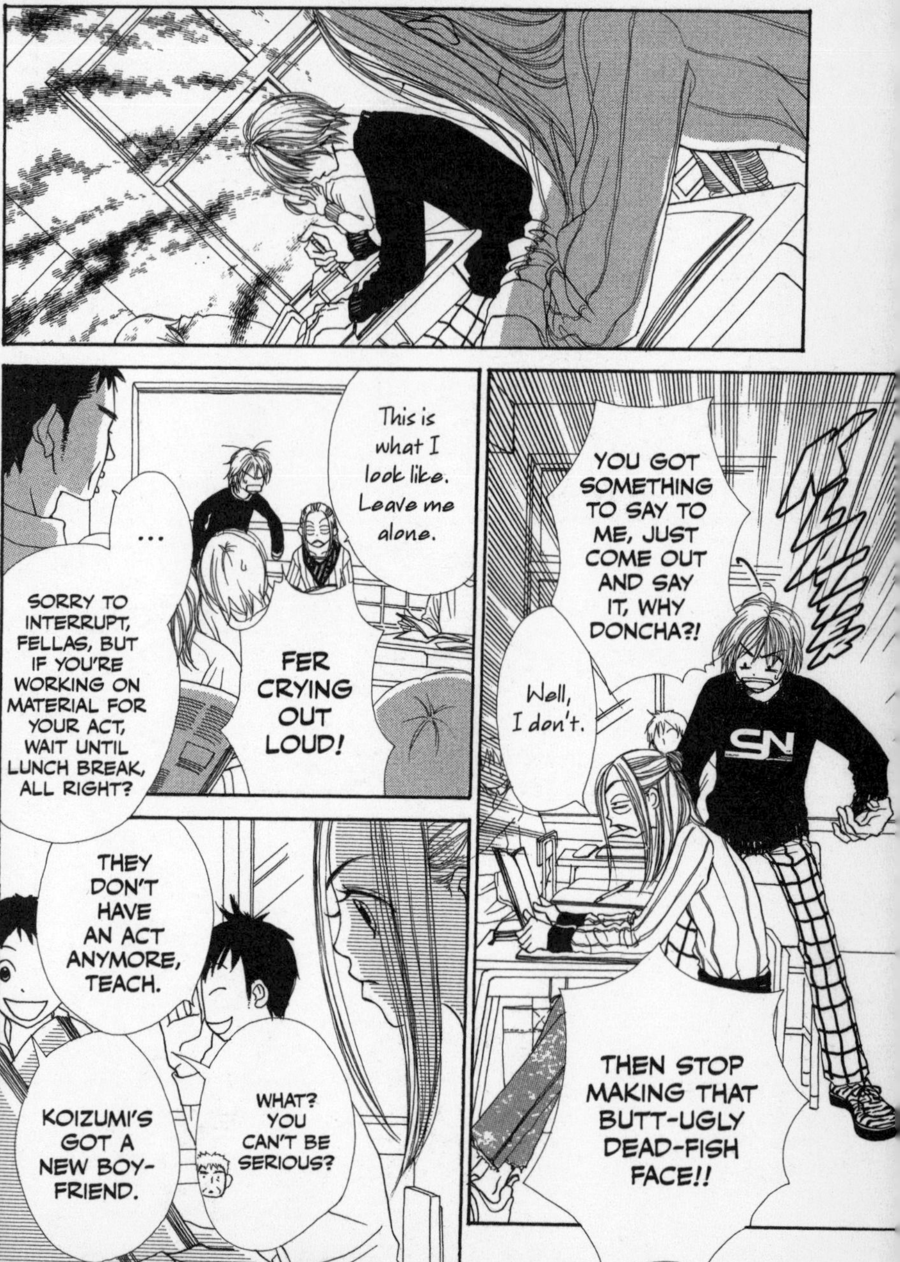

YOU GOT SOMETHING TO SAY TO ME, JUST COME OUT AND SAY IT, WHY DONCHA?!
Well, I don't.
THEN STOP MAKING THAT BUTT-UGLY DEAD-FISH FACE!!
This is what I look like. Leave me alone.
FER CRYING OUT LOUD!
...
SORRY TO INTERRUPT, FELLAS, BUT IF YOU'RE WORKING ON MATERIAL FOR YOUR ACT, WAIT UNTIL LUNCH BREAK, ALL RIGHT?
THEY DON'T HAVE AN ACT ANYMORE, TEACH.
WHAT? YOU CAN'T BE SERIOUS?
KOIZUMI'S GOT A NEW BOY-FRIEND.

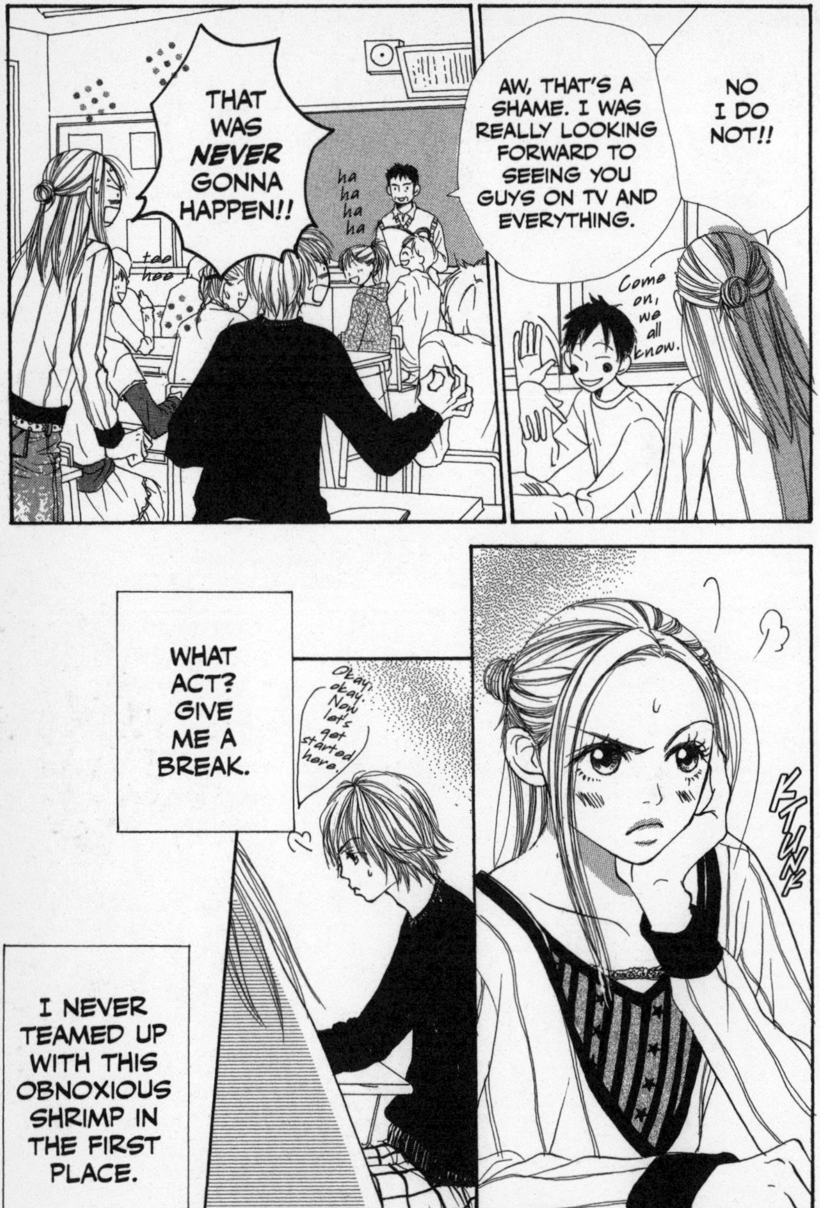
AW, THAT'S A SHAME. I WAS REALLY LOOKING FORWARD TO SEEING YOU GUYS ON TV AND EVERYTHING.
NO I DO NOT!!
Come on, we all know.
THAT WAS ***NEVER*** GONNA HAPPEN!!
ha ha ha ha
tee hee
KTUNK
Okay, okay. Now let's get started here.
WHAT ACT? GIVE ME A BREAK.
I NEVER TEAMED UP WITH THIS OBNOXIOUS SHRIMP IN THE FIRST PLACE.

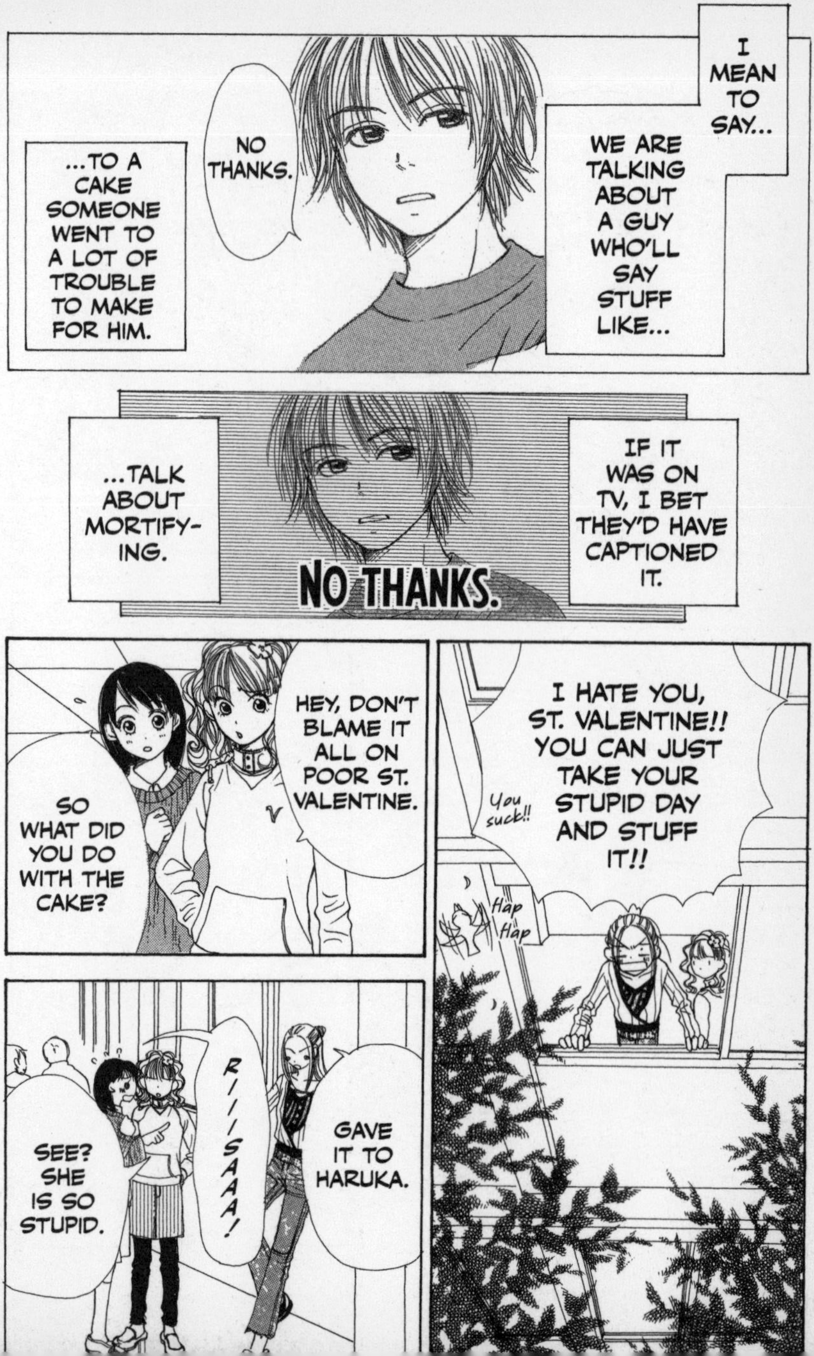
I MEAN TO SAY...
WE ARE TALKING ABOUT A GUY WHO'LL SAY STUFF LIKE...
NO THANKS.
...TO A CAKE SOMEONE WENT TO A LOT OF TROUBLE TO MAKE FOR HIM.
IF IT WAS ON TV, I BET THEY'D HAVE CAPTIONED IT.
NO THANKS.
...TALK ABOUT MORTIFY-ING.
I HATE YOU, ST. VALENTINE!! YOU CAN JUST TAKE YOUR STUPID DAY AND STUFF IT!!
You suck!!
Hap Hap
HEY, DON'T BLAME IT ALL ON POOR ST. VALENTINE.
SO WHAT DID YOU DO WITH THE CAKE?
GAVE IT TO HARUKA.
R//SAAA!
SEE? SHE IS SO STUPID.

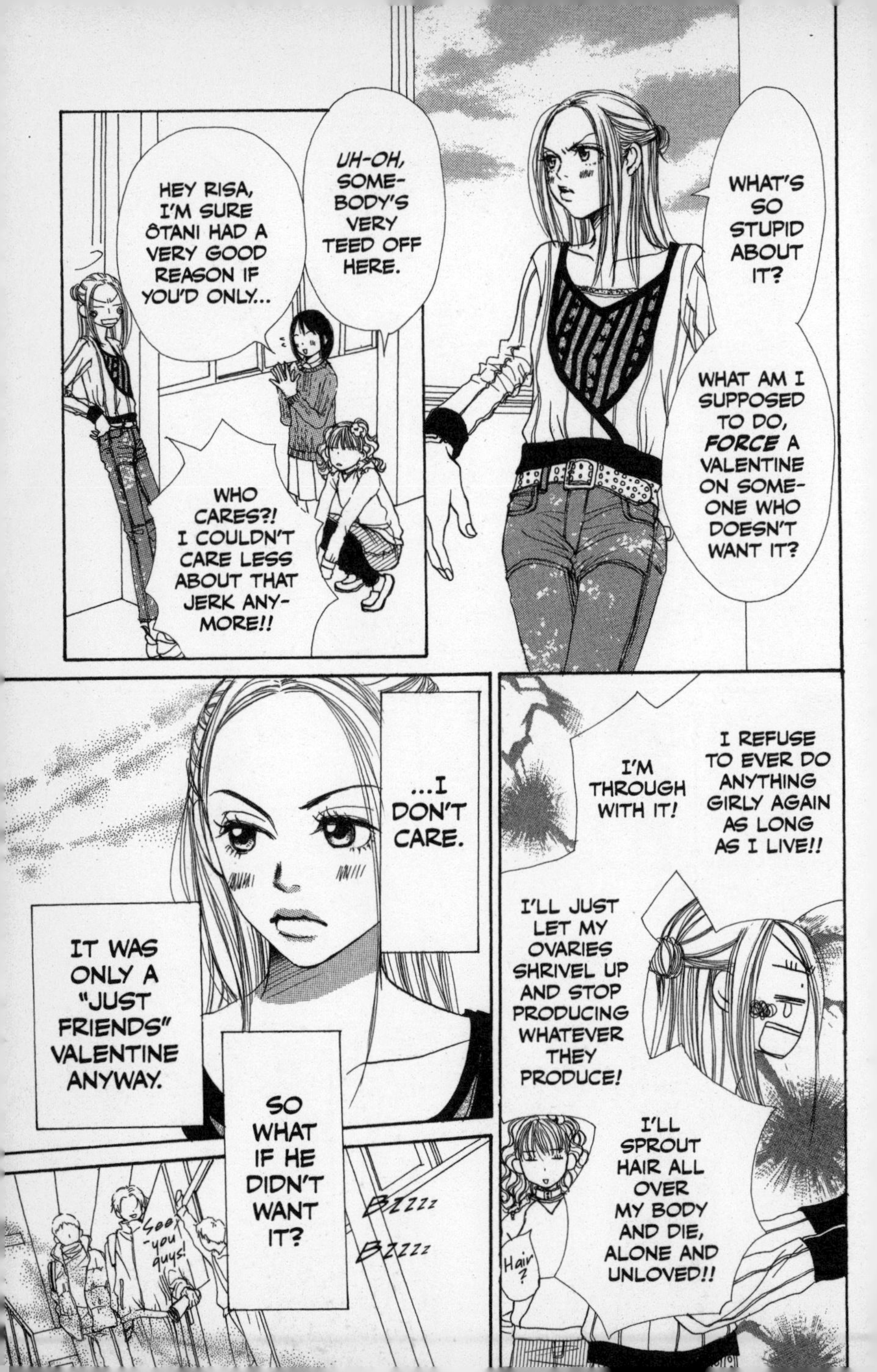
WHAT'S SO STUPID ABOUT IT?
WHAT AM I SUPPOSED TO DO, *FORCE* A VALENTINE ON SOMEONE WHO DOESN'T WANT IT?
UH-OH, SOMEBODY'S VERY TEED OFF HERE.
HEY RISA, I'M SURE ŌTANI HAD A VERY GOOD REASON IF YOU'D ONLY...
WHO CARES?! I COULDN'T CARE LESS ABOUT THAT JERK ANYMORE!!
I REFUSE TO EVER DO ANYTHING GIRLY AGAIN AS LONG AS I LIVE!!
I'M THROUGH WITH IT!
I'LL JUST LET MY OVARIES SHRIVEL UP AND STOP PRODUCING WHATEVER THEY PRODUCE!
I'LL SPROUT HAIR ALL OVER MY BODY AND DIE, ALONE AND UNLOVED!!
Hair?
...I DON'T CARE.
IT WAS ONLY A "JUST FRIENDS" VALENTINE ANYWAY.
SO WHAT IF HE DIDN'T WANT IT?
BZzzz
BZzzz
See you guys!

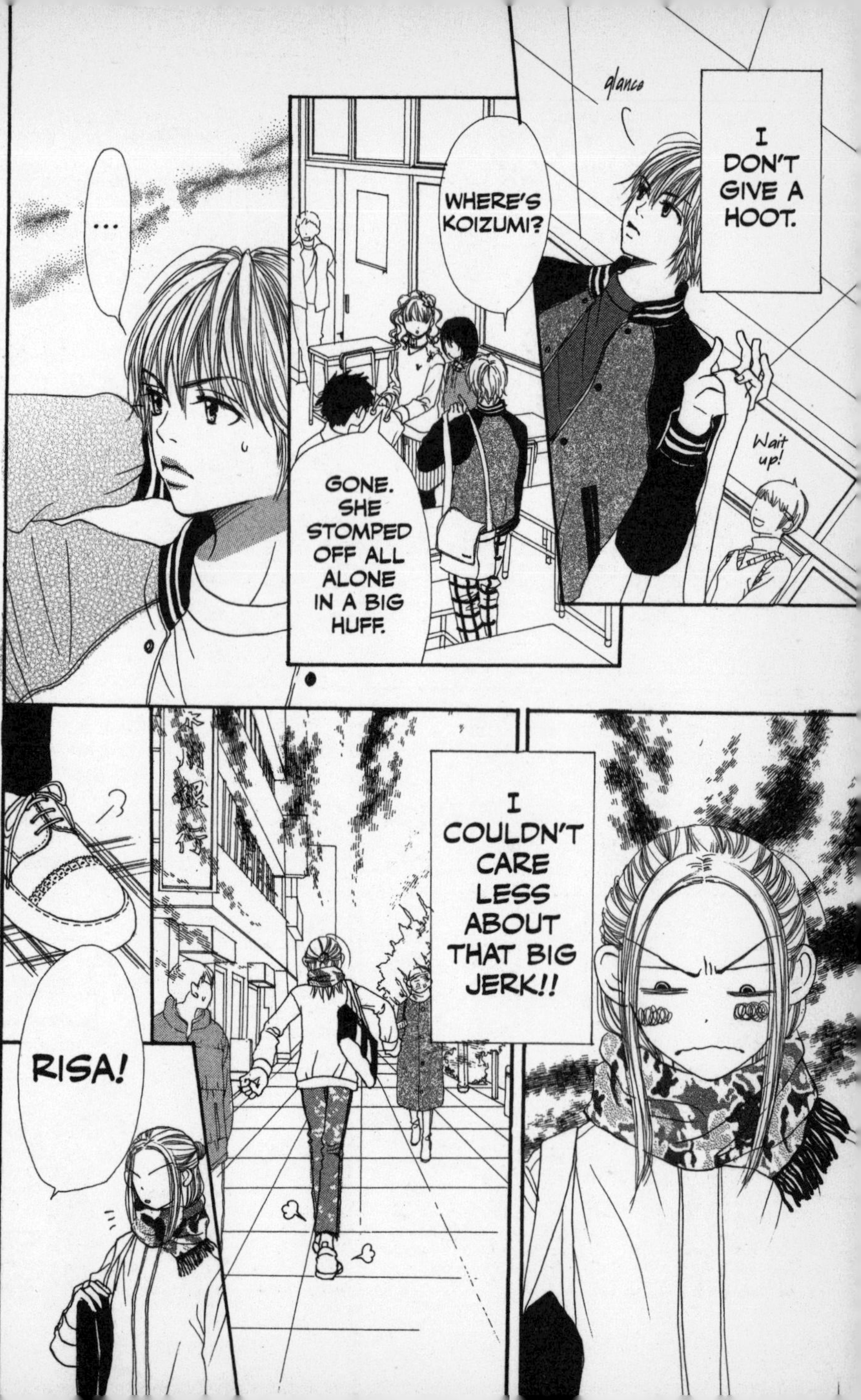

I DON'T GIVE A HOOT.
glance
Wait up!
WHERE'S KOIZUMI?
GONE. SHE STOMPED OFF ALL ALONE IN A BIG HUFF.
...
I COULDN'T CARE LESS ABOUT THAT BIG JERK!!
RISA!

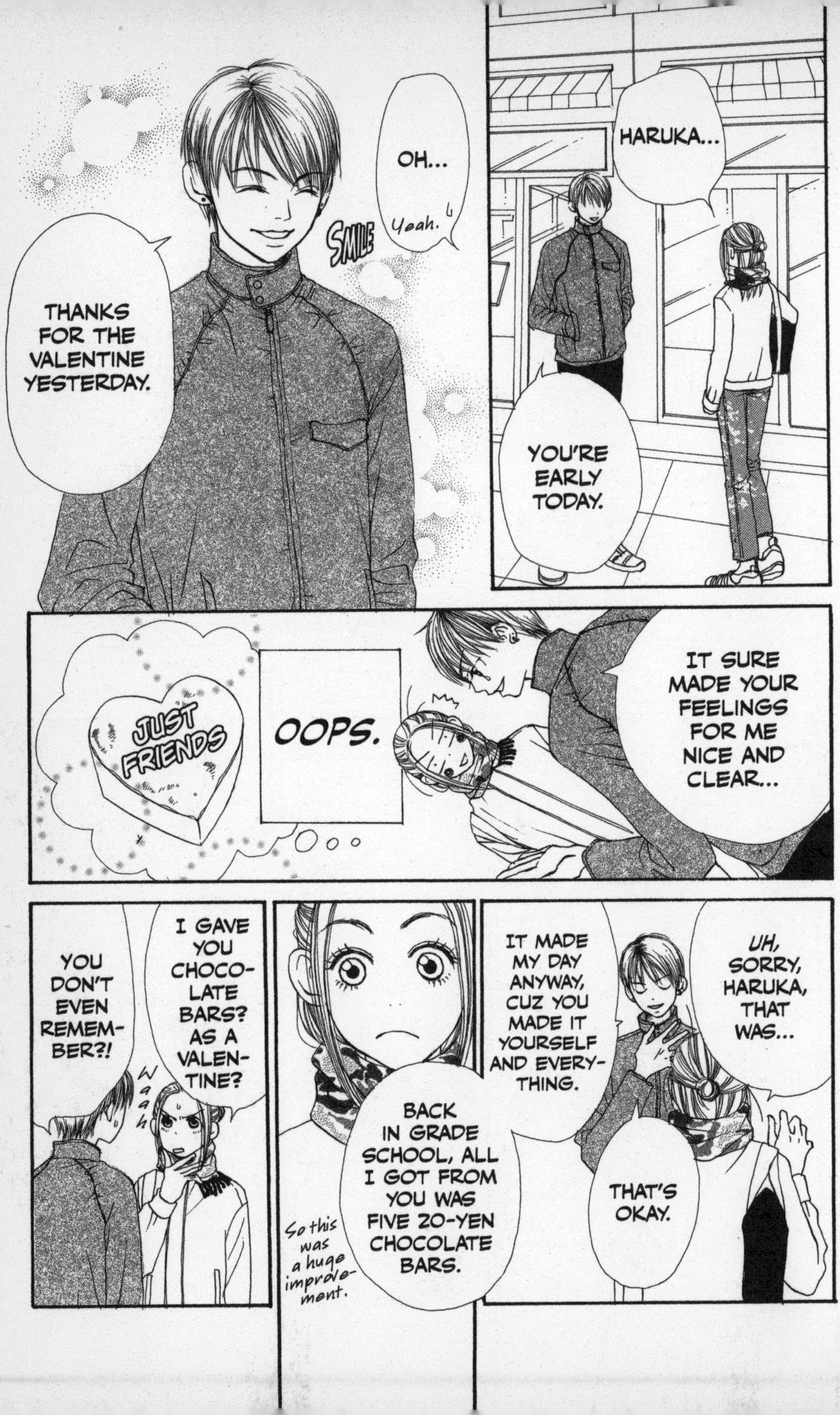
HARUKA...
YOU'RE EARLY TODAY.
OH... Yeah.
SMILE
THANKS FOR THE VALENTINE YESTERDAY.
IT SURE MADE YOUR FEELINGS FOR ME NICE AND CLEAR...
OOPS.
JUST FRIENDS
UH, SORRY, HARUKA, THAT WAS...
THAT'S OKAY.
IT MADE MY DAY ANYWAY, CUZ YOU MADE IT YOURSELF AND EVERYTHING.
BACK IN GRADE SCHOOL, ALL I GOT FROM YOU WAS FIVE 20-YEN CHOCOLATE BARS.
So this was a huge improvement.
I GAVE YOU CHOCOLATE BARS? AS A VALENTINE?
YOU DON'T EVEN REMEMBER?!
Waah

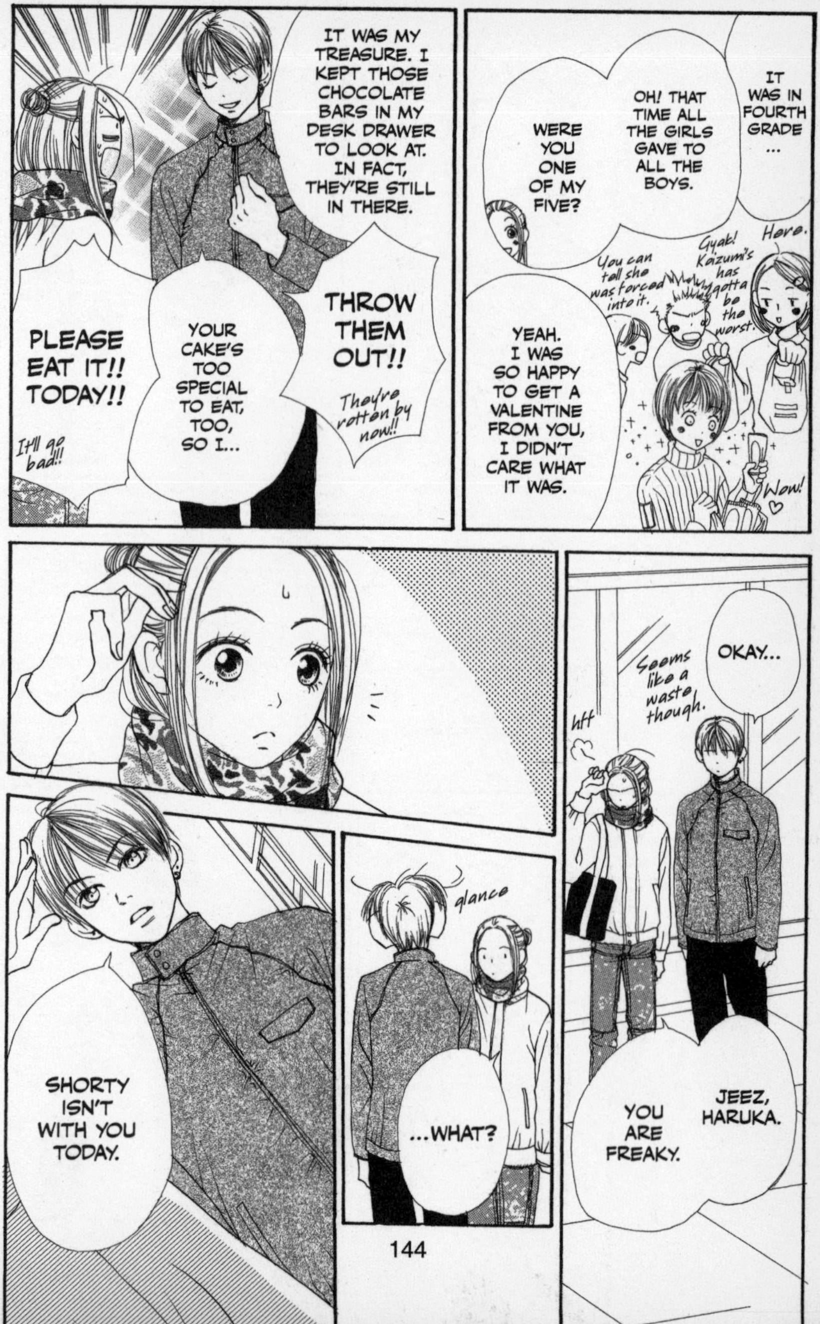
IT WAS IN FOURTH GRADE ...
OH! THAT TIME ALL THE GIRLS GAVE TO ALL THE BOYS.
WERE YOU ONE OF MY FIVE?
Here.
Gyak! Kazumi's has gotta be the worst.
You can tell she was forced into it.
Wow!
YEAH. I WAS SO HAPPY TO GET A VALENTINE FROM YOU, I DIDN'T CARE WHAT IT WAS.
IT WAS MY TREASURE. I KEPT THOSE CHOCOLATE BARS IN MY DESK DRAWER TO LOOK AT. IN FACT, THEY'RE STILL IN THERE.
THROW THEM OUT!!
They're rotten by now!!
YOUR CAKE'S TOO SPECIAL TO EAT, TOO, SO I...
PLEASE EAT IT!! TODAY!!
It'll go bad!!
OKAY...
Seems like a waste though.
hff
JEEZ, HARUKA.
YOU ARE FREAKY.
glance
...WHAT?
SHORTY ISN'T WITH YOU TODAY.

4.

Errrm...

This is the last one.
My apologies to those of you who're bothering to read this.
Why can't I think of anything more interesting to write...?

Well, I really hope I get to meet you all again in Vol. 3.

All's well that ends well!
Thank you for your patience!

Aya

2002. 6

Special thanks to...

Rumiko Sawada
Nana Ikebe
Mimi Murai
Ikuko Matsuo
Etsuko Yamamoto
Aki Nakahara

and
you

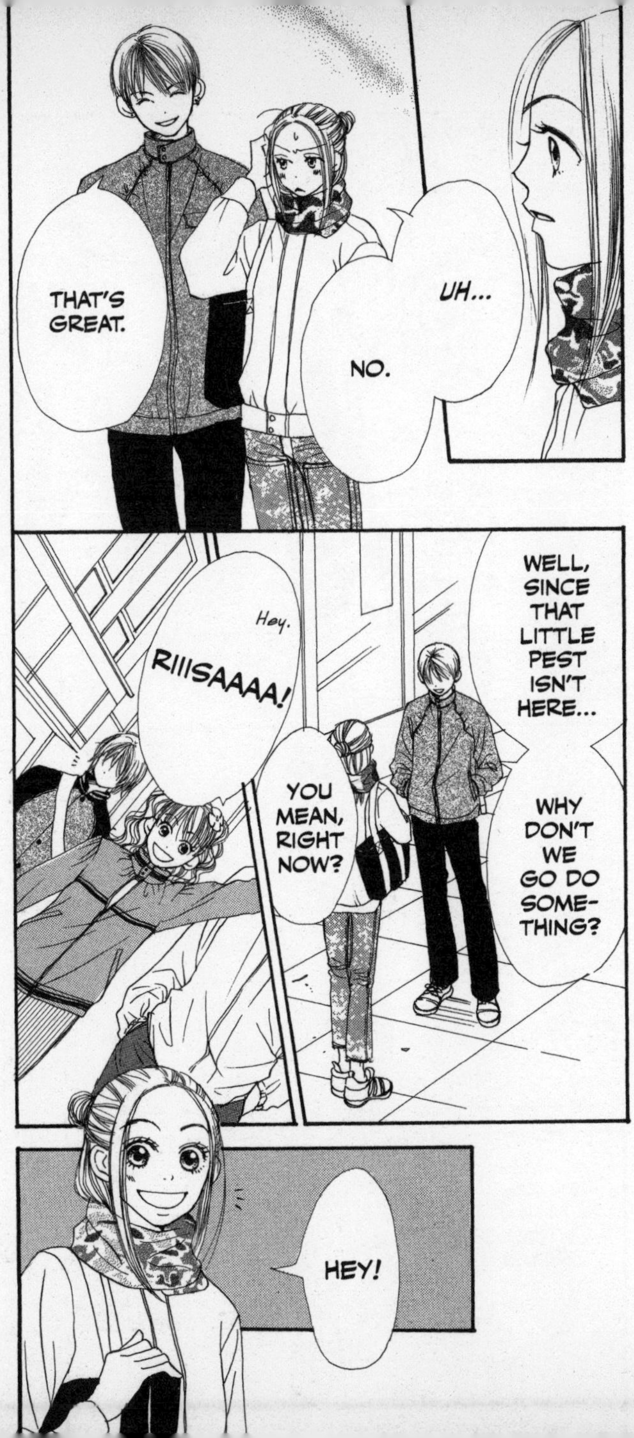

UH...
NO.
THAT'S GREAT.
WELL, SINCE THAT LITTLE PEST ISN'T HERE...
WHY DON'T WE GO DO SOMETHING?
YOU MEAN, RIGHT NOW?
Hey.
RIIISAAAAA!
HEY!

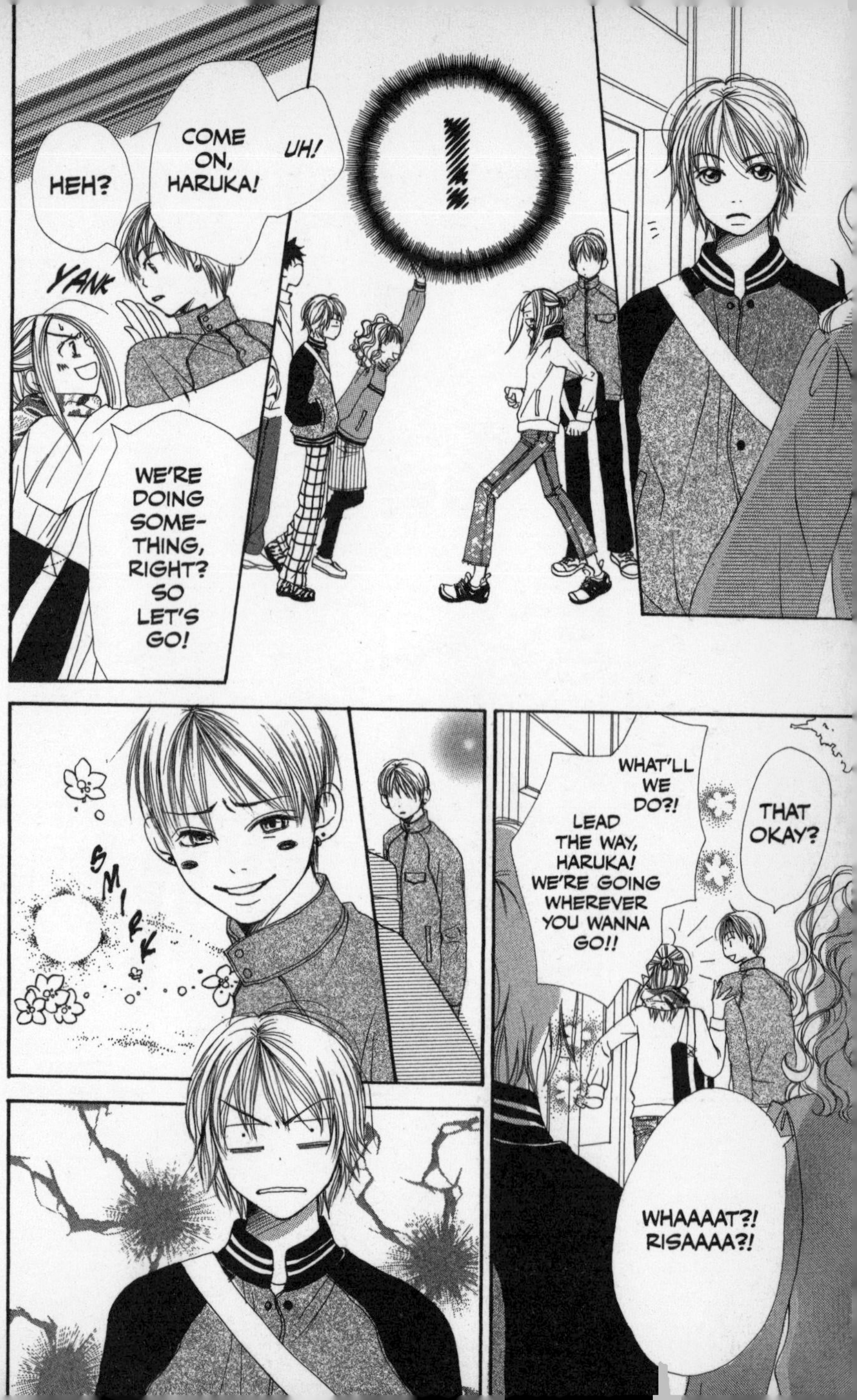
!
UH!
COME ON, HARUKA!
HEH?
YANK
WE'RE DOING SOME-THING, RIGHT? SO LET'S GO!
THAT OKAY?
WHAT'LL WE DO?!
LEAD THE WAY, HARUKA! WE'RE GOING WHEREVER YOU WANNA GO!!
WHAAAAT?! RISAAAA?!
SMIRK

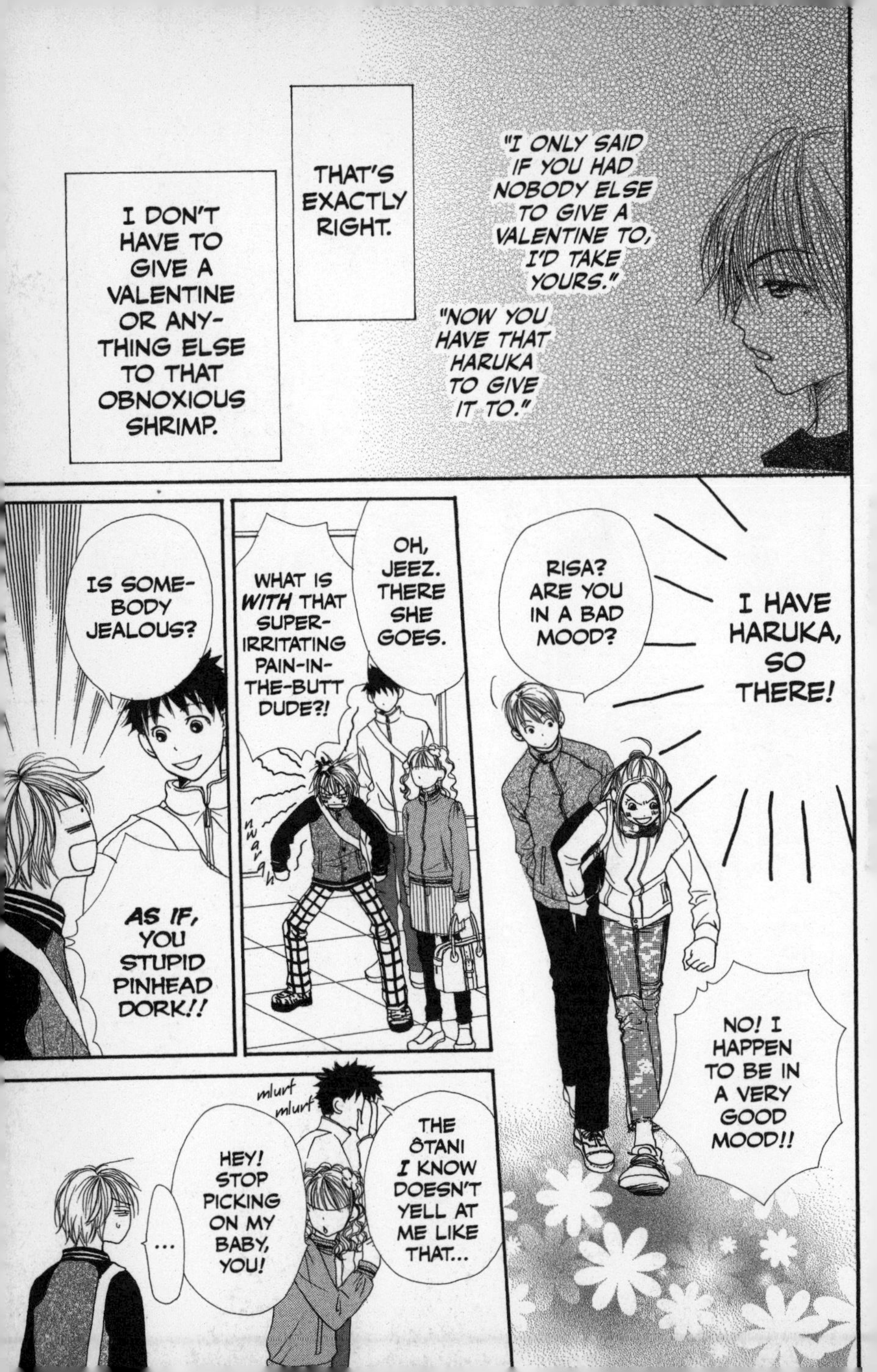
"I ONLY SAID IF YOU HAD NOBODY ELSE TO GIVE A VALENTINE TO, I'D TAKE YOURS."
"NOW YOU HAVE THAT HARUKA TO GIVE IT TO."
THAT'S EXACTLY RIGHT.
I DON'T HAVE TO GIVE A VALENTINE OR ANY-THING ELSE TO THAT OBNOXIOUS SHRIMP.
I HAVE HARUKA, SO THERE!
RISA? ARE YOU IN A BAD MOOD?
NO! I HAPPEN TO BE IN A VERY GOOD MOOD!!
OH, JEEZ. THERE SHE GOES.
WHAT IS *WITH* THAT SUPER-IRRITATING PAIN-IN-THE-BUTT DUDE?!
nwaaah
IS SOME-BODY JEALOUS?
AS IF, YOU STUPID PINHEAD DORK!!
THE ŌTANI *I* KNOW DOESN'T YELL AT ME LIKE THAT...
mlurf mlurf
HEY! STOP PICKING ON MY BABY, YOU!
...

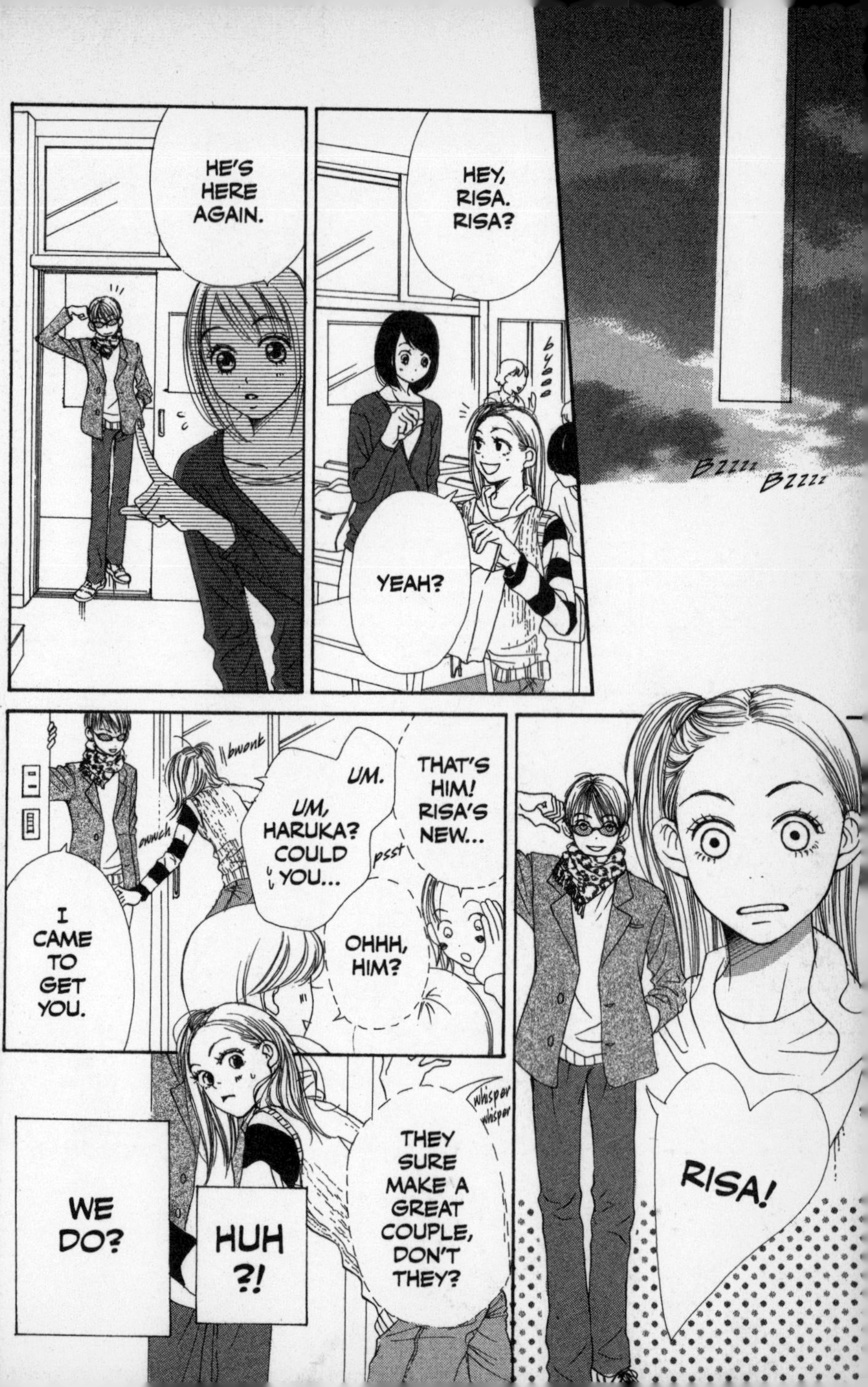
Bzzzz
Bzzzz
HEY, RISA. RISA?
YEAH?
HE'S HERE AGAIN.
RISA!
THAT'S HIM! RISA'S NEW...
UM.
UM, HARUKA? COULD YOU...
psst
OHHH, HIM?
bwonk
I CAME TO GET YOU.
whisper whisper
THEY SURE MAKE A GREAT COUPLE, DON'T THEY?
HUH ?!
WE DO?

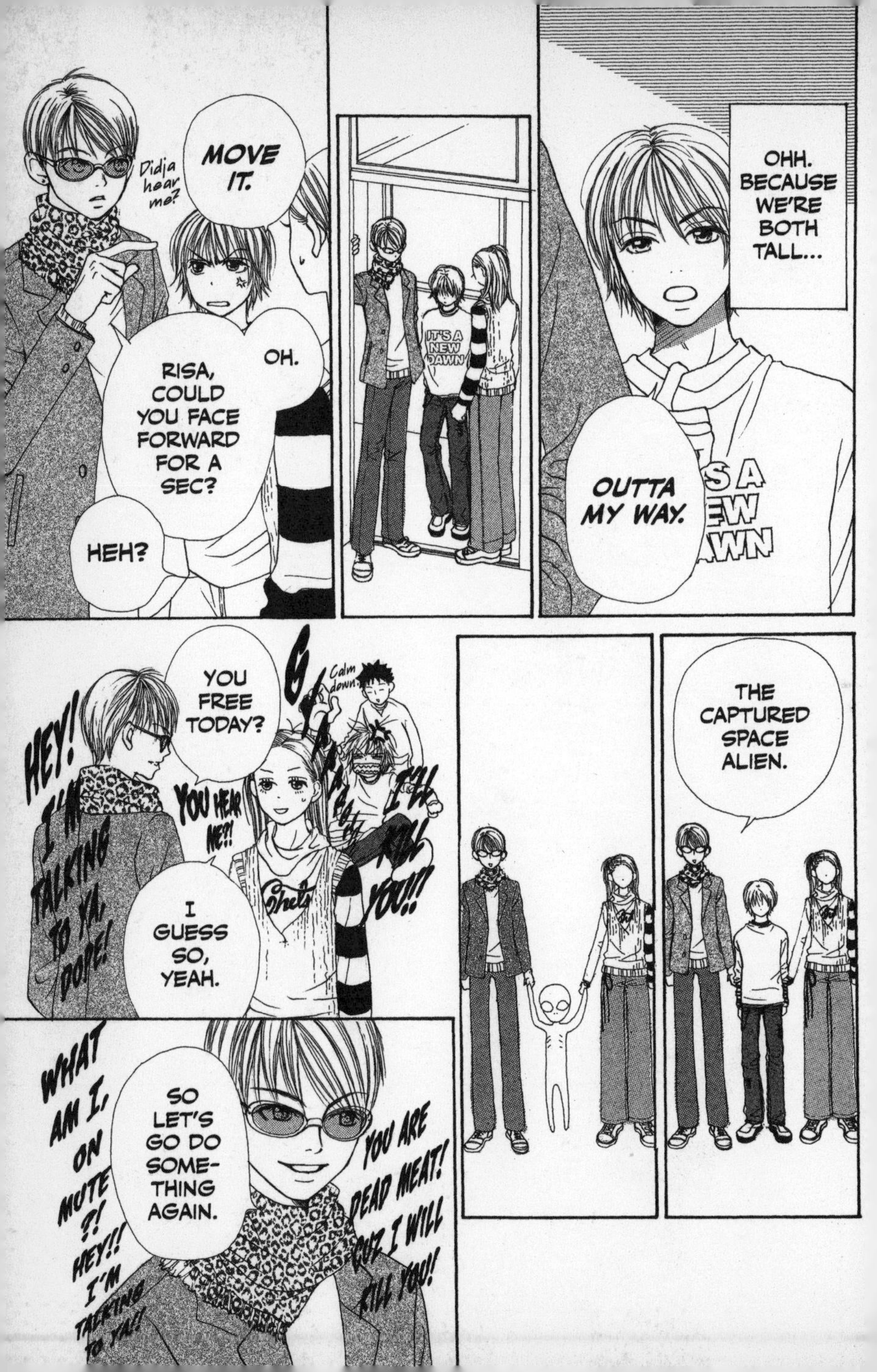
OHH. BECAUSE WE'RE BOTH TALL...
OUTTA MY WAY.
IT'S A NEW DAWN
MOVE IT.
Didja hear me?
OH.
RISA, COULD YOU FACE FORWARD FOR A SEC?
HEH?
THE CAPTURED SPACE ALIEN.
YOU FREE TODAY?
Calm down.
I'LL KILL YOU!!
YOU HEAR ME?!
HEY! I'M TALKING TO YA, DOPE!
I GUESS SO, YEAH.
SO LET'S GO DO SOME-THING AGAIN.
YOU ARE DEAD MEAT! CUZ I WILL KILL YOU!
WHAT AM I, ON MUTE?! HEY!! I'M TALKING TO YA!!

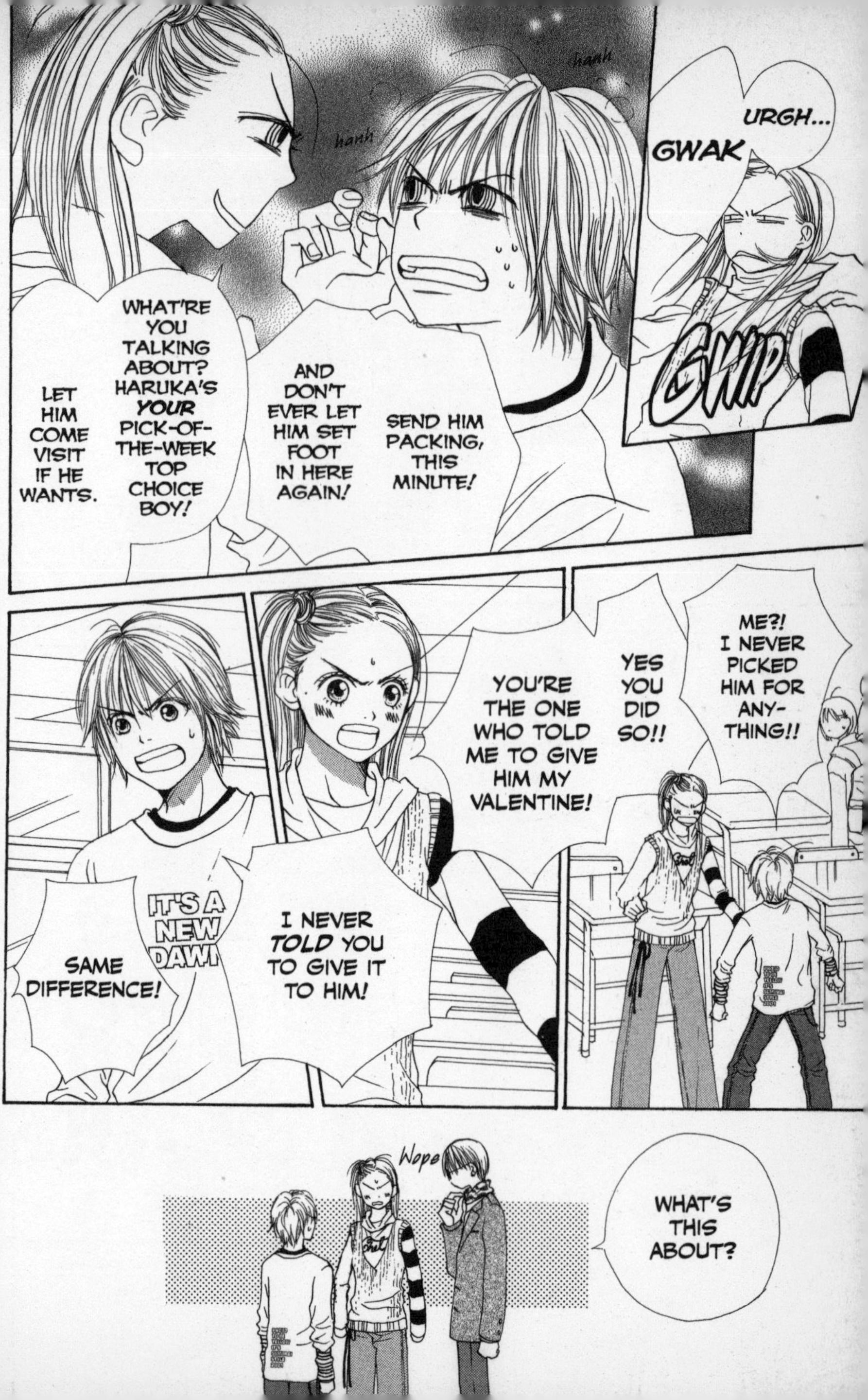
URGH...
GWAK
GWIP
hanh
hanh
SEND HIM PACKING, THIS MINUTE!
AND DON'T EVER LET HIM SET FOOT IN HERE AGAIN!
WHAT'RE YOU TALKING ABOUT? HARUKA'S *YOUR* PICK-OF-THE-WEEK TOP CHOICE BOY!
LET HIM COME VISIT IF HE WANTS.
ME?! I NEVER PICKED HIM FOR ANY-THING!!
YES YOU DID SO!!
YOU'RE THE ONE WHO TOLD ME TO GIVE HIM MY VALENTINE!
I NEVER *TOLD* YOU TO GIVE IT TO HIM!
SAME DIFFERENCE!
WHAT'S THIS ABOUT?
Wope

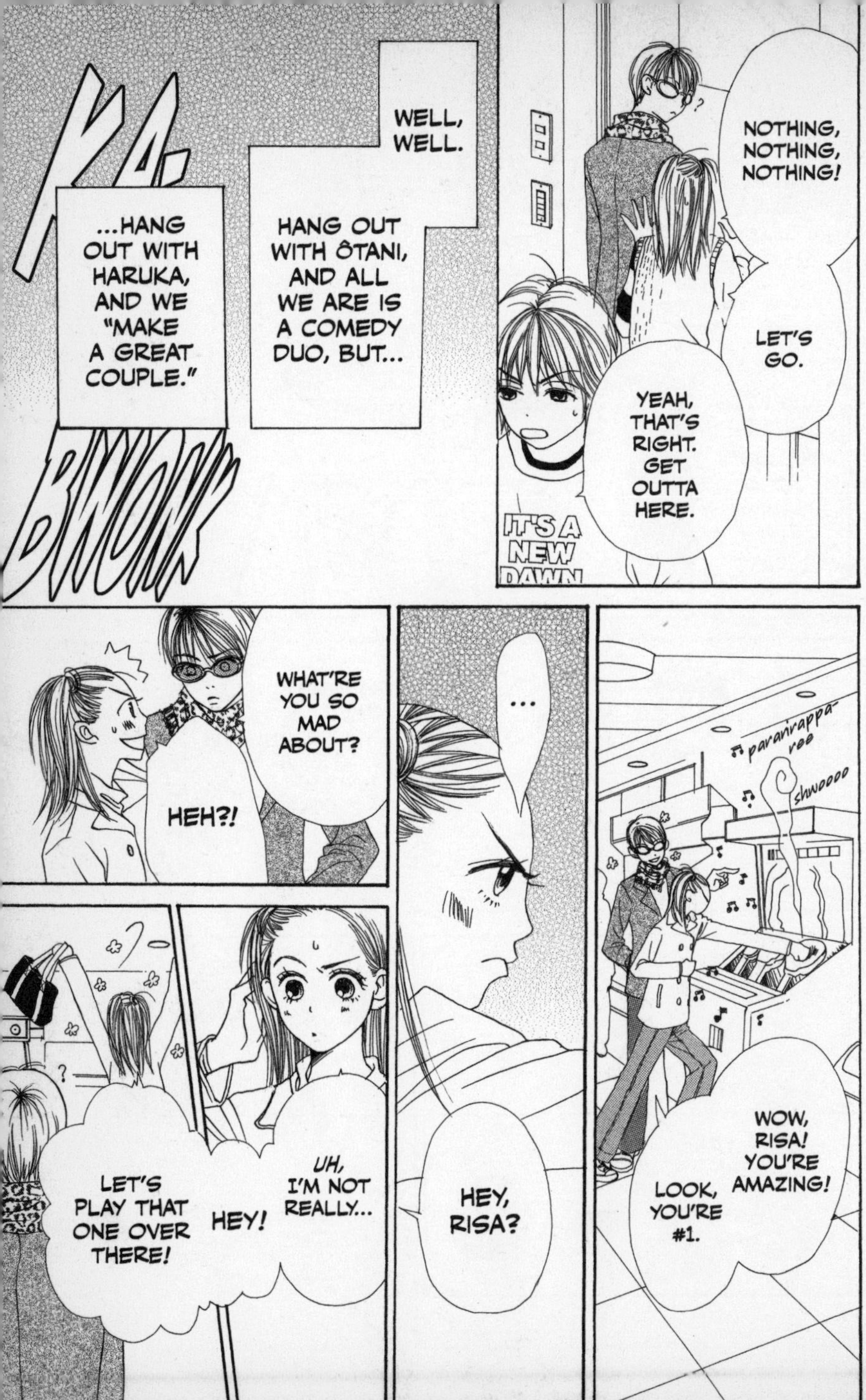
NOTHING, NOTHING, NOTHING!
LET'S GO.
YEAH, THAT'S RIGHT. GET OUTTA HERE.
IT'S A NEW DAWN
WELL, WELL.
HANG OUT WITH ÔTANI, AND ALL WE ARE IS A COMEDY DUO, BUT...
...HANG OUT WITH HARUKA, AND WE "MAKE A GREAT COUPLE."
paranirappa-ree
shwoooo
WOW, RISA! YOU'RE AMAZING!
LOOK, YOU'RE #1.
...
HEY, RISA?
WHAT'RE YOU SO MAD ABOUT?
HEH?!
UH, I'M NOT REALLY...
HEY!
LET'S PLAY THAT ONE OVER THERE!

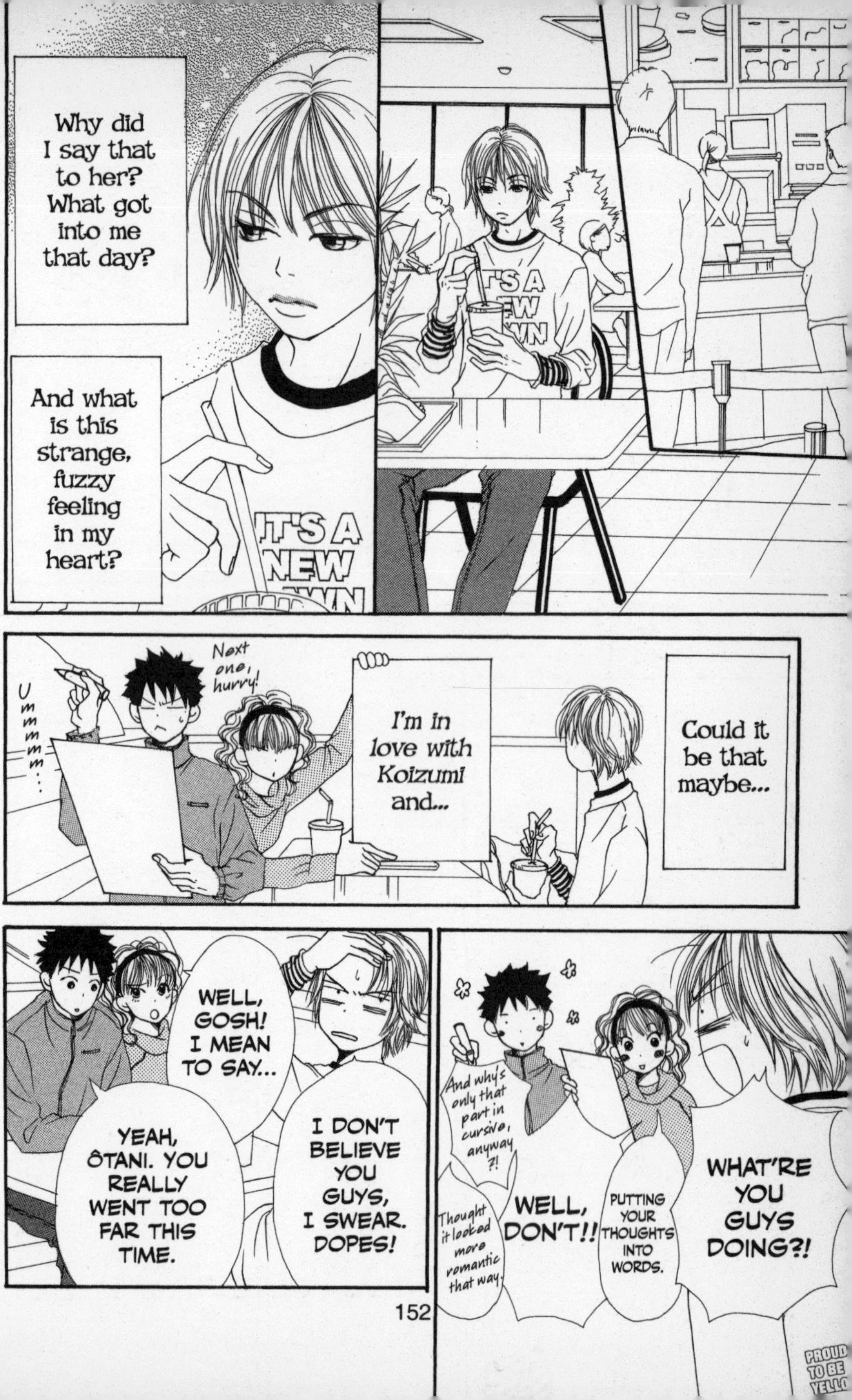
Why did I say that to her? What got into me that day?
And what is this strange, fuzzy feeling in my heart?
IT'S A NEW TOWN
Could it be that maybe...
I'm in love with Koizumi and...
Next one, hurry!
Ummmmm...
WHAT'RE YOU GUYS DOING?!
PUTTING YOUR THOUGHTS INTO WORDS.
WELL, DON'T!!
And why's only that part in cursive, anyway?!
Thought it looked more romantic that way.
WELL, GOSH! I MEAN TO SAY...
I DON'T BELIEVE YOU GUYS, I SWEAR. DOPES!
YEAH, OTANI. YOU REALLY WENT TOO FAR THIS TIME.

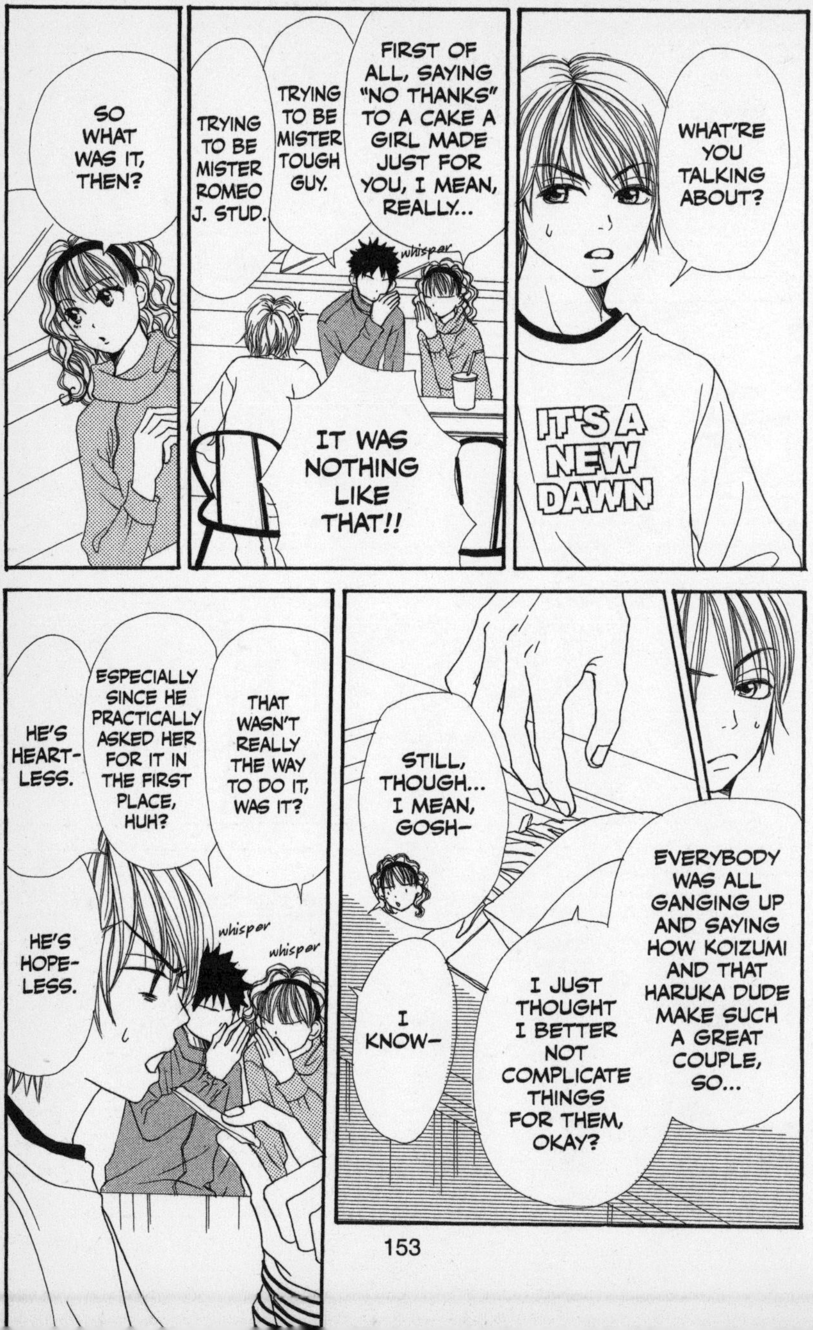
WHAT'RE YOU TALKING ABOUT?
IT'S A NEW DAWN
FIRST OF ALL, SAYING "NO THANKS" TO A CAKE A GIRL MADE JUST FOR YOU, I MEAN, REALLY...
whisper
TRYING TO BE MISTER TOUGH GUY.
TRYING TO BE MISTER ROMEO J. STUD.
IT WAS NOTHING LIKE THAT!!
SO WHAT WAS IT, THEN?
EVERYBODY WAS ALL GANGING UP AND SAYING HOW KOIZUMI AND THAT HARUKA DUDE MAKE SUCH A GREAT COUPLE, SO...
I JUST THOUGHT I BETTER NOT COMPLICATE THINGS FOR THEM, OKAY?
STILL, THOUGH... I MEAN, GOSH-
I KNOW-
THAT WASN'T REALLY THE WAY TO DO IT, WAS IT?
ESPECIALLY SINCE HE PRACTICALLY ASKED HER FOR IT IN THE FIRST PLACE, HUH?
HE'S HEART-LESS.
whisper
whisper
HE'S HOPE-LESS.

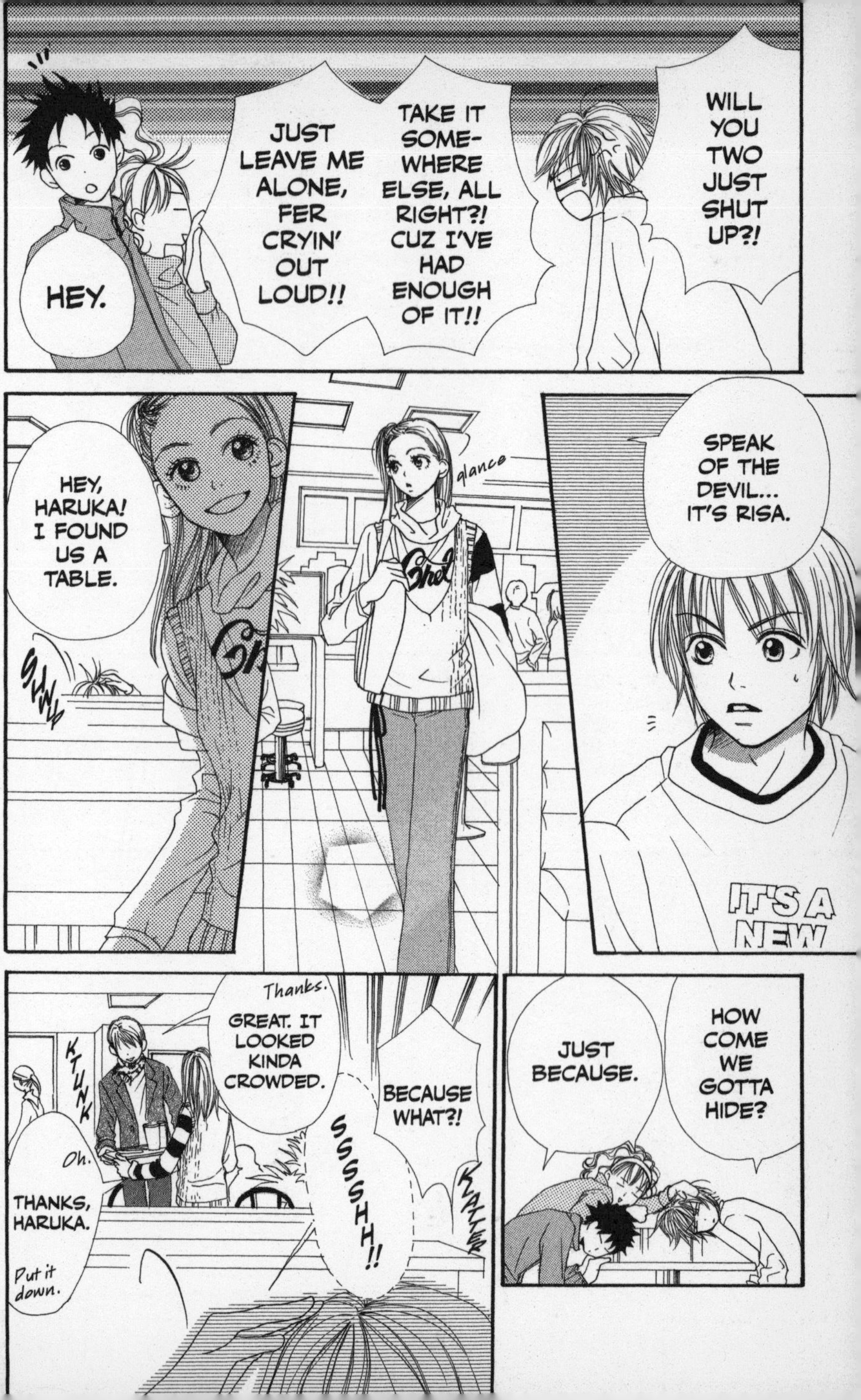
WILL YOU TWO JUST SHUT UP?!
TAKE IT SOMEWHERE ELSE, ALL RIGHT?! CUZ I'VE HAD ENOUGH OF IT!!
JUST LEAVE ME ALONE, FER CRYIN' OUT LOUD!!
HEY.
SPEAK OF THE DEVIL... IT'S RISA.
IT'S A NEW
glance
HEY, HARUKA! I FOUND US A TABLE.
HOW COME WE GOTTA HIDE?
JUST BECAUSE.
BECAUSE WHAT?!
KLATTER
Thanks.
GREAT. IT LOOKED KINDA CROWDED.
SSSSHH!!
KTUNK
Oh.
THANKS, HARUKA.
Put it down.

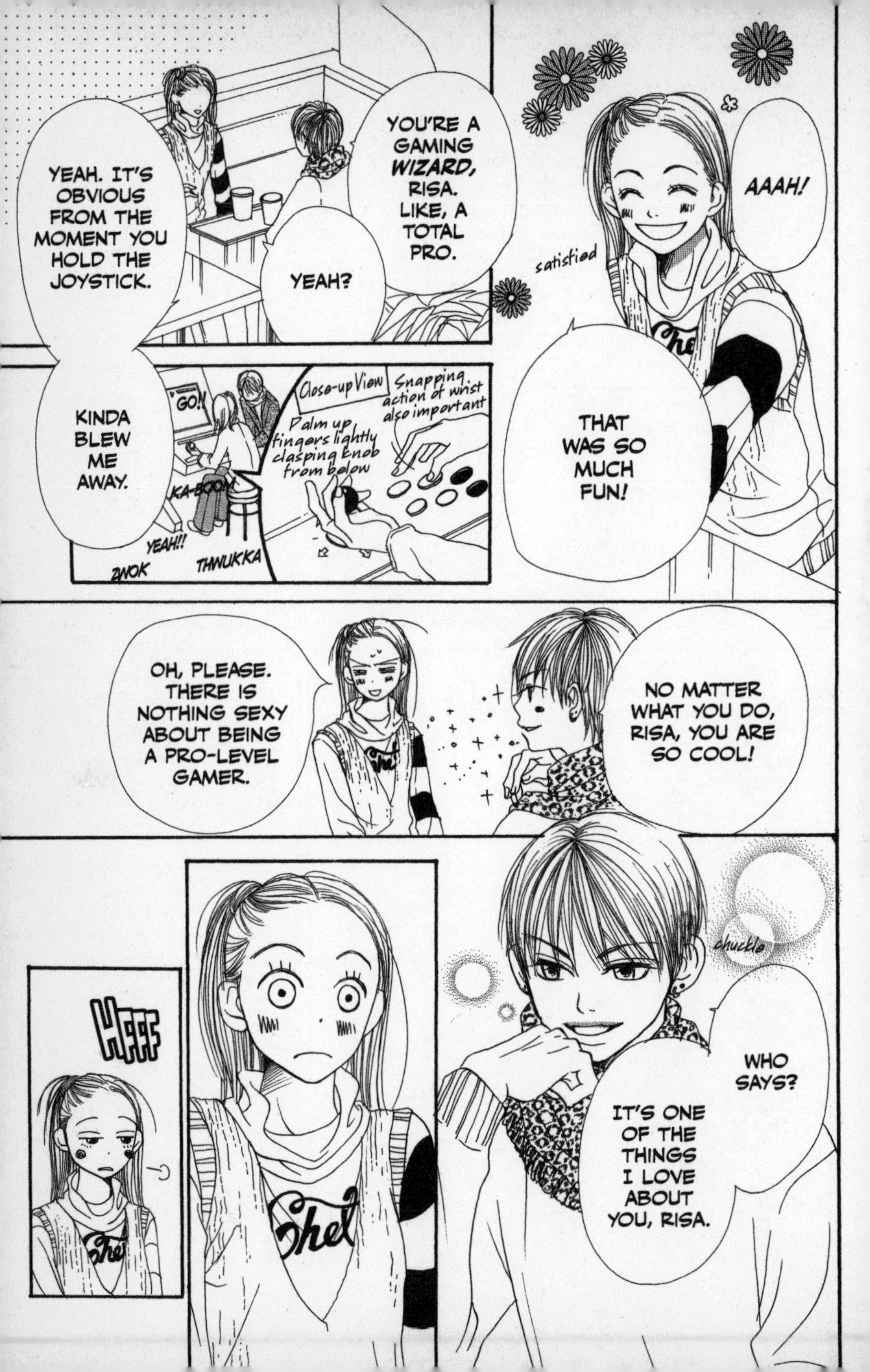
AAAH!
satisfied
THAT WAS SO MUCH FUN!
YOU'RE A GAMING WIZARD, RISA. LIKE, A TOTAL PRO.
YEAH?
YEAH. IT'S OBVIOUS FROM THE MOMENT YOU HOLD THE JOYSTICK.
Close-up View
Snapping action of wrist also important
Palm up fingers lightly clasping knob from below
KINDA BLEW ME AWAY.
GO!
KA-BOOM
YEAH!!
THWUKKA
ZWOK
NO MATTER WHAT YOU DO, RISA, YOU ARE SO COOL!
OH, PLEASE. THERE IS NOTHING SEXY ABOUT BEING A PRO-LEVEL GAMER.
chuckle
WHO SAYS?
IT'S ONE OF THE THINGS I LOVE ABOUT YOU, RISA.
HFFF

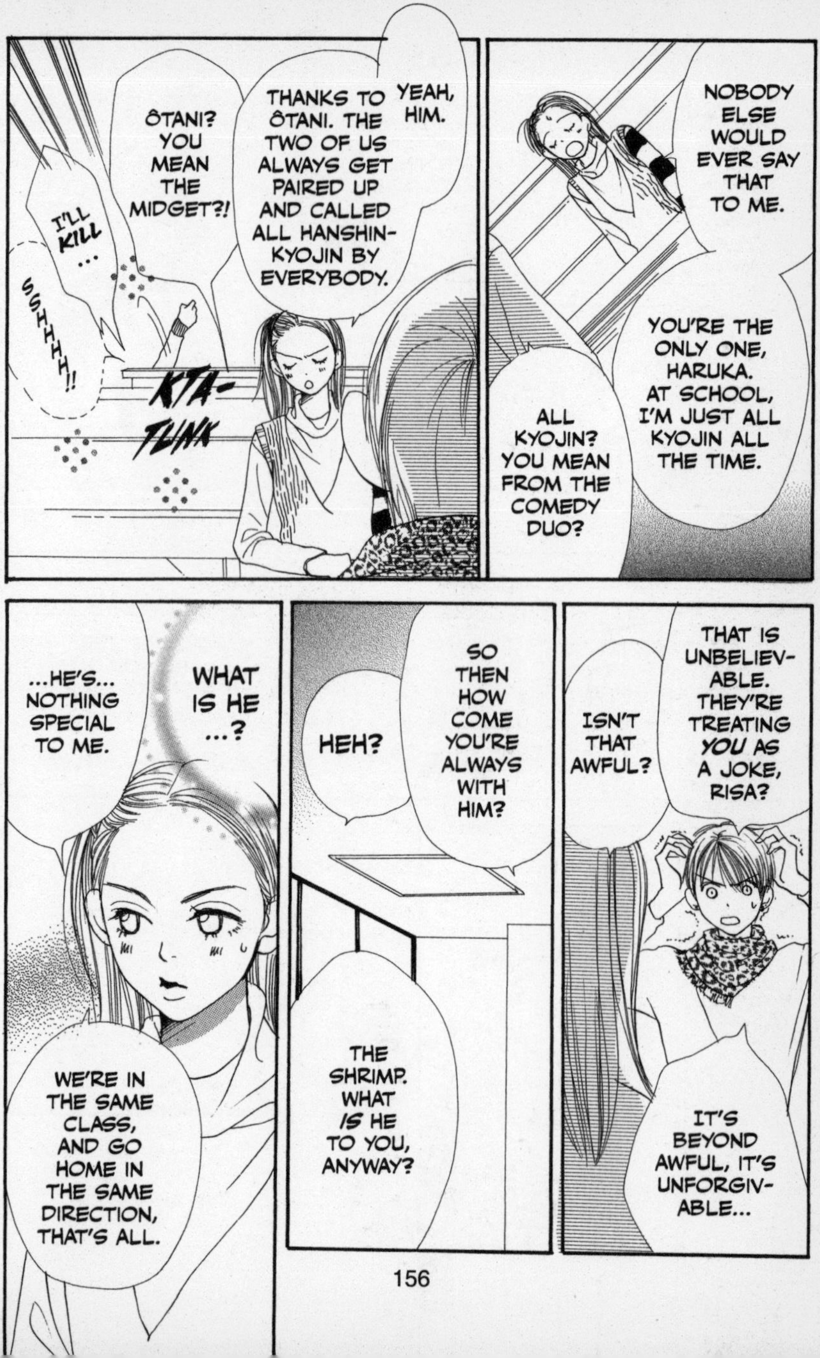
NOBODY ELSE WOULD EVER SAY THAT TO ME.
YOU'RE THE ONLY ONE, HARUKA. AT SCHOOL, I'M JUST ALL KYOJIN ALL THE TIME.
ALL KYOJIN? YOU MEAN FROM THE COMEDY DUO?
YEAH, HIM.
THANKS TO ŌTANI. THE TWO OF US ALWAYS GET PAIRED UP AND CALLED ALL HANSHIN-KYOJIN BY EVERYBODY.
ŌTANI? YOU MEAN THE MIDGET?!
I'LL KILL ...
SSHHHH!!
KTA-TUNK
THAT IS UNBELIEV-ABLE. THEY'RE TREATING *YOU* AS A JOKE, RISA?
ISN'T THAT AWFUL?
IT'S BEYOND AWFUL, IT'S UNFORGIV-ABLE...
SO THEN HOW COME YOU'RE ALWAYS WITH HIM?
HEH?
THE SHRIMP. WHAT *IS* HE TO YOU, ANYWAY?
WHAT IS HE ...?
...HE'S... NOTHING SPECIAL TO ME.
WE'RE IN THE SAME CLASS, AND GO HOME IN THE SAME DIRECTION, THAT'S ALL.

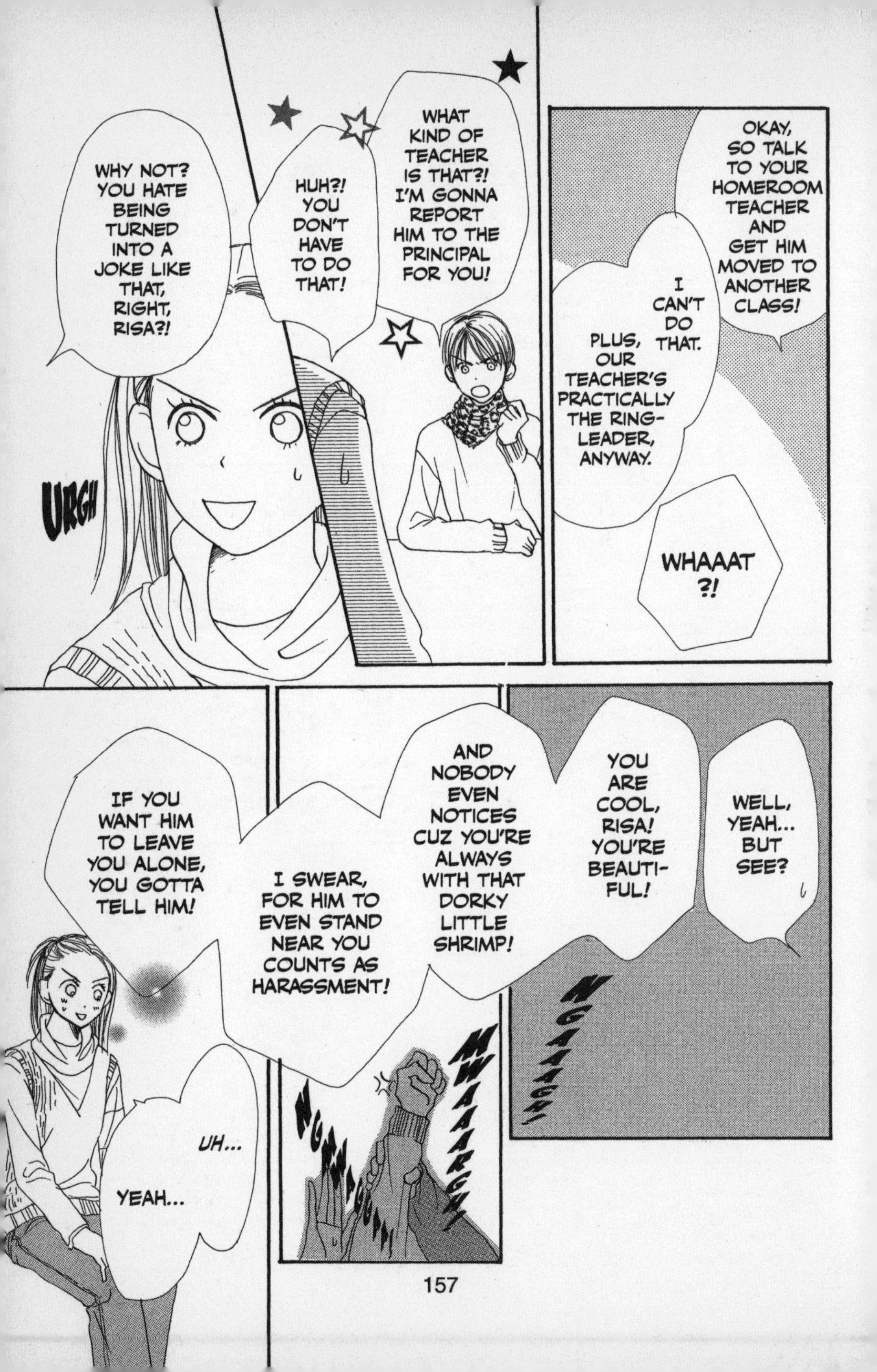
OKAY, SO TALK TO YOUR HOMEROOM TEACHER AND GET HIM MOVED TO ANOTHER CLASS!
I CAN'T DO THAT.
PLUS, OUR TEACHER'S PRACTICALLY THE RING-LEADER, ANYWAY.
WHAAAT?!
WHAT KIND OF TEACHER IS THAT?! I'M GONNA REPORT HIM TO THE PRINCIPAL FOR YOU!
HUH?! YOU DON'T HAVE TO DO THAT!
WHY NOT? YOU HATE BEING TURNED INTO A JOKE LIKE THAT, RIGHT, RISA?!
URGH
WELL, YEAH... BUT SEE?
YOU ARE COOL, RISA! YOU'RE BEAUTI-FUL!
AND NOBODY EVEN NOTICES CUZ YOU'RE ALWAYS WITH THAT DORKY LITTLE SHRIMP!
MGAAAAGH!
I SWEAR, FOR HIM TO EVEN STAND NEAR YOU COUNTS AS HARASSMENT!
MWAAAARGH!
IF YOU WANT HIM TO LEAVE YOU ALONE, YOU GOTTA TELL HIM!
UH...
YEAH...

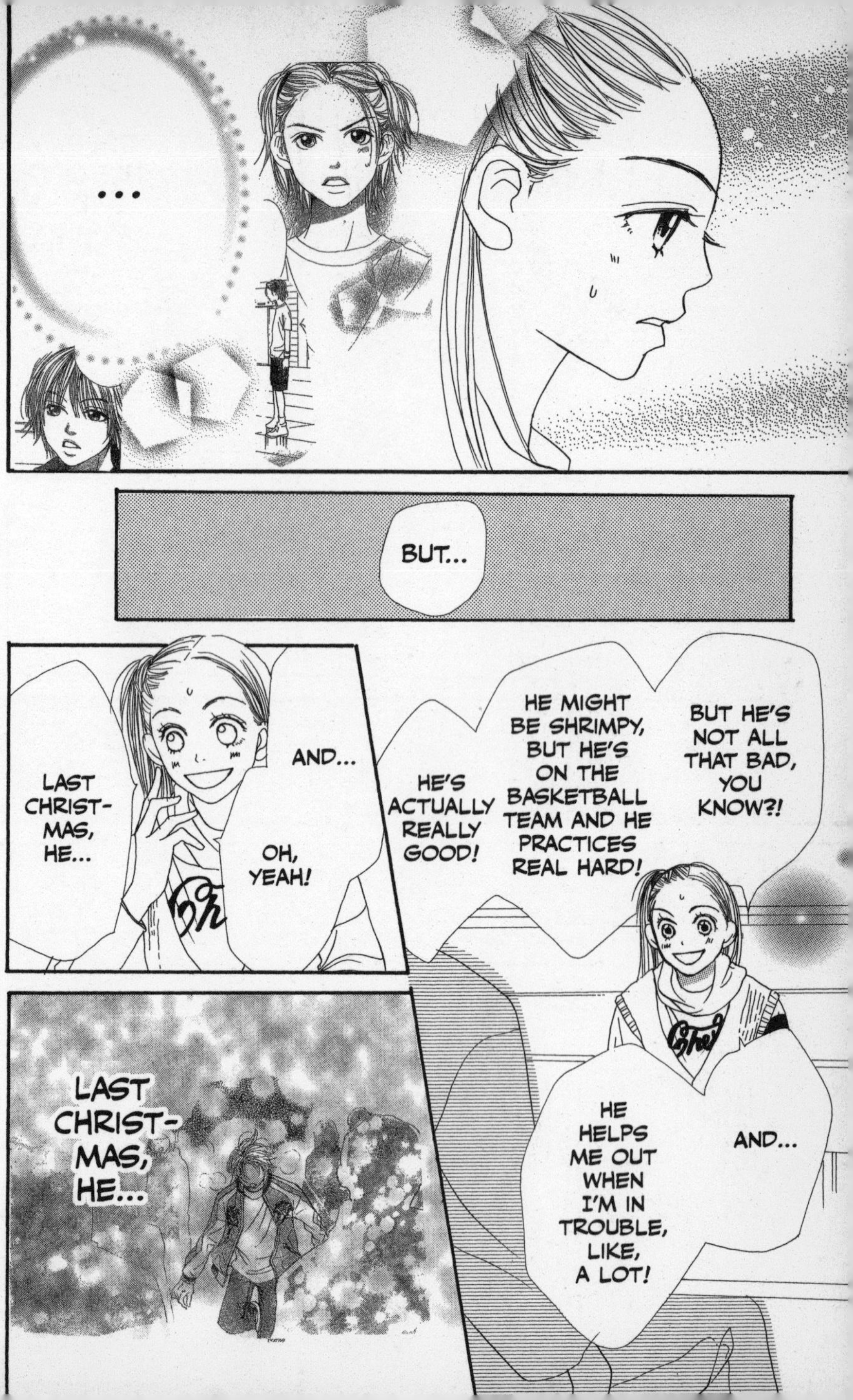
...
BUT...
BUT HE'S NOT ALL THAT BAD, YOU KNOW?!
HE MIGHT BE SHRIMPY, BUT HE'S ON THE BASKETBALL TEAM AND HE PRACTICES REAL HARD!
HE'S ACTUALLY REALLY GOOD!
HE HELPS ME OUT WHEN I'M IN TROUBLE, LIKE, A LOT!
AND...
AND...
OH, YEAH!
LAST CHRIST-MAS, HE...
LAST CHRIST-MAS, HE...

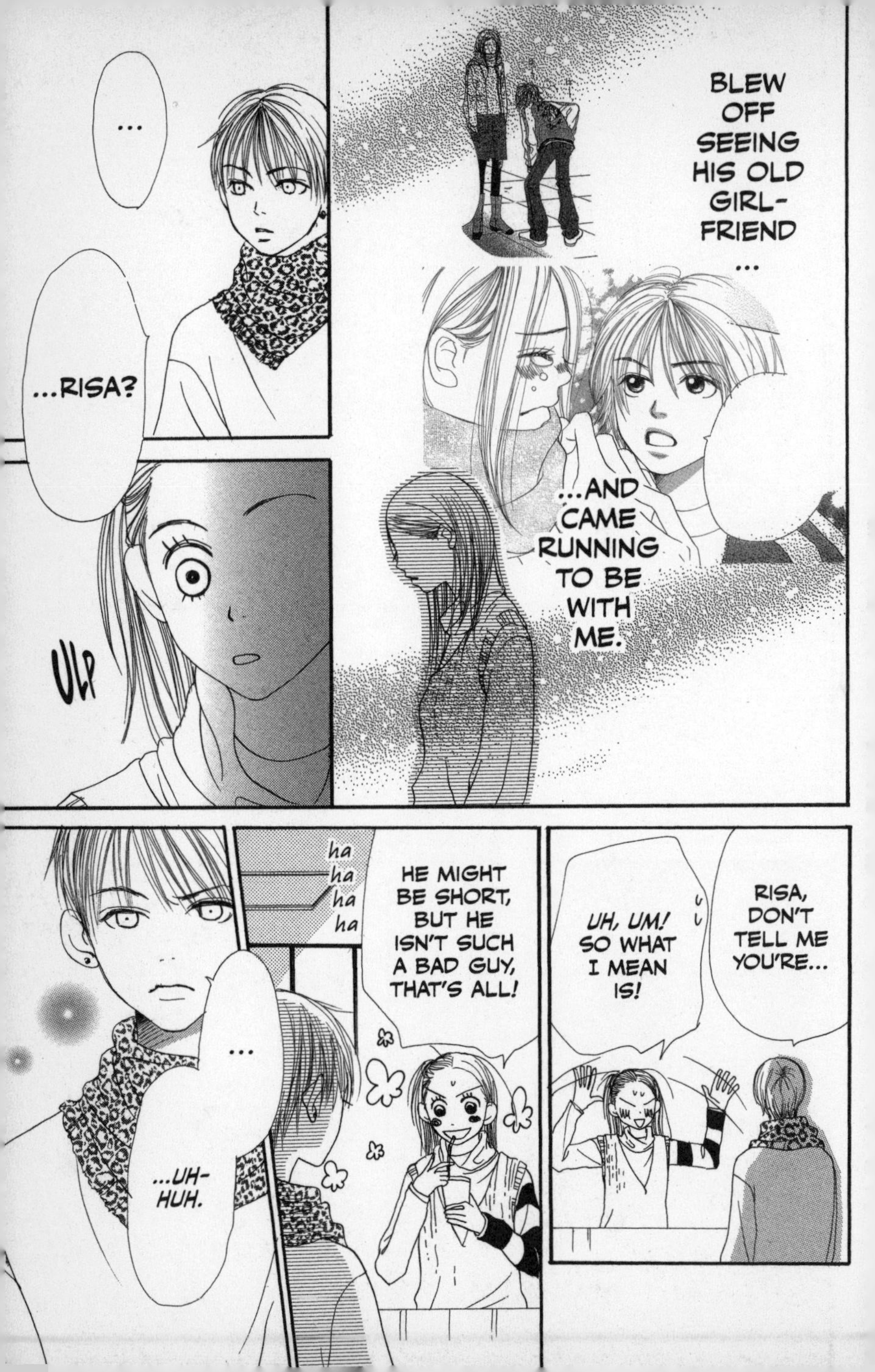
BLEW OFF SEEING HIS OLD GIRL-FRIEND...
...AND CAME RUNNING TO BE WITH ME.
...
...RISA?
ULP
RISA, DON'T TELL ME YOU'RE...
UH, UM! SO WHAT I MEAN IS!
HE MIGHT BE SHORT, BUT HE ISN'T SUCH A BAD GUY, THAT'S ALL!
ha ha ha ha
...
...UH-HUH.

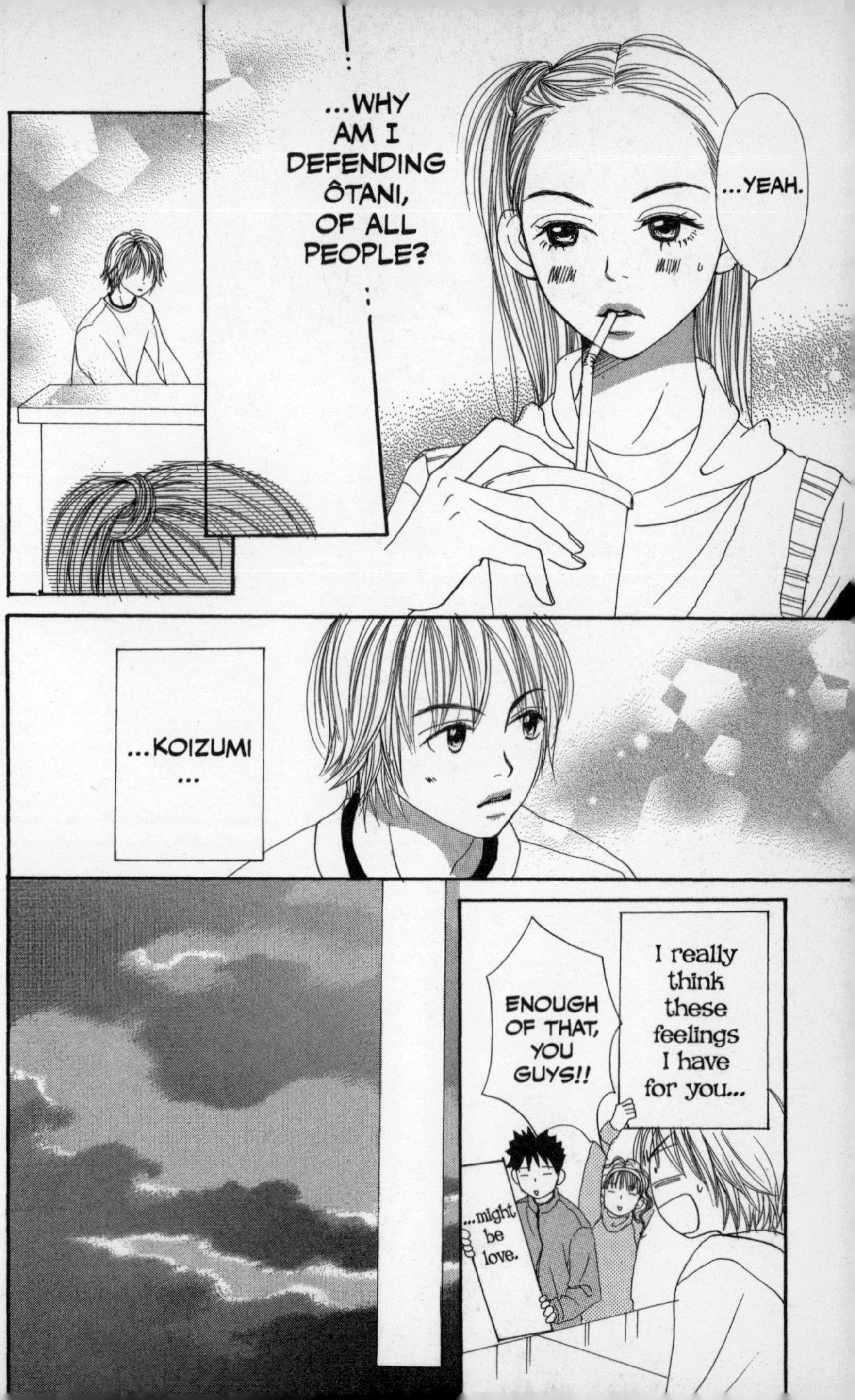
...YEAH.
...WHY AM I DEFENDING ÔTANI, OF ALL PEOPLE?
...KOIZUMI ...
I really think these feelings I have for you...
ENOUGH OF THAT, YOU GUYS!!
...might be love.

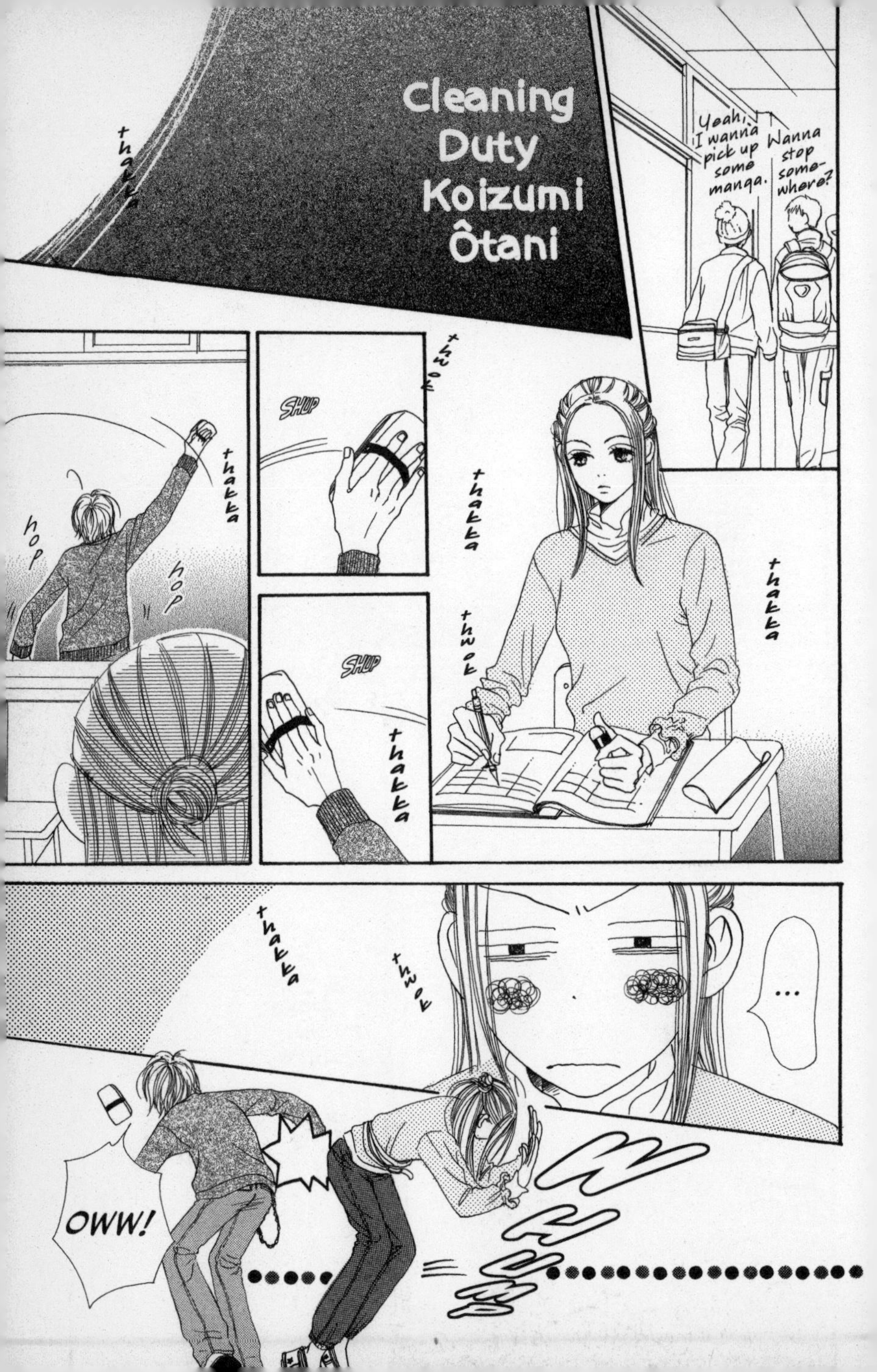

Wanna stop some-where?
Yeah, I wanna pick up some manga.
Cleaning Duty Koizumi Ôtani
thakka
thakka
thwok
thakka
thwok
SHUP
thakka
hop
hop
SHUP
thakka
...
thakka
thwok
WHUMP
OWW!

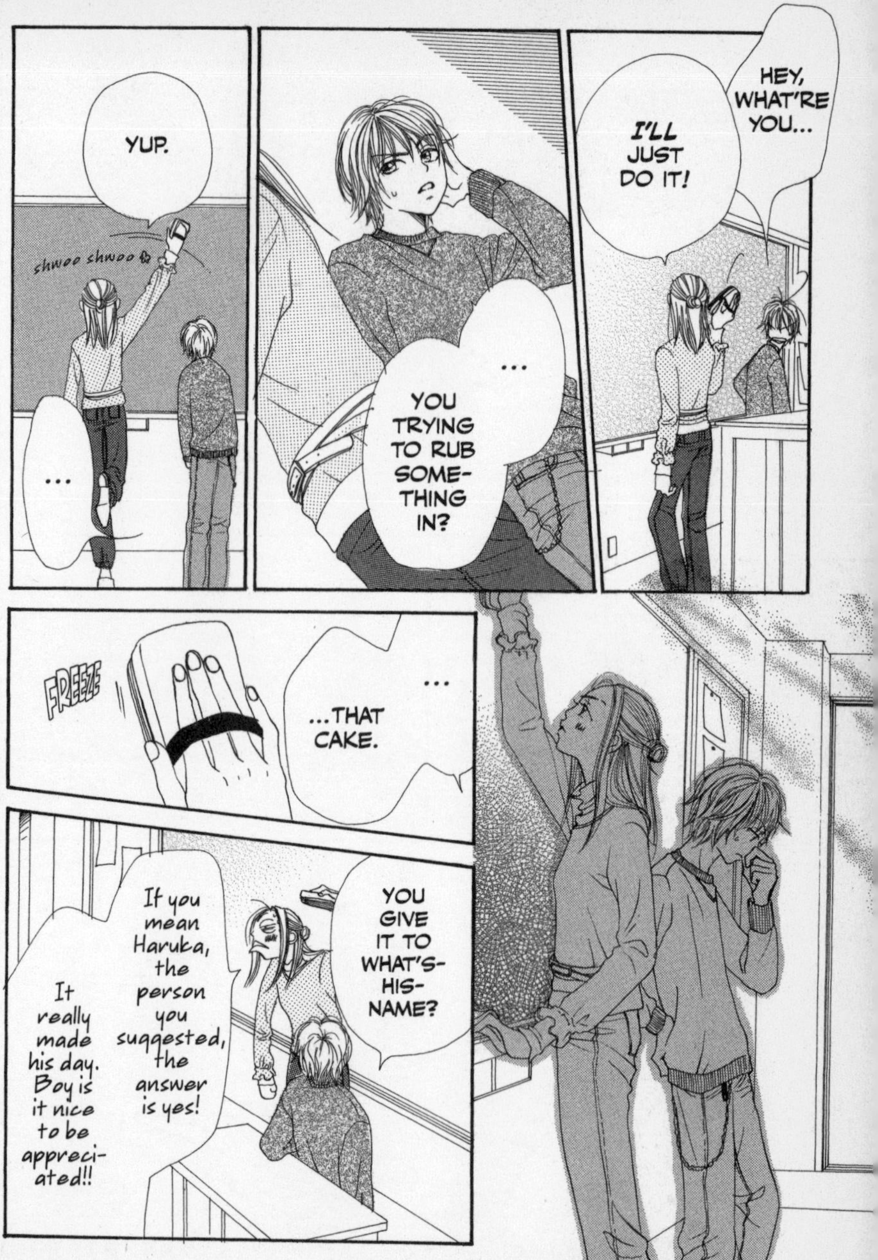
HEY, WHAT'RE YOU...
I'LL JUST DO IT!
...
YOU TRYING TO RUB SOME-THING IN?
YUP.
shwoo shwoo
...
...
...THAT CAKE.
FREEZE
YOU GIVE IT TO WHAT'S-HIS-NAME?
If you mean Haruka, the person you suggested, the answer is yes!
It really made his day. Boy is it nice to be appreciated!!

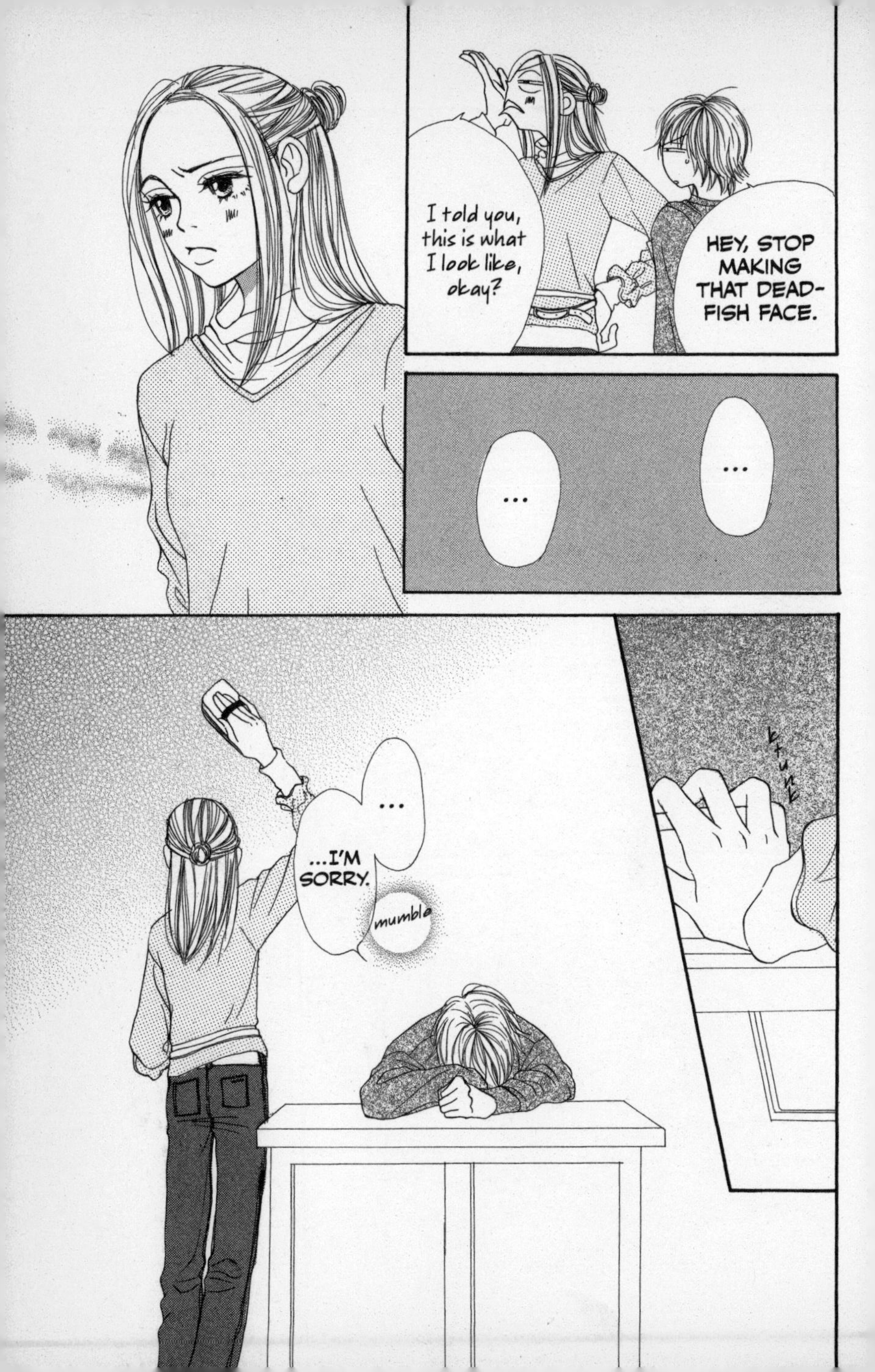
HEY, STOP MAKING THAT DEAD-FISH FACE.
I told you, this is what I look like, okay?
...
...
ktunk
...
...I'M SORRY.
mumble

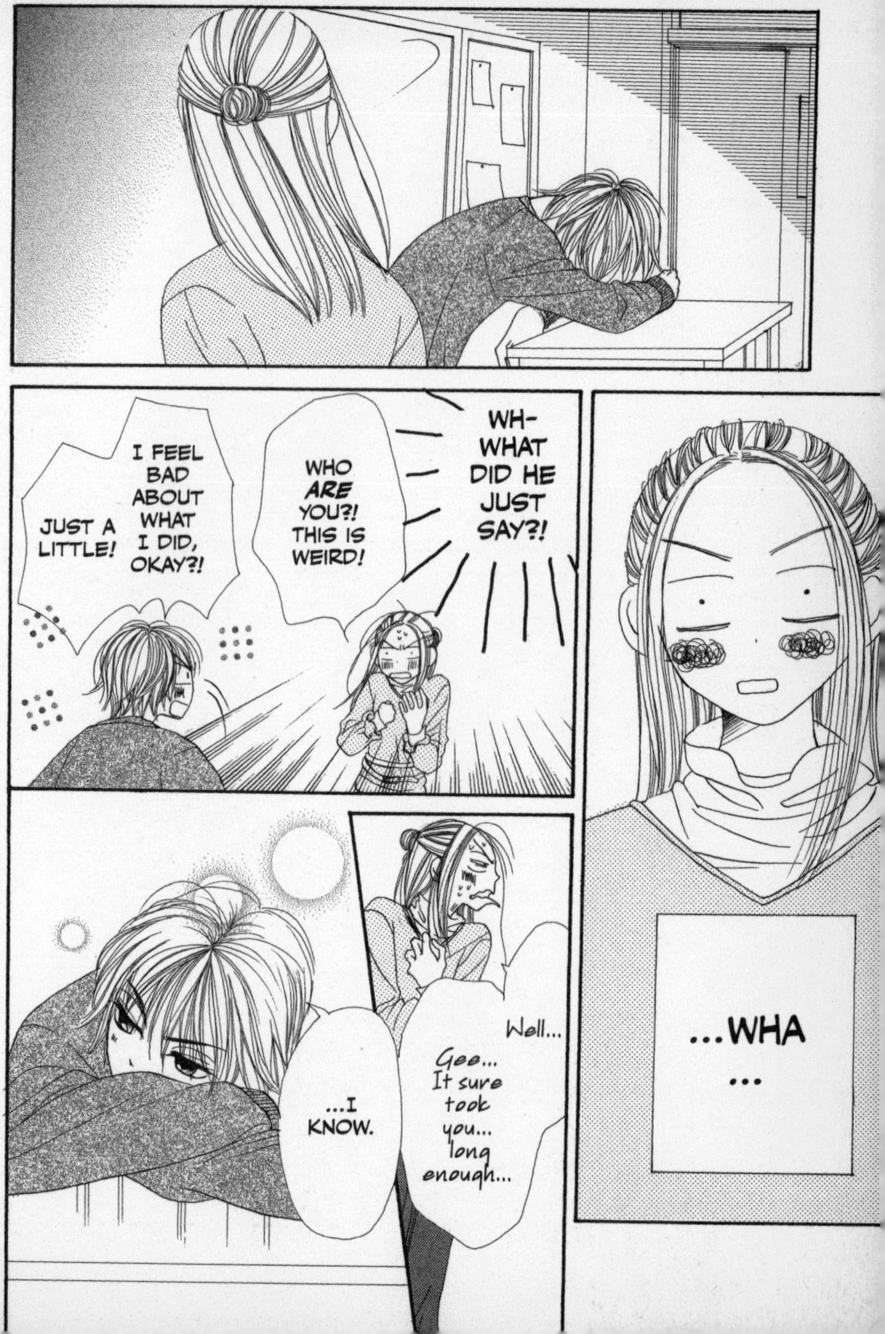
...WHA ...
WH- WHAT DID HE JUST SAY?!
WHO ARE YOU?! THIS IS WEIRD!
I FEEL BAD ABOUT WHAT I DID, OKAY?!
JUST A LITTLE!
Well...
Gee... It sure took you... long enough...
...I KNOW.

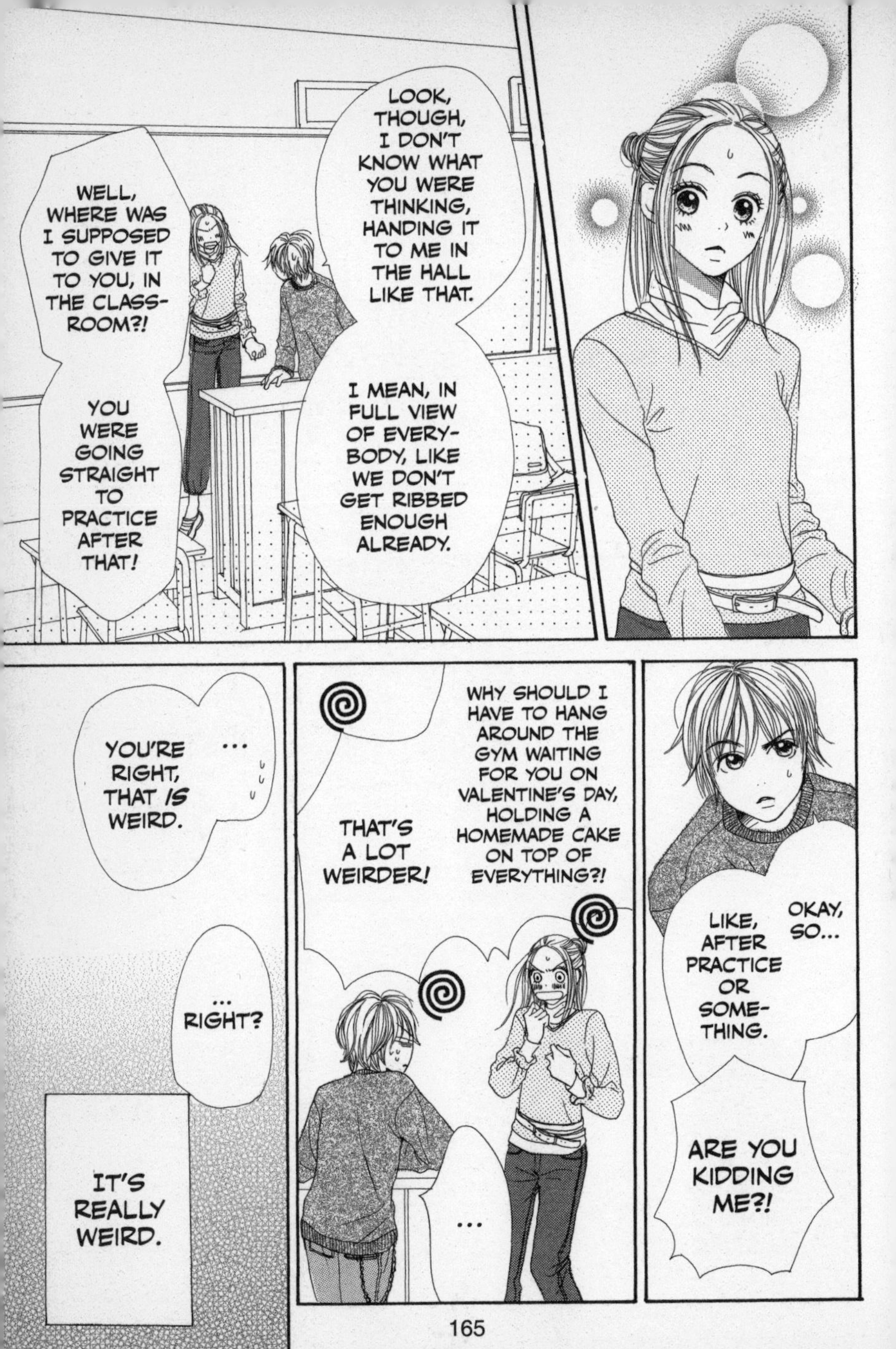
LOOK, THOUGH, I DON'T KNOW WHAT YOU WERE THINKING, HANDING IT TO ME IN THE HALL LIKE THAT.
I MEAN, IN FULL VIEW OF EVERY-BODY, LIKE WE DON'T GET RIBBED ENOUGH ALREADY.
WELL, WHERE WAS I SUPPOSED TO GIVE IT TO YOU, IN THE CLASS-ROOM?!
YOU WERE GOING STRAIGHT TO PRACTICE AFTER THAT!
OKAY, SO...
LIKE, AFTER PRACTICE OR SOME-THING.
ARE YOU KIDDING ME?!
WHY SHOULD I HAVE TO HANG AROUND THE GYM WAITING FOR YOU ON VALENTINE'S DAY, HOLDING A HOMEMADE CAKE ON TOP OF EVERYTHING?!
THAT'S A LOT WEIRDER!
...
...
YOU'RE RIGHT, THAT *IS* WEIRD.
...RIGHT?
IT'S REALLY WEIRD.

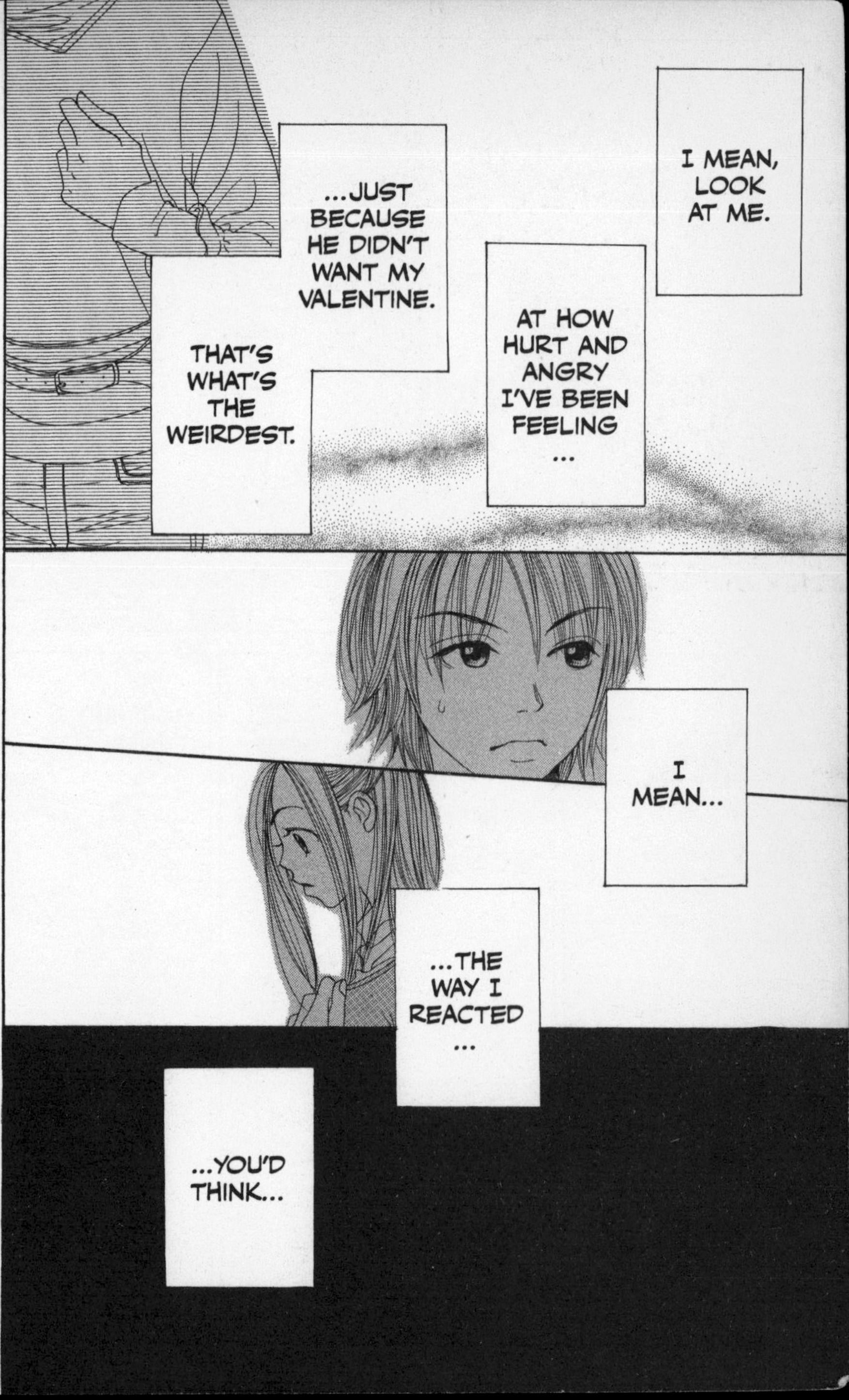
I MEAN, LOOK AT ME.
AT HOW HURT AND ANGRY I'VE BEEN FEELING ...
...JUST BECAUSE HE DIDN'T WANT MY VALENTINE.
THAT'S WHAT'S THE WEIRDEST.
I MEAN...
...THE WAY I REACTED ...
...YOU'D THINK...

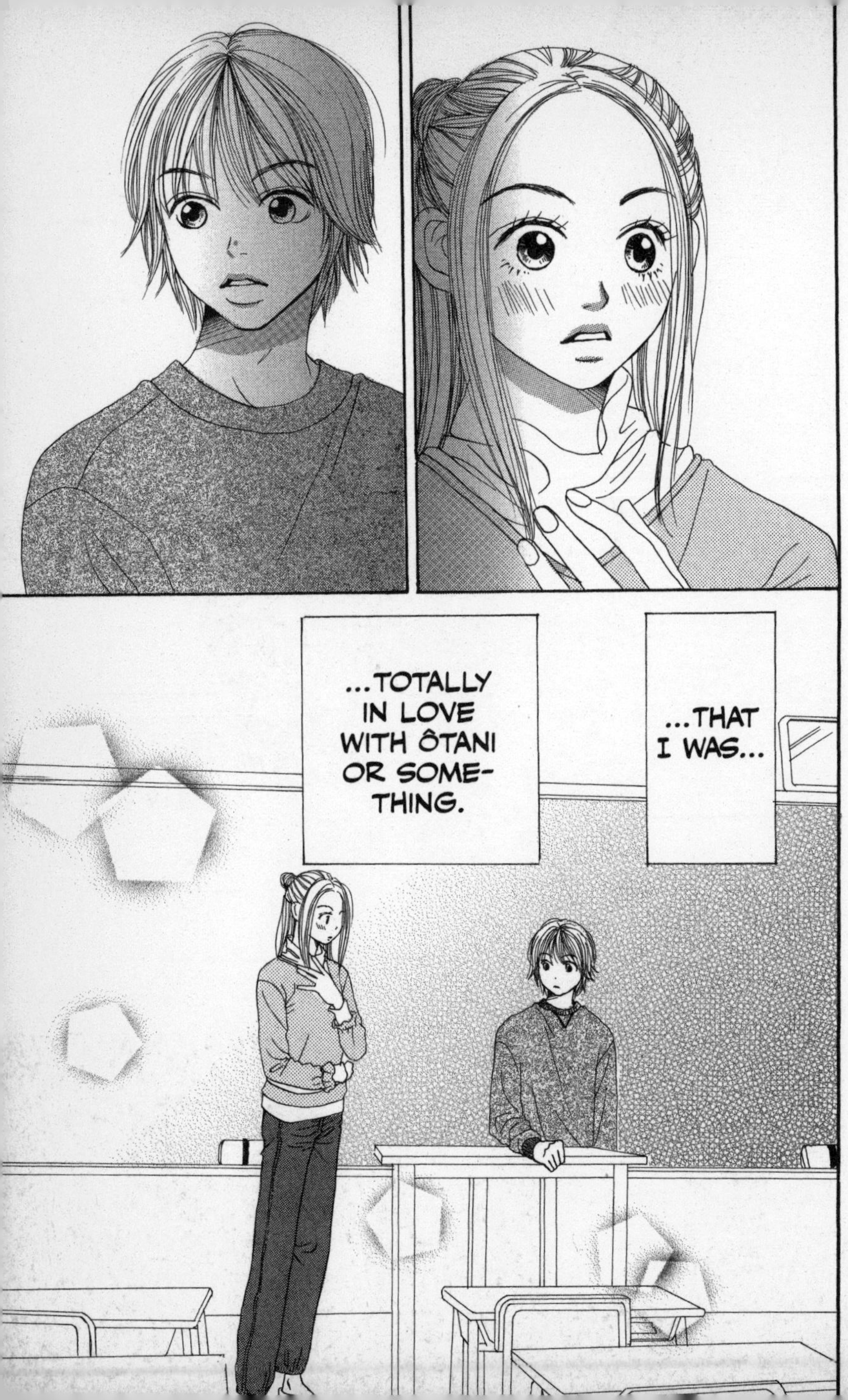
...THAT I WAS...
...TOTALLY IN LOVE WITH ÔTANI OR SOME-THING.

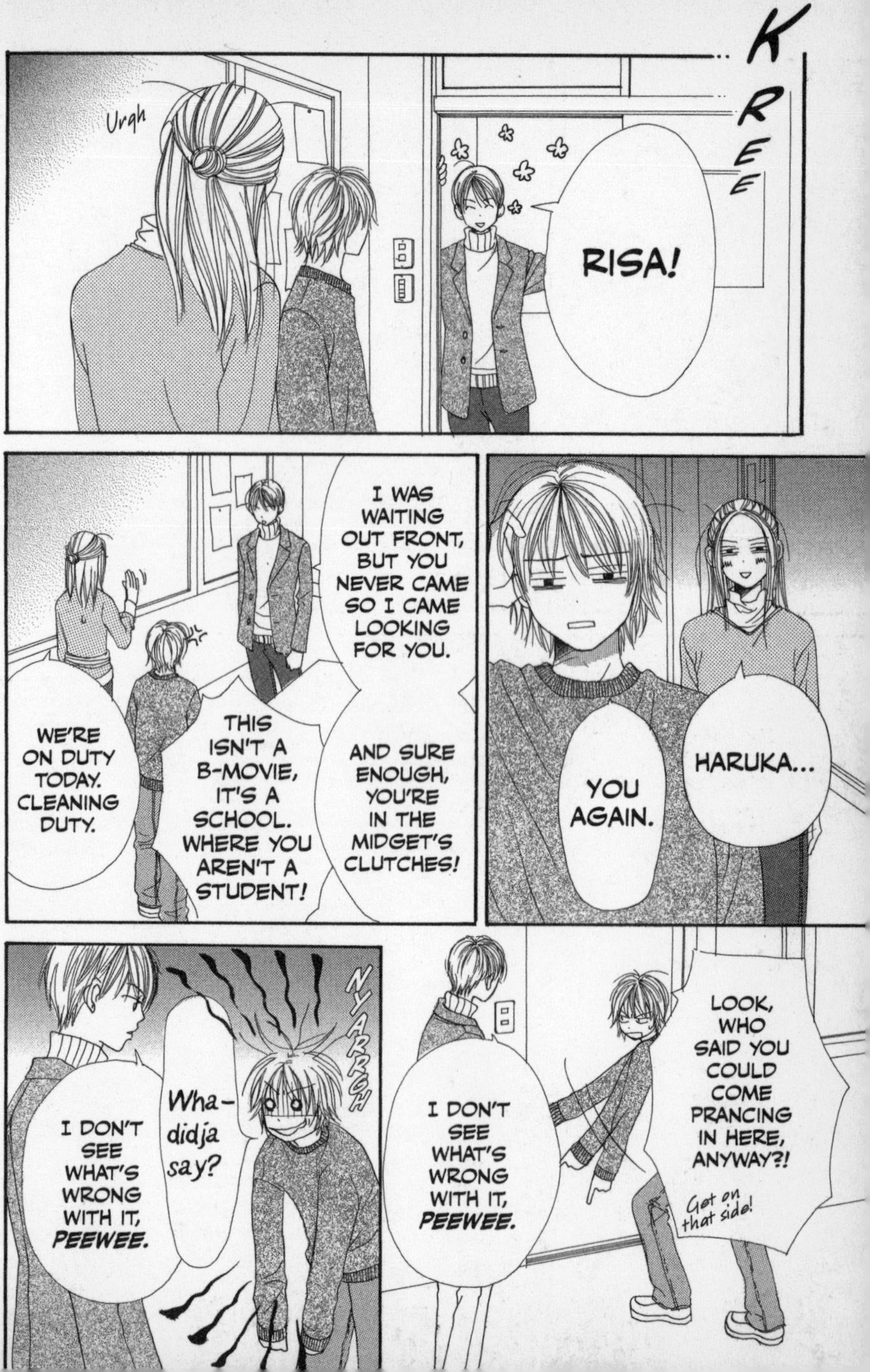
KREEE
RISA!
Urgh
HARUKA...
YOU AGAIN.
I WAS WAITING OUT FRONT, BUT YOU NEVER CAME SO I CAME LOOKING FOR YOU.
AND SURE ENOUGH, YOU'RE IN THE MIDGET'S CLUTCHES!
THIS ISN'T A B-MOVIE, IT'S A SCHOOL. WHERE YOU AREN'T A STUDENT!
WE'RE ON DUTY TODAY. CLEANING DUTY.
LOOK, WHO SAID YOU COULD COME PRANCING IN HERE, ANYWAY?!
Get on that side!
I DON'T SEE WHAT'S WRONG WITH IT, PEEWEE.
NYARRGH
Wha-didja say?
I DON'T SEE WHAT'S WRONG WITH IT, PEEWEE.

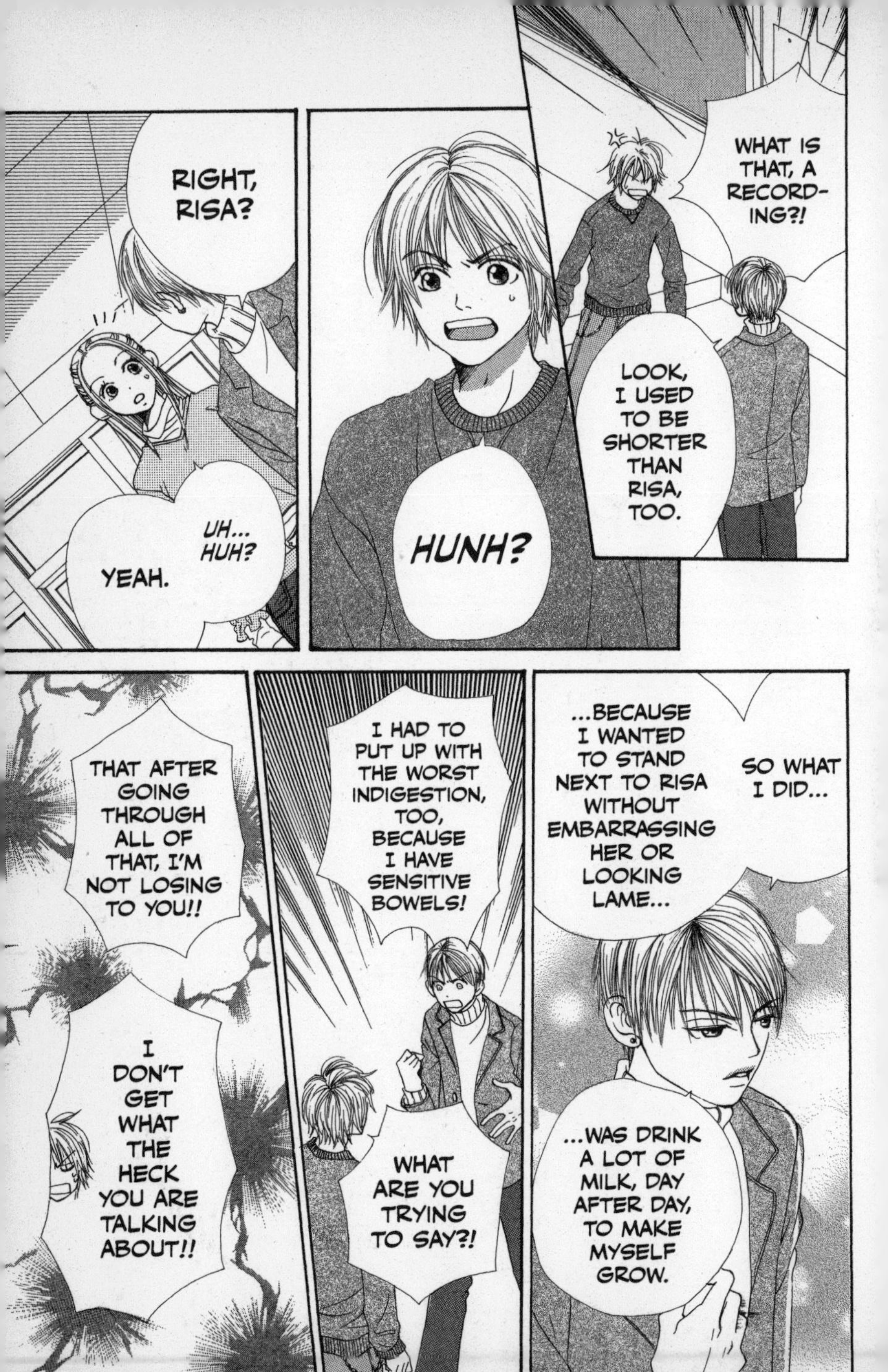
WHAT IS THAT, A RECORDING?!
LOOK, I USED TO BE SHORTER THAN RISA, TOO.
HUNH?
RIGHT, RISA?
UH... HUH?
YEAH.
SO WHAT I DID...
...BECAUSE I WANTED TO STAND NEXT TO RISA WITHOUT EMBARRASSING HER OR LOOKING LAME...
...WAS DRINK A LOT OF MILK, DAY AFTER DAY, TO MAKE MYSELF GROW.
I HAD TO PUT UP WITH THE WORST INDIGESTION, TOO, BECAUSE I HAVE SENSITIVE BOWELS!
WHAT ARE YOU TRYING TO SAY?!
THAT AFTER GOING THROUGH ALL OF THAT, I'M NOT LOSING TO YOU!!
I DON'T GET WHAT THE HECK YOU ARE TALKING ABOUT!!

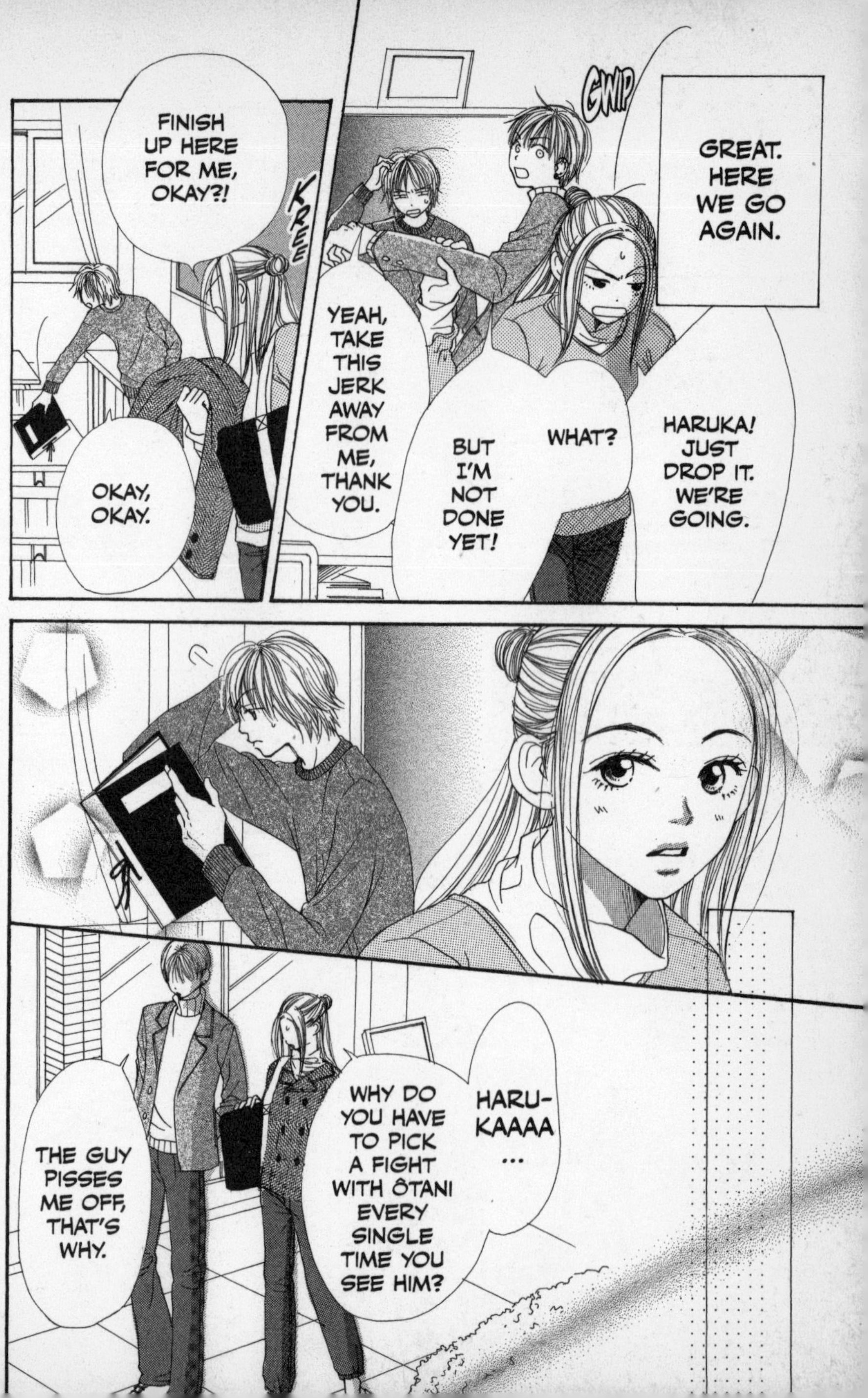
GWIP
GREAT. HERE WE GO AGAIN.
HARUKA! JUST DROP IT. WE'RE GOING.
WHAT?
BUT I'M NOT DONE YET!
YEAH, TAKE THIS JERK AWAY FROM ME, THANK YOU.
KREE
FINISH UP HERE FOR ME, OKAY?!
OKAY, OKAY.
HARU-KAAAA ...
WHY DO YOU HAVE TO PICK A FIGHT WITH ŌTANI EVERY SINGLE TIME YOU SEE HIM?
THE GUY PISSES ME OFF, THAT'S WHY.

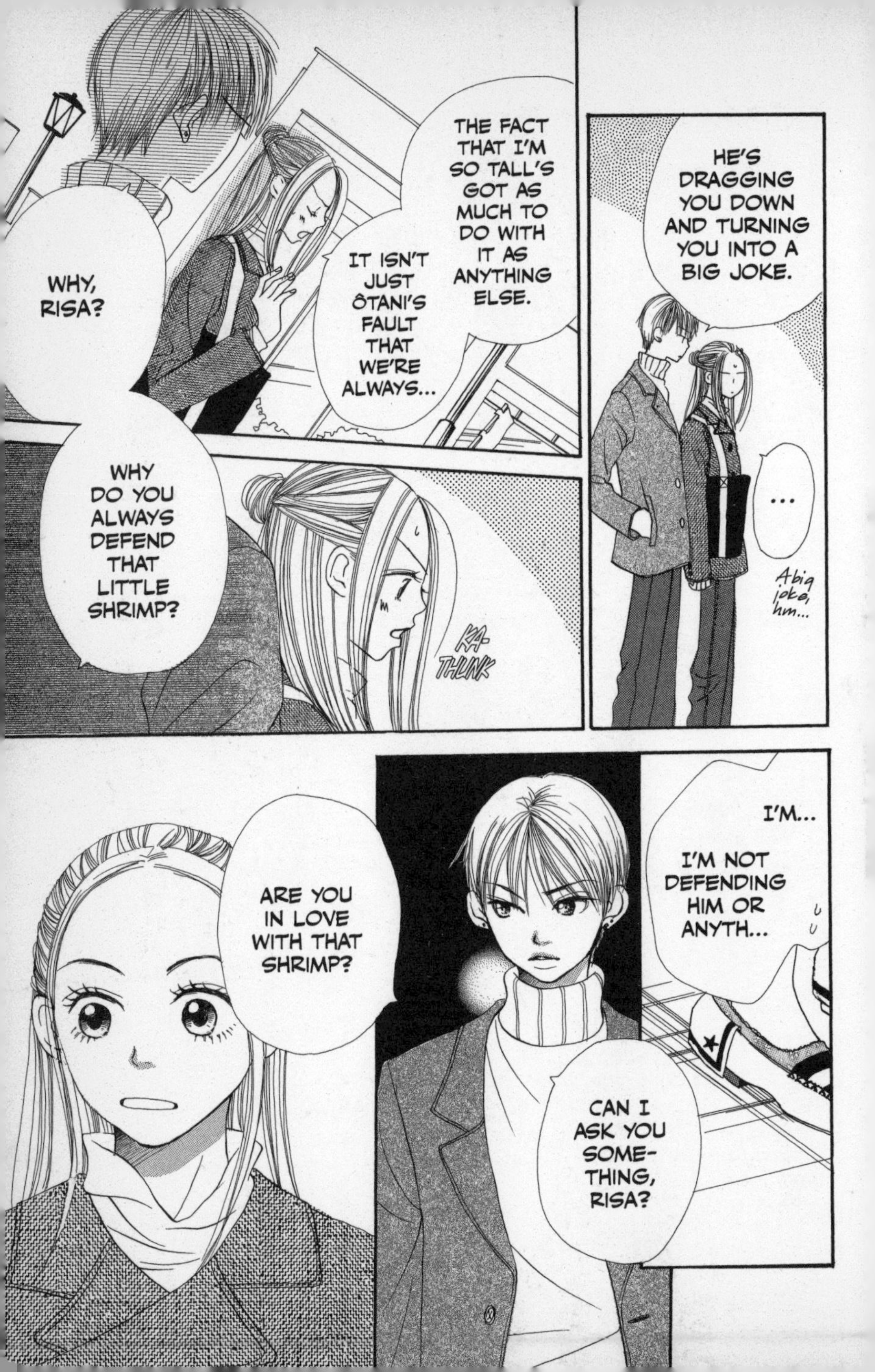
HE'S DRAGGING YOU DOWN AND TURNING YOU INTO A BIG JOKE.
...
A big joke, hm...
IT ISN'T JUST ŌTANI'S FAULT THAT WE'RE ALWAYS...
THE FACT THAT I'M SO TALL'S GOT AS MUCH TO DO WITH IT AS ANYTHING ELSE.
WHY, RISA?
WHY DO YOU ALWAYS DEFEND THAT LITTLE SHRIMP?
KA-THUNK
I'M...
I'M NOT DEFENDING HIM OR ANYTH...
CAN I ASK YOU SOMETHING, RISA?
ARE YOU IN LOVE WITH THAT SHRIMP?

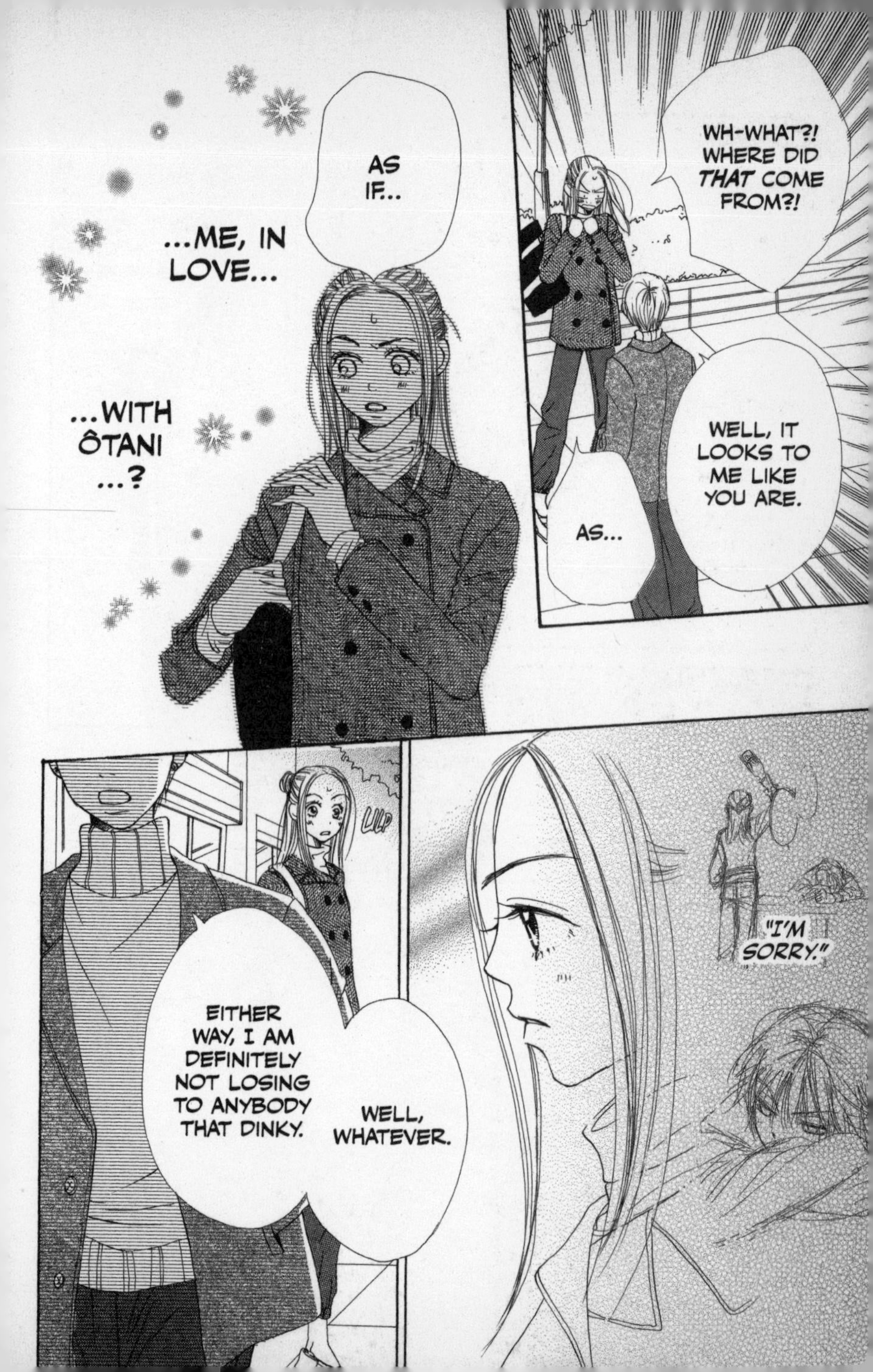
WH-WHAT?! WHERE DID *THAT* COME FROM?!
WELL, IT LOOKS TO ME LIKE YOU ARE.
AS...
AS IF...
...ME, IN LOVE...
...WITH ÔTANI ...?
"I'M SORRY."
GULP
WELL, WHATEVER.
EITHER WAY, I AM DEFINITELY NOT LOSING TO ANYBODY THAT DINKY.

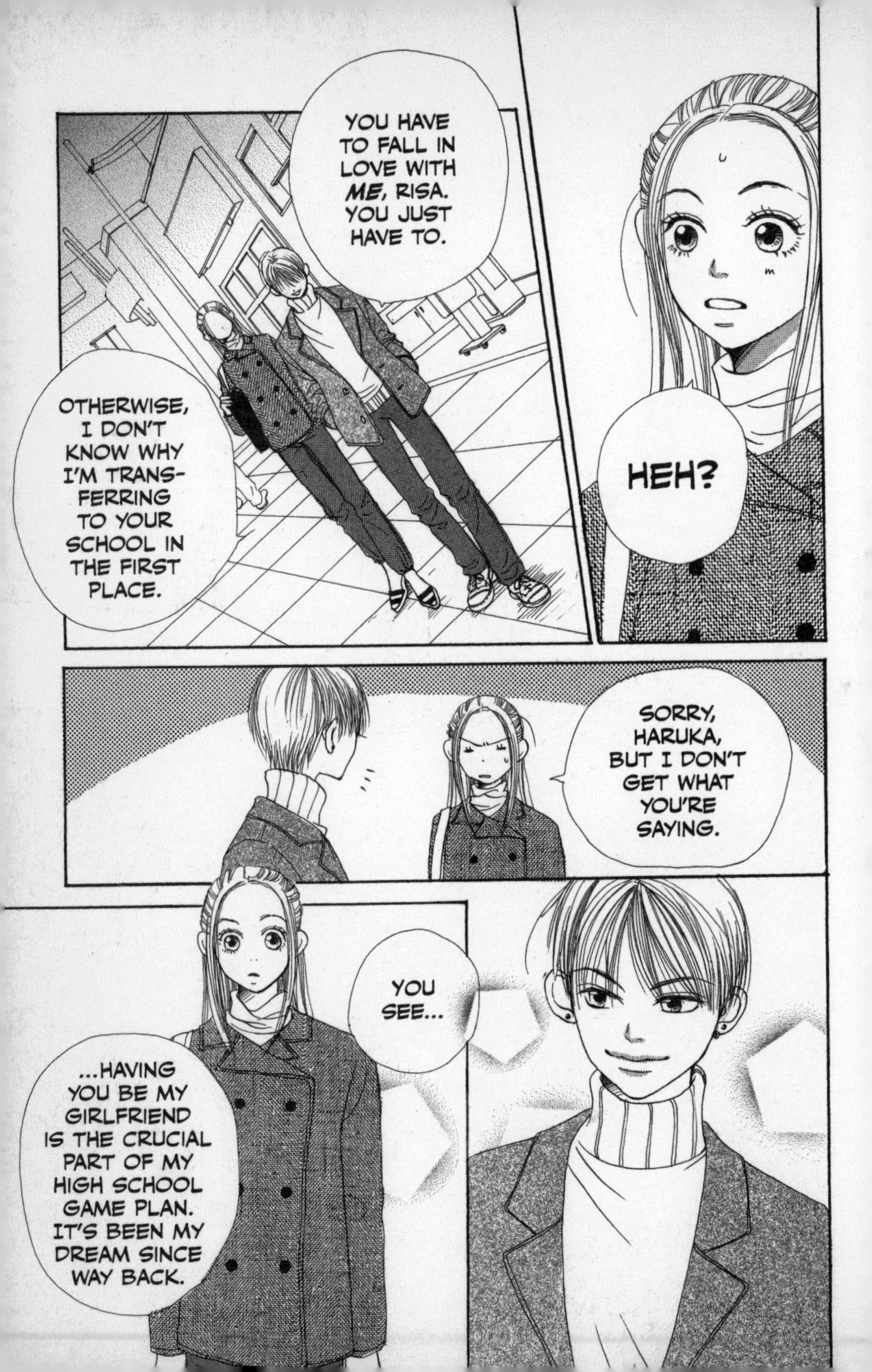
HEH?
YOU HAVE TO FALL IN LOVE WITH *ME*, RISA. YOU JUST HAVE TO.
OTHERWISE, I DON'T KNOW WHY I'M TRANS-FERRING TO YOUR SCHOOL IN THE FIRST PLACE.
SORRY, HARUKA, BUT I DON'T GET WHAT YOU'RE SAYING.
YOU SEE...
...HAVING YOU BE MY GIRLFRIEND IS THE CRUCIAL PART OF MY HIGH SCHOOL GAME PLAN. IT'S BEEN MY DREAM SINCE WAY BACK.

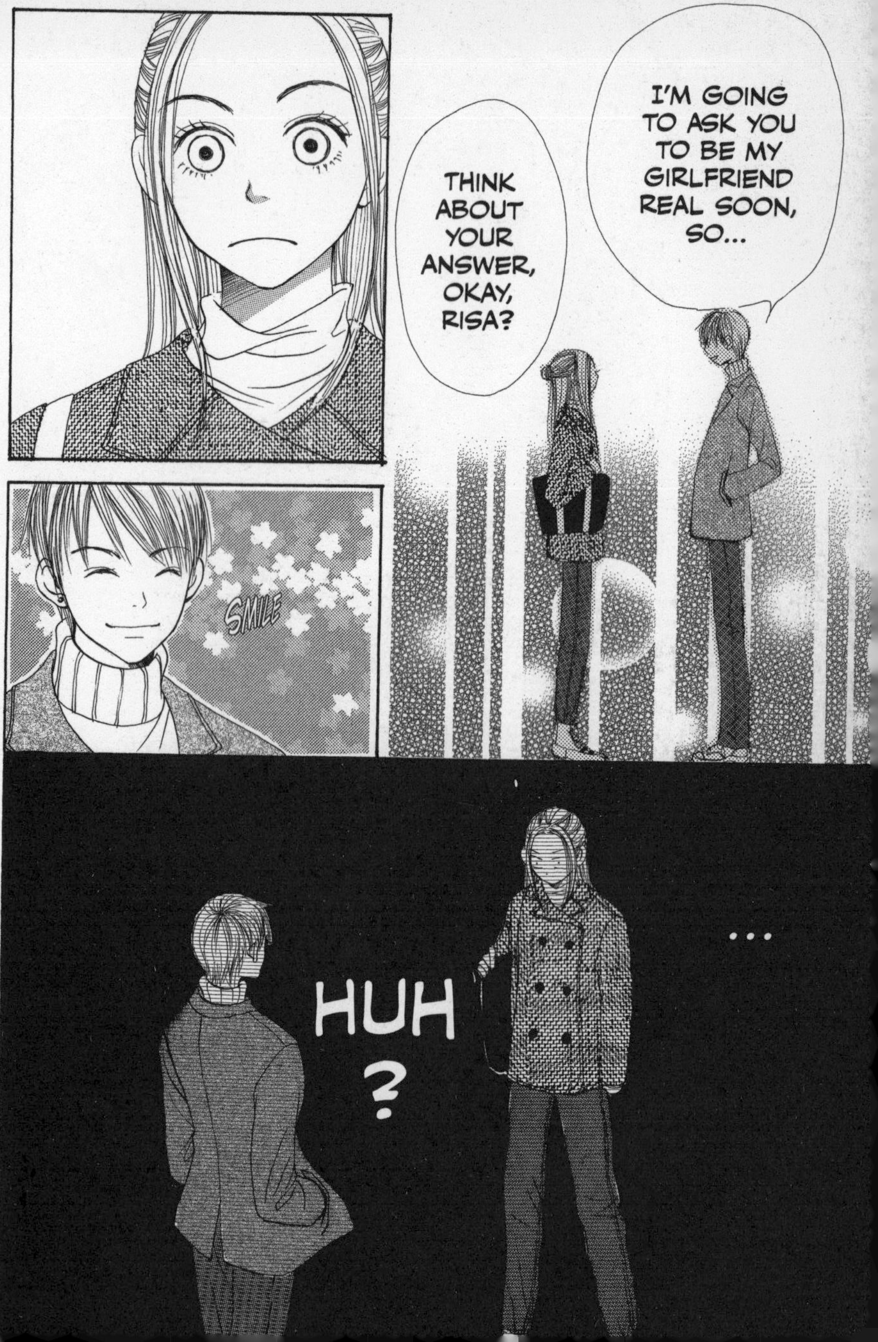
I'M GOING TO ASK YOU TO BE MY GIRLFRIEND REAL SOON, SO...
THINK ABOUT YOUR ANSWER, OKAY, RISA?
SMILE
...
HUH ?

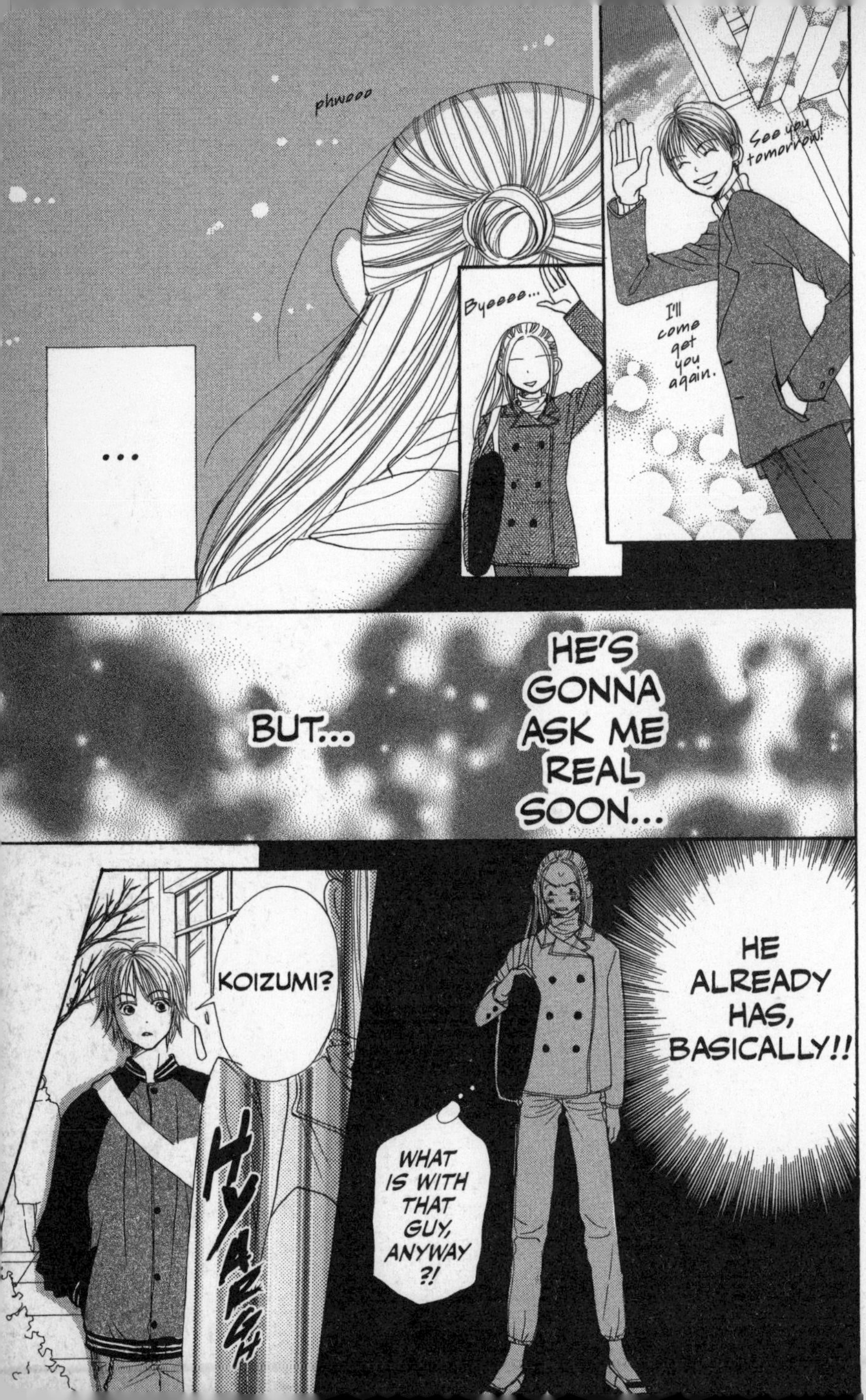
See you tomorrow!
I'll come get you again.
Byeeee...
phwooo
...
HE'S GONNA ASK ME REAL SOON...
BUT...
HE ALREADY HAS, BASICALLY!!
WHAT IS WITH THAT GUY, ANYWAY?!
KOIZUMI?

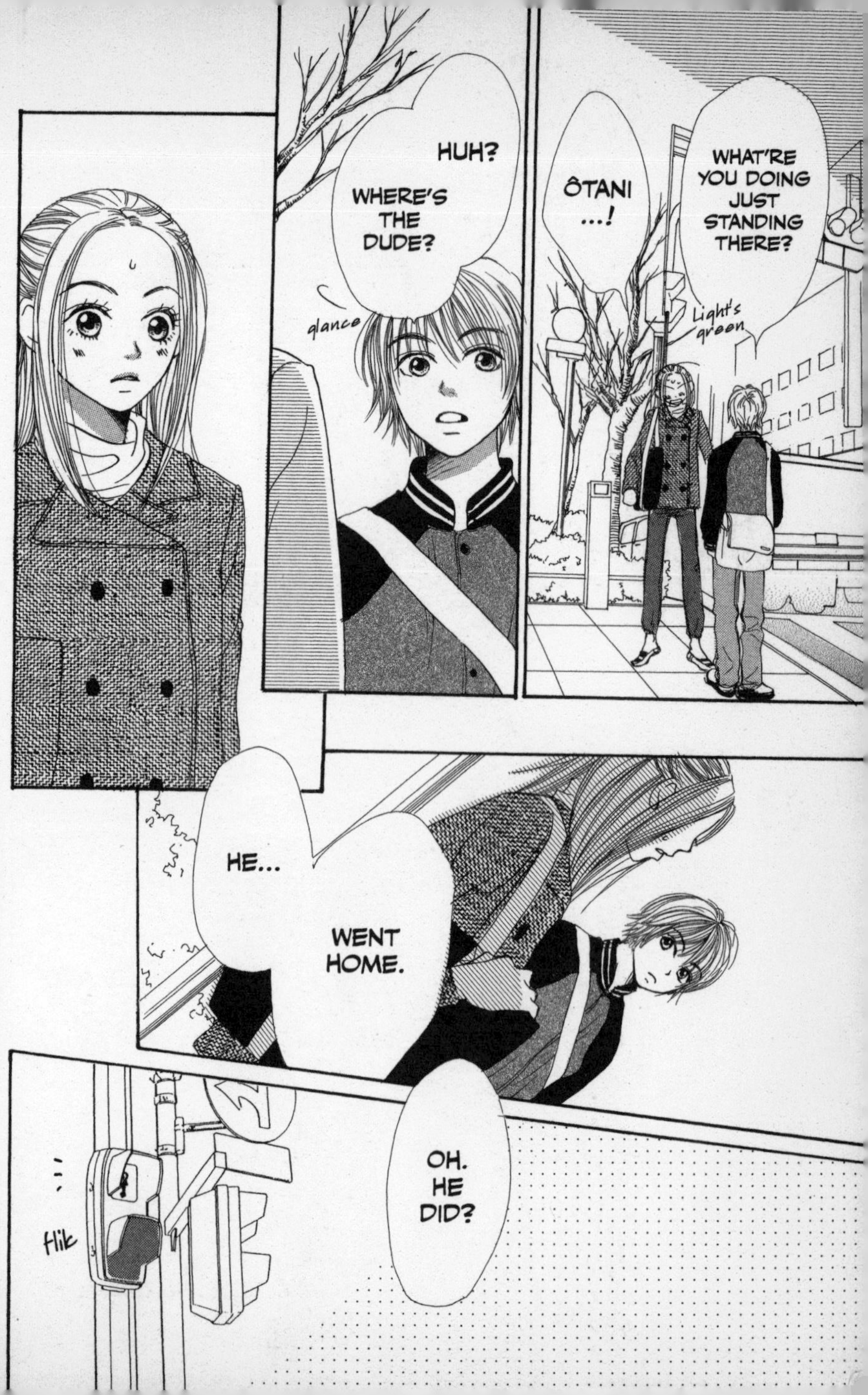
WHAT'RE YOU DOING JUST STANDING THERE?
ÔTANI ...!
Light's green
HUH?
WHERE'S THE DUDE?
glance
HE...
WENT HOME.
OH. HE DID?
...
flik

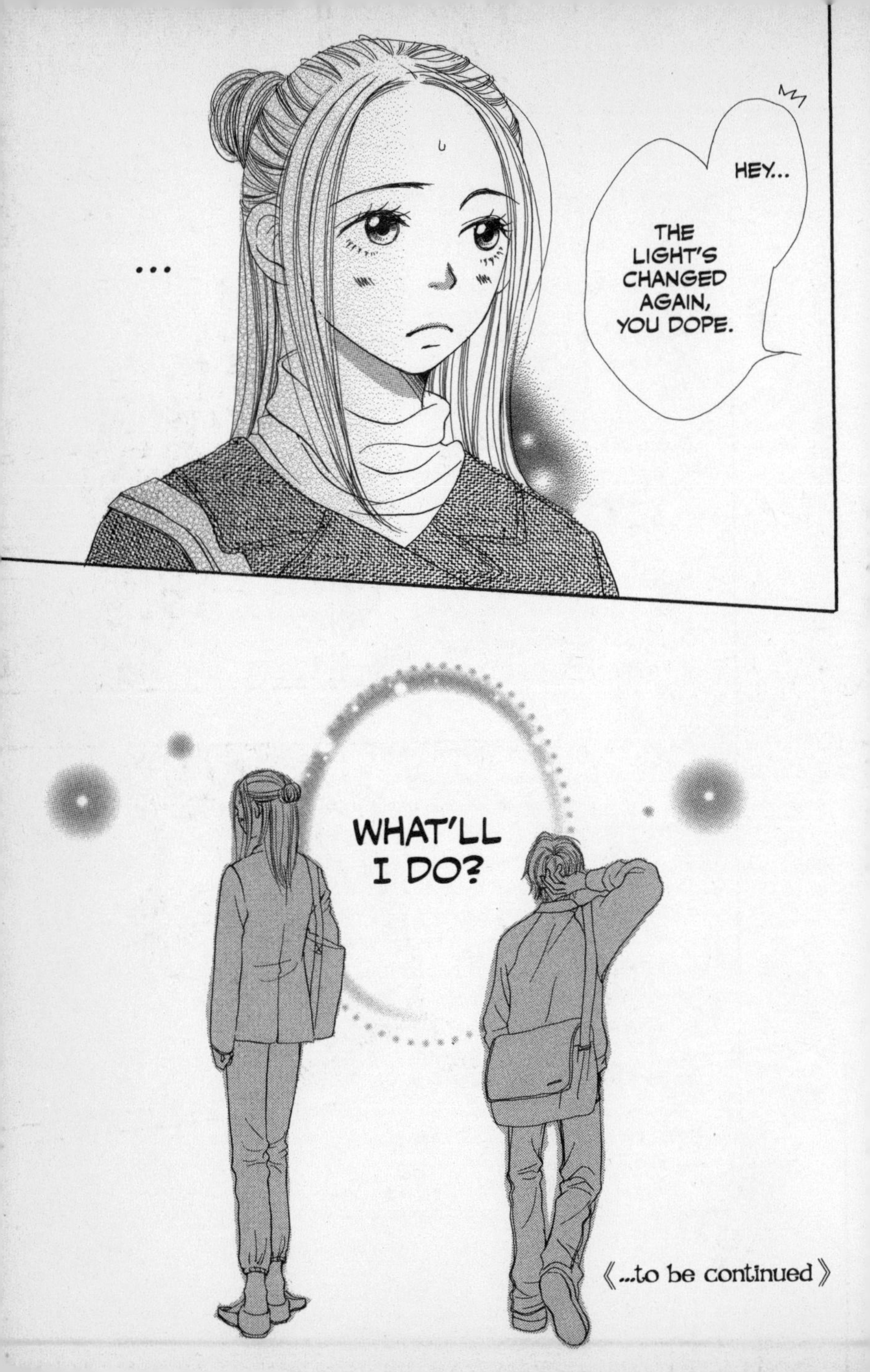
HEY... THE LIGHT'S CHANGED AGAIN, YOU DOPE.
...
WHAT'LL I DO?
《...to be continued》

glossary

Page 11, panel 5: All Hanshin-Kyojin
This is Risa and Ōtani's nickname at school, and refers to a comedy team with one tall member and one short member. See volume 1 glossary for more information.

Page 23, panel 5: Giant Baba
The name of a popular and humongous pro wrestler, similar to The Rock or Hulk Hogan.

Page 53, panel 2: Oden
A Japanese hot pot that includes ingredients like daikon, fish cake, boiled eggs and konnyaku (yam cake), all simmered in kelp broth. It is considered to be a comfort food.

Page 60, panel 6: New Year's wish
New Year's is the most important Japanese holiday, and it is believed that each year is a fresh start. It is traditional to visit a shrine or temple on New Year's Day with family and friends, and make a wish for the coming year.

Page 94, panel 1: Valentine's Day
Valentine's Day is celebrated slightly differently in Japan than it is in the U.S. Women give chocolates (homemade are the best) to their boyfriends or husbands, although sometimes they'll also gift co-workers or fellow students with purely platonic sweets. The men get their chance to shine on White Day (March 14), a Japanese holiday named for the pure and virtuous image of the color, where guys get a chance to give back to the ladies in their lives. When White Day started in 1980, the gifts included white marshmallows or chocolate. These days, White Day gifts include chocolate, sweets, or other small presents.

Page 128, panel 5: Just Friends
The original Japanese literally says "obligation" or *giri*, as in valentines given out of obligation rather than *honmei*, those given out of love.

It's in an episode that wasn't included in this volume, but there's a wristband that just sorta happened to appear in the story, and well, one thing led to another and a real-life version of it is now actually going to be produced. I've been feeling rather remorseful about it, cuz... I mean, I should've put a lot more thought into making it much cooler... So my feelings about this are kinda... well... *mumble mumble*. But I'm stoked!

Aya Nakahara won the 2003 Shogakukan manga award for her breakthrough hit *Love★Com*, which was made into a major motion picture and a PS2 game in 2006. She debuted with *Haru to Kuuki Nichiyo-bi* in 1995, and her other works include *HANADA* and *Himitsu*

LOVE★COM VOL 2
The Shojo Beat Manga Edition

STORY AND ART BY
AYA NAKAHARA

Translation & English Adaptation/Pookie Rolf
Touch-up Art & Lettering/Gia Cam Luc
Design/Amy Martin
Editor/Pancha Diaz

Editor in Chief, Books/Alvin Lu
Editor in Chief, Magazines/Marc Weidenbaum
VP of Publishing Licensing/Rika Inouye
VP of Sales/Gonzalo Ferreyra
Sr. VP of Marketing/Liza Coppola
Publisher/Hyoe Narita

LOVE★COM © 2001 by Aya Nakahara
All rights reserved. First published in Japan in 2001 by
SHUEISHA Inc., Tokyo. English translation rights in the United
States of America and Canada arranged by SHUEISHA Inc.
No portion of this book may be reproduced or transmitted in
any form or by any means without written permission from the
copyright holders.

Printed in Canada

Published by VIZ Media, LLC
P.O. Box 77010
San Francisco, CA 94107

Shojo Beat Manga Edition
10 9 8 7 6 5 4 3 2 1
First printing, September 2007

store.viz.com

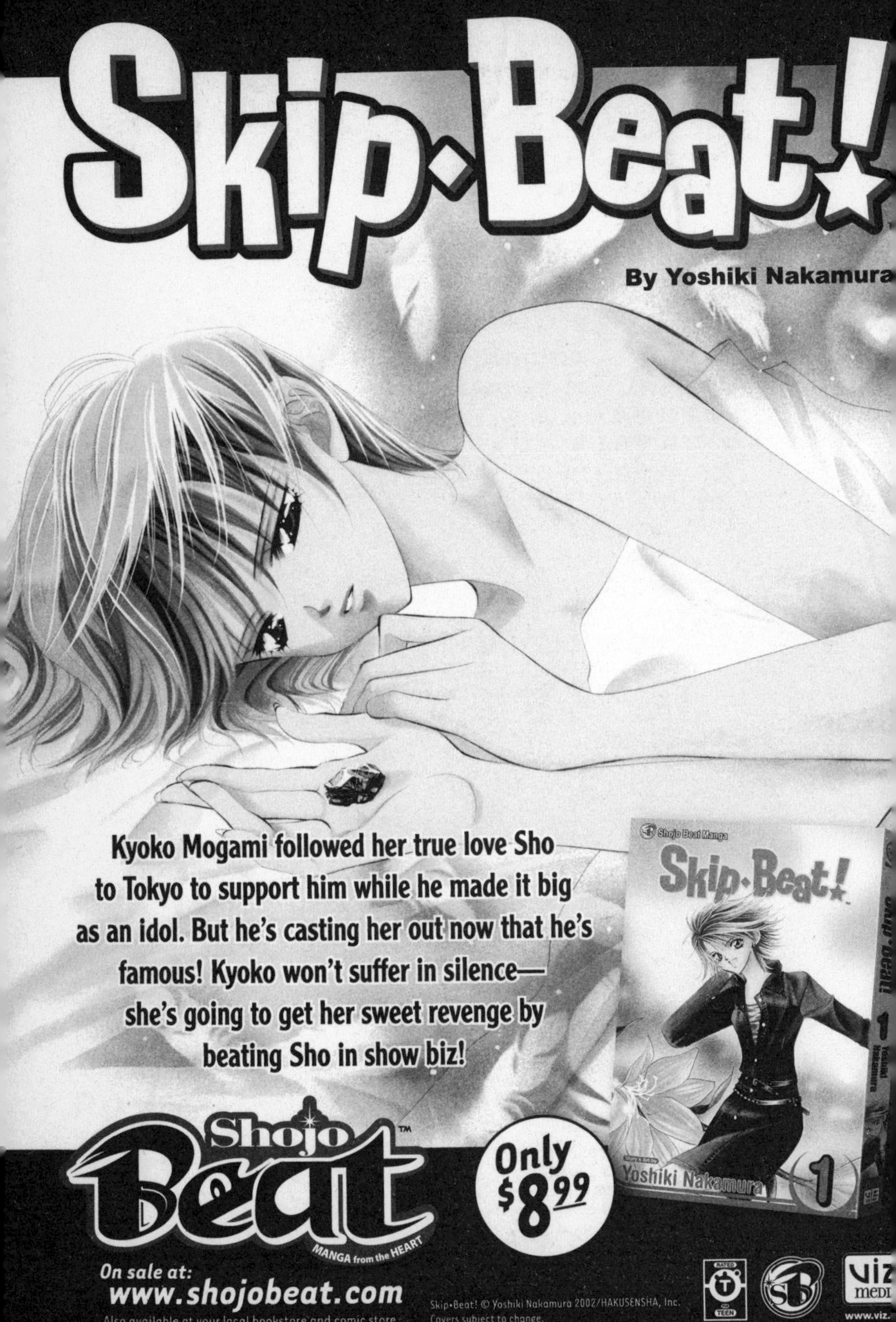
Skip·Beat!
By Yoshiki Nakamura
Kyoko Mogami followed her true love Sho to Tokyo to support him while he made it big as an idol. But he's casting her out now that he's famous! Kyoko won't suffer in silence—she's going to get her sweet revenge by beating Sho in show biz!
Shojo Beat Manga
Skip·Beat!
Yoshiki Nakamura
1
Shojo Beat™
MANGA from the HEART
Only $8.99
On sale at:
www.shojobeat.com
Also available at your local bookstore and comic store.
Skip·Beat! © Yoshiki Nakamura 2002/HAKUSENSHA, Inc.
Covers subject to change.
RATED T TEEN
viz media
www.viz.

Tell us what you think about Shojo Beat Manga!

Our survey is now available online. Go to:

shojobeat.com/mangasurvey

Help us make our product offerings better!